The Dooleys of Richmond

The Dooleys of Richmond

*An Irish Immigrant Family in
the Old and New South*

MARY LYNN BAYLISS

UNIVERSITY OF VIRGINIA PRESS

Charlottesville and London

*Mary Lynn Bayliss
@ Maymont, 2011*

University of Virginia Press

© 2017 by the Rector and Visitors of the University of Virginia

All rights reserved

Printed in the United States of America on acid-free paper

First published 2017

ISBN 978-0-8139-3998-8 (cloth)

9 8 7 6 5 4 3 2 1

Library of Congress Cataloging-in-Publication Data is available from the Library of Congress.

JACKET ART

Front: John Dooley, by Peter Baumgrass, 1859; *back:* James Dooley by William Garl Brown Jr., 1889; *front flap and spine:* Sarah Dooley and child, by Peter Baumgrass, 1859; *back flap:* Sallie Dooley, by William Garl Brown Jr., 1889. (Maymont Mansion, Richmond, Va.)

For John Temple

CONTENTS

Illustrations follow page 160.

ACKNOWLEDGMENTS

A casual conversation years ago with the late lawyer and historian Drew Carneal launched my search for the Dooleys. Then a member of the board and chairman of the Historical Committee of the Maymont Foundation, Drew commented that the work of the foundation was progressing nicely, but, despite great interest in the Dooleys, who gave Maymont to the City of Richmond, very little was known about them because their papers had been burned shortly after Mrs. Dooley's death in 1925. I offered to do a little research to see what I could find, and before long I received a letter from Drew inviting me to join the Historical Committee. Fortunately, another member of the committee, Charles M. Caravati, M.D., had collected what was then known about James Henry Dooley and in 1978 had privately published *Major Dooley,* a brief biography of him. Dr. Caravati's work provided the springboard for my further research into the lives not only of Major and Mrs. Dooley of Maymont but also of other members of their family. I am grateful to both kind gentlemen for encouraging me in my work.

Since then I have become deeply indebted to many people and institutions. First and foremost, I am indebted to Boyd Zenner, Acquiring Editor at the University of Virginia Press, for shepherding my overly long manuscript throughout the prepublication process and trimming it expertly. Her wise counsel sustained me throughout the bumpy process.

I am grateful to two historians who read drafts of my manuscript. John Kneebone, chairman of the History Department at Virginia Commonwealth University, took time out from his own research project to read and suggest helpful revisions of many chapters. Anne Freeman, writer, historian, friend, bravely read the long first draft of the manuscript of this book and gently suggested ways to improve it.

I am very grateful to Nelson Lankford, who alerted me to several sources that I might have missed, and to the archivists and librarians who located the manuscripts and records that form the basis of this work. Among them are Jean Murray, chief archivist at Limerick Archives and Limerick Ancestry, who located Dooley family records in the National Archives of Ireland; Frances Pollard at the Virginia Historical Society; Minor Weisiger, Chris Colby, and Dave Garbarek at the Library of Virginia; Teresa Roane, Meghan Hughes, and Kelly Kerney at the Valentine Museum; Lynn Conway at the Georgetown University Library; Victor Sansone at the Diocese of Richmond; Sister Joanne Gunter at Mount de Chantal School, Wheeling, West Virginia; Jennifer McDaid at the Norfolk Southern Historical Collection; Sister Betty Ann McNeil and Bonnie Weatherby at the Daughters of Charity Provincial House, Emmitsburg, Maryland; Wesley J. Chenault at the James Branch Cabell Library, Virginia Commonwealth University; Jodie Koste at the Tompkins-McCaw Library, Medical College of Virginia; Sandy Monroe, Richmond City archivist; B. Obenhaus at Special Collections, Virginia Polytechnic Institute and State University libraries; Mrs. John Samuel Biscoe at the National Society of the Daughters of the American Revolution headquarters in Washington, D.C.; Mary Ann Quinn at the Rockefeller Archive Center, Pocantico Hills, New York; Margaret Whittington at the C&O Historical Society; Maureen Manning at the University Club, New York City; and Liz Triplett, Skip Stockdon, Shannon Humphreys, Sue Shook, Ellen Parnell, Lynn Vandenesse, and David Kilmon at the main branch of the Richmond Public Library.

I also thank Dale Wheary, Fred Murray, Peggy Singlemann, Nancy Loudon, Kathy Garrett-Cox, Evelyn Zak, Carol Harris, Dot Ruqus, Armistead Wellford, Beth O'Leary, Karrie Jurgens, Dick Cheatham, Dottie Robinson, Geoffrey Platt, and Norman Burns at Maymont.

I owe thanks to the heads and the employees of several organizations whose archives yielded helpful information. They include Sally Warthen, then president of the National Society of the Colonial Dames of America in the Commonwealth of Virginia, who gave me access to its archives; Ray Pardue and his executive assistant, Norma Marshall, at St. Joseph Villa, who gave me access to early records; and Mabel Toney at Hollywood Cemetery.

I greatly appreciate the efforts of the people who provided the photographs for the illustrations in this book: Jamison Davis at the Virginia Historical Society; Dale Neighbors at the Library of Virginia; Meghan Hughes at the Valentine Museum; Ray Bonis at Virginia Commonwealth University; Shaun Aigner-Lee at Dementi Studio; Dale Wheary at Maymont; and Alfred Scott.

I am grateful to Katherine Busser and her staff at Capital One for publishing the keepsake edition of *Will the Real Major Dooley Please Stand Up? and Other "Maymont Moments"* auctioned at Vintage Maymont 2005.

My special thanks go to the James Henry Dooley Chapter of the Ancient Order of Hibernians, whose eagerness to learn about their patron spurred my work, and to AOH member Jack Cassells, who searched for records of the Dooley family in Ireland.

Others who shared information, gave helpful advice, or identified additional source material also deserve thanks, including Mark Cox; Bob Evans; Fitzhugh Elder; Rossie Fisher; Carter Fox; Lang Gibson; Bob Hill; Virginia Wellford Jones; Jack McElroy; Sorrel McElroy; Mac McGuire; Dick Mulligan; John O'Grady; Beth O'Leary; Dr. Lee Perkins, who translated the Latin text of James H. Dooley's doctor of laws diploma; John Peters; Bill Rose; Emily Rusk, researcher extraordinaire; Phil Schwarz; Alfred Scott; Elizabeth P. Scott; Linda Singleton-Driscoll; Rita Smith, Lynn Spellman; Ben Warthen; and Harry Warthen.

I am especially grateful to my husband, John Temple Bayliss, my patient, wise, and encouraging first reader; to Armistead Saffer, Ann Bayliss, Tom Bayliss, and Delores Bridgett, whose expertise solved a number of distressing problems with my computer; and to our son, Temple, who for years listened patiently at the dinner table to my animated reports of new discoveries about the Dooleys.

The Dooleys of Richmond

Introduction

Inside the elegant filigreed gates of Maymont in Richmond, Virginia, lie one hundred acres of beautifully manicured lawns and gardens, a Richardson Romanesque stone mansion with a sumptuous Gilded Age interior, a handsome stone carriage house, and a stone barn. The lower terrace of the Italian garden leads to a hillside fountain topped with a stone lion's head. Nearby, a forty-five-foot-high waterfall plunges dramatically into a serene Japanese garden.

Now open to the public, Maymont was originally the home of a prominent and philanthropic couple, James Henry and Sallie May Dooley, who lived on the estate for more than thirty years before leaving it to the City of Richmond in 1925. Operated for the city by the non-profit Maymont Foundation, the estate attracts more than a half million visitors per year. It was not, however, the Dooleys' only home. They had another, Swannanoa, eighty miles west of Richmond. A marble palace on Afton Mountain, it was built by the Dooleys between 1911 and 1913. It is now a crumbling monument to excess, and its vast terraced gardens are ruins. Even so, both estates are now Virginia Historic Landmarks and listed on the National Register of Historic Places.

Despite the opulence of their two estates and Maymont's popularity with visitors, very little is known about the Dooleys today because relatives ordered their papers to be burned after Mrs. Dooley's death. Probably the question that visitors most often ask is how James Dooley made his money. When told that he was the son of Irish immigrants, most people assume that his story is a variant on the Horatio Alger myth, but recent research reveals that is far from the truth.

James Dooley's parents, John and Sarah, did not fit the usual profile of poor, illiterate day laborers forced to leave Ireland by political upheavals or terrible famines. They were well-educated middle-class people, like thousands of other prefamine Irish immigrants who left Ireland in the 1820s and 1830s, and they brought intelligence and sophistication to Virginia. In 1836 they settled in Richmond, where John Dooley established a hat manufacturing company that grew to be the largest of its kind in the South. During the Civil War John rose to the rank of major in the First Virginia Regiment of the Confederate army. Immediately after ill health forced his retirement from active duty, he founded and led the Richmond Ambulance Committee, whose members served at their own expense while saving thousands of lives on both sides of the conflict. In Richmond's April 1865 Evacuation Fire, Dooley lost the entire manufacturing and retail business he had spent almost thirty years building. The final three years of his life provide a chronicle of his efforts to rebuild while continuing his charitable work.

John's wife, Sarah, was an independent thinker with a keen interest in politics. When the Whig activist Lucy Barbour, widow of the Virginia governor James Barbour, founded the first organized political organization for women in the state in 1844, Sarah became a member. Later she and her five daughters, all ardent advocates for women's suffrage, became leaders in that movement.

John Dooley was devoted to his adopted city, a cosmopolitan place where immigrants from many foreign countries were able to rise to prominence. Dooley's Irish birth and Catholicism were integral aspects of his life, not handicaps. He was active in raising money for causes in Ireland and supported many of his Irish relatives financially. He even advertised his business in Irish immigrant newspapers with circulation throughout the United States. Dooley was a founder of a militia company composed primarily of Richmonders of Irish birth or ancestry, but he was also a close associate of many prominent Richmond men with deep roots in colonial Virginia. Famed for his honesty and business acumen, he gradually became a leader in the financial, educational, and political circles of Richmond before the Civil War.

While following in his father's footsteps, James Henry Dooley—builder of Maymont and the third of John and Sarah Dooley's nine children—practiced law during the difficult transitional period in the South after the Civil War. A graduate of Georgetown College, the younger Dooley became a leader in the Irish Conservatives, a wing of the Conservative Party, and during the 1870s he was elected to three terms in the Virginia House of Delegates. He continued his father's practices of raising money for Irish causes, supporting Irish-born relatives, and advertising in Irish-immigrant-owned newspapers.

Most importantly, James Henry Dooley was one of three Richmond men who in the post–Civil War period led the tremendous growth throughout the South of transportation networks, heavy industry, and finance that transformed the region and created the New South. Their contributions to that development began during the 1880s, when, in an effort to bring prosperity back to Richmond, James Dooley and two other young lawyers, Joseph Bryan and Thomas M. Logan, acquired controlling interest in the Richmond and Danville Railroad. They developed it into the second-longest and the fastest-growing railroad in the country. They also created the first railroad holding company in U.S. history and founded a railroad construction company that built railroads in several states and the Washington Territory. Their success in the industry led the "Virginians" (as they began to be known in the national press) to invest in Alabama's Sloss Iron and Steel enterprise and real estate in both the North and the South. They also bought the patent for the telautograph, the first American fax machine, and obtained a charter for the Gray National Telautograph Company, making Richmond its headquarters.

In the final decade of the nineteenth century, Dooley joined John Skelton Williams in creating the Seaboard Air Line Railway. Making Richmond a center of the global economy was a primary objective for the men, and Dooley frequently articulated their vision in public lectures and essays.

Dooley's marriage to Sallie May, an author whose ancestors included two governors of colonial Virginia (Sir Dudley Digges and his son, Edward Digges), proved to be a union of polar opposites, but they shared a devotion to community service and enjoyed an active life in Richmond social circles. Her 1906 book, *Dem Good Ole Times,* a fictional paean to idealized days of the Old South published in New York by Doubleday, Page & Company, provided an ironic coda to her husband's efforts in the creation of the New South.

The contributions of both Dooley generations had a lasting effect on the quality of life in Richmond and the wider South. Their advocacy of innovation in education is one example. The father was a founder and board member of the Mechanics Institute, a night school that provided education for workingmen well into the middle of the twentieth century. The son, vice president of the Co-operative Education Association for almost two decades, published essays and lobbied vigorously for reform in Virginia public schools. Among the changes he advocated were the laws requiring compulsory education and the nine-month school year that still govern Virginia's educational system.

John Dooley's philanthropic work provided a model that James Henry and Sallie May Dooley followed throughout their lives. With their bequests, they became two of Virginia's great philanthropists.

A	lthough heavy rain and flooding had persisted throughout the last week of August and into September, the sun was shining on September 3, 1836, outside St. Mary's Catholic Church in Alexandria, Virginia. Inside a young couple knelt at the altar rail to receive the blessing of Father John Smith, the Jesuit priest who married them that morning. The groom's widowed mother, sisters, and a brother-in-law, all immigrants who had left Ireland to seek a new life in the United States, looked on.[1]

The newlyweds were John Dooley and Sarah McNamara Dooley.[2] The groom and his family had emigrated from Limerick, a city that had flourished in the late eighteenth and early nineteenth centuries, when Irish commercialization and industrialization had been at their peak.[3] After the Napoleonic Wars of 1800 to 1815, however, a prolonged recession slowed economic growth so much that urban dwellers began to emigrate in large numbers. Between 1821 and 1841 the population of Limerick, which had been a little over fifty-nine thousand, shrank to about forty-eight thousand. Even before his father's death, it was clear to young John Dooley that opportunity lay across the Atlantic.

John grew up in a house on Mary Street in Limerick, where his parents, James Dooley and Mary Margaret McNamara, raised their ten children.[4] His father ran a successful hat manufacturing business that John would later say gave him "a long course of practical experience."[5] The family was Catholic, and all the children were baptized in St. Mary's Catholic Church nearby. A literate man, James Dooley was a leaseholder or possibly the owner of the family home as well as the buildings where his hat manufacturing business was located.[6] He was a British subject who voted in local elections. After James's death, his widow and some of his children emigrated to the United States. John Dooley, his mother, and three girls thought to be his sisters, "Sally," age seventeen, "Anne," fourteen, and "Eliza," twelve, landed in the port of New York on the schooner *Helen Mar* in May 1834 and eventually made their way to Alexandria, Virginia.[7]

It was hardly a propitious moment to immigrate. Andrew Jackson was president at the time, and in 1833 he had fulfilled a campaign promise to abolish the country's central banking system by withdrawing all the public funds from the Bank of the United States. The result was a national financial panic and a depression that continued at least through 1834. John Dooley, however, was bright, articulate, willing to work hard, and not easily discouraged. By 1836 he had determined that Richmond, rather than Alexandria, was the appropriate place to open his hat manufacturing business. Richmond was the only industrialized city of any size in the South, and its import/export business was significant.

During the years he lived in Alexandria, Dooley had fallen in love with Sarah McNamara, an Irishwoman who was probably a cousin on his mother's side. She was intelligent and unafraid to venture to unfamiliar places, so when John proposed moving to Richmond as soon as they were married, she agreed. Less than two weeks after the wedding, the newlyweds arrived in Richmond, then a bustling little city with a population of almost twenty thousand.[8] By September 19, 1836, John, Sarah, John's mother, and his sister Ann had settled into rented quarters in one of Richmond's best neighborhoods. Built on one of Richmond's highest hills, their house was only two blocks from Capitol Square. Sarah and John's first four children would be born there.

The house was next to the First Baptist Church, which a contemporary of their children would later describe as a "low-browed, dingy, brick edifice . . . said to have a seating capacity of two thousand. It was therefore in demand when mass political meetings were convened."[9] The location suited the young Dooleys. They were both interested in politics, and the political meeting-house brought all the important issues of the day to their door.

Seven months before the newlyweds moved to Richmond, an event occurred there that was destined to play an important role in their lives and the lives of their yet-unborn children. On February 13, 1836, a Richmond, Fredericksburg and Potomac train, "the first railway train ever out of Richmond," rolled northwest out of the city. The train was a seven-car affair pulled by a six-thousand-dollar steam locomotive built in Liverpool. A huge crowd gathered along the track for almost a mile to watch as the train left the city. One hundred and fifty passengers were on board for a rough twenty-mile-long ride over the tracks to a celebratory barbeque. The trip took an hour and thirty-one-and-a-half minutes going out and an hour and twelve-and-a-half minutes returning. As one of the passengers presciently declared, "We . . . have seen the light of the age burst upon us."[10]

Despite the introduction of the train, however, Richmond money was still being invested in the James River and Kanawha Canal. Its first section had been built in the late eighteenth century, and it would remain a primary mode of transportation for goods and passengers until after the Civil War despite vast growth in railroads during that period. Competition between the canal and the railroads for investment from both private sources and the Board of Public Works was keen and would remain so for the next forty years.

By September 1836, two more railroad companies—the Richmond and Petersburg and the Richmond and Louisa—had been established. Preliminary work had also begun on a railway running from Richmond to Farmville and Lynchburg. A later recorder of the city's history commented that a "fever for building railroads had seized the city."[11] John Dooley caught that fever and eventually owned shares in at least five railroads: four that served Richmond, including the Richmond and Petersburg, and one that served the Roanoke Valley.[12]

On Monday, September 19, John Dooley's first advertisement appeared—under the heading "Domestic Manufacture"—in the *Richmond Courier and Daily Compiler*. It told what little is known about the twenty-six-year-old entrepreneur's background and training, and also about the business opportunity that brought him to Richmond. It revealed that Dooley had considerable experience in the hat-making business and enough capital to employ other men to make the hats sold under his name. At that time, despite the presence of small manufacturing operations in cities such as Richmond, the South, a predominantly agricultural region, depended heavily on northern and European manufactured goods. In recent years, business had become complicated by sectional politics and mired in issues connected with tariffs on imported goods and the extra expense required to ship such goods southward from northern ports. Some southerners reacted by developing manufacturing operations below the Mason-Dixon Line, in an effort to make the South independent of the North. John Dooley arrived in Virginia at just the right moment to take advantage of these conditions, and he was astute enough to alert his potential customers to the political implications:

John Dooley, respectfully informs the citizens of Richmond and the public generally, that he has commenced the manufacture of fur and silk Hats, on Main Street, opposite the Market House, where he will constantly keep an extensive assortment of all shapes and qualities. As he has by a long course of practical experience, acquired a perfect knowledge of the trade, and being determined to employ none but men whose capacity to perform good work is unquestionable, he can with confidence recommend any work manufactured by him—His prices will invariably be low, which the public can easily ascertain by a trial. He respectfully solicits a share of patronage, which by the most assiduous attention to business and the most active exertions to please, he hopes to merit.

He would beg leave to say that gentlemen who are disposed to encourage domestic industry, will have ample opportunity of doing so with considerable interest, for while the quality of his article will be of the best, the prices (he being the original manufacturer) will of course be lower than they generally are on imported goods. He has also on hand and will be supplied for the fall and winter with an elegant assortment of fur and seal caps, made by the most celebrated manufacturer in the union, which he will sell at a very small advance on cost.[13]

The optimism evinced by his ad, which ran almost daily for the next three months, would be tested in 1837, when yet another financial panic caused a nationwide economic depression. Overextension in financing canals and railroads was said to lie at the bottom of the difficulty.[14] In the spring, Richmond banks suspended specie payment, and the governor called for an extra session of the legislature. Work continued on railroads, however, even though hard times extended well into the following year and the banks didn't resume specie payment until August 1838. Despite the panic, John Dooley's business began to grow.

He and Sarah had been in Richmond for only a little over a year when their first child, a son they named George, was born on October 2, 1837. He was baptized at St. Peter's Catholic Church on Grace Street, a block west of Capitol Square, on All Saints' Day, November 1.[15] The boy flourished, but his forty-nine-year-old grandmother, Mary Margaret Dooley, did not. She suffered what seems to have been a stroke and died in mid-August 1838.[16] John bought a plot in Shockoe Cemetery northwest of the city, where he and Sarah buried his mother just ten days before their first daughter, Mary Helen, was born.

On November 15, Dooley took the first step required for an immigrant seeking to become a citizen of the United States. He appeared in Richmond's Hustings Court to make his "Alien Report." The Minute Book of the court records that he paid the fee and took an oath renouncing "forever all allegiance to any foreign prince, potentate or sovereignty whatever and particularly to Victoria Alexandrina queen of Great Britain and Ireland."[17]

Two years later the 1840 census of the United States reported that, after only four years in Richmond, John Dooley owned four slaves.[18] Two were women who helped Sarah take care of the children and the house. The two men, one a teenager, the other over thirty, did the heavy work of the household.

That same year John and Sarah had their first exposure to the American way of politicking. In the 1840 presidential campaign two Virginians, William Henry Harrison and John Tyler, headed the Whig ticket. The local Whigs built a block-long log cabin in Shockoe Bottom not far from Dooley's business and called it a "Tippecanoe Club." They stocked it well and plied passersby with hard cider during the campaign.[19]

The Dooleys' rented house, only two blocks from the Capitol, was an ideal observation post for anyone interested in the campaign, and later events suggest that Sarah was, even though her husband had not yet become an American citizen. During the campaign, women were, for the first time, invited to attend political rallies.[20] Since many of those rallies were held in Capitol Square, only a few steps from her home, they provided Sarah with the opportunity to participate in American political life.

When the Whig Party held its state convention in Richmond in October 1840, between six thousand and eight thousand delegates attended. Among the speakers they heard in Capitol Square was Daniel Webster of Massachusetts, who, after giving speeches to huge crowds, agreed to deliver a "special address" on women and politics.[21] About 1,200 women turned out for the event.

Politics was not the only source of excitement in 1840. On November 25, almost exactly two months before the Dooleys' third child and second son, James Henry, was born, the president and directors of the James River and Kanawha Canal Company took what then seemed to be a giant step in the history of transportation in Virginia. They boarded a Richmond packet boat bound for Lynchburg for the first-ever trip on the canal between the two cities. Travel time for the 147-mile trip was estimated to be thirty hours.[22] As a later historian of the canal would point out, 340 more miles would have to be built before the canal could reach the rivers in Ohio and begin to carry valuable cargo from the fields of the West.[23]

The year 1841 brought important changes in the Dooleys' lives. Their second son, James Henry, whom they would call Jim, was born on January 17. Shortly thereafter, John Dooley and a group of other men founded a new educational establishment, which they called the Richmond Mechanics Association. The association was officially incorporated on March 26, 1842, for the purpose of "forming a library, securing public lectures, and establishing a school for apprentices and others."[24] The fundamental objective was to provide educational opportunities to workingmen wishing to improve their skills. Twelve years later it would change its name to the Virginia Mechanics' Institute. It continued its work into the mid-twentieth century.

In October, members of the First Baptist Church next door to the Dooley house decamped for a new Greek Revival building on Twelfth Street. The old building was turned over to the black members of the congregation and was renamed the First African Baptist Church. As the largest hall in the city, the building remained the scene of some of the major political gatherings of the period, as well as the destination for many a torchlight parade during presidential election years.

On July 11, 1842, John and Sarah welcomed their third son. Named for his father, he was called "Jackie." Their frail second daughter, Alice Irina, was born in February 1844 but died only two months later.

That year Dooley's commitment to encouraging the intellectual life of the city led him to join approximately eighty other men in becoming a member and stockholder in the Richmond Library Company. In March he paid a three-dollar "assessment" levied on members and then, in May 1845, ten dollars for one share in the company.[25] He remained a member and stockholder until 1861, when the company transferred the library to the Virginia Historical and Philosophical Society, which by then was familiarly called by its later official name, the Virginia Historical Society.

Despite his many investments in Richmond, it was not until 1844, ten years after his arrival in the United States, that Dooley bought his first piece of Virginia real estate. Both his growing family and the construction work going on at the corner of their quiet block may have prompted him to buy the property. The medical branch of Hampden-Sydney College, which since 1838 had been using the old Union Hotel at Nineteenth and Main Streets for its classes, was building a spacious new Egyptian-style facility across from their house on what was soon to be called College Street. The chemistry lecture hall, finished in June 1845, had a 750-student capacity.[26] During the years the Dooleys lived on that street, Sunday services, evening lectures, and torchlight parades at the First African Baptist Church were occasional disturbances, but the Medical College would be busy and noisy all day, every day. Accordingly, when eight lots a block or two west across Broad Street were put up at auction in May 1844, Dooley bought one of them. The parcel was the second lot from the corner of Broad and Tenth Streets and ran the full length of the block between Broad Street and Capitol Square.[27]

Dooley's second big step that year occurred in November. Almost exactly six years to the day after he made his "Alien Report," he became an American citizen. He and his sponsors, I. Carrington and R. Hill Jr., appeared in Henrico County Quarterly Court before its four "Gentleman Justices."[28] Carrington and Hill each swore an oath that Dooley had lived in the United States for more than five years, more than one of them within the State of Virginia, and that "during that time . . . had behaved as a man of good moral character, attached to the principles of the constitution of the United States & well disposed to the good order of happiness of the same." After Dooley swore that he would "support the Constitution of the United States" and renounce all other allegiances, he was "admitted a citizen of these said United States."

In the presidential campaign of 1844, Richmond's favorite, Henry Clay, ran on the Whig ticket against the Democrat James K. Polk of Tennessee. Despite Clay's strong showing in the city, Polk carried the rest of the state and the nation.[29] In the Dooley household, however, Henry Clay remained an important figure, and John Dooley purchased the two-volume *Collection of the Speeches of the Hon. Henry Clay* when it was published in 1857. The books are now on the shelves of the library in Maymont mansion. But even before that not only John but Sarah, too, had a keen interest in Henry Clay.

Much of the credit for Sarah's interest lay with Lucy Barbour, widow of the late governor James Barbour, who in a letter published on November 14, 1844, in the *Richmond Whig* proposed that the "Whig women of Virginia" give some "token of respect" to Clay. The token Mrs. Barbour had in mind was a statue of her hero. When she and a group of Richmond women met at the First Presbyterian Church on December 9, they founded an organization they called the Virginia Association of Ladies for Erecting a Statue of Henry Clay, which later they simply referred to as the Clay Club.[30] They elected Mrs. Barbour their president and decided that a membership fee "costing no more than one dollar each" would be used to raise the money needed for the statue. They also decided to establish branches of their association, "with women as officers and collectors," throughout the state to raise additional funds. Sarah Dooley contributed her dollar and joined Mrs. Barbour's Whig women.[31] It was her first known participation in Virginia political life; it would not be her last. By this time women, perhaps including Sarah, were going in large numbers to Clay Club rallies and public political meetings.[32] By November 1845 they had raised enough money to commission the sculptor Joel Tanner Hart to design and execute the Henry Clay statue.

While Sarah was taking her first steps into political affairs, John Dooley had located a piece of land double the size of the one he had bought earlier. The new parcel was large enough to allow him to build not only a bigger house for his growing family but also a second one to sell. He sold the first lot and bought the larger one.[33] He built two houses on it and in 1847 sold the one on the corner to Sarah Bohannon, wife of Dr. Richard L. Bohannon, the obstetrics professor at the Medical College.[34]

By 1845 Dooley had built a solid reputation in the Richmond business community. His credit rating was excellent. The handwritten account in the notebook of the Richmond representative for the national credit-rating company R. G. Dun & Co. even reflected Dooley's recent real estate transactions.[35] The reporter wrote on January 15 that Dooley had "been here 8 or 10 years & made his money in the business. Owns 1 or 2 houses Character. Good. industrious. & safe." The following July the Dun reporter jotted in his notebook that Dooley was "age 35 been in business 10 years business clear. Capital & habits very good." Happily, his new house across Broad Street had room to spare even after Sarah gave birth that fall to another baby girl, this one strong and healthy. They named her Alice Elizabeth.

When the Mexican War broke out in July 1845, the United States awoke to the need for trained reserves who could be called up in times of military crisis.[36] The formation of several new volunteer companies in Richmond during the war had some impact on local businesses, including John Dooley's. Before the Mexican conflict, his contracts with militia companies involved supplying only enough hats for monthly drills and occasional ceremonial service.[37] In the decade to come, however, manufacturing military hats and caps would become big business for him, with orders coming in from other states as well as Virginia. Years later, during the Civil War, the excellent quality of Dooley's hats and the large capacity of his manufacturing works would lead to even bigger military contracts. The Mexican War ended in 1848, but Richmonders continued to form new militia companies, and within a year John Dooley had joined one of them.[38]

Meanwhile on the domestic scene, railroads, the newest and most technologically advanced form of transportation, roared ahead. Rail travel was a primary focus of attention in the Virginia legislature when it chartered new businesses in 1847, among them four railroad companies. One of these was the Richmond and Danville Railroad, for which the stock subscription books opened March 23. John Dooley subscribed for three shares and held on to them through the mid-1850s, gradually acquiring more. By 1856 he had twenty shares.[39]

Dooley's business continued to grow as the economy improved. In his report for December 1846, the R. G. Dun & Co. representative made note that Dooley's business was worth at least ten thousand dollars, "doing well & making money."[40]

CHAPTER 2

Richmond Responds to the Great Famine
and Politics in Ireland

The wintery blasts of January 1847 seemed less chilling the night the Irish novelist, poet, and songwriter Samuel Lover performed in the concert room of Richmond's Exchange Hotel. Lover's comic novel *Handy Andy* had been a best seller in the United States ever since it first appeared in 1842. Its hero, Andy Rooney, had kept the country laughing at his antics by doing everything wrong. That night in Richmond Mr. Lover presented his "favorite Irish Evening." He illustrated "the National Characteristics Mirth and Melody of his Country . . . with . . . [an] original comic story of 'The Cow that ate the Piper.'"[1]

The lighthearted picture Lover painted contrasted sharply with the actual situation in Ireland, where famine had followed the potato blight that had invaded the country in 1845. The harvest had failed the previous fall, and the American papers were filled with dark news of widespread suffering. Immigrants like John and Sarah Dooley were not the only readers who were distressed by news of the famine. As reports spread throughout the country, Americans responded with generous donations for Irish relief. In Richmond the mayor, Gen. William Lambert, called a meeting of those willing to help raise money to aid the starving in Ireland and appointed leading citizens to spearhead the fund raising. Under the headline "The Poor Irish," the March 3, 1847, issue of the *Enquirer* reported that the meeting had "raised near 3,000 dollars to send provisions to the starving Irish."

A notice published by the mayor's committee on March 10 dramatically addressed the enormity of the problem: "Famine . . . is wasting the nations of Europe. France, Belgium, Scotland, and especially Ireland, are suffering the ravages of want. In Ireland the calamity seems to be greatest, the means of relief the most remote and uncertain. The entire failure of the potato crop, and the want of other supplies, have brought millions of her people to the verge of starvation."[2] The notice also announced the establishment of "central committees" in counties across the Commonwealth to receive and forward donations to Richmond, and it promised to publish regular reports on the donations.

John Dooley, who had sisters and brothers-in-law with young families back in Ireland, must have taken very little comfort from the news in the March 25 *Whig* that there were fewer deaths "by actual starvation in Dublin, Cork, Limerick, and the other large towns."

At the end of March a proposal was made in Congress that the federal government finance ships to carry stores of food across the Atlantic.[3] After hearing news of the proposed legislation, the Richmond committee chartered its own ship, the "fine Barque *Bachelor*," to sail directly from Richmond to Dublin.[4] Loaded with provisions, the *Bachelor* sailed for Dublin on May 10 under the command of a Captain Horton. Although there is no record of Dooley contributions, his later generosity to Irish causes suggests he may well have helped provision the ship. Once it arrived in Ireland, the Quakers, who had organized soup kitchens throughout Ireland, distributed the cargo.[5]

The following year John Dooley's well-known interest in education led to another call on his generosity, this time from the nuns of the Sisters of Charity, who had decided to add a school to the "orphan asylum" for girls that they been running since 1834. Although the nuns had operated the asylum without an official charter, a board of trustees and a charter were required before they could add the school. Dooley was named one of the five original trustees in the charter for "St. Joseph's Female Academy and Orphan Asylum," granted by the Virginia General Assembly on March 27, 1848.[6]

The combined complex was a substantial one. The trustees held full financial responsibility for St. Joseph's, which the charter specified as "the power to take and hold property . . . to the amount of thirty thousand dollars"—about three-quarters of a million dollars in present-day funds.[7] John Dooley's selection as one of the five trustees is evidence of his standing in his church as well as in the city of Richmond. It was also the first indication of his commitment to the education of young women.

In early summer 1848, Sarah gave birth to another daughter. The Dooleys named her Florence Catherine. She and her sisters would eventually study at St. Joseph's Female Academy.

In July 1848 construction began on the Richmond and Danville Railroad, of which John Dooley owned three shares.[8] When the R. G. Dun & Co. representative wrote John Dooley's credit report the following September, he not only noted that Dooley "Stands well and doing a fine business" but added that Dooley had five thousand dollars invested in railroads and estimated that he was worth between twelve thousand and fifteen thousand dollars in all.[9]

Meanwhile, Irish politics figured increasingly in the international news in papers throughout the United States. The movement to repeal the Act of Union binding Ireland to control by the English Parliament was led by a popular barrister, Daniel O'Connell. The repeal initiative had been in the news for years, but more recently the papers mentioned a group of younger activists who advocated the violent overthrow of British rule. Calling themselves the Young Ireland movement, they were led by men like the newspaper editor John Mitchel, and his compatriots Thomas Francis Meagher and Smith O'Brien. In the summer of 1848, violent clashes in Limerick, John Dooley's birthplace, between government forces and members of the Young Ireland movement figured prominently in the news.

In response to the reports of political strife in Ireland, groups sprang up throughout the United States whose primary purpose was to raise money to send to the militant nationalists.[10] In August a pro-Irish faction in Richmond called on the "Friends of Ireland" to express their "sympathy" for Ireland by raising money to aid the Irish rebels. John Dooley was prominent in this new group and was elected its treasurer.[11]

The network of sympathy groups also served another purpose closer to home. They provided the basic units for Irish American militia groups.[12] The militia movement initiated by the call for volunteers to serve in the Mexican War received added impetus from the American response to Irish radicalism. Within a year such a group was organized in Richmond.[13] It was called the Montgomery Guard in honor of an Irish aristocrat, Gen. Richard Montgomery, who served in the Colonial army during the American Revolution. From its beginning, John Dooley served as a Montgomery Guard officer.

That spring the tempo of political life in Richmond quickened. It was an election year, and political party conventions were being organized. On Tuesday evening, March 20, Dooley attended a large and "most enthusiastic" meeting of Whig Party members across Broad Street at the First African Baptist Church.[14] Two thousand people filled the seats that night to choose delegates to the Whig convention, which would nominate a candidate to run for their district's seat in the U.S. Congress. When two hundred delegates to the convention were chosen at the meeting, Dooley was among them.

By the end of the 1850s John Dooley was both prominent and financially comfortable. His personal property tax records for the early 1850s reveal that by 1852 he had acquired two gold watches, two clocks, a piano, thirty-five pieces of gold or silver "plate," six hundred dollars' worth of household and kitchen furniture, three slaves, two "horses or mules" valued at $125, and a "pleasure" carriage worth $150.[15] In 1859 five slaves appear on the list. The piano and harp added by 1855 indicate that the Dooley children were growing up in a household that was not only prosperous but also cultured.[16]

Dooley's 1849 decision to send his eight-year-old son Jim to Dr. Socrates

Maupin's Classical and Mathematical Academy for Boys supports that suggestion. Maupin was an erudite medical doctor with extraordinary credentials. In addition to his medical degree, he had a master's degree in classical languages and literature. He was one of the founders of the Medical College of Virginia and had served as the faculty president. There were many good schools for boys in Richmond in the 1840s and 1850s, but Dr. Maupin's was considered the very best.[17] One of Jim's classmates at Dr. Maupin's was Edward Valentine, who became a friend and later a renowned sculptor.

Educational opportunities for the Dooley children were not limited to the hours they spent in school. The location of their house diagonally across Broad Street from the First African Baptist Church and just two blocks east of Capitol Square made it easy for the family to keep abreast of current politics and take part in ceremonial events. The children and their parents had to walk only a few steps to hear great orators like Daniel Webster and Henry Clay or to see in person the governors of Virginia and the presidents of the United States, who made a point of speaking on the south portico of the Capitol Building even if their visits in Richmond were only a few hours long.[18] An education in American political activism and the duties of citizenship thus was readily available to every member of the family. Not surprisingly, the family library contained many biographies and books of speeches by the best-known political figures of Ireland, Great Britain, and the United States.[19] The location of their house also guaranteed that no one in the family could possibly miss the firing of minute guns and cannons, the fireworks, or the parades.

Ceremonies in honor of national heroes, martial music, and fireworks did not, however, distract John Dooley from the demands of his manufacturing business or from opportunities to invest his capital. On February 1, 1850, he bought another residential property in the neighborhood, this time strictly for investment purposes. Dooley's purchase, which cost him $4,500, was a brick house on the north side of three-block-long Ross Street. At a time when mortgages were paid off quickly, Dooley put $1,138 down and promised to pay the remainder plus interest in three installments due in six, twelve, and eighteen months.[20] His new property lay next door to an imposing four-story house on the corner of Ross and Governor Streets owned by another Irish immigrant, Dr. John Cullen, a distinguished member of the Medical College of Virginia faculty with a large and profitable private practice.[21]

During the next decade Richmond's population rose to almost thirty-eight thousand, and its industrial base grew significantly as well, in large part because of the railroad.[22] When the Louisa Railroad prospered sufficiently to extend its tracks, it changed its name to the Virginia Central Railroad, and Dooley bought a share of stock in the new company.[23] His hat manufacturing business was thriving as well. At the end of 1849, R. G. Dun & Co. estimated Dooley's worth at fifteen thousand dollars or more; by January 1853, it had risen to thirty thousand dollars.[24]

Taken together, the Dun & Co. credit reports offer an impressive thumbnail portrait of Dooley's character. He was "very honest and worthy," and he had made a "snug little fortune even tho' he is easy & indulging." The reporter even commented on Dooley's short stature, noting that he stood "high in every respect (except in size)." In June 1857 the Dun reporter noted approvingly that Dooley "does the largest wholesale and retail business in his line," that he was very "attentive," "prudent," and "of strict integrity." When a financial panic hit the nation in 1857 and many businesses tottered and fell, Dooley continued to win praise as "a very clever man of good business capacity . . . pays very promptly and has throughout the pressure in some cases anticipated payment before maturity. He enjoys deservedly good Credit. And is perfectly safe for his contracts, no danger with him."[25]

In July 1850, Richmonders witnessed a benchmark event in southern industrial history. Until then, locomotives for Virginia railroads had been purchased abroad in Liverpool, England. In 1850, for the first time, a railroad locomotive was built locally.[26] Talbot & Bros. foundry, a manufacturer of steam engines for canal boats, produced a steam engine named the *Roanoke* for the Richmond and Danville Railroad for $7,500. As a Danville stockholder and a supporter of the "home" manufacture movement from the date of his first newspaper ad in 1836, Dooley must have been delighted that the company had given the commission for its first locomotive to a local firm. The trip of the *Roanoke* from the foundry to the canal basin was a noisy and exciting event for the whole city.

Another indication of the rapid growth of the railroads and subsidiary industries in Richmond is that by 1853 a Talbot & Bros. competitor, the Tredegar Iron Works, had contracts for twenty locomotives for a variety of railroad companies.[27] The new mode of transportation was still, however, considered a risky investment. When a bill to incorporate the Richmond and York River Railroad passed the Virginia legislature in January 1853, it included a provision that the state would invest in the company only after five hundred thousand dollars' worth of stock had been sold to other investors.[28] John Dooley paid five hundred dollars to acquire his five shares.[29] When in March the

General Assembly transformed the Richmond and Petersburg Railroad from a wholly owned entity of the Board of Public Works into a stock company, Dooley bought twenty shares of it as well.[30]

The expansion of the railroads and the burgeoning prosperity of the city could not, however, obscure rising political tensions between the North and the South over whether to allow slavery in newly admitted states. Talk of secession escalated as debates grew more heated in Congress and across the country. Even after a compromise proposed by Henry Clay and guided through Congress by Illinois senator Stephen A. Douglas was passed in September 1850, some Virginians were still so angry that they formed a state-wide organization called the Southern Rights Association of Virginia. Richmonders formed their own branch—the Southern Rights Association of Richmond—and drew up a list of "Articles of Association for the Defence of Southern Rights," which was duly published in the *Enquirer.* According to the article, the list was "intended as a guide for such of our citizens as may be disposed to unite in forming associations for common defence against the aggressive spirit of the North." The very first provision on the list asserted, "We will not hereafter, knowingly . . . buy any commodity produced in or imported from any non-slaveholding State of this confederacy; provided as good, or sufficient substitutes, produced elsewhere, can be bought in our neighboring towns."[31]

Although John Dooley continued to travel to the North frequently on business, he joined the association. In the years to come, his advertisements often reminded customers that although he did business throughout the United States, his allegiance lay with the South. By 1856 Dooley's advertisement in Ellyson's *Richmond Directory and Business Advertiser* not only indicated that the company had grown considerably during the interval since 1852 but also reflected his political sentiments. Its new name, the Great Southern Hat and Cap Manufactory Depot, appeared in the advertisement above Dooley's name.

A few months after the formation of the Richmond branch of the Southern Rights Association, a meeting of merchants from across Virginia demonstrated the degree to which politics and business prospects had become intertwined. The subject was "direct trade." It stemmed from their impatience with problems relating to the import and export of goods through northern ports and had been festering even before the enmity between the North and the South over the slavery issue had grown venomous. Railroad expansion had made it possible to bypass northern ports and ship goods directly to foreign markets through southern ports. The convergence of the developments in railroad service with the rise of political tension made direct trade seem not only feasible but highly desirable. At stake for the merchants was nothing less than "the commercial independence of the South."[32]

The demands of business did not prevent John Dooley from taking an active role as an officer in the Montgomery Guard. The company grew slowly at first and did not have sufficient numbers to participate in militia events until 1851, when it adopted an emerald-green uniform and readied itself for service. That May, the Montgomery Guard joined the other militia groups of the city in becoming a part of the First Regiment of Virginia Volunteers.

In December 1852, Senior 1st Lieutenant John Dooley agreed to the pleasant duty of serving as one of forty "managers" of the Montgomery Guard's first Civic and Military Ball.[33] Among the others were Virginia's first popularly elected governor, Joseph Johnson; the mayor of Richmond, Gen. William Lambert; and the captains and lieutenants of the other militia companies in the city. The "committee on arrangements" promised "good music and plenty of it," as well as supper and other refreshments provided by an "experienced caterer [of] known skill." Tickets for men were $2.50; there was no charge for ladies. The *Dispatch* carried a full account of the event right down to the decorations, declaring the ball "a star in the horizon of our social enjoyment."[34] Subsequently, the Montgomery Guard ball became an annual event in Richmond, with John Dooley always serving among the managers.

Some months later, the Montgomery Guard discharged another kind of duty when the First Virginia acted as host for the one-day visit of a Baltimore regiment called the Law Greys. It was one of many such visits of militia from one state to another. John Dooley marched at the front of his company at one o'clock on a mild spring day when the First Virginia paraded down Broad Street. The Greys responded with a light infantry drill of military maneuvers to the "tap of the drum"—a performance greatly admired by the members of the First. After the review both regiments marched to the Military Hall, where they heard speeches and were served "a sumptuous collation."[35]

A speech delivered by a captain of the Greys reflected the growing sectional tensions. The officer declared that he "hoped that this Union might never be dissolved, and [said] that as Marylanders they were with the South, if it must come to that—and that if a fanaticism of the North rendered it necessary, Maryland would go heart to heart and shoulder to shoulder with Virginia and with the entire South."

That same evening, Richmond had its first peek at an Irish political refugee. Several exiles were traveling in the United States after escaping from the British penal colony in Van Diemen's Land (present-day Tasmania), to which they had been sent after being convicted of treason for their roles in the Young Ireland movement. In part because they claimed to have modeled their movement after the American Revolution, Thomas Francis Meagher and John Mitchel were received as heroes when they arrived in the United States, and their sagas were widely reported in the American press.[36] Meagher, the first to visit Richmond, arrived to give a lecture at the First African Baptist Church just as the mild weather turned cold and snowy. The fifty-cent tickets to Meagher's lecture had been available the previous week at the American Hotel, where he was staying, and also at several stores in the city, including John Dooley's.[37] When Meagher entered the hall on the appointed night, the audience, including "several" women, rose to its feet and clapped enthusiastically. Alluding to Patrick Henry's famed "Give me liberty, or give me death" speech, Meagher proclaimed that "these words, when I was but 12 years old, struck the chords of my heart and caused them to vibrate, and the vibration has not yet ceased."[38] An admiring account of the event in the *Dispatch* described Meagher as a young man with "handsome features, black hair, and . . . fine muscular development—The countenance, frank and fearless. . . . His delivery is clear, deliberate and strikingly effective." Unmentioned was the fact that the revolutionary hero had a habit of borrowing money he never repaid, from John Dooley among others.[39]

Home life became difficult for the Dooley family that spring as John's younger sister, twenty-seven-year-old Ann, who had lived with them since their arrival in Richmond, began to show signs of mental illness. By June 1853, John had taken her to Baltimore for what was to have been a yearlong rest cure at Mount Hope, a retreat center for the mentally ill operated by the Sisters of Charity. Ann remained there for the rest of her life, first at her brother's expense and eventually at her nephew Jim's. She died on February 2, 1894, at the age of sixty-nine, after thirty-seven years in the institution.[40]

Dooley faced a different sort of problem in midsummer, when Dr. Socrates Maupin closed his Classical and Mathematical Academy to accept an invitation from the University of Virginia to head its chemistry department. By that time Jim had been studying at Dr. Maupin's for four years. Fortunately, an Irish schoolmaster named Richard Tighe arrived in Richmond to fill the vacuum left by Dr. Maupin's departure. Tighe's advertisement, three times longer than any of the others in the *Enquirer*'s "Schools and Colleges" column, announced the opening of the "College Grammar School, Richmond; Richard H. L. Tighe, A.M., Principal" and revealed that Mr. Tighe was a graduate of Trinity College in Dublin, Ireland.[41] The advertisement proclaimed Tighe's intention of educating boys for "professional and commercial life." Importantly for the young Dooleys, it also declared that "the course of instruction will furnish a complete preparation for any class in College." At the bottom of the ad was an impressive list of references for Tighe from such personages as the bishop of New York and other clergymen in New York City, Brooklyn, and Philadelphia. The advertisement also included a short letter of recommendation from the rector of St. John's Church on Richmond's Church Hill. This letter alone hinted that Mr. Tighe himself was a clergyman and, interestingly for the education of the Catholic Dooley boys, an Episcopalian, not a Catholic, priest.

When Richard Tighe's school, located "in a pleasant part of Franklin street, between 6th and 7th streets," opened, the faculty included a Mr. Murfee, "a distinguished graduate of the Virginia Military Institute" who taught mathematics; and a Mr. Michard, who taught modern languages, in addition, of course, to Tighe himself, who taught classics and English and made "Reading, Writing and Spelling the objects of his special attention."[42] Jim's record at Georgetown College, which he entered three years after he began his studies with Mr. Tighe, suggests that he was not only bright but also well prepared. He became the first student in the history of the college to be first in his class each of his four undergraduate years.

I n late January 1854, John Dooley's sister Mary Byrne, her husband, Michael, and their three small children left Ireland for New York. They boarded the United States mail steamer *Pacific* in Liverpool and traveled first class (thanks to the generosity of Mary's brother, who paid their way). The advertisements for the *Pacific* declared it "unequaled for elegance and comfort" and boasted that "an experienced surgeon is attached to each ship."[1] Unfortunately, the surgeon couldn't save the life of Mary Byrne, who died on board of complications following a miscarriage.[2] Dooley went to New York to accompany Mary's body, Michael, and the children on the steamer *Jamestown* for a record-breaking thirty-hour trip from New York to Richmond. They left New York at 4:00 p.m. Saturday, February 11, and arrived in Richmond early Monday morning, February 13, after a stop in Norfolk.[3] The funeral was at three thirty that afternoon at St. Peter's. John buried his sister in the Dooley family plot next to his mother, who had been interred there in 1838.

Dooley then faced the task of helping his bereaved brother-in-law and his young children settle into life in their new country. The substantial real estate investments he had begun to make in Chicago—then a raw town on the edge of the western frontier—provided a solution. He had an account with a Chicago bank and a lawyer in Chicago to handle his legal work, but his property was of sufficient size and complexity to require on-site management that he could not personally provide. Although Byrne was a farmer, he was not a laborer but rather a farm manager of some sophistication, and Dooley decided that he was just the man to manage his growing real estate holdings in Chicago.[4]

The rest of 1854 was brighter for the family. In late May, John agreed to serve on a committee appointed by Mayor Joseph Mayo to invite another Irish political exile, John Mitchel, to speak in Richmond. Dooley and Mitchel were destined to become close friends, and the Dooley and Mitchel family histories intertwined for many years to come. Mitchel had escaped from Van Diemen's Land not long after Thomas Meagher and had been in the United States for just seven months before he was invited to Richmond. Like Meagher, he had received a hero's welcome in San Francisco and New York, and his opposition to the abolition movement and to the Know-Nothing Party quickly brought him nationwide renown.[5] Since Mitchel had already decided to take a southern speaking tour, he readily accepted the invitation to speak in Richmond.

When he arrived, the reception committee tucked him into the carriage of the lawyer James Lyons for the ride to the hotel. The Montgomery Guard in full green and white summer uniform, the "lively airs of the Armory Band," and the "deafening cheers of thousands of persons" accompanied him.[6]

There was a banquet in Mitchel's honor the next night that many complained cost too much, but the governor, the mayor, and some 150 others, including John Dooley, managed to find the money. The dining room of the Exchange Hotel was decorated with the flag of Richmond's oldest militia company, the Light Infantry Blues, as well as that of the Montgomery Guard. After dinner, the host for the evening, John M. Patton, a lawyer and former three-term U.S. congressman who had been acting governor of Virginia in 1841, introduced Mitchel. In the course of his remarks, Patton referred to "the large number of emigrants annually arriving in this country . . . and congratulated them . . . that here they were . . . free to enjoy life and liberty after their own notions, with none to make them afraid." Patton welcomed Mitchel as "our distinguished guest" and added, "We . . . cheer him in his exile." Mitchel stood as the band played a tune then popular called "Exile of Erin."[7]

Mitchel left Richmond the next day, no doubt with gratifying memories of its hospitality. His acquaintance with John Dooley eventually grew into a close friendship, fostered in part by Dooley's business trips to New York. Mitchel edited a newspaper there called the *Citizen* that became so successful it was distributed nationwide. John read it in Richmond, and Michael Byrne, in Chicago, where it was readily available in men's reading rooms.

Mitchel, however, was uncomfortable in New York and decided to move south permanently. He and his family decamped for Knoxville, Tennessee, where in 1857 he began to publish a new paper called the *Southern Citizen*. John Dooley not only read it but advertised in it.[8] Thanks to the Virginia and Tennessee Railroad, he had been able to expand his business territory well beyond the confines of Virginia. The *Southern Citizen* was a perfect vehicle for advertising in this new territory.

Although John Mitchel had been warmly welcomed in Richmond, there were men in Virginia and across the United States who did not share this hospitable view of new arrivals. In the winter of 1854 a new and disturbing political movement had begun to take shape. Secretive and nativist in its leanings, the Know-Nothing Party aimed to terrorize immigrants rather than welcome them. Not surprisingly in light of the religion practiced by a large portion of the Irish and German immigrants then pouring into the United States, it was virulently anti-Catholic. The party's presence in Virginia had been recognized in a March 1854 meeting of the Democrats of Henrico County, which issued some resolutions expressing the platform they favored for the coming statewide elections. Among them was a condemnation: "The principles of the new party which has sprung up among us . . . do not commend themselves to our approval. Though a large majority of us are protestants and native born citizens, yet we can not consent to make either the accident of births, or the profession of any particular religious faith the sole tests of patriotism or official capacity."[9] Although Know-Nothingism was challenged in Virginia by Governor Henry Wise and others, the situation for new immigrants over the next several years was not as comfortable as it had been for earlier arrivals.

During the summer of 1854, Dooley once again was one of a group of citizens involved in expanding the educational opportunities for workingmen, this time by transforming and enlarging the Mechanics Association, soon to be known as the Mechanics' Institute. Dooley and the others who established the association remained among the officers and managers of the institute.[10] Under their auspices its expanded curriculum provided instruction in chemistry, English, and architectural drawing; by 1858 more than 150 men were enrolled. The board of the institute also established a school of design, a chemical laboratory, a library, public lectures, and an annual exhibit of students' work. Within two years, the institute had five hundred students.[11] The oldest such school in the South, it would provide low-cost evening school for generations of workingmen in Richmond well into the mid-twentieth century.

The summer of 1854 also saw a cholera epidemic break out in Richmond, and from early July until late August death struck black and white, rich and poor alike. Those who could, left the city, and business came almost to a standstill. The Dooley family was spared, though there was considerable concern because Sarah was once again in a "delicate condition." Finally in September, a tiny but healthy baby girl named Sarah Evelyn—called Saidie by the family—arrived safely six years after her nearest sibling.[12]

In November 1854 the Virginia Democratic Party held its convention in Richmond, well aware that the Know-Nothing Party had won elections in Massachusetts and Delaware and had helped defeat the Democrats in Pennsylvania, Ohio, and Indiana. After "heated polling" the Democrats nominated Henry A. Wise to run for governor. A former Whig, Wise was an articulate and experienced politician with a cosmopolitan outlook. He had served six terms in the U.S. House of Representatives, from 1832 to 1844, and three years as the U.S. minister to Brazil, from 1844 to 1847. He had already written a 1,200-word manifesto denouncing the Know-Nothings for their attacks on immigrants and Catholics, and after his nomination he ran a vigorous campaign against them in the early months of 1855.[13] Wise's campaign found a convert in another former Whig, John Dooley, who joined the Democratic Party and later became a friend of Wise's.

Although 1855 opened "with a gloomy outlook for business," Dooley kept his employees occupied making hats at a faster-than-usual rate. His March advertisement did not reflect any doubts about the economy.[14] On the contrary, it was rather chatty: "NEW AND FASHIONABLE HATS, FOR SPRING 1855— JOHN DOOLEY 81 MAIN STREET, RICHMOND, VA. . . . Having kept in constant employment during the past dull and hard winter, all his hands, (male and female) he has accumulated a much larger stock than is usually on hand at this period of the year." This ad is the first-known evidence that Dooley employed women as well as men in his manufacturing operation. During the Civil War, the serious shortage of manpower in all aspects of manufacturing in Richmond would require him to employ a great many women.

St. Patrick's Day 1855 was celebrated in Richmond with a dinner in Corinthian Hall. Approximately seventy men were present, "the majority being Irish citizens," for dinner, speeches, champagne toasts, songs, and "wit of a high order."[15] There were at least seventeen toasts, among them one by Thomas Jefferson's grandson George W. Randolph. When the others called on him "vociferously" to give a toast, he responded by giving a very graceful one: "The Commonwealth of Virginia and her Adopted Sons. Whom the law hath joined together let no man put asunder."

Although the men at the St. Patrick's Day dinner represented the anti–Know-Nothing feeling current in Virginia, there was at least one episode on St. Patrick's Day that suggested nativism was not completely absent from the capital. A brief item in the *Dispatch* under the heading "Paddies" gave an account of some "mischievous boys" who had placed small, probably straw, figures wearing necklaces strung with potatoes in front of the houses belonging to some Irish immigrants. The newspaper reported that "such jokes have become too stale even to create a laugh, unless some son of the Emerald Isle gets into a pet on seeing the caricature, which did not occur. . . . About 1 o'clock a number of boys passed up Governor street with a 'Paddy' astride a stick, but no one appeared to be offended at their sport."

Later in March, at the invitation of the Democratic Association, Illinois senator Stephen A. Douglas came to speak. He was well received by the large audience at the First African Baptist Church, who heard him denounce the Know-Nothing Party for making "birthplace instead of merit, the standard for office." He also insisted that religion should not be a qualification either. He urged "those democrats who had joined the [Know-Nothing] order, to withdraw from it and return to their first love."[16]

In the summer of 1855, a yellow fever epidemic spread quickly and devastatingly in Virginia. The first cases hit Norfolk and Portsmouth in July. By the time the death toll had mounted to nearly a hundred victims per day, business had shut down. There were only a few cases in Richmond, but enough to worry the city fathers. On August 9 the Richmond City Council adopted quarantine regulations forbidding anyone from Norfolk or Portsmouth to enter the city.[17] Richmonders held a public meeting and raised almost ten thousand dollars to help the other two cities.

At the height of the epidemic, Dooley took his usual business trip up north. He also visited Chicago to check on his real estate holdings and to purchase wholesale goods such as furs for his hat manufacturing business. By then Michael Byrne was investing large sums for him in Chicago real estate, contracting to have houses built on Dooley's lots, overseeing those projects, and suggesting future investments. Correspondence on business matters between the brothers-in-law in the years that followed provided not only a record of Dooley's financial commitments in Chicago and a picture of the extended Dooley family's life but also revealing glimpses of life in Chicago and the nationwide Irish immigrant network at that time.[18]

After returning to Richmond, Dooley sent his power of attorney to Byrne to enable him to handle the paperwork required when purchasing property on his behalf. In the accompanying letter, he authorized Byrne to invest no more than twelve thousand dollars in real estate for him at that time. In his August 15 response to Dooley's letter, however, Byrne, who couldn't resist a deal, admitted to exceeding Dooley's instructions and putting one-fourth down on a property for sale for $2,800 while still in the preliminary negotiation for a large piece costing twelve thousand dollars. It was only the first of many occasions when Byrne cavalierly disregarded Dooley's instructions. Inside Byrne's letter was a letter from a member of the extended Dooley family in Ireland, Denis Heaton, the farmer husband of Dooley's sister Sally. The Heatons were preparing to emigrate to Illinois. By the fall Dooley had bought farmland for them near the Illinois Canal southwest of Chicago and also sent them money to pay for their trip across the Atlantic that winter.[19] By spring he had paid to have a house built for them and paid a portion of the subscription to their church.[20]

Sometime during 1855, George Dooley, who turned eighteen that October, joined his father's business. Apparently uninterested in continuing his education, George became a salesman in his father's firm, and his name appeared the following year in the Richmond directory, right under his father's entry: "Dooley, George J. salesman with J. Dooley, 81 Main; res. Broad, be. 12th and 14th."[21]

His fourteen-year-old brother Jim continued at Mr. Tighe's school. Like his father, he loved to read and treasured his books. A tattered copy of a book now on the shelves of Maymont mansion suggests that he even treasured his schoolbooks. Its title page is torn. The insides of the front and back covers and its flyleaves are covered with scribbling, some of it in Latin and some of it in English. The second flyleaf declares in block letters, "Latin Exercise Dictionary 1855." Below it in small, plain, and neat handwriting is the name "James H. Dooley, Richmond, Virginia." Something written on the last flyleaf in the back of the book suggests the daydreams of its owner: "When I have $5.178.360 I will stop making money J. D."[22] Daydreams about becoming rich are not unusual in the young, but this dream is different. It is a dream of retiring from the quest for wealth and suggests that as a teenager Jim was unusually thoughtful.

By late autumn yellow fever had almost disappeared from Virginia, but the two thousand deaths among adults in Norfolk during the epidemic had left many children orphaned. Since facilities there were insufficient to handle the number of orphans left behind, many were sent to Richmond to be housed. John Dooley was keenly aware of the influx. As winter drew near, many of the poorest boys who had no homes became street urchins, and their dire situation prompted John to serve as president of a newly established branch of the Young Catholic Friend Society, one of several such groups in Virginia.[23] The purpose of the local organization was to provide the orphan boys not only warm clothing and shoes but also education in a Sunday school especially designed to serve their needs. The school eventually became a five-day institution called St. Peter's Cathedral School for Boys. The group could not have begun its work at a more critical moment for the orphans, because the new year brought a terrible cold spell that caused great suffering among the poor of the city.

Sometime during the winter, both George Dooley and his mother fell seriously ill.[24] They were both still sick in late April when Dooley received a letter from Michael Byrne, who was then in New York preparing to board ship for a voyage to Ireland. The ostensible purpose of his trip was to bring to the United States the three oldest children he and his wife had left in Irish boarding schools when they had immigrated. Byrne planned to spend three months in Ireland, for which, as he explained in the letter, he expected John to provide at least $1,500. When Byrne ran out of money while there, he wrote to ask for more. Each time Dooley provided the requested funds, but the demands of the extended family on his pocketbook must have seemed unending.[25] He was still sending money to the Heatons in Illinois, who were settling into the house and farm he had bought for them. Nonetheless he kept Byrne in his employ and supported the other members of the family for years.

By summer, Sarah Dooley was at last strong enough to take George to one of the Virginia springs renowned for its curative powers. By the end of the summer, Sarah seemed to have fully regained her strength. George, however, remained very ill.

Financially, at least, the Dooleys were thriving. John Dooley's hat business continued to prosper. Just how prosperous it had become was apparent in 1856, when Dooley's firm was one of only two hat manufacturing businesses in the United States featured in a nationally distributed mercantile guide. Published in Philadelphia, the guidebook had an extraordinarily long title that summarized its contents: *Leading Pursuits and Leading Men. A Treatise on the Principal Trades and Manufacturers of the United States. Showing the Progress, State and Prospects of Business: and Illustrated by Sketches of Distinguished Mercantile and Manufacturing Firms.* Dooley was described as "the proprietor of one of the largest and most elegant hat establishments in the Union." His entry further observed that "twenty years ago he arrived in Richmond with very little other means than a knowledge of his trade and a cheerful disposition and buoyant spirits. Though an entire stranger in that community, he was not long without friends; for the citizens of Richmond, who are proverbially hospitable, generously encouraged him in his new enterprise."[26]

By late 1856, when the first rumblings of the financial panic of 1857 could already be felt, some others in the hat manufacturing business in Richmond and other cities turned to Dooley for help. Fortunately, his business was so successful that he had money to invest, and lending funds to others in the industry, though not risk-free, was an attractive option for him. He became a kind of banker for other hatters in Richmond and elsewhere and lent a good deal of money to them.[27]

One of those Dooley could not save was a hat manufacturer named James Collins, a member of the Montgomery Guard, who had borrowed two thousand dollars in 1854 to help him finance the introduction of a new hat-making invention in Richmond. Collins's business was a small one aimed at a niche market, primarily customers whose heads were hard to fit. In early 1852 he had purchased a new kind of confirmator, the device used to shape and size hats during the hat-making process. His advertisements in the city directory boasted that he had "a beautiful French typographical confirmateur" and declared that complaints about "ill-fitting hats" and "prejudices of some to wearing silk hats in consequence of some malformation of the head" had "induced me to procure . . . one . . . at much trouble and expense." His ads also appealed to "The Medical Faculty and lovers of the Sciences generally," who were "respectfully invited to call and examine the INSTRUMENT, which, from its peculiar construction . . . will . . . simplify facts hitherto intricate and abstruse in the science of Phrenology."

Unfortunately, by 1856 Collins was over his head in debt to creditors in New York, Philadelphia, Baltimore, Norfolk, and Richmond. He was forced to declare bankruptcy in August 1856 and had to turn over all the assets of his hat shop and all his other property to a trustee. John Dooley was named "first class" creditor in the bankruptcy suit, which meant that he would have been the first creditor to be repaid if there were any proceeds from the bankruptcy auction, but he was a soft touch as usual and willing to be regarded as one of the second-class creditors to the extent of his "open account of two thousand dollars or thereabouts," a huge sum in those days.[28]

In September 1856 an Irish hatter in Philadelphia named John O'Byrne, whose situation was similar to Collins's, wrote to Dooley, "Embarrassments come thick on me, my gross liabilities are between $10,000 & $11,000 against that I have about $14,000 good assets in Stock . . . due bills and notes." O'Byrne's debt to Dooley accounted for one thousand dollars of the liabilities.[29] By the following May, despite Dooley's help, O'Byrne was in even worse financial shape and unable to meet his obligations.[30] It is a measure of the stability of Dooley's firm that despite those bad loans his net worth continued to increase.

Bank stock was by now included in Dooley's investment portfolio, and he had been named to a seat on the board of the Commercial Savings Bank. (A couple of years later, Dooley would also invest in the Bank of the Commonwealth. He had twenty-five shares for which he had paid one hundred dollars each.)[31] Among the other members of the Commercial Savings board was a prosperous young shopkeeper named Lewis Ginter.[32] Of Dutch extraction, he had come to Richmond from New York City. Several decades later, he was to figure prominently in the life of Richmond's business community as president of one of the city's largest tobacco manufacturing enterprises. By then he had become a friend and associate of Dooley's son Jim.

In the late summer of 1856, Dooley had decided to send both Jim and Jackie away to school. Jim was ready to enter Georgetown College; Jackie, Georgetown's preparatory school. The burden of taking care of his invalid eldest son, George, may have been a factor in his decision.

Because the dates for the opening of Georgetown College and its preparatory school were a week apart, John Dooley, who accompanied the boys to their new schools, had to make not one but two lengthy trips from Richmond to the District of Columbia that September. On the twenty-first, he took his Jim, age fifteen, and a large trunk containing Jim's belongings by train to Aquia Creek, where father, son, and trunk boarded a ferry to cross the Potomac to Washington. Once there, they boarded yet another train for a hilly little neighborhood on the western side of the District of Columbia, where the spires of Georgetown College overlooked the Potomac. A hack deposited them and the trunk at the gate of the imposing main building. There John enrolled Jim for a five-month term in "First Humanities."[1] They had brought with them, as required by the college, a written recommendation from Mr. Tighe.[2] But even so Jim had to be examined by the prefect of studies to determine the appropriate level of study. The full cost of the term was two hundred dollars, much of which John had apparently paid in advance.[3] That day he also paid seventy-five dollars for board and $2.50 for medical aid.[4]

Meanwhile Jim's large trunk had been hauled to his room. In it were the black frock coat, two vests (a black one and a white one), a pair of white pantaloons for summer wear and a blue pair for winter that constituted the required college uniform to be worn for special occasions as well as whenever a student left the college. There were also, as required, two other suits for daily wear on campus, six shirts, six pairs of stockings, six pocket handkerchiefs, three pairs of shoes, a hat, and a heavy coat or cloak.[5] Tucked in among his clothes were the silver spoon and fork required by the college. Both Jim and Jackie had misplaced their spoons by the end of their first year, and the $3.12 cost of a college-supplied replacement appeared on the bills for each of them in the Georgetown ledger book for September 1857. Although Irish American students constituted the third-most prominent ethnic group from the South at Georgetown in the 1850s, the Dooley boys were unusual because very few of the others were the sons of immigrants.[6] Most of the others were sons of young professionals, mainly lawyers and doctors. Only 8 percent of the students' fathers were businessmen.

Both the Dooley boys did well that first year. Jim, in addition to taking the regularly required classes in First Humanities, also took piano lessons all year. By the end of the strenuous spring term, his eyes were bothering him, but he had earned the first-place medal in the First Humanities class as well as the first-place medal in first-level mathematics and honorable mentions, called "Accesserunts," in third-level French and "First Class of Music."[7] It had not been all work and no play for either boy that year, however. Georgetown offered a full complement of extracurricular activities for its students, and they took advantage of those opportunities, too. During his first year Jim joined the Reading-Room Association, which gave students interested in current events a place where they could find reliable information on the leading topics of the day by reading "the principal journals published in the country . . . together with the most popular, interesting, and instructive of the foreign and domestic Reviews and Magazines." Jim remained a member throughout his four years at Georgetown, serving as an officer in his second and third years.[8] During his first year he also joined the Philonomosian Society, a debating club for first- and second-year students. Jim's enthusiasm for debate was surpassed only by his love of acting. Both he and Jackie joined the Dramatic Association.[9]

By June, when Jim and Jackie were finishing their first year at Georgetown, their father had become the founder and officer of another charitable organization, this one intended to help the immigrants who continued to pour into Richmond. Although most if not all of its founders were Irish and they called themselves the Hibernian Society, they did not limit themselves to helping Irish immigrants: their purpose was to help all immigrants, regardless of "birth, religion or politics." According to the *Dispatch* report the Monday after its first meeting, "If an emigrant comes to the city, friendless and moneyless, in search of employment, he will be sought out, his immediate necessities relieved, and good counsels given him, so that he may, with proper exertion, obtain an honorable livelihood. It is believed that in this manner many a poor fellow may be saved from degradation, if not utter ruin."[10]

Jim and Jackie had only been home for a few days of summer vacation when their mother and father became parents for the ninth and last time. Josephine Estelle Dooley was born on July 15. The family called her "Josie," and John asked Michael Byrne to be her godfather.

A month later John took Jim with him on a business trip to New York and Chicago. While in Illinois Jim had a chance to see for himself the substantial investments his father had made in residential property in the suburbs. On August 12, 1857, John wrote to his wife:

We came by way of the beautiful Hudson River and Niagara Falls . . . Jim you know is a good deal of a stoic—he expresses very little wonder at those great wonders of the world but probably feels and I believe he does feel great astonishment—he certainly has a mind capable of drinking in and appreciating great and stupendous works of Nature like these—and can when he talks descant in very apropos language on the merits and demerits of most things that come under his observation. . . . I am glad I brought him for I might never have the same opportunity at home—I have so little time there of talking to him as freely as I have done since we commenced our trip. I find he possesses a great deal of information on a great many subjects and can form a very clear and good sense judgement in matters that you would scarcely think he knows any thing about. . . . I think he is greatly benefitted by the Trip—he finds no eating tho any where as good as the Astor house New York—that's Jim's "Beau Idea" of a Hotel—and so it is a great house in the eating line—it would make you laugh to see with what a gusto Jim enjoy'd it.[11]

Dooley concluded the letter with observations about Chicago itself and the changes it had undergone since his last visit: "It really is wonderful to see the energy enterprize and determination evinced to make the Place great," he wrote. "And great I do really believe it must be in a few Years . . . from the situation of the Place its back country capable of almost feeding and producing for a world—its fine Lake where any amount of shipping can be harbored and any amount of Commerce carried on it seems to me to be destined for a great Place."

Jim for his part took the lessons of his trip to New York and Chicago to heart. Years later he followed his father's footsteps and bought real estate in suburbs of cities on the verge of development in three states: Virginia, Alabama, and Minnesota.

Shortly after father and son returned to Richmond, John Dooley faced and survived what a local historian later described as "one of the worst financial panics that had ever visited" Richmond.[12] The Panic of 1857 was felt nationwide, and banks in cities throughout the country suspended specie payment. John Dooley, whose position on bank and insurance company boards gave him an insider's perspective on the nation's finances, calmly rode out the storm. As usual his business continued to grow even as others around him were failing. It was at this point that, thanks to the extension of the Virginia railroad network beyond its own borders, he was able to expand the territory of his Great Southern Hat and Cap Manufactory and Depot into Tennessee and take out large ads in John Mitchel's *Southern Citizen.*

Despite the financial panic, in mid-October the Mechanics' Institute held its annual fair, at which Richmond-made articles were featured. Praise of the fair in the *Dispatch* had a Southern Rights Association ring to it, including a comment that the exhibits of locally made items strengthened "a feeling in behalf of Southern independence that no true Virginian can despise or disregard."[13] In fact, the institute was doing so well that on October 28, it laid the cornerstone for a building of its own. Formerly, its classes had been scattered in locations throughout the city. Now they would be consolidated in one place.

Spring found both Sarah and George Dooley sick again. Throughout most of April Sarah was quite ill, and although she slowly began to recover, John wrote to Byrne that George was "rather worse if anything."[14] Jackie added to his father's burdens when he wrote that he had decided to become a priest. The decision upset his father, who said so in a letter to Byrne. Byrne replied, "I can hardly join your dread of his becoming a priest. . . . I wish I had a son worthy enough to devote himself to so holy a calling."[15]

Meanwhile, Jim's academic success during his second year at Georgetown led to his being chosen to give a speech at the moving-up ceremonies for first- and second-year students during the college's July commencement festivities. Unquestionably, hearing Jim give his first public speech would have been a proud moment for John Dooley, but his duties in the Montgomery Guard prevented his attending the ceremony.[16] He also missed seeing both boys receive first-place medals, Jim in the Class of Poetry and Jackie in the First Division of the Class of Second Humanities.

Back in Richmond, their father and the rest of the Montgomery Guard participated in a ceremony of a different sort. They marched in an elaborate funerary procession in Richmond for the reburial of President James Monroe, whose body had been moved from a cemetery in New York City to be reinterred in Richmond's Hollywood Cemetery. When the steamship *Pocahontas* carrying the president's casket docked, along with its escort ship, the *Ericsson,* bringing the Seventh New York Regiment, thousands of people, the Henrico Guard, and seven companies of the First Regiment of Virginia Volunteers were waiting. As Monroe's casket was transferred to an open hearse pulled by six white horses, a band played a dirge and minute guns fired. Church bells began to toll as the procession of pallbearers, honor guards, New York and Virginia regiments with weapons reversed, and special guests in carriages followed the hearse moving slowly along crowded streets on the long trip toward the cemetery. After reaching the hilltop gravesite, the military companies snapped to order, Governor Henry Wise spoke, and prayers were offered in Monroe's honor.[17]

On August 7, 1858, Dooley had arrived in New York on business. He was at the Astor House as usual when he received a letter Michael Byrne had written two days before, giving an account of the reaction in Chicago to the successful laying of the first transatlantic cable. Byrne reported that "the news of the arrival of the 'Niagara' *safely* with the Atlantic Cable" had reached Chicago at eight o'clock. Byrne was just finishing his letter ("I must close and run off") when he was interrupted: "There!—the first gun of a hundred is let off. Adieu." Chicago's celebration had begun.

In mid-August Byrne joined Dooley in New York City to settle some banking business. In addition to ironing out those financial matters, Byrne tried to find some household help for John's sister Sally Heaton out in Illinois, who, according to Byrne, had "too much to do for one person." The task was difficult because, despite the Heatons' precarious financial situation, Sally had high standards for hired help. When he looked for someone among the Irish immigrant girls, Byrne discovered that he "could not get a girl in New York for Sally. . . . I could get girls at the Immigrant Depot North st who had been at service in New York for longer or shorter periods . . . [but] they would not I was afraid suit Sally."[18] Byrne didn't seem to think it strange that a family member financially dependent on Dooley would want to hire a servant, but he seemed astonished to learn that before Dooley returned to Richmond he had had a visit from the Irish ex-patriate Thomas Francis Meagher, who still owed him money and was bold enough to ask for more.[19]

By January 1859, the population of Richmond had grown so much that the absence of house numbers made it difficult for strangers to navigate.[20] When city authorities decided to remedy the situation and the process of numbering began, the official whose job it was to number the houses on the south side of Broad Street approached the Dooley house. Sarah Dooley, who had spent much of the 1850s steadfastly welcoming Irish political exiles and members of her husband's extended family to her home, reacted politely but unexpectedly. "We do not wish to have our house numbered," she is reported to have said.[21] Despite her response, the house was given the number 1225. From then on, anyone on Broad Street could find it.

That spring John Dooley and Lewis Ginter were elected to seats on the board of the Merchants' Insurance Company, as were Joseph R. Anderson of Tredegar Iron Works and John Purcell, owner of Purcell and Ladd Pharmaceutical Company.[22] The company wrote marine insurance policies on vessels, cargo, and freight; inland insurance policies "on goods transported by rivers, canals or land carriage"; and fire insurance policies "on Merchandise generally, Dwelling Houses, Warehouses and other Buildings in town or country."[23] The company's May 1862 advertisement declared that it had "Capital $200,000—surplus $75,000." Dooley remained on the board throughout the Civil War, and the company prospered.

Meanwhile up at Georgetown College, Jim—still at the head of his class— was chosen to recite a poem and Jackie to participate in a "Dialogue on Woman's Rights" during the summer commencement celebration on July 6. (Unfortunately, history does not record which side he took.) Jim also won a medal in rhetoric that year.[24]

Mental illness struck the Dooley family again the following August. This time the victim was another of John's sisters, Eliza. She had been living with another branch of the family since coming to the United States, but John moved her to Baltimore, where she joined their sister Ann at Mount Hope, where Ann had been since 1853. Eliza returned briefly a year later before being readmitted in August 1860. Both sisters spent the rest of their lives at Mount Hope.

Just before Jim returned to college, an exchange of letters with his uncle in Chicago revealed both the young man's interest in Dooley business holdings and also just how wealthy his father had become. Jim asked a number of questions about his father's property in Illinois, which Byrne answered frankly. Later, Byrne reported to Dooley that his son was "very anxious to know all about your property here. In my last letter to him in reply to a direct question I stated that you had $30,000 worth of real estate here, though it would not fetch that amount just now."[25] The 1860 census listed the worth of Dooley's Virginia properties at fourteen thousand dollars,[26] and the December 1858 report by R. G. Dun & Co. estimated Dooley's worth in Richmond at thirty thousand dollars.[27] By the standards of the time Dooley was a rich man—but also, it appears, he was still a soft touch who seldom refused to lend money to a friend.

In 1859 Dooley commissioned two portraits, one of himself and one of Sarah, by a well-known German-born portrait painter named Peter Baumgras, who had emigrated to New York in 1853. Just how and when Dooley found him is unknown, but since Baumgras signed John Dooley's portrait and dated it "Richmond 1859," he must have come to the city at least for the sittings. The fur stole Sarah is wearing in her portrait suggests that the artist painted it during the fall or winter.

The highlight of September 1859 for Jim and Jackie was their return to

Georgetown for Jackie's first year as a college student and Jim's last. Less than a month later, however, a raid by a small band of men on an arsenal many miles away suddenly interrupted the routines of daily life. When John Brown and his men raided Harpers Ferry, Governor Wise called out the militia companies and sent them after the raiders. John Dooley and the Montgomery Guard left by train but were sent back from Washington when the governor learned that U.S. Marines, under the command of Col. Robert E. Lee, had captured the insurgents. The men of the Montgomery Guard quickly settled back into their workaday lives and monthly Monday evening drills. The First Virginia infantry and mounted ranks were filling rapidly, however, and plans were being made to establish artillery and howitzer companies. It seemed that men all over Virginia were preparing not simply for maintaining civil order during the upcoming trial at Harpers Ferry but for war.

In early November, John Brown and all but one of his associates were sentenced to be hanged in December. On November 20, the officer in command at Harpers Ferry telegraphed the governor that he needed five hundred men immediately to guard the prisoners against an attempt to free them by "a large force, armed with pikes and revolvers . . . marching from Wheeling."[28] The bells of Richmond rang shortly after six o'clock that evening to alert the volunteer companies to prepare for departure. By nine o'clock the Montgomery Guard had joined the Grays, the Blues, Company F, the Young Guard, the Howitzers, and the Virginia Rifles at the Richmond, Fredericksburg and Potomac Railroad depot on Broad Street. Governor Wise joined them for the trip to Charlestown. Thousands of people came to see the military off, and the eight railroad cars rolled westward a little before ten o'clock. New dispatches indicated that the threat of an armed force from Wheeling was erroneous, but the train full of soldiers steamed off toward the west nonetheless. John Brown was hanged on December 2 without incident. The Virginia troops stayed on, however, at strategic places in the vicinity. The Montgomery Guard remained by the ferry itself and was the last of the Richmond companies to return.[29]

The evening the Montgomeries arrived home, the Southern Rights Association, which had receded into the background in recent years, reasserted itself at a large meeting in the Henrico County Courthouse and won enthusiastic endorsement from the people there. By the end of the meeting the men had passed fifteen resolutions to send to the Virginia legislature. The first one asserted the duty of southerners to encourage home manufacture and discontinue "as soon as practicable all dealings with those States which tolerate abolitionists, or have any law to prevent directly or indirectly the execution of the fugitive slave law." Another not only advocated foreign trade through southern ports but specified that "no vessels owned by the citizens of a State which tolerates abolitionists ought to be employed for any purpose by southern men." Another resolution hit directly at families and at least one schoolmaster: "The practice of sending our children to the North to be educated ought to be discontinued and also the practice of employing Northern teachers, male or female, in the South."[30] If John Dooley attended the meeting, he might have objected to that resolution. In any case he did not follow its recommendation. The Dooley boys returned to Georgetown for the winter term, and Jackie even stayed on for another year. However, Richard Tighe, the Dooley boys' former schoolmaster, must have sensed what was under way. After the bombardment of Fort Sumter, he closed his school and moved back to New York.

That meeting marked a beginning of sorts. The Central Southern Rights Associations of the city and of Henrico County, which had been slumbering, began to meet almost weekly. New military companies sprang up. Articles encouraging "Home Industries" and advertisements trumpeting southern loyalties appeared in the newspapers.[31] In his ads Dooley stopped mentioning that his stock included northern-made hats and instead emphasized the manufacturing capacity and regional scope of his business. "Purchasers will find it to their interest to call at his house previous to going further North," read the text of one typical Dooley advertisement, "as he is leaving nothing undone, sparing no expense or pains to keep the Southern trade at the South."[32]

Sectionalist feeling pervaded student life at Georgetown College as well. Jim was still a member of the Reading-Room Association, which he had joined his first year. He and the other members were devoted to reading about and discussing current issues on both domestic and foreign fronts. In his senior year he also became a member of the Georgetown Debate Club. Both organizations had been following the news about Harpers Ferry and press coverage of the secession issue closely even before the Debate Club decided to take up the topic "Should the South Secede Now?" The club had been debating the issue for a week when on the afternoon of December 18, 1859, the debate exceeded the allotted time and was renewed in the college basement after the evening meal. The professors upstairs had already sent down messages asking the club to debate more quietly when, according to one of the students, a "climax was finally reached, and a scene followed not unlike some of those then frequently occurring in [the U.S.] Congress—a free fight" broke out. A student from Mississippi sprang at the vice president of the club; students from Louisiana and Maryland "rushed" at some from

Washington, D.C. In the center of it all was "Jim Dooley of Virginia" with companions from Maryland, Louisiana, and Georgia "mixed up in the melee in inextricable confusion when somebody suddenly put out the lights and left us in total, ludicrous darkness. A lull in the storm ensued . . . at this moment, the door . . . opened [and the astronomy professor appeared] in skull-cap descending the stairs . . . holding a candle above his head and shading his eyes as he peered in dubiously to the quarters of the contending hosts."[33] That ended the fight and the debates for the rest of the year.

T he atmosphere in Richmond was tense during the weeks after its volunteer military companies returned from Harpers Ferry. In his newspaper advertisement for December 6, Richmond's rhyming clock- and watchmaker, W. J. Bartholomew, described the situation succinctly in verse:

> All Classes now are in suspense to know
> Which way the winds from Harper's Ferry blow.
> Some whisper peace, and some allude to war,
> Which all alike must equally abhor.
> 'Tis said that this suspense does injure trade,
> And very many people feel afraid[.] [1]

The anxiety extended well into the new year. The "Commercial" column of the January 10, 1860, *Dispatch,* which carried the wholesale market prices for commodities sold the previous week, reported that, thanks to the "unsettled condition of national affairs," business between the South and the North had been disrupted: "The falling off in the purchases from the North in this city alone is very large."

The two Dooley boys returned to Georgetown in January just as the new year brought increased responsibilities for their father, who was elected captain of the Montgomery Guard. In February he was obliged to make a trip north on business despite the unfavorable political implications of doing so. The strain upon him began to show and led to an uncharacteristic lapse: he forgot to pay the boys' tuition, room, and board for the new term. Father Duddy, treasurer of the college, finally wrote on February 16, but Dooley remained away on business until February 23. The next morning Sarah showed him the letter, and he sat down immediately to write both a check and a letter:

> Rev'd Dear Friend
>   This morning Mrs. Dooley called my attention to Your favour of the 16th inst — received while I was absent at the North — You will please find enclosed my check on the Farmers Bank of Va for Amt of afc $388.92 to Your order as Treasr.

With best regards to Yourself and Revd Father Earley and all the Professors. I remain very sincerely

Your Friend John Dooley[2]

Jim and Jackie continued to thrive at Georgetown. Jim was now vice president of the Dramatic Association and played the leading role in Shakespeare's *Richard III,* while Jackie had a small part in the comedy *Paul Pry.* Jim also continued the fencing lessons he had begun taking the previous November. In late spring he was again selected to be one of the speakers for Georgetown's July commencement celebration.

As the months passed, pro-southern sectionalist reaction to Harpers Ferry stimulated the creation of various new business ventures in Richmond, among them the Virginia Life Insurance Company. The Virginia Senate passed the act to incorporate the company on January 10; the House of Delegates, on January 23.[3] John Dooley was one of the twenty-six men elected to its first board of directors, along with Lewis Ginter, Joseph R. Anderson of the Tredegar Iron Works, and Dooley's fellow Irish immigrant P. T. Moore.[4] The company's first advertisement made no secret of its sectionalist leanings: "The chief object of the Company is to aid in re-taining [*sic*] at home the immense amount of money which goes annually from our State for Life Premiums to Northern Companies."[5]

Several new banks were chartered in early 1860, among them the Old Dominion Savings Bank. Its name not only trumpeted its southern identity but announced its goal to keep money "at home." John Dooley was elected to its first board of directors.[6]

Plans were being made to start a woolen mill, a broom factory, a sewing machine factory, a hoop skirt factory, and a sugar refinery. A new brewery had just been opened. Expansion of the manufacturing capacity of existing businesses was also encouraged, and Dooley's manufacturing operation was among those responding. Crowed an article in the *Dispatch,* "Let the spirit be kept alive, and Virginia will soon be independent of the North."[7]

On April 12, 1860, businesses in Richmond closed in honor of the eighty-third birthday of the late Henry Clay and the unveiling of his statue in Capitol Square. For Sarah Dooley and other members of the Whig Ladies Clay Association, the day was especially significant.[8] The association was the first statewide women's political organization, and Virginia women had been raising money to erect that statue since 1844. At last they had achieved their goal, and nearly twenty thousand people crowded into the square for the ceremony.

Despite the political tensions that spring, to a large degree business was conducted as usual in Richmond.[9] John Dooley continued to find investment opportunities in Virginia's burgeoning railroad industry. On May 15, he invested five hundred dollars for five shares in the Roanoke Valley Rail Road, a company whose newly extended tracks ran between Clarksville, Virginia, and Ridgeway, North Carolina. The twenty-two-mile-long extension provided a transportation link for a productive tobacco region needing an efficient way to ship its hogsheads to market. It also provided Dooley's Great Southern Hat Manufactory with rapid transport for its goods to merchants in towns along the route in North Carolina, a growing market for them.

Cannon fire jolted the Dooleys and their neighbors out of their beds at dawn on July Fourth, as the Fayette Artillery on Capitol Square commemorated the eighty-fourth anniversary of American independence with an opening volley. Shortly after eight o'clock patriotic music and the sound of marching filled the warm air as the companies of the First Regiment, with Captain Dooley leading the Montgomery Guard, paraded through the streets behind Smith's Band and Drum Corps. The *Dispatch* reported that the anniversary was celebrated with "unusual military spirit by the citizen soldiery of Richmond." Salutes were fired off again at midday and sunset, just as they had been in years past; but in some respects it was a more sober sort of celebration. There were no long-winded speeches or exuberant patriotic outbursts. As one *Dispatch* writer put it, "Silent thankfulness for the past is none the less heartfelt because not boisterous."[10]

A few days later, Jim Dooley graduated from Georgetown, one of seventeen students who graduated from the Greek Academy of the college. Later that day, at the "Annual Termination of the Course of Moral Philosophy," Jim was one of five new graduates who gave a public oration, called a "dissertation." The orators had to be "prepared to answer in Latin or English, any questions proposed by the Audience, on the subject of each Dissertation and the Theses connected therewith." Jim's topic was "Divine Providence." He spoke again the following day on "The Influence of Religion on Society."[11] Although the college had previously invited the president of the United States to award the diplomas and medals on graduation day, that year the college chose a southern clergyman well known to the Dooleys, the Rt. Rev. John McGill, bishop of Richmond, to do the honors.[12] Before the middle of July, Jim and Jackie were back at home in Richmond and ready for an August trip to the mountains with their sister Mary.

The heated four-way race in the presidential election of 1860 and the politicking in Virginia's capital city must have been of considerable interest to Jim, who had immersed himself in current events and political issues all through his college career. Now he was living at home again, only two blocks away from the Capitol. As a later chronicler of the city's history wrote: "With four tickets in the field and with the future welfare of the country depending upon the issue, the interest manifested was intense. . . . On the streets, in the offices, in the homes, everywhere the subject of conversation was politics and the relation of the North and the South."[13] At night the streets were ablaze with torchlight processions. Many passed the Dooleys' house on their way to and from the First African Baptist Church.

Of the four candidates for the presidency that year, two were Democrats, thanks to a fracture between the northern and southern branches of the party. The southern Democrats' candidate, John C. Breckinridge of Kentucky, and the northern Democrats' candidate, Stephen A. Douglas, were running against the Constitutional Union Party's candidate, John Bell of Tennessee, and Republican Abraham Lincoln. Years earlier, after Douglas had condemned the Know-Nothings in a Richmond speech, his enthusiastic followers formed a political support group called the Douglas Association, so it was not surprising that he came to speak in Richmond on August 30.[14] The event was of such interest nationally that an account of it later appeared in the *New York Times*.[15]

Partisan politics even spilled over into the hat business in Richmond that fall. Binford's hat store advertised three new styles inspired by the presidential campaign: the "Douglas," the "Breckinridge," and the "Bell and Everett."[16] A customer had only to use his head to give a boost to his favorite candidate. Binford did not carry a stovepipe hat, associated even then with candidate Abraham Lincoln. Although John Dooley was an active member of the Breckinridge Committee for Madison Ward, he did not mix his campaigning with his business.[17]

During the summer, George Dooley, who had been chronically ill for several years, grew progressively weaker. He finally died on Sunday, September 30, 1860.[18] The newspaper announced that friends and acquaintances of the family were invited to attend his funeral at St. Peter's Cathedral. And the day before their oldest child's twenty-third birthday, John and Sarah buried him in the family plot at Shockoe Cemetery.

Sometime later that fall, Jim began to read law in the Richmond law office of William Green. Reading law with Green might at first seem an odd choice for a well-educated young man. William Green had never attended a university, never even finished school. He was, however, an excellent choice as a mentor for Jim Dooley. He was the oldest of the seven sons of John Williams Green, a lawyer who had served on the Virginia Supreme Court of Appeals. Although William's formal schooling ended at fourteen because his family could not afford to send him to university, he had by then already begun to study Greek and Latin classics and read the law under the guidance of his father.[19]

William Green began practicing law at the age of twenty-one and quickly won renown for his devotion to "profound study and research."[20] Green was not, however, simply an expert in his field; he was an intellectual. He read widely and published essays in a variety of fields. His personal library contained more than seven thousand books by the time he moved to Richmond, and almost ten thousand by the time he died in 1880.

Green exerted a profound influence on Jim. Not only did he provide him with a thorough professional grounding, but he also became Jim's model in his life as well as in law. Eventually Jim, too, had a vast library, although not as large as Green's. He read widely in fields other than the law, wrote fluently, and published articles in newspapers and pamphlets on politics, finance, and education as well as the law. It was a particular stroke of good fortune for Dooley that Green was a specialist in municipal law, which then included corporations, property, contracts, and pleading.[21] Undoubtedly he encouraged his young protégé to do what he later advocated in an address to his law students at Richmond College: "pursue the single goal of 'love of excellence.'"[22] Jim read law with Green through the winter into the spring of 1861, but his study was destined to be disrupted by the Civil War.

Meanwhile John Dooley was playing an increasingly active role in political life during that election year. He attended the Grand Democratic Rally the Saturday before Election Day to hear Patrick Henry's grandson, P. H. Aylett, and others speak on behalf of the Breckinridge ticket. Just how heated the election campaign had become in Richmond can be deduced from the November 3 "Political Notices" column of the *Dispatch*. Under the heading "Attention Voters," an ominous note cautioned: "Every vote for Breckinridge is a vote for a Dissolution of the Union, because the great bulk of his supporters in the southern states are disunionists. If you vote for Breckinridge you vote for Civil War and all its attendant horrors."[23]

Although Abraham Lincoln and not Breckinridge was elected president of the United States on November 4, the warning was prescient. Six weeks after the election, on December 20, South Carolina seceded from the Union.

Shortly thereafter, Mississippi, Florida, Alabama, Georgia, Louisiana, and, in February, Texas followed suit. Two days after Christmas, a large contingent of Richmond men met at the First African Baptist Church to consider what course of action Virginia ought to take in light of those developments.[24]

The economic ramifications of Lincoln's election were quickly becoming apparent in Richmond. On November 20, the board of the Farmers' Bank suspended payment in specie. It was the first bank to do so, but not the last. A few hours after the announcement, John Dooley and a group of other businessmen gathered for an "informal" meeting at the office of the Virginia Life Insurance Company to discuss the anticipated impact of the Farmers' Bank decision. Dooley was one of seventy-five representatives of various firms in the city who signed a series of resolutions intended to encourage the other banks in the city to follow the lead of the Farmers' Bank.[25]

Indications of an impending depression were also apparent in the retail end of Dooley's hat business. The clientele who in previous years patronized his store before Christmas were not buying in 1860. On December 4, he ran a notice: "The Public is hereby notified that my unusually large stock of Hats, Caps and Ladies' Furs, shall be sold from now to the 1st of January at very reduced prices."[26] Significantly he appended another sentence to the notice even more emblematic of the financial state in the country that month: "Uncurrent Virginia and North Carolina Bank Bills taken at par," which meant at face value no matter how much they had been discounted in the market. When by the end of the month the economy still hadn't recovered, Dooley cut his prices even more drastically, selling at cost "without regard to profit or loss."[27]

The plight of those forced into unemployment by the financial slump prompted a group of concerned men to establish a Volunteer Relief Association. They set up an elaborate system that divided the city into eight sections. Each section had "visitors" responsible for identifying the needy and ensuring that they received aid. Among the volunteers were John Dooley and Lewis Ginter, who served together as visitors in Division No. 2.[28]

In early January 1861, despite the pervasive unease in the city and the increasing emphasis on military preparedness, the Montgomery Guard took time out to have a little fun by holding its ninth annual ball. A news item the morning after the event expressed the hope that the Montgomery Guard might "enjoy their happy festival" for many years to come.[29] That afternoon, John Dooley led the Guard in the First Volunteers' annual parade commemorating the Battle of New Orleans. The reporter for the *Dispatch* observed that the band, "instead of playing National airs, as on similar anniversaries heretofore, played the Marseillaise." It was a tune that would be played with increasing frequency.

Even John Dooley's advertisements reflected preparations for war. He advertised the wholesale phase of his business under a new name, the Southern Hat Mart. His ads for it included the statement, "I am now supplying a great part of Virginia, North Carolina, and Tennessee with Military Goods."[30]

In February, Governor John Letcher sent a long message to the Virginia legislature on the issues facing the Commonwealth, and the legislature voted to open a constitutional convention on February 13 to decide whether Virginia should secede. Their deliberations took place at the Mechanics' Institute, and the public was allowed to listen to the debates. Although there is no record indicating that Jim Dooley was an observer, it seems very likely that anyone in the vicinity who was reading law at the time would have found the debates compelling. The secession convention, as it came to be called, moved slowly, through February, March, and early April. At that point three "peace commissioners"—A. H. H. Stuart, William Ballard Preston, and Thomas Jefferson's grandson George Wythe Randolph—went from the secession convention to Washington to confer with President Lincoln but were unsuccessful in forging a peaceful settlement.[31]

Meanwhile, strident advocates of secession decided to hold their own convention. By April 1 they had named it the "Southern Rights Convention" and issued a call throughout the Commonwealth to appoint delegates. A widely distributed circular announced, "Your presence is particularly requested at Richmond, on the 16th day of April, to consult with the friends of Southern rights as to the course which Virginia should pursue in the present emergency."[32] John Dooley accepted the invitation. Despite the careful neutrality of the circular's language, it was clear that if the official convention had still not voted for secession by April 16, the Southern Rights contingent would do so without delay. In order to maintain order, the sessions were held in secret, and any delegate entering Metropolitan Hall was obliged to present a ticket to the doorman.[33] In a show of corporate support, the Richmond, Fredericksburg and Potomac Railroad offered discounted tickets for those traveling to Richmond for the event.[34]

Then, on April 12, 1861, at 4:30 a.m. Confederates opened fire on Fort Sumter. When news of the attack reached Richmond by telegraph Friday morning, "crowds thronged the streets all day discussing the situation and eagerly waiting for more news."[35] By Saturday evening, when they heard that the Union forces at Fort Sumter had surrendered, the young wife of a Presbyterian minister visiting family in Richmond was writing a letter. Her husband suggested they go for a walk, but just as they were ready to go, "a terrific report split the brooding air and rent the very heavens. Another and another followed."[36] She later wrote: "We stood transfixed, without motion or speech, until we counted, silently, seven. It was the number of the seceding states! As if pandemonium had waited for the seventh boom to die sullenly away . . . the pause succeeding the echo was ended by an outburst of yells, cheers, and screams that beggars description." She and her husband had heard the seven-gun salute at Tredegar Iron Works when the seven-star flag of the Confederacy was raised there. Later that night a one-hundred-gun salute of the Fayette artillery on Capitol Square could be heard throughout the city. It would have been deafening at the Dooleys' house, where five-year-old Saidie and three-year-old Josie must have had trouble sleeping. A crowd said to have been ten thousand strong swarmed through the streets and eventually up the hill to Capitol Square. Politicians gave speeches at the newspaper offices, on the steps of the Spotswood and Exchange Hotels, and in Capitol Square. Bonfires burned throughout the city, and many buildings and houses in the business district were illuminated.[37]

The official secession convention met again on Monday, but still the delegates failed to come to a decision. Finally they agreed to go into secret session the following morning. Then the news came that President Lincoln had ordered all the states of the Union to send troops to help put down the rebellion in South Carolina and given each state a quota to fill. A powerful negative reaction throughout the Commonwealth overcame the hesitancy of many in the pro-Union contingent at the Virginia secession convention. Suddenly regional loyalties overruled all others.

When the Southern Rights Convention opened, four hundred delegates poured in from every part of the Commonwealth. John Dooley was one of the ninety-one Richmond delegates who appeared at 11:00 a.m., when the door of Metropolitan Hall opened. They handed their tickets to the doorman, who stood there with his sword drawn.[38] The demeanor of the participants offered a stark contrast to that of the celebrants who had paraded through the streets several evenings before. The *Dispatch* reported "an earnestness in the expression on every countenance. . . . No badinage prevailed—no empty compliments were passed; but a more earnest pressure of the hand . . . gave an almost painful impression that the present was a solemn occasion, and the impending danger such as only brave, stern, self-sacrificing men could encounter and avert."[39]

Following an opening prayer, the task of electing officers and appointing committees occupied most of the secret session that day. Dooley and the other delegates were preparing to leave when there was a commotion on the stage and a newcomer announced that the river channel past Norfolk had been blocked to prevent U.S. Navy ships from sailing away from the Gosport Navy Yard. A delegate named J. B. Jones later wrote in his diary that the hall filled with "shouts of joy. Young men threw up their hats and old men buttoned their coats and clapped their hands most vigorously."[40]

The convention met again at ten o'clock the following morning, but its offices were not needed because Lieutenant Governor Latane Montague arrived with the news that the official convention had finally passed the Ordinance of Secession. Before long, former president John Tyler and Governor Wise arrived arm in arm and walked down the center aisle "amid a din of cheers, while every member rose to his feet."[41]

Early the following Sunday morning the roll of military drums melded with the clanging of church bells. Fully armed men in uniform rushed through the streets to join their companies for regimental drills. The Montgomery Guard under Capt. John Dooley joined the First Regiment, a thousand men strong, on Broad Street where they stood in formation for inspection before being mustered in for state service.

At Georgetown College, the southern students, including the Richmonders Jack Dooley and his friend Jimmie Cowardin, successfully petitioned the college administration to let them return home to join the war effort.[42] On April 23, the college treasurer's office gave Jack six dollars to cover the cost of his travel to Richmond.[43] In May, the treasurer sent his father a bill for $209.22 to cover Jack's expenses for the term through April, but the postal service couldn't pass it over the state line into the Confederacy. It went to the dead letter office for a while before being returned to the college, where it remained in the treasurer's office until after the war.

O n April 27, 1861, Capt. John Dooley and his slave Ned Haines marched with the regiment to the new fairgrounds just west of the city for its annual target-shooting practice. What the regiment did there contrasted vividly with its previous target practices. Those had featured a bit of target shooting early on a single day that was mostly a social occasion. This year, however, the event was a "Camp of Instruction" lasting several weeks. The men pitched their tents and set about learning how to manage camp life, heading home only on weekends.[1]

Preparations for war were also evident in Dooley's manufacturing business. The Confederate government had given his Great Southern Hat Manufactory a contract to make thirty thousand caps for the newly established Army of the Confederate States. The newspaper article announcing the contract alluded to the "more than thirty young ladies" in Dooley's employ, reflecting the manpower problem he faced as men left in great numbers to join the army.[2]

In late May the First Virginia left for Manassas. Their families and hundreds of other Richmonders gathered at the train station on Broad Street to see them off. On the train with the First Virginia that night were Dr. John S. D. Cullen, son of Dooley's late neighbor, fellow Irish immigrant, and Medical College of Virginia faculty member Dr. John Cullen; Father John Teeling, Catholic chaplain from St. Peter's Church; and three young men who eventually became very close friends of the Dooley family: John Mitchel's son, Pvt. James Mitchel; Pvt. John Keiley, the son of an Irish immigrant schoolteacher, who had grown up in Petersburg; and Sgt. Robert "Tantie" McCandlish Jones, a store clerk who, before the war was over, would marry the Dooleys' oldest daughter, Mary.[3]

Remaining in Richmond was one of Dooley's hat salesmen, Philip Dornin, who in early June made a surprising sale to Mr. D. Y. Murphy. The ninety-four "Grey Fatigue Caps" sold at $1.25 each were to be expected, but the ninety-four "cartridge boxes" at $1.25 apiece suggested that Dooley might have a new business sideline.[4] Actually, he didn't. The cartridge boxes belonged to his friend and fellow immigrant, Col. P. T. Moore, a hardware merchant who sold guns as well as cutlery and tools. Moore now depended on Dooley's firm to handle his business while he was away on the battlefront. The war often placed strains on small businesses that obliged them to enter into unusual agreements if they were to survive. Even with such cooperative arrangements, however, remaining open often became impossible. Such was the case with Moore's hardware business. The following year (1862) it closed entirely.[5]

Through most of July, the Montgomery Guard drilled, paraded, and waited. The first anniversary of Jim's graduation at the top of his class and his commencement oration at Georgetown passed with the family separated and Jim at home in Richmond trying to run the Southern Hat Manufactory. On July 17, the First Virginia finally received orders, as one participant later wrote, "to meet the enemy, who was then advancing from Washington. . . . We marched to Bull Run, crossed at Blackburn's Ford, and halted during the night on the north bank of the Run."[6] Before dawn the next morning, Captain Dooley drafted a holograph will that exhibited his characteristic tendency for understatement as well as his respect for his wife's judgment:

> I, John Dooley, of the city of Richmond, but now at Bull Run river, (expecting hourly a Battle with the Northern enemy), knowing at all times, but particularly under present circumstances, the uncertainty of life, do make this my will, which is all in my own hand writing. Having the fullest confidence in the sound discretion of my wife, Sarah, I do hereby give, devise, bequeath and dispose of unto her all my property, real and personal, and of every description and kind, with power should she find it necessary to sell all or any portion of my real estate and to convey the same to any purchaser or purchasers trusting to my dear wife in the management of everything and to the making of such disposition of my estate at such times, in such manner and in such proportions among our children as she may deem best for their interest.

In the final sections of the will, Dooley added:

> It is especially my wish and desire that my mercantile business shall be carried on as usual if it is at all practicable, but of this my wife must be the judge.
>
> I appoint my said wife Sarah my Executrix and desire she shall not be required to give security as such.
>
> Given under my hand and seal this morning of the 18th of July 1861.[7]

When he had finished writing, Dooley took a few moments more to write a brief document in which he conveyed his power of attorney to his son Jim. He also scribbled a note to the editor of the *Dispatch,* asking him to announce that he had done so. Then he tucked the will, power of attorney, and note into a regimental dispatch pouch and sent them on their way to Richmond. The announcement duly appeared in the "Special Notices" column every day for a week.[8]

For the next eight months James Dooley, who turned twenty-one in January, was in charge of the manufacturing and retail operations of the Great Southern Hat Manufactory, the largest business of its kind in the South. With his father away at war, Jim was initiated into the business world at a time when the company held large contracts from the Confederate government and also faced a manpower shortage. Additional government contracts required a concomitant expansion of manufacturing operations, over which the young Dooley also presided. As a result, he emerged from the war years with a sophisticated understanding of the business world unusual for men in their mid-twenties.

A week after being given the power of attorney, Jim Dooley signed his first contract with the Confederate government—a small one, to be sure: 130 black wool hats at one dollar each, to be delivered to the Quartermaster Department. Jim may have been new to running the business, but he followed in the footsteps of his efficient father. The receipt for the hats shows they were delivered in two boxes on July 30 to J. B. McClelland, assistant quartermaster of the Confederate States army. McClelland, however, was more leisurely in paying. He didn't sign the voucher authorizing payment of $131.25 for the hats and boxes until September 30.[9] Even then, the military was a bureaucracy's bureaucracy.

Meanwhile, the elder Dooley and the First Virginia were at Bull Run and engaged in their first battle. A private in the Montgomery Guard named Frank Potts, who had immigrated to Virginia from Ireland just a year earlier, kept a detailed diary in which he gave vivid descriptions of John Dooley in command that day: "Our brave captain [Dooley], as cool and stern as ever Roman was, gave the word, 'Take arms. Remember boys, fire low.' . . . each man held his breath. . . . Suddenly the fire came . . . and the entire discharge passed over us. 'Down men,' and down we went to mother earth, and . . . they gave us three volleys."[10] Later, when "the command devolved on Maj. [Frank] Skinner . . . [h]e took a particular fancy to our Co., was all the time calling for Capt. Dooley, and seemed to think that we Irish were the very boys to fight, and to do him justice. He certainly gave us all the honor he could, and put us in as much danger as possible. . . . I can now see our Captain, in our rear, with a pistol in each hand, his lips compressed and his eye as stern as eye ever shone, standing right out in open places disclaiming [*sic*] the shelter of a tree. 'That's the way boys,' 'Fire at the hill top.' 'Come from behind that tree you blackguard.' 'Now my boys, do them so again.'"

Two days later, when the battle reopened, Captain Dooley—once again with a cool disregard for his own safety—led the Montgomery Guard through a "storm of lead and iron."[11] According to Potts: "Soon after sunrise, our Captain came along the line, and told us, 'To keep cool men and fire low should they attempt to cross, jump over the ditch and give them the bayonet. Let each of us commend ourselves to God, and pray to him for courage, and with our hopes and confidence in Him we cannot be beaten.' The cannonade began soon after."[12] Before the battle ended, Dooley was ordered to report to General Longstreet, who gave him command of additional men that day. According to Potts, as the battle began again, he "saw Capt. Dooley coming toward us, and . . . [t]he Capt. roared 'Come on Montgomeries' and we were beside him, in a moment, just then right over our heads came a volley of musketry, and before we could think, right among our feet, crushing and tearing the trees right and left came a discharge of grape. 'Take shelter, men. Duffy send down & tell Gen. Longstreet that they have the range on us . . . and ask him what we shall do.' This was the Captain's order, given as coolly as if on parade."

The entire regiment later received highest praise from General Longstreet for its role at Bull Run: "The heavy part of this fight was made by the old First regiment, so that it can well claim to have done more toward the success of the First Manassas than any one regiment. . . . I can say that its officers and men did their duties as well, if not better, than any troops whose service came under my observation."[13]

Back in Richmond, anxiety ran high as people waited for news. Large crowds gathered at the railroad station whenever the Virginia Central arrived. There were no special ambulance trains, so the wounded arrived in whatever regularly scheduled cars passing through Manassas Junction had enough room to accommodate them. No lists of casualties were posted or printed. When a train arrived in Richmond, the crowds on the platform pushed and shoved to get close enough to see if husbands, sons, or brothers were among those being carried off. The crush made it difficult to unload wounded soldiers, and rumors and mistaken information flew. The Sunday after victory was announced, the churches filled in thanksgiving, and at St. Peter's, the Dooleys' church, three hundred soldiers crowded in with the congregation to hear Bishop McGill preach on "Divine Providence."[14]

John Dooley and the First Virginia remained in northern Virginia for months after the battle at Bull Run, engaging the enemy at Centreville, Mason's Hill, and Fairfax Courthouse, where much-appreciated new uniforms sent by the City of Richmond arrived. A member of the city council had introduced a resolution in January 1861 to appropriate fifty thousand dollars to "arm and equip volunteer companies," but the proposal had been tabled until April 15, when it finally passed.[15] Not until fall, however, were the new uniforms delivered.

On November 18, Dooley was promoted to the rank of major, and Major Skinner to the rank of colonel.[16] The promotions were well received by the men. In fact, the regiment's newspaper correspondent described the promotions in a letter to the *Dispatch* as "the most popular that could possibly have been made."[17]

For the first, intensely cold months of 1862, the First Virginia camped at Centreville, and morale waned. Dooley, upon whom command of the regiment largely devolved, began to suffer ill health thanks to the dismal weather and the primitive conditions of camp life. Heavy colds that went into his chest and the deep bronchial coughing to which he was susceptible took their toll. Nonetheless, when morale was at its lowest, he found ways to boost the men's spirits. One observer wrote: "Though not much of a military genius, [Dooley] was one of the kindest and most generous of men. Often on a bitter, cold night, he could be seen bringing the men on guard a drink, saying with a smile: 'Boys, I saw you wink at me.'"[18]

Despite such gestures, however, men began to leave—some on furlough, some not. On one occasion a sergeant dutifully reported that some of the troops had made off to Richmond without leave. "And have they?" replied Dooley. "The bad fellows! Let me know when they come back, and I will punish them severely." A few days later the sergeant told Dooley that the miscreants had reappeared. "Have they come back? The good fellows!" Dooley replied. No further action was taken.

Depletion in the ranks was not just the result of personal whim. Illness played a significant role. Dysentery and pneumonia struck the army in epidemic proportions that winter. An added complication was that the industries essential to the war effort frequently requested that skilled workers be relieved of military duty. In one such case, a tug-of-war broke out between Joseph R. Anderson and the regiment over John McDonald, first sergeant in the Montgomery Guard and a key worker at Tredegar Iron Works. By dint of a letter-writing campaign, Anderson succeeded in having McDonald released from active duty in July just a few days before Bull Run.[19] For these and other reasons, by March the ranks had thinned from seven hundred to three hundred men.

Large Confederate contracts continued to arrive at the Great Southern Hat Manufactory, but the labor-force shortage in Richmond was acute. Jim Dooley placed advertisements in the newspapers for fifty new hatmakers, offering "best wages and constant employment," but because able-bodied men — and women — were in such short supply, he paid to run the ad for three months.[20] In late March he was faced with an even larger problem: conscription. Jefferson Davis had sent a message to the Confederate Congress recommending that all men between the ages of eighteen and thirty-five be required to don uniforms and serve in the military. The news traveled quickly. Suddenly the whole Dooley family became aware that Jim's days for reading law and running the company were numbered. He did not wait for the legislature to debate the issue. On April 1, he caught the train to Orange Court House, where he signed on for a three-year hitch as a private in Company D under his father's old friend Capt. William English.[21]

By then his father, whose health had not improved, had decided to resign at the end of April, when the regiment was scheduled to be reorganized, but he remained in northern Virginia with the regiment as it moved about on outpost duty. On March 8 the regiment began a series of marches so long and hard that within days, most of the men had thrown away some of their gear.[22] They covered as many as sixteen or seventeen miles some days and spent nights sleeping in woods or pastures. By April 3 the entire First Virginia had finally arrived at Orange Court House and encamped about a mile outside the town. Jim's service only overlapped with his father's through April 26, the official date for the reorganization.

Jim's enlistment left a void in the management of his father's business. Despite the fact that his brother Jack was only eighteen and not particularly interested in business, the day after Jim arrived in Orange Court House, Major Dooley sent a "card" to the *Dispatch* from "Headq'rs 1st Reg't Va Vols. Near Orange C. H. April 2, 1862," announcing that "My son, John E. Dooley is hereby authorized by me to execute, as my attorney in fact, any paper, in any way necessary to the prosecution of my business." The announcement did not appear under "Special Notices" as Dooley intended but in the "Amusements" column on April 7. Luckily for Jack, and probably for the company, his tenure at the head of his father's business was short. In less than a month, his father returned to resume his civilian duties.

Older brother Jim had joined the Confederate army just in time to march to Louisa Court House with the regiment through intermittent hail, snow, and rain. Then it was on to Richmond, where on April 16 the regiment boarded the steamboat *Glen Cove* and journeyed down the James to King's Mill on the Peninsula. Here they disembarked at 2:00 a.m. and marched to Winn's Mill, where they did picket duty and strengthened the works while enduring heavy shelling.[23]

Ten days later the regiment underwent a complete reorganization and held elections for officers. John Mitchel's son James was promoted to captain of Company C, and Jim Dooley changed companies in order to become one of its members. Maj. Lewis Burwell Williams was elected colonel to replace Colonel Skinner, who had been wounded. Exhausted and unwell after a full year of service, John Dooley returned to Richmond and his business at the Great Southern Hat Manufactory, leaving his slave Ned Haines behind to look after Jim.

By the beginning of May, Gen. Robert E. Lee had ordered Confederate troops on the Peninsula to move westward to defend Richmond against a possible attack by the Union army. All through the night of May 3, 1862, Company C First Virginia, A. P. Hill's Brigade, Longstreet's Division, and the rest of the Army of Northern Virginia marched westward. Their orders were to slow down the Union forces, which they did by digging sham earth-works at intervals in the middle of the road and making it look as though they had planted torpedoes there. Whenever one of the army wagons got hopelessly stuck in the mud, the men transferred its cargo into other wagons on firmer ground, pushed the empty one over, and hacked up its wheels with axes. One Union soldier wrote in his diary that near the place called the Half-way House, Confederate soldiers had left "lots of dead mules strung out on the road for a mile or more lying on their backs, half smothered in mud, with their feet sticking up out of it."[24]

On May 4, the weary members of Company C reached Williamsburg and camped in the field beside the Insane Asylum on the western edge of town. They awoke the next morning to heavy rain, stirred their fires, somehow managed to cook their breakfasts, and packed their tents to the sound of gunfire from a skirmish about a mile and a half away.

At about ten o'clock the company was ordered to fall in, and the First, Seventh, Eleventh, and Seventeenth Virginia Regiments marched through Williamsburg.[25] Close to the colonial Capitol they halted, took off their knapsacks, and deposited them in the front room of one of the nearby houses. The ladies who lived there promised to take good care of them. The knapsacks and military paraphernalia they left behind almost filled the room to the ceiling.

A short distance farther on, the men marched east to the right of the Capitol into the woods toward Fort Magruder, an earthwork fort they had been deployed to defend. The troops soon came under fire, and some of the companies ahead of them broke and ran back through their ranks, with Union forces close behind. As a sergeant in the First Virginia later wrote: "At first we thought they were . . . our men until we were fired upon by them. . . . Now, the enemy, having been reinforced, swarmed all around us. The bullets seemed to come from all directions. We lost a good many of our men." The severely wounded were left on the battlefield because there were no ambulances to remove them. Among them were Jim Dooley; his colonel, Lewis Burwell Williams; and almost three hundred other men.

The next morning the able-bodied members of the regiment reclaimed their knapsacks from the house where they had left them before the battle and left Williamsburg.

On May 5, Dr. John Cullen left Richmond for Williamsburg with a group of medical personnel and traveled all night under a flag of truce. Upon their arrival in Williamsburg, as the *Enquirer* reported over a week later, "these surgeons . . . were, by the blundering of the [Union] official, placed under a tent and guard until midnight of Tuesday before they were released."[26] Among those they belatedly treated was Jim Dooley, whose right wrist had been shattered in battle. Whether because of the severity of the injury or the delay in treatment, the bones would never heal properly.

Back in Richmond, the Dooley family waited anxiously to learn of Jim's fate. For the next several days they and the rest of Richmond waited, but the newspapers reported only rumors, not facts, to ease their anxieties. The Thursday morning *Dispatch* lamented that, despite the proximity of Williamsburg and the Peninsula to Richmond, "our information is almost as imperfect and incomplete as that from the Southwest."[27] The next day, however, finally brought news. The Friday morning editions of both the *Enquirer* and the *Dispatch* printed accounts of the battle that listed the dead and the wounded by the regiment and company. Jim, his family learned, was "severely wounded in the right arm"—but still alive.[28]

What the family didn't know might have comforted them. Fortunately, Jim was one of the Confederate wounded brought to Bruton Parish Church, which—like other churches in Williamsburg—had been transformed into a hospital. There he was discovered by a young widow, Cynthia Tucker Washington, whose many Richmond relatives included Dr. David Tucker, a faculty member at the Medical College.[29] Jim was almost the same age as Cynthia's brother Beverley St. George Tucker, and they may have known one another.[30]

If so, that could explain why, although care in family homes generally was extended only to officers, the Tuckers took in Jim—only a private—along with Colonel Williams and two other wounded Confederate officers. Cynthia and her mother attended to the four until they were sufficiently recovered to be sent to Hampton Roads, where they were incarcerated as prisoners of war.[31]

All the Dooley family knew, however, were the few details that appeared in the Saturday paper. It was reported that although the Confederate army had worked quickly during a lull in the battle to carry the wounded off the battlefield, the lack of ambulances forced them to leave many of them.[32] A rumor swept the city that the Yankees planned to send all the Confederate wounded from Williamsburg to Richmond, but it proved to be false.[33]

Inexplicably, the Confederate government had taken no official measures in the year since the conflict began to provide for the wounded. Although some units, such as the First Virginia, had a physician on staff, the government had provided neither field hospitals nor ambulances. All those too grievously wounded to walk were left to fall into Union hands. In March the "Local Matters" column of the *Dispatch* had reported that "Captain John Herbig . . . is raising a company to be known as the Infirmary corps. Their duty will be to remove the wounded from the battle field and render them prompt and skillful medical aid. . . . The number of men that have offered to Captain Herbig are more than he required, but being desirous of only procuring those who are really efficient, many were rejected."[34]

Although Herbig's Infirmary Corps was badly needed at Williamsburg, its members were still inadequately prepared for removing the wounded from the battlefield. In fact, it would be a case of "too little, too late" for the Infirmary Corps for the rest of the war. The "really efficient" members proved not so efficient after all, and although the Corps saw some action, its men frequently deserted.[35]

By Sunday, May 18, the company of Richmond surgeons had left Williamsburg to accompany the wounded to Union-controlled Fortress Monroe, where officers were imprisoned; and to its neighboring island, Rip Raps, where Jim Dooley and the other infantrymen were incarcerated. The news brought great anguish to the Dooley household. John Dooley's distress propelled him to try to prevent other wounded soldiers from suffering Jim's fate.

CHAPTER 7 | The Ambulance Committee

On May 23, Confederate and Union forces clashed mightily at Hanover Courthouse, twenty miles north of Richmond. By then John Dooley, intent on preventing more wounded soldiers from being left on the battlefield, had found thirty volunteers with carriages or spring wagons who were willing to help rescue the wounded and carry them back to the city. Dooley had also conferred with John Enders, the businessman whom Mayor Joseph Mayo had appointed chair of the city council's "Committee of Arrangements" to find houses in the city that could be used as hospitals.[1] Coordination of the two men's efforts would be vital.

In planning his strategy for the evacuation of the wounded, Dooley drew on both his battlefield experience and his expertise as a shipper of dry goods. He knew that an efficient logistical framework was necessary for the work of what would soon be known as the Ambulance Committee. Manassas had made him keenly aware of the need for both horse-drawn vehicles and railway transport for the conveyance of wounded men. Although trains had brought many of the wounded back to Richmond after the battle, no advance planning had gone into the effort, and as a result there had been prolonged delays on station platforms and inadequate care for the men once they were on the trains, especially for those who could not sit up. Fortunately, because he held stock in several railways with headquarters in Richmond, he was in a good position to persuade those companies to provide not just passenger cars but also freight cars in which wounded men unable to sit could lie on pads. He also convinced the railways to add special trains to transport the wounded. Called "ambulance trains," these appeared on railroad schedules for the rest of the war.

The first test of the system came at a place called Seven Pines. Dooley's plans for the rescue of the wounded were detailed and meticulous. Members of the Ambulance Committee were stationed at the rear of the battlefield, watching the action intently. As the wounded fell, committee members dashed onto the field and carried them away to wagons and carriages that took them immediately to a nearby railroad crossing. There the injured men were loaded into waiting railroad cars for the trip into Richmond, where other wagons and carriages were standing by, ready to transport them to hospitals.

Rainy weather complicated the work. The following Thursday the *Ex-aminer's* "City Intelligence" column provided a vivid account of the Ambulance Committee's "energetic and untiring exertions": "Throughout the terribly dark night after the first battle, the squads of the committee, lantern in hand, traversed the woods and swamps for miles around the Seven Pines, hunting up the fallen and bearing them to the roadside hospitals, where even the candles by which the surgeons plied their profession were furnished by the forethought of the committee."[2]

More difficulties ensued when the wounded arrived in the city. Initially, the drivers weren't told in advance which hospitals and houses had beds available, which meant they wasted time driving from place to place before they could deliver their injured passengers. Further, there weren't enough hospitals to begin with, even though more were opening in warehouses and private homes almost every day.[3] And on Sunday came yet more unpleasantness, when enemy shells rained down on the Richmond and York River Railroad cars as they carried the wounded away from Seven Pines. The artillery was so accurate that shells were exploding directly overhead, until someone in the Ambulance Committee finally thought to fly a yellow flag on the locomotive and the firing ceased.

Nonetheless, the Ambulance Committee's work received high praise in the Richmond press. A *Dispatch* reporter on the scene commented that "our medical staff . . . could very well learn a salutary lesson from the complete arrangements and system practiced on the field in conveying dead and wounded."[4] Public recognition of Dooley's role in this first systematic mass removal of the wounded by train came from Lt. Col. Frederick G. Skinner of the First Virginia, who declared in a letter to the editor of the *Dispatch* that, "with the invaluable assistance of Major Dooley, our wounded were removed from the field without an instant of unnecessary delay."[5]

Before the month was over, the Ambulance Committee had discharged its duties at such places as Mechanicsville, Gaines Mill, and Malvern Hill. The men may have been noncombatants, but their work was both difficult and extremely dangerous. Meanwhile, the Confederate government's official arrangements for the care and transport of the wounded continued to lag behind. Not until after the Battle of Seven Pines did the office of the Confederate surgeon general publish its first "Regulations for the Care of the Wounded in Battle," which belatedly decreed that ambulance wagons be held in the rear of any military action.[6] Even so, there were never enough government-supplied ambulances during rest of the war.[7]

During the period when John Dooley was organizing his volunteer ambulance corps, he still had to discharge his responsibilities in civilian life. In May 1862 he attended the annual meeting of the Virginia Life Insurance Company and was elected to his third term on the board of directors. Much of the meeting focused on a new war-related business opportunity that had arisen. Life insurance companies north of the Mason-Dixon Line had decided not to honor the policies of men on the Confederate side of the conflict. After considering the matter, the board responded with a May 30 advertisement in the *Examiner:* "INSURE YOUR LIFE AT HOME—THE VIRGINIA LIFE INSURANCE COMPANY . . . The Yankee companies, having made known their intention to repudiate the policies of our fellow-citizens who may be killed in defense of their homes . . . every prudent man insured by them, ought at once to . . . insure at home."[8]

Dooley also attended board meetings of the Merchants' Insurance Company. The primary aim of the company was to protect businesses from the full spectrum of problems endemic to shipping and storing merchandise. Despite the Union's naval blockade of southern shipping, the company prospered during the war. Its capital in 1862 was a healthy two hundred thousand dollars. By the time of its February 4, 1864, annual report, it could announce: "CAPITAL (ALL PAID) $1,000,000" as well as an "accumulated surplus" of another $1 million.[9] Even accounting for the inflation of Confederate currency by that time, the company was doing very nicely indeed.

Toward the end of June 1862, the Seven Days Battles raged within five miles of the city, and the Ambulance Committee was again called to service. Like other Richmond residents whose houses were built on one of the city's hills, the Dooleys could stand on their roof and see the smoke and fire of battle in full color. There were weeks then, and during the next three years, when the family heard what a young Richmond woman named Sallie Brock described as "the dread music of artillery" and inhaled air "mingled with the vapor of war."[10]

The Ambulance Committee's work during the Seven Days Battles gave evidence of its increasing sophistication in the use of the railroad and also in coping with some of the problems that continued to plague it. To speed transport of the wounded, the Virginia Central turned over a train to the committee, which transformed it into a series of rolling emergency rooms by taking out many of the seats so the severely wounded could lie down. The committee also fitted up the Virginia Central depot in Richmond as a fully staffed receiving hospital and brought along mules carrying kegs of fresh water for the wounded.[11] The crush of visitors on the outskirts of battlefields and at railroad stations was great enough to oblige the committeemen to wear badges on their hats to identify themselves.

During the month between Seven Pines and the Seven Days Battles, John Dooley undertook a new project on behalf of the war wounded. Recognizing the need for more hospital beds than Richmond had been able to provide, he and a fellow merchant on Main Street, William Richardson, established a hospital in a warehouse they shared at Fourteenth and Main. They called it simply "Dooley and Richardson's Hospital" and hired Dr. William Allen Carrington as chief surgeon-in-charge.[12] Carrington often accompanied the Ambulance Committee and later became an honorary member.

Thanks to conscription, the scarcity of able-bodied men in the city was becoming ever more pressing. Vexingly, Dooley's Confederate government contracts meant that he had plenty of orders for hats at the very time he could not find skilled laborers to make them. In July he addressed the problem by advertising in the newspaper for "twenty young LADIES, to sew on caps. None but experienced hands are wanted."[13] As the shortage of manpower worsened a year later, Dooley responded by increasing the number of women workers on his payroll. John Mitchel noted in his journal that "my friend Mr. Dooley ... employs forty girls in cutting and sewing soldiers' and officers' caps."[14] Rosie the Riveter wouldn't exist for another eighty years, but at the Great Southern Hat Manufactory, her predecessors were already doing men's work.[15]

During those summer months in 1862 the complicated intertwining demands of his business and volunteer work must have left John Dooley exhausted. Unfortunately, none of his humanitarian efforts had any effect on the plight of his own son Jim, who was still languishing as a prisoner of war. Luckily, however, the Confederate and Union governments had been busy negotiating a prisoner-of-war exchange cartel, and Jim was chosen to participate in the first exchange.[16] On Sunday, August 2, he and thousands of other Confederate prisoners of war were loaded onto crowded steamboats, each flying both a flag of truce and the Stars and Stripes, for a trip up the James River to Aiken's Landing in Varina, twelve miles east of Richmond, where the prisoners were to be exchanged.[17] As soon as the returning Confederates disembarked, Union soldiers who had been prisoners in Richmond filled the steamboats for the return trip downriver.

Because there was no official group waiting to welcome the returning prisoners, they had to find their own way to Richmond, and it took some of them several days to do so. The lack of organization was particularly hard on soldiers not from the Richmond area. They had no one to greet them and no place to receive them. "Unhappily," reported the *Enquirer,* "they are sent to adjacent camps or suffered to stroll or lie about the city, without a morsel of food and liable at any time to arrest by the military police. . . . [S]o they straggle in, cluster about the corners, stray off in search of unknown camps, making their beds anywhere, if without money . . . doing no better than if they were upon hostile ground."[18]

The lack of preparation was not lost on John Dooley, who arranged with Exchange Commissioner Gen. Robert Ould that in the future the Ambulance Committee would provide escort and medical aid for released prisoners of war. In the years to come, when exchanges took place, the committee accompanied Union captives on the boats to Varina and Confederate prisoners of war on the return trip.

Jim's return had an immediate impact on his younger brother. Jack, thought to be too frail for combat, had joined the Home Guard in Richmond a month and a half earlier, but as he put it in his diary: "Tired of remaining in the City catching deserters & Conscripts, I resolved at once to enter the field where I considered it the imperative duty of every young man to be. Altho' repeatedly warned that I was doing a rash thing, that I would never be able to undergo the fatigue & hardship of a soldier's career, and that I would come back in a very few weeks 'kilt entirely,' nevertheless I was resolved to make the experiment cost what it might."[19]

Six days after his wounded older brother returned, on a morning that Jack described as "broiling hot," he and John Mitchel's son James rode out of Richmond on the roof of an overcrowded railroad car.[20] Jack took with him only a blanket, in which he rolled a change of clothes and a "tolerably respectable Springfield musket." When they arrived at Gordonsville, Jack joined Company D, in which his brother had so recently fought. By early September, his worried father had sent his slave Ned Haines to look after Jack, who wrote in his diary that Ned had "declared himself forthwith ready to take care of me as he had done of my father before."[21]

Back at home, Jim spent the next two months recuperating, but his wrist failed to heal. Although he had been eager to serve out the remainder of the three years for which he had signed up, in mid-October he applied for a certificate of disability and an honorable discharge from the regiment. Dr. David H. Tucker signed the required certificate confirming that Jim had suffered a "Gun Shot wound fracturing the Bones of the forearm (right) involving the wrist Joint So as to render him incapable of performing military service," but the disability request was not granted.[22] Instead, the request was returned with a note inquiring if the "patient [might] be useful in another capacity than field service." In November Dr. Tucker resubmitted the certificate with a second explanation of Jim's disability that showed some impatience with red tape: "As the patient'[s] right wrist is seriously and probably permanently impaired in its function I can hardly imagine any military service for which he could be fitted." Even though the letter arrived in the proper office on November 18, Dooley had to wait for his discharge until May 1863, when Col. Lewis B. Williams finally caught up with his paperwork and signed the certificate.

Jim developed a tremor in his right arm and would struggle "all the rest of his life to use the wrist and hand."[23] He carried a cane, not to help himself walk but to steady his hand. Despite the difficulties and the delay, he studied for and passed the exam required to become a noncombatant officer in the Confederate Ordnance Corps and continued in his off hours to read law with William Green.[24]

The previous autumn, while Jim was recuperating, the members of the Ambulance Committee decided to impose a formal structure on their efforts by organizing a chain of command and electing officers. They divided the officers' responsibilities and elected John Enders of the Mayor's Committee for Hospitals as their president. He was to be responsible primarily for the committee's work in Richmond. John Dooley was elected captain, responsible for leading the fifty or so men who regularly traveled to and from the battlefields. Dooley also continued to recruit new volunteers and organized the work of the Ambulance Committee for the remainder of the war.

Meanwhile, on the other side of the Atlantic, John Mitchel was avidly following news of the war in the American papers that found their way to Paris four or five times a week. Restless after reading accounts of the Battle of Williamsburg and the Seven Days Battles, Mitchel broke up his household, sent his wife and two of his daughters back to Ireland, and decided to return to Richmond. Mitchel tried to send his youngest son, fifteen-year-old Willy, to Ireland with his mother too, but the boy refused to go, telling Mitchel "resolutely that he must go and join his brothers in the Southern army."[25]

By the end of October, John and Willy Mitchel were ensconced at the Powhatan Hotel in Richmond. After breakfast on their first morning, they called upon John Dooley, who insisted that father and son come to live at the Dooley house.[26] Within a few months, John Mitchel settled into editing the *Enquirer,* which he described in his memoirs as "an old established daily paper . . . that supported the Government and sustains the measures (generally) of President Davis; while the *Examiner,* another daily sheet, owned and conducted by John M. Daniel often bitterly censures the Administration."[27] Over the next two years, Mitchel, too, became disenchanted with Davis, eventually leaving the *Enquirer* to write for the *Examiner.* Willy Mitchel joined the Montgomery Guard as color-bearer shortly after he and his father arrived, and a few months later Mitchel joined the Richmond Ambulance Committee.

I n November, while Jim Dooley was waiting for his discharge, his father and John Mitchel took a train to Fredericksburg. There the First Virginia and the rest of Longstreet's Division were digging into the hills just south of the town in anticipation of an attack by Union forces. Their ostensible purpose was to visit their sons Jack and Willy, encamped there with the First Virginia, but in actuality Dooley's primary purpose was to assess the situation prior to the expected battle and plan the rapid removal of wounded soldiers to Richmond by train.[1]

Once the two men left the train, they had to find their way over several miles of hilly terrain just to reach their sons' campsite. When they finally arrived at the First Virginia's encampment, Col. Lewis Burwell Williams welcomed them as guests and provided "comfortable quarters" for them.[2] The fathers spent a happy evening visiting their boys by the campfire, and the following morning the colonel invited Jack and Willy to his tent for breakfast with their fathers.

Several days later, however, the Union forces arrived, and Dooley and Mitchel came under fire as they stood at the center of the Confederate line on a hill overlooking the Rappahannock River.[3] According to Mitchel: "[A] splendid battalion of Yankee artillery was right opposite upon the plain. . . . Soon we found that the knoll on which Major Dooley and I were standing seemed to become a special object of the enemy's shot: they evidently took us for two officers of distinction. The horrible screaming missiles came very close to us, and tore up the earth near to where we stood. Dooley and I descended a few paces on the safe side of the hill, and lay down showing only the tops of our heads. The shells came thick and fast, sometimes throwing some of the earth over us." Fortunately, the shelling stopped just as suddenly as it had begun.

Before dawn on December 13, Dooley and Mitchel, having reconnoitered sufficiently to plan for the removal of the wounded, left the Confederate encampment. According to Mitchel, as they walked toward the railroad station, "we became aware of a most tremendous artillery fire. We were too far off already to hear the musketry, but knew that the battle was engaged."

Meanwhile the rest of the Ambulance Committee had arrived at Summit, a small town southeast of Fredericksburg. Here they spent the night, rendezvousing with Dooley and Mitchel early the following morning on the way to the battlefield. The committeemen began removing the wounded from the battlefield as soon as they arrived, working swiftly and methodically. The overwhelming number of casualties, however, made it impossible to rescue all the wounded quickly. One hundred and eighty wounded rode on the first train to Richmond that night. The estimate of the total wounded that day, however, was 2,500.[4]

Reinforcements for the Ambulance Committee on Monday included Governor Letcher and Captain Alexander, the assistant provost marshal, who brought fifty men with him. Although four trains loaded with casualties—both Confederate and Union—left Fredericksburg on Tuesday, more men remained at the railroad station at Summit for another full day before being taken to Richmond. The *Dispatch* reported that committee members tried to ease their wait by "distributing some food to the poor fellows, who had been wet through by the terrible rain of the night before, and, lying about in their rags, hardly looked like human beings."[5] The last of the wounded finally arrived in Richmond on Wednesday.

After the Confederate victory at Fredericksburg, the First Virginia spent Christmas and the first cold and snowy month of the new year about five miles from the last stop on the railroad south of Richmond. There Jack Dooley, Willy Mitchel, Tantie Jones, and the Dooleys' slave Ned Haines built a log cabin, which they plastered over with mud to keep out the biting wind.[6] Since the camp was near the railroad station, Richmond families could visit. When John Dooley and several others visited their soldier sons in January, they brought enough home-cooked food to feed the regiment. Jack recorded in his diary that his father supplied the "drinkables" and that "such a night of enjoyment [was] I think . . . rarely experienced in a soldier's camp."[7] His father entertained the troops by singing a Samuel Lover ballad called "'Molly Carew' in such an affecting way that the company was convulsed. Afterward one of his father's friends whispered in Jack's ear that he had known John Dooley "for twenty five years and never knew that he loved a joke."

In mid-February, after the First Virginia had been ordered to move near Yellow Tavern and the weather was particularly miserable, John Dooley, worried about Jack's uncertain health, returned to camp with the intention of bringing his frail younger son home with him. Jack recorded in his diary that although his father was "a special pleader of the highest order," he only succeeded in getting permission to take Jack home for one night by promising that he would bring him back early the next morning.[8] John Dooley returned to camp several more times during that bitter winter to request leave not only for Jack but also for Willy Mitchel.[9]

In March, Dooley turned his attention to making arrangements for his fourteen-year-old daughter Florence to transfer from St. Joseph's Female Academy in Richmond to the Ursuline Academy in Columbia, South Carolina, where he thought she might be safer. The wisdom of sending Florence to South Carolina was clear in early May, when panic swept through the city of Richmond as Union cavalry raided along its northern edges, wrecking railroad bridges, tearing up track, stealing horses and mules, and terrifying the inhabitants.[10] On May 3, Federal forces attacked near Ashland, eight miles north of Richmond, burning a hotel and about thirty small houses.[11] At about four o'clock that afternoon a Federal detachment waiting in ambush near the Richmond, Fredericksburg and Potomac Railroad tracks captured a Confederate ambulance train, with 198 sick and 69 wounded aboard.[12]

Rumors about raids to the west of the city in Fluvanna, Goochland, and Louisa Counties kept Richmonders' nerves on edge. According to the *Dispatch,* several thousand people gathered at the railroad depot to wait for the news that the ambulance train would bring.[13] When the train did not arrive, hundreds of people willing to help defend the city against attack by Union raiders gathered on Capitol Square in regimental formation. Undoubtedly it was alarming to Sarah Dooley and her little girls—Saidie, now eight years old, and Josie, now five—when they heard the shouts, the rattling of muskets, and the banging of the iron gates around the square.[14]

Meanwhile, a battle had begun at Chancellorsville, and the Ambulance Committee had left the city by night to bring back the wounded. Raiders having cut telegraph lines and railroad tracks north of the city, details of the subsequent victory didn't reach Richmond for days. Among the wounded the Ambulance Committee brought back to Richmond was James Mitchel. Instead of delivering him to one of the hospitals, John Dooley brought him to his own home, where he recovered under Sarah Dooley's supervision.

By spring the Ambulance Committee counted five doctors among them and began to receive some help from the Confederate Commissary. Years later Mitchel described their work: "The Richmond merchants, bankers, clergymen ... [were] sometimes seen ... laboring the whole day and the whole night through, carrying stretchers laden with their groaning burden, helping tottering men to their places in the cars, washing and dressing wounds, administering soup, coffee, stimulants or milk; occasionally, too, we ... relieve[d] each other, some working while others snatch[ed] a sleep."

The landscape they traveled through on their way to battlefields, he wrote, was "sadly wasted . . . by the passage and repassage of two great armies; fences destroyed, vast breadths of forest cut away and . . . lying in wild confusion and ugly nakedness; houses sometimes burned, sometimes pulled down for firewood; ruined old planters, whose sons [were] in the field, dwelling gloomily in their dilapidated homes . . . in county after county."[15]

As a result of the recent raids, the Richmond City Council decided that it was time to create official military companies "for the defense of the City in case of any sudden and unexpected attack from the enemy."[16] Each company was to have at least fifty but not more than seventy-five men, and George W. Randolph was appointed commander over all the companies. He and three members of the city council were appointed to choose twenty captains to serve under his command. Among those chosen were John Dooley and Philip Wright, both of the Ambulance Committee. Each captain was to recruit fifty men for his company.[17] Not surprisingly, Dooley appointed fifty members of the Ambulance Committee to his company. From then on they attended regular drills on Capitol Square. John Mitchel later noted that in addition to being "armed as a company connected with the city guard. . . . we . . . [were] several times called out to take share of guard duty on the trenches around the city."[18]

Despite the increased demands of his service as captain of one of the city's official military companies, Dooley continued to conduct his business affairs in the usual orderly manner. On April 18, for instance, he paid the auditor of public accounts $870, the license tax due on his firm's gross sales receipts of $199,000.[19] That amount represented a tremendous increase in his gross receipts from the year before, which totaled only $40,000.[20] The increase may not have reflected his continued contracts with the Confederate government so much as the inflation of Confederate currency by this point in the war. Nonetheless, in 1863 Dooley still had sufficient surplus capital to invest. That year, he invested again in insurance companies — one thousand Confederate dollars, for example, for forty shares of the Old Dominion Insurance Company, which had been one of the first group of new insurance concerns chartered in 1860.[21]

In June, when the Ambulance Committee learned that the Army of Northern Virginia was planning to campaign in Pennsylvania, a field surgeon of the First Virginia named St. George Tucker Peachey wrote to Gen. Robert E. Lee to express the Ambulance Committee's willingness to accompany the army.[22] Lee responded that he was "under great obligations to them for their services to the sick and wounded of this army, from the battles around Richmond to the present time." He added, however, "I do not see that it would be of any benefit to the service for the committee to accompany the army in any movement which the campaign may render necessary."

As a result, on July 3, 1863, the third day of the Battle at Gettysburg, when Jack Dooley and Willy Mitchel were within sight of each other at the start of Pickett's Charge, their fathers and the rest of the Ambulance Committee were camped about four miles outside of Richmond waiting for a signal from Gettysburg that the committee's services were needed. Both fathers wanted news of their sons.[23] They wouldn't know for weeks that Willy had been killed or that Jack had been severely wounded by a bullet that traveled through both his thighs. By a strange coincidence, Jack lay unattended on the battlefield beside Col. Lewis B. Williams, the same officer who had been left on the battlefield in Williamsburg with his older brother, Jim.[24] By July 12, Jack's twenty-first birthday, he was a prisoner of war in a railroad cattle car rattling its way to Fort McHenry in Baltimore.[25]

When the signal that the Ambulance Committee was waiting for finally came, they made the long trek to Williamsport, Maryland, where they met the defeated army as it crossed the Potomac River.[26] Those wounded in the three-day battle numbered 18,735, and a seventeen-mile-long wagon train carrying the wounded had left Gettysburg in the pouring rain on July 4.[27] Neither John Dooley nor John Mitchel could learn anything about his son. They got word that the First Virginia had been "almost annihilated in the attempt to gain the Cemetery Heights," and Mitchel finally heard that his son James, who had also been in the battle, had not been wounded. Yet even James knew nothing of Jack's fate.[28] On July 29 Mitchel wrote to his son John, then a captain in a South Carolina artillery regiment, to say that he had "been delaying to write to you in the hope that I might have some news of poor Willy. . . . I begin to be very anxious about him, for it is now near four weeks since the battle, and if he and J. Dooley were in any hospital or place of confinement at the North, one would suppose that one or other of them would have found means to get a note slipped through the lines to let us know they are alive."[29] Then John Dooley, desperate for news, finally found a way to send a letter through the lines to the North, and on August 30, the two fathers learned the grim news. Jack was alive and a prisoner, but fifteen-year-old Willy was dead. Mitchel wrote again to his son John: "I know poor Willy's fate at last. He was killed on the field at Gettysburg. It was only to-day I learned it, by a letter from a gentleman in Philadelphia, to whom Mr. Dooley had written to make inquiries about his own son Jack, [and] about Willy."[30]

Jack, whom the family had thought too small and frail to endure the hardships of army life, suffered greatly from the wounds in his legs. They still hadn't healed by late August, when, after six weeks in the prison hospital at Fort McHenry, he was shipped to Johnson's Island in Lake Erie near Sandusky, Ohio. There he contracted the tuberculosis that would shorten his life.

CHAPTER 9 | Fame

Letters from Jack arrived sporadically in September and October. In view of the seriousness of his injuries, the family undoubtedly hoped he might be chosen for the prisoner-of-war exchange and sent home within a few months, as Jim had been in 1862. Jack, however, harbored no such hopes and made a point of letting his father know that in a November 20 letter in which he wrote that he was "resigned to remaining here as long as I can do nothing else."[1]

Meanwhile, the work of the Ambulance Committee was coming to the attention of newspapers on both side of the Mason-Dixon Line. In early November, the *New York Times* reprinted an article from the *Enquirer* describing an occasion when 185 Union prisoners were exchanged at City Point for an equal number of Confederates.[2] The article reported that the committee "received the grateful acknowledgments of the Yankee officer in command of the boat, for the care and tenderness with which they moved and handled the dismal freight which they put on board his ship," none of whom was fit enough to be moved. The article was not the last about the work of the committee to appear in the northern press.[3] By the war's end, the Richmond Ambulance Committee was famous. Its work brought it such fame that the Richmond commission merchant firm Harvey, James and Williams named a new blend of tobacco in its honor. "The Ambulance Committee Smoking Tobacco" probably began as a palliative in the supplies the committee packed along with splints and bandages for its rescue missions, but by the end of the war the company had sold thousands of pouches to regular customers as well.[4]

By the beginning of 1864, Richmond prisons had become terribly overcrowded. The Confederate government addressed the situation by shifting prisoners of war to cities farther south. In light of its extensive experience accompanying prisoners of war under the exchange cartel, the Ambulance Committee was now called upon to conduct prison-to-prison transport. In late January, for example, it was ordered to ferry Union prisoners to a prison in Danville.[5]

On the last day of February, however, the Ambulance Committee's duty as part of the Home Guard took precedence. The alarm bell in the bell tower on Capitol Square rang repeatedly as Union general Judson Kilpatrick's forces attempted a raid on the city from the north along Brook Road. The city fathers correctly anticipated an additional attack from the west and sent out the city guards including the Ambulance Company. As John Mitchel recorded in his diary, "we had a night or two under canvas" along the Westham Plank Road five or six miles west of the city.[6] There they clashed with a five-hundred-man Union cavalry detachment led by Col. Ulrich Dahlgren that had separated from Kilpatrick in western Goochland County.

Dahlgren's men had swept through eastern Goochland, burning houses, mills, and barns (and making off with horses, mules, and silver) while on a mission to kidnap Gen. Henry Wise, the former governor of Virginia. Wise had been in Goochland visiting his daughter and her husband at Eastwood, very near Sabot Hill, the plantation of the Confederate secretary of war, James Seddon. He escaped—just barely—with Dahlgren in furious pursuit.

At dusk on Tuesday, March 1, at the western edge of Richmond, Dahlgren's forces encountered unexpected resistance from the Ambulance Committee and the rest of the Home Guard near the farm of Ben Green. The skirmish lasted until after dark before Dahlgren and his men pulled out. By morning they had moved north and east to rejoin Kilpatrick. "At first the whole scope and main object of this raid were not understood in our city," Mitchel wrote. "We only knew that flying bodies of cavalry were breaking our James River Canal, and plundering some of the homesteads of the rich James River valley."

Dahlgren's mission, Mitchel later noted, "was, first to release the ten thousand prisoners on Belleisle [sic], and let them loose on the city; then to open the jail doors, and . . . set fire to the city itself, and in the general confusion to seize the President and the Ministers of State—and ride away. We in Richmond did not discover the whole of this plan until it had failed."[7]

A few days later, the Confederate government, faced with a continuing shortage of fighting men, issued a new Conscription Act that canceled all previous exemptions and required all white men between the ages of seventeen and fifty to serve in the military.[8] The fifty or so men of the Ambulance Committee, even those who, like its president, John Enders, had been officially exempted, were now required to serve not just in the Home Guard but also in the Confederate army. The committee petitioned the secretary of war to exempt the men, but their petition was refused.[9] The *Examiner* took a strong stance against the conscription of the committee on its front page that morning, declaring that its "services . . . are equivalent to a brigade in the field. . . . Some of our worthiest and most liberal citizens organized this corps[, which] has done a service of conspicuous usefulness and generosity. . . . [I]t would be a sorry expedient indeed if, for a most insignificant addition to the conscription, this organization should be crippled and re-paid with such ingratitude.[10] Despite such protests—and a letter from Governor William Smith expressing his intention to withhold from conscription men "necessary" to the state—on March 23 the members of the committee were mustered in and sent to Camp Lee to prepare for service in the field. After the *Dispatch* published the governor's letter, however, Secretary of War James S. Seddon relented somewhat and declared that the reserves "under State authority . . . need not at once be called into Confederate service, but may be allowed to remain as they are *until further orders*."[11]

In mid-May, while the Ambulance Committee was away at Guiney Station south of Richmond, robbers burglarized a number of Richmond businesses. Among them was Dooley's hat shop in Main Street's Eagle Square. The *Dispatch* reported that the thieves, who entered the shop by forcing open the front door, took "a considerable number of hats and caps—the exact amount not known."[12] Despite the robbery and the threat of raids on the city, however, the Dooleys' oldest daughter, Mary, and her fiancé, Robert "Tantie" McCandlish Jones, sergeant major of the First Virginia, decided to postpone their wedding no longer. During a lull in hostilities, on May 21, 1864, Mary and Tantie were married by Bishop McGill in a 6:00 a.m. wedding at St. Peter's Catholic Church on Grace Street, a block west of the Capitol.[13]

By late June the Union army under Grant's command had laid siege to Petersburg. The Petersburg correspondent for the *Dispatch* noted that the "good Samaritans" of the Ambulance Committee were "ministering to the suffering and the dying. In their good work they are nobly seconded by the fair women of this good city."[14]

As the siege of Petersburg continued, the Richmond and Petersburg Railroad announced changes in its regular train service between the two cities: "On and after Monday the 7th instant, the trains on this road will run as follows: Mail Train—Leave Richmond at 6:55 A.M. and arrive at 8:43 A.M. Ambulance Train—Leave Richmond at 9 A.M. . . . . The Ambulance Train will transport passengers South but not North."[15] Unmentioned but universally understood was that the northbound train brought back the wounded.

In the fall of 1864, Florence Dooley returned to boarding school at the Ursuline Convent in Columbia, South Carolina, but by mid-November, when the Union army under Gen. William Tecumseh Sherman was marching from Atlanta to Savannah, her father had decided to bring her back home to Richmond. Fortunately for the Dooleys, the Ambulance Committee was designated to travel southward, first to Savannah and then to Charleston to deliver

Federal prisoners of war and bring paroled Confederate prisoners back. Accordingly, while in South Carolina, John Dooley took a side trip to Columbia to pick up Florence and several other Richmond girls.[16] In order to smuggle them through the Union lines along the way home, he hid Florence and her friends in the back of a wagon covered with piles of burlap bags, where they stayed for the entire eight-day journey.[17] Many years later one of Florence's daughters would recall her mother's description of "the terror felt by the girls" during the trip.

Around this time, Dooley decided to invest in real estate as a hedge against the spiraling inflation of Confederate currency. The day after Christmas he paid $16,500, an outrageous sum even in light of inflated currency, for a piece of land on the south side of Main Street between Adams and Jefferson in the western reaches of the city. He may have intended the site as the location for a new manufacturing works.[18] Early in the new year he also bought a lot on Ninth Street for $10,000. He held on to it for only six months, selling it in June.[19] By then his numerous large government contracts had prompted him to expand his manufacturing enterprise. To do so, he created a new company he called simply the Richmond Hat Manufactory. The incorporation process provided Jim, still under the tutelage of the lawyer William Green, with his first personal experience of corporate law. His father enlisted W. H. Haxall, president of Richmond's largest manufacturing business, the Haxall Flour Mills, to be the company secretary. Haxall brought extensive corporate experience that complemented Dooley's, and he kept the firm running while Dooley continued to serve as captain of the Ambulance Committee. Just how big the Richmond Hat Manufactory became during the war years is reflected in its newspaper advertisements during December and early January: "Wanted—The Richmond Hat Manufactory wishes to purchase one hundred thousand pounds of sheep and lamb's wool for which the market price will be paid in cash. The Company also wants several competent HATTERS who are not liable to the conscript law."[20]

The new year brought with it yet another task for the Ambulance Committee. Despite the serious food shortages in Richmond that winter, a group of women decided to give the soldiers encamped near the city a festive New Year's dinner. They spent much of the week between the Christmas and New Year's holidays gathering sufficient supplies to give the men a decent meal and special treats like the pouches of Ambulance Committee Smoking Tobacco that someone probably tucked into the packages. On January 4 the "War News" column of the *Dispatch* mentioned that Ambulance Committee members were still out distributing the dinners in the field.

In February 1865, a close confidant of Abraham Lincoln's named James P. Blair arrived in Richmond. Blair conferred with Jefferson Davis about the possibility of emissaries from the North and South meeting to try to negotiate a peace. Davis agreed to send them, and on January 29 they left to meet with Lincoln on board a steamship at Fort Monroe. After a four-hour conference, however, negotiations broke down. A telegram delivered the bad news before the committee returned. The *Dispatch* reported in its February 6 issue: "There is no prospect of peace. Mr. Lincoln's only terms were unconditional submission to the laws and Constitution of the United States."

Reaction to the news in Richmond was swift and angry. There were calls throughout the city for a public meeting so people could hear from the peace commissioners in person. Governor Smith obliged and scheduled the meeting for seven o'clock that evening in the First African Baptist Church diagonally across the street from the Dooleys' house. There was so much interest in the meeting that the *Dispatch* predicted, "No room in the city will accommodate one fifth of the people who would crowd to hear Mr. Stephens." Even before five o'clock that evening, "every seat and position where a man could stand was occupied, and with each moment the crowd became greater."[21] So many people crammed into the galleries that there was fear they might collapse. The *Dispatch* declared that the purpose of the meeting was "to hurl back into Lincoln's teeth the insult put upon the Southern people by his answer to the Confederate commissioners." John Dooley was one of those who managed to squeeze in to hear Jefferson Davis give "what many would say was the best speech of his life," which was interrupted "frequently . . . with the wildest outbursts of applause."

There were calls for another meeting, and Senator R. M. T. Hunter agreed to serve as president for it. Governor Smith, John Dooley, Joseph R. Anderson, John Purcell, Judge William H. Lyons, and William H. Macfarland were six of the twenty vice presidents. John Mitchel and James A. Cowardin were secretaries. The speakers were all members of the Confederate Congress. Notices published in the newspaper announced "A Great Meeting of the People" to be held once again at the African Church at noon on Thursday, February 9. Despite all the speeches, however, the "great" meeting, like its predecessor, served only to underscore the futility of the situation, as one by one the speakers aired their anger and frustration.

Several weeks later, Jim Dooley was one of the volunteers accompanying the Ambulance Committee as it steamed down the James. More than a thousand men on each side were to be exchanged. At Aiken's Landing, the Confederates burst forth with "deafening cheers" as they boarded the flag-of-truce boat.[22] Suddenly, Jim caught sight of his younger brother. As Jack later wrote, "brother James . . . [was] among the first to hail me and bid me welcome, being one of the Committee to look after the wounded." John Mitchel recognized Jack, too, "amongst the forlorn troop who came on board to us at Varinas [*sic*], a slender young man in an officer's faded uniform, and a face sadly worn by suffering."[23]

The committee fed the returnees and made the wounded and sick comfortable. According to Jack, when they arrived at Richmond "a little before 2 a.m. . . . my brother and I proceed[ed] together to the house where to a surety there . . . [was] great rejoicing over the long lost prisoner."[24]

Despite the gloom of those waning months of the war, the Dooleys did not forget to celebrate St. Patrick's Day. As Jack later told it, he went to church on the evening of March 17 and returned home to find guests waiting for his father, "who, having invited them, forgot it and went to church."[25] When John Dooley finally arrived home, he joined his sons and his company in lifting glasses of "wine and apple brandy in *honour* of the Day, and having quite a social evening."

Later in March, Jack accompanied Jim to a real estate auction at which the elder brother successfully bid on their father's behalf for a piece of undeveloped property. Like the other lots John Dooley had bought recently, this one passed through several hands during the war. Dooley paid $21,920 in Confederate dollars for the property.[26] Like many other Richmond businessmen, as the war neared its close, he was keenly aware that when peace came, Confederate currency would be worthless. On the other hand, real estate, purchased now and sold after the war, would yield United States currency. It was a lesson that served Jim well in his postwar business career.

At the beginning of April, a Union breakthrough on the rail line south of Petersburg finally convinced Lee that his army had to retreat. He sent a telegram to the War Department on Sunday morning April 2, 1865, reporting his decision to pull out at once and recommending that the government evacuate immediately.

After Jefferson Davis abandoned the city that night, John Mitchel's instincts as a journalist told him that the big news would occur wherever the president established a new seat of government. So he, too, left the city, traveling southwest on foot for fourteen miles until his path intersected with the Richmond and Danville train carrying Davis.[27] However, he couldn't have been more wrong about where the big news would happen.

D uring the night of April 2, 1865, looters prowled the streets of Richmond's business district, guided by the light of the flames that were devouring it. Earlier that evening, twenty-five men — under orders from the Richmond City Council — had broken open barrels of whiskey and poured their contents into nearby gutters.[1] Meanwhile the Confederate provost marshal ordered the tobacco stored in the city's warehouses burned so it wouldn't fall into the hands of the enemy. Thanks to the wind that blew through the city streets, the flames from the burning tobacco ignited the liquor.

When news of the fire reached the Dooley family house, Jim left immediately to retrieve important papers from the office over his father's shop. He hurried downhill toward the business district through a maelstrom that the Home Guard, armed only with "flintlocks and rusty sabres," could not control.[2] Jim managed to enter the door under the sign of a gilded hat and lock it behind him before going upstairs.

A few minutes later a young Confederate courier, who later wrote an eyewitness account of what he saw that night, encountered a large group of men walking rapidly toward him. He heard one of them shout, "Here is a hat store! Who is for a new head-gear?" and watched as two of the men who had obviously seen Jim enter grabbed the doorknobs and "shook them savagely, crying: 'Let us in! Open the door!'" Others kicked and banged against the shutters closed over the windows. Suddenly the courier heard a shot that seemed to have been fired from a second-story window; he saw the men give the door a "series of rapid and powerful blows with the butts of their muskets" before they broke the glass and rushed inside. He watched as "with a yell one man cleared the breach . . . [and] ran to the shelves to make his choice." By then, "a dozen more were in the room," including the courier. While "men were busily . . . ransacking drawers, overturning boxes, and stripping shelves," he grabbed several hats for himself and made his way back out to the street. He didn't see Jim make his escape and head home.

It's doubtful that anyone in Richmond slept that night, but if they did, they awoke the next morning to a new and terrible world. Ninety percent of Richmond's business district was a blackened ruin. For John Dooley, what became known as the Evacuation Fire brought stupendous losses. His hat shop in Eagle Square and his manufacturing operation were gone.

Before dawn, Joseph Mayo, the elderly mayor of Richmond, and three other men left the city in an open carriage waving a white flag and intending to surrender the city to the Union forces. A few hours later the official surrender took place on Capitol Square. The fire, which had destroyed eighteen blocks and nine hundred businesses, was still raging even though Union troops under Gen. Godfrey Weitzel had set to work to help put it out as soon as they entered the city. Sallie Brock later reported that the "roaring, hissing crackling" of the fire could still be heard when the U.S. flag unfurled from the pole on top of the Capitol and a military band played "The Star-Spangled Banner."[3] She commented that, although before the war the tune "was wont to awaken a thrill of patriotism . . . now . . . [f]or us it was a requiem for buried hopes."

By three o'clock in the afternoon the fire was finally under control.[4] A layer of smoke hung over the city for days while the smell of the fire and burning tobacco permeated the air. It would be hard for some to draw a breath in that part of the city for a long time to come.

The business that John Dooley had spent almost thirty years building was a total loss. Not even a vestige of the golden hat sign remained to indicate where the company's retail store had been. Along the whole eighteen blocks, only the Custom House and a few partial walls remained standing. Not a bank building was left in the city. Only one newspaper, the *Whig,* was left to record what the eye could see. The paper reported one ironic aspect of the situation: "For the first time during the war the city may truly be said to be quiet, and life and property safe."[5]

The following morning President Abraham Lincoln and his son Tad arrived at the city dock to pay a visit to Richmond. The president, Tad, and their U.S. Navy escorts walked from the dock uphill to the house left two days earlier by Jefferson Davis. Anyone in the Dooley home who happened to be looking out the window might have seen the president and his party as they crossed the street. Two days later, the Dooleys probably heard a boisterous "Jubilee" meeting at the First African Baptist when two thousand or more former slaves and black soldiers of the United States Colored Troops filled the building "to capacity" to celebrate Emancipation.[6]

The *Whig* did offer one piece of good news. Mail service between the South and the rest of the country had been reestablished. For John Dooley, that news was particularly welcome. He was anxious to hear from his brother-in-law Michael Byrne, who managed his real estate ventures in Chicago.

Communication between the two of them had been cut off by the war. No doubt the news was also welcomed at Georgetown College, where the administration was eager to hear from John Dooley about the bill they had sent him in 1861 for Jack's last term. During the war, the bill had been returned to them through the dead letter office.[7]

With the *Examiner* now gone, John Mitchel returned to Richmond to find himself jobless. His strongly held pro-southern sympathies prevented him from joining the shorthanded staff of the *Whig*, which had been given permission to publish as long as it supported the Union. Mitchel felt he had no choice but to leave his family behind in Richmond and head north to find a job in New York, where he was well known. Only a few days after arriving, he wrote to his sister that he was now editor of the *Daily News*, "a staunch southern newspaper, which was opposed to the war from the beginning," and that he was not certain that he was safe in New York because, "when I came . . . here, several of the more violent newspapers called for my arrest."[8] Mitchel's worry about his own safety was justified. Two weeks after writing that letter, he was arrested and sent to prison at Fort Monroe, where he was confined to a cell near the one holding Jefferson Davis.

Meanwhile, an exhausted John Dooley faced the prospect of starting his business all over again. Nevertheless, he retained his sense of civic duty. He agreed to serve on the newly organized Relief Committee. Although by the Thursday after the fire the farmers' markets in Richmond were offering fresh fish and vegetables for sale to those lucky enough to have specie or greenbacks, many in the city, both white and black, had neither and had to do without.[9] The newly established occupation government quickly responded to the plight of the hungry. It divided the city into thirty districts and appointed "visitors" to go door to door to determine who needed ration tickets for food from the government commissary stores. John Dooley was appointed a visitor for the district between Eighth and Seventeenth Streets from Broad to Main.[10] By April 17, the visitors had distributed 17,367 ration tickets for 86,555 packages of food.

A few days after Lee surrendered to Grant in Appomattox on Tuesday, April 9, the *Whig* published a list of businesses lost in the Evacuation Fire. "John W. Dooley Hatter" appeared on the Main Street list.[11] The paper did not include the estimated financial losses for individual businesses but noted that "they must sum up many millions, the amount destroyed ranging in each case from thousands to hundreds of thousands."

On Sunday, April 16, Richmonders awoke to the news that President Abraham Lincoln had been assassinated. Flags in the city and on the ships in the harbor were lowered to half-mast. The full impact of his death would not be felt in Richmond, however, until federal regulations governed the city.

By April 21 rebuilding had begun on the edges of the burned district.[12] But John Dooley wasn't ready to rebuild quite yet. Instead, he was looking for a space to rent where he could reopen his retail shop.

Three weeks later, the First National Bank, helped by an infusion of northern capital, reopened for business in "a small room in the fire-blackened customhouse and post office, the only structure standing in the financial district."[13] As the ruins were cleared away, the vaults of several other banks were uncovered. Several of them were found intact, and a flicker of life returned to the financial quarters of the city.[14]

Elsewhere in Richmond, however, problems dogged the work of the Relief Committee. Beginning on April 18, Gen. Edward O. C. Ord, then in command of the city, ordered the publication of lengthy notices "To the Unemployed Poor of Richmond."[15] They opened with the assertion, "It is not intended that the assistance furnished to the poor . . . shall be permanent." The notices described people taking ration tickets even though they actually had food and visitors being threatened by "men and women of the vagrant sort." The notices warned, "While the United States authority is anxious to relieve entirely the suffering existing here, it is equally determined not to allow its benevolence to be abused or misapplied." Despite the *Whig*'s assurance that General Ord's orders were "excellent . . . and will meet the approbation of every citizen," their brusque tone exacerbated the tensions and despair in the city.

The military presence in Richmond was not felt solely in City Hall and Capitol Square. The citizenry endured numerous military parades through the streets, some of which seemed extraordinarily long and intended to intimidate. One occurred on a beautiful Saturday, May 6, when the Second and Fifth Corps of the Army of the Potomac marched through the streets. The "long blue line" of an estimated forty-five thousand to fifty thousand men, led by Gen. George Meade and his "splendidly mounted staff," began in Manchester and snaked across the James River on a pontoon bridge to the foot of Seventeenth Street with flags waving, accompanied by the sounds of "joyous music" and drum rolls.[16] From there it proceeded in a complicated path through the eastern and the northern edge of the burned district before marching up Governor Street to Capitol Street. The parade took almost six hours to pass by any given point in the city. Sallie Brock commented that as "vast armies of our conquerors . . . began to pour through the streets of Richmond . . . they seemed to us interminable legions of the enemy, against which our comparatively little army had so obstinately, and all but successfully held out for four years. . . . [T]he question that arose in our minds was not why we were conquered at last, but 'how we could have so long resisted the mighty appliances which operated against us.'"[17]

Life in the conquered city may have brightened just a little bit on May 18, when St. Joseph's Female Academy put on its May Festival. It is likely that the Dooleys' daughter Florence was one of the 150 students dressed in white and bedecked with flowers for the festival. Some of the girls gave short addresses, and they all sang and danced. The newly established *Richmond Times* described the festival as "decidedly one of the most lovely and interesting scenes which have occurred in this city for a number of years past."[18]

On May 26, Francis H. Pierpont arrived in Richmond to serve as governor of Virginia under the military command. Four years earlier, when Virginia seceded from the Union, it split in two parts, and Pierpont served as governor of the part that remained in the Union and made its capital in Wheeling. In 1863, when the new state of West Virginia was established there and Wheeling became its capital, Pierpont continued to serve as governor of the remaining portion of Virginia still loyal to the United States, called the "Restored State of Virginia." Its capital was Alexandria. In 1865, Pierpont, aware of the awkwardness of his new position as governor under the military, made concerted attempts to conciliate Virginians, in particular by encouraging leniency in the granting of pardons to former Confederates. His leniency became especially important after May 29, when President Andrew Johnson issued an Amnesty Proclamation that required any person wishing to be reinstated as a citizen not only to take an oath of allegiance to the United States and admit that slavery had been abolished but also to state that he or she had never willingly given aid to the Confederacy. Another of its provisions was aimed at those who, like John Dooley, had property worth more than twenty thousand dollars. These individuals were forbidden to take the Amnesty Oath and faced the possibility of having their property confiscated.[19] It didn't take long for Richmond businessmen to realize that excluding the very men who had enough capital to rebuild endangered the future of the city. They gathered together and appointed a committee to go to Washington to persuade the president to change his mind and drop the restriction.[20]

In late May or early June, having apparently written to Michael Byrne and received no response, Dooley wrote to Daniel O'Hara, the clerk of the Cook County Court in Chicago and a fellow Irish immigrant, to find out whether the taxes on his real estate were paid up and the houses in good order. He also asked about the advisability of selling his holdings. O'Hara's return letter brought the shocking news that Michael Byrne had apparently been lost at sea. He not been seen since October 1863, when, according to his second wife, he was on the dock in New York City waiting to board a steamer headed for Havana. Fortunately, Dooley's houses were in good shape and the taxes paid. O'Hara had taken care of everything during the war years and been paid his fee for the work by Dooley's bank, "the White's," in New York.[21] O'Hara had, he wrote, consulted with "a number of friends" who had "informed [him] that real estate will certainly increase in value as the city extends and increases in population . . . now that the calamitous war is ended."

Dooley decided to put some of his Richmond real estate on the market instead. Two weeks later, he sold the lot on Ninth Street that he had bought the previous January for ten thousand dollars cash in Confederate dollars for only $427.50 in U.S. greenbacks.[22] The sale generated some of the capital he needed to start rebuilding his business.

Even before selling the Ninth Street property, Dooley had managed to rent and stock a place for his shop in an iron-front building on Governor Street untouched by the fire. On June 17 the *Whig* printed his first advertisement since the fire: "JOHN DOOLEY Has just received a large lot of hats of the newest and most fashionable styles and qualities, from the lowest to the highest grades. He is at present over the store of Mr. D. S. Huffard, Governor street, where he will be happy to see his old friends." The fact that he paid to run the advertisement for only one week offers evidence of just how little ready capital Dooley had, and how careful he had to be with it.

Reestablishing his manufacturing works was complicated and would take much longer than stocking his rented shop. First Dooley had to take the required Amnesty Oath; second, he had to apply for a presidential pardon. He conferred with a group of other Ambulance Committee members in the over-twenty-thousand-dollar category, and together they sought the advice of a member of the Pierpont administration, Martin F. Conway. A former U.S. congressman, Conway had connections in Washington that might help expedite the pardon application process. On June 21, Dooley and the committee members went to the provost marshal's office in Capitol Square to take the Amnesty Oath together. Each man received two copies of a certificate attesting to his oath, one copy of which he attached to a letter explaining his credentials for restored citizenship and noting that he had served on the Richmond Ambulance Committee.[23]

Dooley addressed his letter to John Speed, then the U.S. attorney general. As was the case for many of the letters written by Ambulance Committee members, his was more remarkable for what it didn't say than for what it did.

There was, for instance, no mention of his having been an officer on active duty in the Confederate army. Instead, he simply wrote:

> Sir: My property was assessed at over twenty thousand Dollars ($20000). I am thereby not embraced in the Proclamation of President Johnson of the 29th of May 1865. (I may say here that I have devoted this property to the liquidation of my debts due in the Northern Cities.) I have taken the Amnesty Oath as therein prescribed (certificate herewith enclosed) and design to comply with the obligations thereby imposed. Under these circumstances I respectfully ask under the provisions of the Act of Congress of July 1862 to be restored to my rights as a citizen of the United States.

The application letters and certificates were bundled together with a letter from Gen. John Mulford, who had served as the U.S. commissioner for prisoner of war exchange, to verify the applicants' service in the Ambulance Committee. Then Conway took the bundle and left on the train for Washington.

Around the same time, the *Whig* published a notice signed by John Dooley and thirty-three other business owners calling for a meeting "to consider and adopt the best means" of rebuilding the burned district and reestablishing "trade, commerce and manufactures." Their notice proclaimed rebuilding to be of "vital importance to all classes of our people."[24] A sentence at the bottom of the notice was the only indication that the meeting had official sanction. "I cordially commend the objects of the above petition," it read, and was signed simply "F. H. Pierpont." The morning after the businessmen's notice was published, the *Whig* commented that it was "glad to see the call for the meeting. . . . The incertitude of the enforcement of the Confiscation Act is the chief cause of the paralysis which has thus far kept the best portion of our city a mass of ruins."[25]

Meanwhile Conway had gone to the White House not once but twice to present the Ambulance Committee's letters. His diligence paid off quickly when on Saturday he learned that all the men had been pardoned. The telegram he sent announcing the favorable outcome of his efforts arrived in Richmond Sunday morning: by the following day it was national news.[26] Both the *New York Herald* and the *New York Times* covered the story.[27] The *Whig* commented that the presidential pardons "will disembarrass a large amount of business tact and energy, which will be developed ere long, in enterprises of pith and moment."[28]

Among Governor Pierpoint's duties that summer was making appointments to statewide offices. At the end of June he announced that "James H.

Dooley" had been appointed one of two new notaries public for the City of Richmond and County of Henrico.[29] The appointment gave Jim his introduction to public service, and the small fee he collected for fulfilling its duties probably gave him the first income he had ever earned outside of his father's business.

A week later, on July 6, Jim received his master's degree at Georgetown College's fiftieth graduation ceremony.[30] By then his father had hired the contractors Green and Allen to build a new manufacturing plant on Main Street between Eighth and Ninth Streets, a two-story structure running back a hundred feet.[31]

Several weeks earlier the *Whig*'s Fort Monroe column carried some news that must have come as a shock to the Dooleys. John Mitchel had been brought to Virginia on a steamer called the *Henry Burden* and imprisoned at Fort Monroe.[32] A front-page article in the *Norfolk Post* reported that Mitchel had been arrested at his *Daily News* office in New York quite suddenly and unexpectedly "by order of the government," and that the reason for his arrest was unknown but apparently Mitchel would be tried for treason. The Dooleys and Mrs. Mitchel and her children learned no more until a week or so later, when the *Whig* mentioned the possibility that Mitchel would be tried in Richmond, "where all the witnesses will be available."[33] But that was only a rumor.

In September, when Farmers' National Bank of Richmond, Virginia, organized with an authorized capital of five hundred thousand dollars, John Dooley was one of eleven men elected to the board of directors. The amount of capital authorized for the bank was much smaller than the amounts authorized for Richmond's prewar banks: in 1860, for example, a predecessor with a similar name, the Farmers' Bank of Virginia, had authorized capital of over $3,150,000.[34] The new bank opened a temporary office at 7 Fourteenth Street under the Exchange Hotel. Farmers' National was an ambitious, full-service bank established primarily to serve the business community in Richmond, and advertisements announced that it would "receive deposits, buy and sell exchange on all the principal cities in the United States, Canada and Europe." It "respectfully tendered" its services to "all banks, bankers and others for the transaction of business" and offered "Highest price paid for Government securities," with special attention to "Collections on all available points in the South" and "prompt returns."[35] The bank also offered service for the individual depositor, no matter how small or short-term the customer's deposits might be: "With a view to encourage a spirit of economy especially among the laboring and salaried classes, this Bank will receive deposits and grant certificates . . . payable with interest and on demand without notice. This system is in extensive operation in the Northern cities and in Europe, and its advantages are so apparent that none having idle capital should fail to avail themselves of its benefits."

In October 1865, John Mitchel was released after spending four months in Fortress Monroe without being charged with a crime. He headed straight to Richmond, where his wife and daughters were living. The evening he arrived, the Dooleys were undoubtedly among the many friends who gathered at his house at the corner of Fifth and Canal to welcome him back.[36] The next day he returned to New York, where the Fenians, an Irish political group committed to the violent overthrow of British rule in Ireland, offered him a job as their treasurer in Paris. He accepted and on November 10 sailed from New York to Le Havre. The following autumn, however, disillusioned with the Fenians, he returned to Richmond, where he spent most of 1867 writing his *History of Ireland since the Treaty of Limerick* before returning to New York City to found another newspaper. This one he called the *Irish Citizen*.[37]

Meanwhile, in the early fall of 1865, while John Dooley was working to reopen his hat business, Jim had received William Green's approval to take the formal steps necessary to obtain a license to practice law. There was no such thing as a written bar exam in those days. A would-be lawyer simply had an interview with a judge friendly to his application who would ask him a few questions before giving his approval.[38] Since Green was then serving as a judge in the Court of Conciliation, Jim had no need to seek support from anyone else.

The rather startling absence of any requirement demonstrating an applicant's reasonable fitness to practice law meant that many unqualified lawyers represented clients in the courts of the time. There were, however, some pro forma steps required for a license, and Jim took those. He appeared in Henrico County Court, where it was certified "that James H. Dooley, Esquire, who wishes to obtain a license to practice as an attorney in the Courts of this Commonwealth, has resided in this county for one year next preceding; that he is a person of honest demeanor, and is over twenty one years of age."[39] Two months later he returned to take oaths enabling him to plead cases in the court.[40] The following week he took similar oaths in Richmond's Hustings Court, where criminal cases were heard.[41] Then, almost a year later, he appeared before Justices Richard C. Moncure, William A. Joynes, and Alexander Rives to qualify as counsel before the Virginia Supreme Court of Appeals.[42]

During this period Jim was invited by an established Richmond lawyer, A. Judson Crane, to join his practice as junior partner.[43] Partnership in the firm was an auspicious start for the young lawyer's career: Crane was renowned for his agility in debate and his excellence as a writer.[44] Like Dooley, he had received a classical education at one of Richmond's best schools before going away to college and was considered something of a polymath. He contributed articles in Richmond newspapers for over two decades, and his poetry, essays on literature, and book reviews had appeared in the *Southern Literary Messenger*.[45] Like William Green, Crane provided a strong model for Dooley to emulate, and he would do so throughout his career. There was one conspicuous difference between Crane and Green, however: Crane was a politician, and he may have inspired Dooley's own eventual entry into politics and his career in public service.

In November 1865, John Dooley, who had found that having a shop in a second-floor walk-up was not entirely satisfactory, moved his merchandise to one of the shops on the ground floor of the newly refurbished Spotswood Hotel. His November 29 advertisement in the *Richmond Times* trumpeted the new location "UNDER THE SPOTSWOOD HOTEL," but his manufacturing arm was still not yet up and running.[46] Nevertheless, he also advertised in his friend James Cowardin's *Dispatch,* beginning with the very first issue after the fire. In fact, a Dooley ad appeared in every issue for the next three months. Cowardin thanked Dooley and his other loyal advertisers by giving them a free front-page plug in an article on "Christmas and Christmas Presents" a few days before the holiday. "Notwithstanding the stringency in the money market," Cowardin wrote, "we expect that Santa Claus and Kriss Kingle [*sic*] will have a merry anniversary on Monday."[47] However, the cold reality that Christmas season was that merchants' stock did not move.

By the end of the year the continuing distress evident among the poorest citizens of the city prompted the Catholic bishop of Richmond to encourage the members of St. Peter's and St. Patrick's to establish a St. Vincent de Paul Society in each parish to help the poor. During January the bishop met several times with men of St. Peter's but to little avail. Then one Sunday in early February, a group of six men, including John Dooley and James Cowardin, agreed to try to recruit more men for the society. Jim Dooley was one of eleven new members to join, and he was elected secretary, a position he would fill for many years.[48] The membership grew slowly but surely, and at each meeting a collection for the poor was turned over to the treasurer. Jim's minutes recorded contributions from outsiders as well members, including fifty dollars in March from the bishop of Baltimore. In April the members of the St. Vincent de Paul Society at St. Peter's found that their expenditures for the poor exceeded their receipts. The society held an election to replace its provisional president, Father Becker, and John Dooley was unanimously elected, in part because of his fiscal soundness.

During those early months of 1866, Dooley's advertisements reflected all too clearly the financial problems he and other merchants were facing. From January through March, for example, they carried a line noting that he had, "in consequence of the scarcity of money, reduced considerably the prices of" the hats and caps he had in stock for men, boys, and children. In the middle of March he was selling ladies' fur capes, half-capes, and muffs "at cost."[49] By the end of the month, however, his new manufacturing building was finished, and his ads once again opened with the name, "John Dooley, Hat Manufacturer and Dealer." By July his ad noted that he was "manufacturing the fine MOLESKIN DRESS HAT for gentlemen."[50] Dooley's retail shop, however, remained at the Spotswood Hotel for six months more. He finally opened a new store at 1211 Eagle Square on New Year's Day, 1867.[51]

Despite the continuing postwar depression, there were signs of financial recovery in the banking community that spring. By the beginning of May, the First National Bank had received authorization to increase its stock. Sixty-nine businesses, including John Dooley's, subscribed for it.[52] Its long list of stockholders, however, contrasted with the value of its authorized capital, which was only $156,000, much less than Farmers' five hundred thousand dollars.[53] A short sentence at the bottom of the notice announcing the subscriptions boasted, "The stock of this Bank is owned almost exclusively by the citizens of the State." The operative word was "almost." The Richmond business community took pride in reestablishing the bank but was honest enough to admit that help from outside the state made it possible. A week later, Farmers' National Bank, which had moved from its temporary quarters under the Exchange Hotel, opened for its first day of business in the beautiful new iron-front Wickham Building, next door to and east of the Custom House.[54] On the same morning, a third "national" bank in the city, the National Bank of Virginia, opened in another iron front, a centrally heated building on the corner of Main and Eleventh, with an authorized capital of two hundred thousand dollars. The total capital of the three new banks, however, didn't match the resources of a single one of their prewar predecessors.

Financial issues of a different kind cropped up rather unexpectedly a month earlier. The U.S. Congress appropriated funds to maintain the graves of Union soldiers who had died during the Civil War—but not those of Confederate soldiers. The reaction in Richmond was swift and resentful, especially because both Oakwood and Hollywood Cemeteries, where thousands of Union as well as Confederate soldiers were buried, were in very poor condition. The *Examiner* suggested that Richmond churchwomen take up the cause and organize to remedy the situation.[55] Women responded quickly and established an auxiliary for each of the cemeteries. When the president of Hollywood, Thomas H. Ellis, invited anyone who wanted to help clean up the cemetery to meet at St. Paul's Episcopal Church on May 3, women flocked to the church to form the Hollywood Memorial Association. At another meeting on the evening of May 14, Sarah Dooley was among the women elected to the association's board of managers, and the women set May 31 as the date for a Confederate Memorial Day.[56] The elaborate plans they made for the commemoration included a parade of military companies. When the veterans of the First Virginia met to organize for the parade, John Dooley was appointed to two committees, one to find a band and the other to draft an organizational plan for the regiment's participation.[57]

At eight o'clock in the morning three days before the scheduled event, more than eight hundred men, most of them Confederate veterans, arrived to put in a day's work cleaning the cemetery. Many of them had been given the day off by their employers.[58] The following day, five hundred more arrived to continue the work. On May 31, the city's businesses closed for Hollywood's Memorial Day. At nine o'clock that morning, the First Virginia led off a parade of military companies followed by a procession of more than twenty thousand people walking or riding in carriages. They arrived at Hollywood just before noon. Veterans were obliged to wear their old uniforms without the buttons and military insignia, which had been outlawed by the government.

At two o'clock that afternoon, two companies of Federal soldiers arrived at the Richmond, Fredericksburg and Potomac depot—not to attend the memorial ceremonies but to supplement the local Union forces in maintaining order.[59] They were too late, but that didn't matter. Their services had not been needed on that solemn occasion.

J im Dooley had been practicing law for only a year when, on a Tuesday
evening in early October 1866, a number of Richmond's lawyers met
in the city council chamber to organize a bar association for the city.[1]
They called it the Marshall Association in honor of the first chief justice of the U.S. Supreme Court and elected several of the city's distinguished
older lawyers as officers of the association that night.[2] Recognition of Jim as
a promising member of the profession came when they elected him corre-
sponding secretary.

Later that month, Jim's reputation received another boost when he defended a client who had stabbed another man during an argument. The particulars of Jim's plea in Henrico Circuit Court are lost to history, but the *Dispatch* reported that it was "a forensic effort of great merit, evincing much legal
ability on the part of the young advocate."[3] Despite the growing reputation of
the junior partner and the well-established one of the senior, it was hard for
Crane and Dooley to make a living in the immediate postwar years. Most of
their clients were people of modest means, and the lawyers' fees often went
unpaid. Some of the clients were like Martha Johnson, who couldn't read,
write, or afford to pay for their services. She made her "mark" on a September 24, 1866, IOU.[4]

On January 3, 1867, A. Judson Crane died unexpectedly, and with the loss
of his partner, Jim became an inexperienced single practitioner. Fortunately,
he continued to acquire new cases, but making a living was hard. On January 19, 1867, for example, he represented a man named West Wyatt in Hustings Court on the charge of selling liquor without a license. Dooley's fee for
the case was fifteen dollars. Wyatt paid five dollars in cash toward the fee, but
a receipt in Dooley's law office papers shows that Wyatt never paid the full
amount.[5]

During the early postwar years, Jim shared the general conviction that immigration could help alleviate the acute labor shortage complicating Virginia's efforts to recover from the devastation of the war. As the editor of the *Dispatch* commented: "We console ourselves with the thought that as soon as we
are fairly restored to the Union and peace and civil government once more
reign in the South, immigration will come to people our cities, to settle our
deserted farms, and to restore life and prosperity to our suffering country."[6]

Jim saw many companies that had relied on immigrant labor to build railroad beds and canals before the war turn again to immigrant labor to replace them. He watched as new companies sprang up on both sides of the Mason-Dixon Line to entice European immigrants to settle in the South.[7] He knew that the Virginia legislature had established a Board of Immigration and that the governor had appointed a commissioner of immigration, whose duties included making land available for immigrants to lease or to buy.[8] In the early months of 1867 those developments prompted Dooley to join a group of men, most of whom were either Irish immigrants or descendants of Irish immigrants, who incorporated a company called the Irish Emigrant Aid Society of Virginia.[9] The main purpose of the society was "to afford aid and information to emigrants and generally to promote their welfare," but its February 26, 1867, charter also gave the society the power to acquire and "rent out or lease, mortgage, sell, transfer or convey, real and personal estate" to attract immigrants to Virginia.

Meanwhile, in March 1867, the U.S. government designated Virginia as Military District No. 1, and Reconstruction officially began.[10] In October, Gen. John Schofield, the commander of Military District No. 1, ordered that elections be held for delegates to a convention to write a new constitution for Virginia. The Reconstruction Acts passed by the U.S. Congress required a new constitution for each state that had seceded as a prerequisite for readmission to the Union. When the elections for delegates to the convention were held across Virginia on October 22, the combined number of black delegates and Radical Republican delegates from the North or foreign countries elected was almost three times larger than the number of Virginia-born white delegates.[11] The reaction was a groundswell of political activism among conservatives across the state, who formed the Conservative Party from an alliance of prewar Whigs and Democrats. They called for a political party convention and decided to hold it in Richmond.

The constitutional convention opened in the House of Delegates on December 3, and a little more than a week later, the Conservative Party opened its convention at the Richmond Theater. The *Dispatch* opined that the Conservative delegates included "some of the greatest men of the State, some of whom (in advanced age) speak to us as ambassadors from the heroic and virtuous age which achieved the independence of the United States."[12] There were also a number of young businessmen and lawyers in attendance, Jim Dooley among them.

Six weeks later, family matters demanded Jim's attention. His father was suffering from what seemed to be a bad cold, but at 6:30 a.m. on Tuesday morning, February 18, 1868, he managed to escort his daughter Florence down the aisle to marry William Lynn Lewis of Sweet Springs.[13] On Thursday, however, an item in the *Enquirer* revealed that John Dooley was very sick. The Friday morning *Whig* offered the further information that "Maj. John Dooley is lying dangerously ill, from pneumonia, at his residence . . . little hope of his recovery is entertained. Richmond could not lose a better man."[14] But Richmond had already lost him before the paper hit the street. John Dooley had died at 4:00 a.m. on February 21, 1868, at the age of fifty-six.

The affection that the citizens of Richmond felt for John Dooley was confirmed by the large crowd that gathered in front of the Dooley family house and accompanied the funeral procession to St. Peter's Church. The horse-drawn hearse left from the house around two thirty.[15] Following it were the orphans of the St. Joseph's Female Asylum, the boys of St. Peter's Sunday schools, the members of the Ambulance Committee, the surviving members of the First Virginia, the members of the St. Vincent de Paul Societies of St. Peter's and St. Patrick's, the Pastime Baseball Club, "of which the deceased was an honorary member," and the carriages of family and friends. The doors of the church stayed firmly closed until the procession arrived shortly after three o'clock. An "immense" crowd had been waiting patiently outside the church, and it filled quickly, but most of the crowd couldn't get inside. When the funeral Mass ended, the procession continued to Shockoe Cemetery. The *Dispatch* reported that "the procession extended for very many squares, and constituted one of the most impressive tributes to the memory of one departed that was ever beheld in this city. Thus has passed away John Dooley, one of the most useful of our citizens—philanthropist, friend, Christian."

With his father's death, Jim became the head of the Dooley family, and eventually the primary support of his mother, brother, and sisters (along with their husbands), as well as his mentally ill aunts, Eliza and Ann, at Mount Hope in Baltimore. Among his first acts was to settle his father's estate. Although his mother was nominally the executrix, he acted as her attorney. The work required was to take years.

His father had provided an exemplary model for the role Jim Dooley would fill for the rest of his life, one for which his legal training had prepared him particularly well. The financial acumen that had enabled John Dooley to build a manufacturing business into an interstate operation and invest astutely in real estate, banking, insurance, and new technology soon became evident in the son as well. For the rest of 1868, however, Jim Dooley was still just a young lawyer trying to make a modest living for himself in Military District No. 1.

As before, he represented clients with an array of legal problems ranging from charges of petty theft and public drunkenness to civil cases. Despite its generally low profile, Jim's practice was beginning to bring him some acclaim, especially through the legal work he did for the Irish immigrants who had begun to pour into Richmond. He was a popular choice for citizenship cases, in which his role was to ascertain whether his clients had lived in the United States long enough to fulfill the residency requirement, whether they had the papers to prove it, or whether they had witnesses who could back up their claim. If they did, he presented them to Judge John A. Meredith, who presided in Richmond's Circuit Court. The elections scheduled for 1868 were a prime factor driving applications for citizenship that winter. Hundreds of immigrant men who had resided in the United States for more than two years and filed declarations of intent to become citizens flocked to the Circuit Court's February session to be naturalized so that they could vote.[16]

In April the constitutional convention finished its work and proposed a constitution that proved to be anathema to Conservatives. One of its provisions granted universal manhood suffrage; another disenfranchised former Confederates who refused to take what was called a "test oath" declaring that they had not given aid to the Confederate cause. That requirement was dropped in July when President Johnson declared general amnesty. In the meantime, naturalization quickly became something of a political football. Some members of the Radical Party, fearing that immigrant voters would align themselves with white Conservatives and vote against the proposed new constitution, took aim at Judge Meredith, charging him with naturalizing immigrants who had not fulfilled the residency requirement and asking for his impeachment.[17] The impeachment proceedings were heard by a military commission consisting of Gen. R. S. Granger, commander of the Sub-District of Richmond, and Col. W. W. Clapp, acting assistant adjutant-general.[18]

The hearing opened at eleven o'clock on June 6, 1868. Early in the proceedings one witness declared that the Irish immigrants in question were represented by James Dooley, and he was called to the witness chair.[19] Jim testified on Judge Meredith's behalf and said that he had represented a "large number" of immigrants, although he couldn't remember how many. Later in the trial, however, another lawyer commented that so many Irish men sought services of this kind from Dooley that on one occasion "the business of the court was suspended in consequence" while the judge questioned the applicants.[20] Jim's own testimony gave a fairly clear picture of that portion of his legal practice. According to the *Dispatch,* he described himself as "a regular practicing attorney in the Circuit Court here" who "was often interested in getting foreigners naturalized [and had] clearly examined the law upon the subject." He maintained that he had "never known an applicant to be admitted to citizenship, when, in my judgment, the requirements of the law were not strictly complied with. My opinion of Judge Meredith, founded upon my practice in his court, is that he is a very particular judge, and on all occasions requires the forms of the law to be rigidly observed."[21] In the end, Meredith was not convicted. Subsequent events, however, proved that the Radical Republicans' fear that newly naturalized citizens would vote with the Conservatives or be recruited by them to vote against the new constitution was justified.

The day after Dooley testified, the self-described "Irish Conservatives" met in the Odd Fellows Hall for what was styled "A Grand Conservative Irish Mass Meeting." The notice announcing the meeting mentioned that "American, German, and other fellow-sufferers are cordially and respectfully invited." The following day a small news item noted that the purpose of the meeting was "to organize and cooperate with others for the purpose of defeating the monstrosity called 'Constitution,' soon to be submitted to the suffragans [sic] of Virginia." The *Dispatch* reported that "a large and enthusiastic meeting of the Irish and other foreign citizens" heard Dooley give the first-known political speech of his career that night. In it he voiced anger and frustration. It was, according to the paper, "an eloquent speech, in which he urged upon his hearers the necessity of combined and untiring exertions 'to defeat the miserable production of twenty-four Negroes, scarcely able to read their own printed work, fourteen renegade Virginians, fit associates for them, and twenty-seven scalawags, carpet-baggers, and miserable political adventurers from the North.' . . . [H]is remarks . . . were received with enthusiastic applause."[22]

Anthony Keiley had then read a list of resolutions that were unanimously approved, including a frankly racist expression of their "struggle for the maintainance [sic] of the political supremacy of the white race." Another resolution declared that "in the contest soon to arise on the so-called Constitution of Virginia . . . the good citizens of the Old Dominion may confidently rely on the unfaltering support of their Irish fellow-citizens." The sixth resolution attacked nativism, declaring that "this meeting recognizes the implacable hostility of Radicalism to the foreign-born population." A seventh pledged "to use every exertion to induce the naturalization of every qualified resident of foreign birth among us." The final resolution swore "untiring efforts" in support of the Conservative ticket for the state legislature.[23]

Before the meeting adjourned, T. W. McMahon proposed that "a committee of five persons from each ward be hereafter appointed by the chairman to perfect a 'permanent' organization of Irish citizens in Richmond."[24] Jim's political career was launched when, despite the fact that he was born and raised in Richmond, he was appointed one of the five "Irishmen" to organize Madison Ward.[25] Anthony Keiley—born in New Jersey, raised in Petersburg, and educated at Randolph-Macon College in Boynton—was also appointed an "Irishman" organizer for that ward. He and Dooley soon became identified as the twin leaders of the young Irish Conservatives and would appear together as speakers at countless future meetings.

Before the summer was over, Jim became an active member of several other Irish political organizations including the Hibernian Seymour and Blair Club and the Democratic Hibernian Club. The goal of the Seymour and Blair Club was to rally enthusiasm for the presidential and vice presidential candidates on the national Democratic ticket, Horatio Seymour and Francis Preston Blair, who were running against the Republican candidates, Ulysses S. Grant and Schuyler Colfax.[26] The appeal of Seymour and Blair rested on a number of factors, the first and most important being the plank in their platform that called for general amnesty for all Confederates.

The Irish were not the only Seymour and Blair enthusiasts in Richmond that summer. The German Conservative Club also organized a number of Seymour and Blair meetings where speeches and resolutions "endorsing the nominations of the national Democratic convention" were made in both English and German.[27] As these rallies indicated, immigrants were growing more deeply involved in Richmond's political life.

Sometime in August, Jim took his brother Jack, who had recently arrived home from Georgetown for summer vacation, to one of Virginia's health-giving mountain springs. Jack was still suffering from the tuberculosis he had contracted while a prisoner on Johnson's Island. Unfortunately, as Jack later put it, "Six weeks of mountain life . . . made scarcely any sensible improvement in my body."[28] Nevertheless, it had a great impact on his brother Jim, who spent part of his vacation courting a young lady from Staunton named Saidie May. Their backgrounds were very different. Jim, a first-generation American, was courting a girl who traced her ancestry to members of Virginia's colonial Council and two colonial governors.

That fall Jim saw one of his father's heroes, former governor Henry Wise, in action again on the political scene. On September 29, 1868, he heard Wise's two-hour-long address at a meeting of the Democratic Hibernian Club.[29] Wise's success in helping put down the Know-Nothing Party in the 1850s had earned him the devotion of the immigrant community, which, after the war, responded sympathetically and generously to his financial difficulties.[30]

Jim also continued to fulfill his responsibilities as head of the Dooley family. In May 1869, he wrote a letter to his mother, who was staying with his sister Florence and her husband in Sweet Springs. In it, he gave her advice on how to manage finances for his aunts at Mount Hope and mentioned, "I am very well & am about to settle up Your Accounts as executrix of the estate." Accompanying his letter was a draft for a hundred dollars he had drawn on his father's bank in Baltimore.[31]

In the summer months of 1869, several deaths in Richmond shaped Jim Dooley's future and paved the way for his candidacy for political office. The first of these was that of an Irish "sporting man" named Joseph Kelly. Jim's role as a notary public was the ostensible reason he became acquainted with Kelly, but clearly his reputation as a lawyer who helped immigrants came into play as well.

In the middle of the night of Thursday, June 25, the Dooley household was awakened by the sound of someone pounding loudly on the front door of the family's four-story brick house. The visitor demanded to speak with the young lawyer who lived there. When Jim came to the door, he heard that his legal services were needed at the St. Charles Hotel, where a man shot by a policeman wanted to make a deathbed statement.[32] Jim emerged a few minutes later and made his way quickly toward the hotel.

At the time, Richmond was languishing not only under the hand of a conquering army but also of a police force appointed by an occupation government. Nonetheless, its future looked brighter as it geared up for the first gubernatorial elections since the war—and the chance to vote on the newly drafted constitution. Voter registration sites had opened ten days earlier in each of the city's five wards, and political parties had been urging their faithful to register before the coming July 6 election.

Tensions had been running particularly high in the Old Market Place, where both a registration office and the police court were located. The day before Jim was summoned, a fishmonger named William Peasley was arguing with a black acquaintance named James Bratt about the fairness of registration, when Peasley gave Bratt a shove. The chief of police, who happened to be standing nearby, promptly arrested Peasley and put him in a cell despite the protests of Bratt, who insisted that Peasley had not done anything to him.[33] Peasley's friend Joe Kelly, who was also nearby, "loudly denounced the arrest as unnecessary and unwarrantable." The *Dispatch* reported that "high words followed," and in the blink of an eye two policeman began dragging

Kelly downstairs toward the police station. While he lay flat on his back on the steps, an officer named Callahan drew a pistol and "fired several times at the prisoner." Though wounded in the stomach and one arm, Kelly managed to pull out a gun and wound the other policeman. When the police left to tend to their slightly wounded colleague, some bystanders led Kelly to a nearby doctor's office.

Later that afternoon Officer Callahan was suspended from the police force by the chief, who ordered him arrested and charged with felonious assault. The *Dispatch* reported that "this is not the first time that such charges have been made against this officer, and the people have a right to demand a thorough and impartial investigation of his conduct." Joe Kelly, the paper made note, "is by no means the best man in Richmond; but . . . if he is the worst he has no less the right to be protected from the cruel malice of a brutal police officer." Meanwhile, Kelly was taken to the more comfortable quarters of his room at the St. Charles Hotel.

When Dooley arrived at Kelly's room at the hotel, he found him lying on a bed looking pale and clammy, with beads of perspiration dripping down his forehead. Dooley sat beside the bed and wrote down the requested statement in longhand after penning the following formal preface: "The dying declaration of Joseph Kelly, taken before me, James H. Dooley, at twenty minutes to 12 o'clock, on the 25th day of June, in the year 1869."[34] After finishing the preface, Dooley asked Kelly to begin. It took an hour for Kelly to give his two-paragraph-long account of the events of the afternoon. Dooley struggled to hear him and had to erase and cross out words as he made the transcription. Then he read the completed document out loud to the wounded man, who had to struggle to sign the statement. Two hours after Dooley left the room, Kelly breathed his last.

When the news of his death spread that morning, there was "universal indignation intensified by the prevailing impression that he was a martyr." The inquest called for by the police took two full days. Dooley's transcript of the Kelly statement was introduced on day two, and a parade of witnesses corroborated Kelly's account. By then Officer Callahan had been remanded for trial by a military commission. Almost a month later, on August 17, a communiqué from military headquarters announced that charges against Officer Callahan had been dismissed and that he had been released on the grounds that he had done "no more than his duty required."[35] In early September the *Dispatch* reported that someone had been passing the hat among the police to raise the money to cover the cost incurred in Callahan's defense. The one-paragraph article noted, "The contributions are reported as liberal, although several officers have refused to give a cent."[36] Dooley's role in the episode, although small, contributed to his growing reputation as a defender of the little man.

The second death in the city that summer that shaped Dooley's future was that of forty-one-year-old James R. Branch, Conservative Party candidate for the state senate and a Dooley neighbor on Broad Street. Branch was killed when a suspension bridge to Vauxhall Island collapsed as a crowd was crossing over it to attend a ticketed political rally and barbeque organized by black Conservatives. Branch, a popular businessman, broker, and banker, had been an advocate for reconciliation between the city's black and white populations. He had worked tirelessly to build the ranks of black Conservatives, and the rally at the island indicated his success.[37] The event was completely integrated. Before the bridge collapsed, more than one hundred of the "most prominent white citizens" had arrived, including Colonel Branch's father, Thomas Branch. The loss of Branch was a setback to attempts by men of both races to achieve racial harmony. Now in the spotlight as a successor to Branch in the hierarchy of Conservative leaders, Jim Dooley joined other party members who wore mourning badges to Branch's funeral at St. Paul's the following Sunday.[38]

Later in the summer Jim returned to the mountains, where he renewed his ardent courtship of Saidie May. By the time his vacation was over, he had proposed to her. The second-youngest of the nine children of Dr. Henry May of Lunenburg Courthouse, Saidie had lost her mother when she was about eight years old. She had been living in Staunton with her oldest sister, Anna, and Anna's lawyer husband, T. C. Elder. Jim and Saidie made plans to be married in September at the Elders' home.

By the time Jim was back in Richmond, with their wedding only two weeks away, the two had quarreled, and Jim had written to apologize. Saidie responded on August 27 using the form of address customary to the ever-so-decorous women of polite society in those days. She began her letter, "My dear Mr. Dooley."[39] It was a hurried letter sandwiched into a busy day and interrupted, as she would write, not just once but "twenty" times: "Your most precious letter was duly recd & healed all the wounds inflicted by the bitterness of those preceding it, not even leaving a scar. Why do you speak in such a way of my love, as if you still doubted its existence? Is it because I do not write in as affectionate a strain as you do?" Saidie then proceeded to give Jim a lesson in the deportment of young ladies: "Whilst it is entirely proper & most becoming in you to assume that style, I cannot divest myself of the impression that it would be a little unmaidenly in me to express the feelings I entertain for you. But when I have a right to show the world the love I glory in, you will be fully satisfied with its strength and depth. This love & the knowledge of its power, are not likely to awaken in me a desire to change you for our creator has saved me the trouble by making you all that the most fastidious & exacting could wish." Saidie's letter smoothed over the quarrel. They didn't cancel their wedding plans.

Two days before the wedding, Jim was overwhelmed by attempts to finish work at his office and prepare for the work he planned to do to settle his father's estate while he and Saidie were honeymooning in Chicago. As a result, he did not arrive in Staunton early enough to apply for the necessary marriage bond. Luckily, a crisis was averted when Saidie's lawyer brother-in-law enabled her take the unusual step of signing the bond herself and authorizing the clerk of the corporation "to issue a license for the celebration of a marriage between Mr. James H. Dooley and myself."[40]

On September 11 Saidie and Jim were married in the Elders' parlor by a Catholic priest, Father Ambler Weed, formerly of Richmond. Father Weed was an ecumenical man of the cloth who had grown up in the Episcopal Church and been confirmed at St. Paul's in Richmond but had been ordained in St. Peter's Catholic Church after his conversion to Catholicism.[41] By the evening of their wedding day, the couple had arrived at the first stop on their honeymoon, Washington's elegant Willard hotel. Here Jim did something most men do not do on the first night of their honeymoon: he sat down to write a brief but important letter to his mother. "My Dear Mother[,] As soon as Tantie returns," he requested, "ask him to go to my office & look in the tin box for the bundles of papers, in Envelopes, marked Chicago papers. . . . I wish him to forward this . . . at the earliest possible moment, to James H. Dooley Care of Moore & Caulfield Atty's at Law. Chicago. Ill."

A little over two weeks later he wrote again, this time from Chicago on Moore and Caulfield stationery:

> I expect to leave here to-morrow morning, for Baltimore, & will probably get home by Saturday. . . . We have been here, since last Thursday, I am afraid Saidie does not enjoy this part of her trip very much, as I have to leave her, from Breakfast until Dinner, by herself. We will go home, by easy traveling to Baltimore, & from there to Richmond down the Bay & up the York River to West Point & from there by R. R. to Richmond. We will go first to the Ballard House. I will suggest to you some things, upon my return, which will place your affairs always, plainly before your eyes, & prove more satisfactory to us both than for me alone to keep your

accounts. I will shew you how to open accounts for yourself: so that you will see exactly how much you receive from each source & how much altogether. . . . We will talk over these matters, as soon as I return. I am going to make a fresh start in my affairs, & hope to make some money. . . . Give my love to all at home. Your loving Son James H. Dooley[42]

CHAPTER 12 | A Young Politician

B y spring there were numerous signs of renewed energy in Richmond, including the formation of a spate of new organizations. Jim Dooley was active in one of them, the Hibernian Benevolent Society. Early in March, notices appeared in the "Meetings" columns of the local newspapers inviting "Irish residents of this city, and those of Irish descent" to a meeting in City Hall for the purpose of forming a Hibernian Society and making plans for a St. Patrick's Day celebration.[1] One such notice exhorted, "Now that we are restoring all things else to an *ante bellum* status, let us welcome the revival of the time-honored observance of that day sacred to the memory of the patron saint of dear old Ireland."[2] As chairman of a committee, Dooley "made a most eloquent address" proposing a St. Patrick's Day parade.

The idea took hold, and the first of many such postwar parades stepped off from Capitol Square at 9:00 a.m. on March 17.[3] Five hundred people, all sporting rosettes of green ribbon on their chests, fell in behind a band headed to St. Patrick's Church on Church Hill, where at 10:30 a.m. High Mass was celebrated. Afterward, Jim joined the governor and Anthony Keiley on the speakers' platform on Capitol Square, where the marchers returned to listen to speeches.

Although by May 1870 Dooley had been active in Conservative Party politics for several years as an "Irishman" ward organizer, he hadn't yet had been a candidate for public office. Then, at a Conservative Party meeting in the Chamber of Commerce headquarters on May 10, he was nominated to run in the party primary to become the candidate for Commonwealth attorney. In the twelve days before the primary, a number of Conservative Party mass meetings were held in prominent public locations.[4] At one such gathering in front of the Custom House on May 15, and another on Capitol Square on May 25, Dooley and the other candidates all spoke. The morning of the mass meeting on Capitol Square, the *Dispatch* predicted a large crowd since "the invitation to this meeting is extended to every citizen of Richmond, of whatever color; and the colored people will be cordially welcomed, colored Republicans as well as colored Conservatives, who are sure to be there. It is desired particularly that the colored people shall hear what may be said on the occasion, whether they are Conservatives or not."[5] James R. Branch's work for racial reconciliation had not been lost at his death. The racial enmity that had dominated Conservative politics in 1868 and early 1869 had been replaced by appeals for biracial support after the Underwood Constitution had been formally adopted the previous July. In the end, Dooley lost the race for Commonwealth attorney, but his speeches had drawn popular attention, and his political visibility began to increase steadily.

Meanwhile, the international news columns in the local newspapers had frequently focused on King Victor Emmanuel's attempts to unify Italy. After the king had occupied Rome, deposed Pope Pius IX as ruler of the Papal States, and isolated him in Vatican City, Dooley very briefly became a figure in international politics when he and Anthony Keiley spoke at a protest meeting at St. Peter's Church.[6] Despite the location of the meeting, interest in the situation was not confined to Richmond's Catholics.[7] The general public was following it, too. Pope Pius IX had been a popular figure in the South since 1863, when Jefferson Davis had, with the blessing of Bishop John McGill of Richmond, commissioned a Catholic priest to approach the pope for official recognition of the Confederacy. Attempts to obtain such recognition from other European countries had failed, and ultimately so did this one, but the pope responded cordially to a letter from Davis presented by the commissioner. When the pope's letter, addressed to "the Illustrious and Honorable Jefferson Davis, President of the Confederate States of America," was made public, it was perceived throughout the South and Europe as a diplomatic coup for the Confederacy, even though it fell far short of official recognition.[8] Accordingly, the pope was viewed with sympathy in 1870, when he lost his temporal throne to Victor Emmanuel.

On January 12, with St. Peter's filled to capacity, Keiley and Dooley joined Bishop John McGill in front of the altar. Keiley was the first to speak, and he lashed out at Victor Emmanuel, calling him a "weak and wicked king." Then Dooley entreated the audience "to lift up our voices . . . against the most glaring wrong, the most atrocious outrage of modern times." A letter of sympathy went eventually to the pope, and that seemed to be the end of the matter in Richmond. Years later, however, Keiley's words came back to haunt him when, in 1885, President Grover Cleveland appointed him "Envoy Extraordinary and Minister Plenipotentiary of the United States to Italy."[9] His credentials were refused by the Italian government, which cited his speech that evening at St. Peter's as the basis for his rejection. In Dooley's case, however, the impact was immediate and positive. His participation in the protest meeting raised his profile as a politician and undoubtedly helped him win the votes he received later that year in his successful race for a seat in the Virginia House of Delegates.

The protest meeting was the first of many occasions in 1871 on which Dooley and Keiley appeared together on a speakers' podium. Another occurred on St. Patrick's Day, when between six hundred and seven hundred people, undeterred by the rainy weather, paraded through the city streets. The plans for the day once again originated with Dooley, who convinced the Hibernian Benevolent Society to organize the parade and presided over the planning meetings held in his office.[10] His only official role the day of the parade was that of assistant parade marshal on Broad Street, but at the end of the parade, Jim joined Anthony Keiley on the speakers' platform—even though Keiley, who had been elected mayor of Richmond in 1870, was the only person scheduled to speak. Keiley spoke at length, tracing the 1,400-year history of Christianity in Ireland and the life and influence of St. Patrick. By the time the speech finally ended, there were loud calls for "Major" Dooley to speak. Jim gave a short, rousing, and obviously prepared speech on Ireland's heroes and their attempts to gain freedom for their country. It was so well received that it was printed in full in the next day's *Enquirer*.[11]

By this time Jim and Saidie, after starting their married life in Richmond's Ballard House Hotel, had settled in at a boardinghouse, as did many other young married couples in those difficult times. Situated on the corner of Eighth and Clay Streets, the establishment was run by H. T. Cook.[12] The confusion of having two Saidie Dooleys in the same generation of the family had prompted Jim's new wife to call herself Sallie instead, a nickname she used for the rest of her life. She and Jim moved around a bit during the next few years. By 1876 they were living at 623 East Franklin. Eventually they shared a house—first at 1 West Grace and then at 316 East Grace—with a number of other couples. Their personal property tax records for 1870 suggest that they had begun to accumulate more than just clothing.[13] At that date Jim paid tax not only on his pocket watch but also on five hundred dollars' worth of books, which were the start of a library that would grow rapidly in the coming years. Sallie had become used to life in a big city as the wife of a young lawyer and rising politician. She attended St. Paul's Episcopal Church across the street from St. Peter's and gradually became active on its committees and in other charitable work.

In the early 1870s much of Dooley's burgeoning law practice was devoted to routine chancery and civil cases: writing wills, providing guardianship for orphans, settling inheritance disputes, and representing clients in real estate transactions, along with a smattering of minor criminal cases for such offenses as petty theft and assault.[14] Occasionally, however, he represented clients in felony cases. In the spring of 1871, one of his more sensational cases was tried in Richmond Hustings Court. The events leading up to it began very early on a cold and blustery Monday morning in early March, when a deckhand on a schooner moored at Nineteenth Street spotted a body floating under the dock. Papers found on the body revealed the deceased to be John Christie, a Scottish mechanic about forty years old, who had disappeared without a trace after leaving his home in Richmond's west end five days before Christmas. His wife had reported him missing, and as weeks passed the mystery of his disappearance had deepened with suspicions of foul play. The city newspapers had kept public concern alive with short bulletins throughout January. The mayor offered a $100 reward for the recovery of Christie's body and a $250 reward for information leading to the conviction of the murderer.[15] A police investigation located witnesses who swore they had last seen the deceased in the company of a certain John Smith on the evening of the day he had disappeared.

Shortly after Christie's body was found, the police arrested Smith, a young sawmill operator, at his house near Savage's, about fourteen miles outside of Richmond. By evening, Smith had hired Dooley to represent him before the Police Court judge. His bail was set at two thousand dollars, an enormous sum for those days.[16] As soon as the date for Smith's trial was set for April 3, Dooley set out to find witnesses who could corroborate Smith's alibi. The search was prolonged and difficult. He requested a continuance, which was granted, and later another one while he continued his investigation.[17] By then he was also searching for an older and more experienced lawyer to join him as co-counsel in the case. Finally, he landed Robert "Judge" Ould, renowned for the logic of his courtroom arguments and for his meticulousness in the preparation of cases.[18]

The prosecution's case in the Christie murder trial hinged on the claim by a witness named James Beatty that he had read documents that proved Smith had killed the victim. While deposing Beatty in the weeks leading up to the trial, however, Dooley discovered that Beatty couldn't read and realized that he had found the key to defending his client. Ould and Dooley jointly pleaded the case during a gripping three-day trial that was covered in great detail by the city newspapers.[19] When the prosecution called its star witness, James Beatty, he swore that Christie had shown him the papers he had in his pocket. During cross-examination by Ould, Beatty emphasized that he had read the order for the amount the defendant owed the victim. His assertion provided just the opportunity the lawyers for the defense needed to discredit him. Ould approached him with one of the papers found on the victim's body and asked him to read it. Beatty refused, but Ould insisted. Beatty replied, "I ain't going to try." Only when the judge insisted did Beatty take the paper, and "after examining it closely admit[ted] that he could only read two words—'John Smith.'" After Beatty failed several more tests of his reading skill, it was clear to everyone in the courtroom that he had been lying all along in an attempt to obtain the $250 reward. The case drew attention to Dooley as the defender of an innocent workingman—a reputation that would serve him well in both his legal career and his political one.

Dooley's legal practice was only one of his professional interests in the early 1870s. In those stringent economic times, real estate offered him welcome opportunities to increase his income. Years later Dooley would say in a speech that the first money he ever made he invested in "Richmond dirt." A small newspaper item announcing his election as an officer of the Hibernia Building Fund Company in March 1871 gives some indication that real estate was becoming a serious form of investment and income for him.[20] The Richmond City Deeds Books for the period also show that Dooley was investing in real estate frequently at this period even though he and Sallie were still living in a boardinghouse.[21]

That fall Jim's mother sent his sister Saidie, then seventeen, to boarding school at Mount de Chantal, the Visitation Academy in Wheeling, West Virginia, where "great attention is given to perfect the pupils in writing and speaking French with fluency. For those sufficiently advanced it is the language of their recreation hours. The purity of accent and correctness of pronunciation acquired in this institution have long been a subject of surprise to the native Parisian."[22]

Since Mrs. Dooley could just as easily have sent Saidie to the Visitation Academy in either Richmond or Georgetown, economic considerations probably played a significant role in the decision. Mount de Chantal had a "Southern Fund" that offered financial aid to southern families in postwar financial distress who could no longer afford to send their daughters to boarding school.[23] After the war, the nuns of the Mount, as it was called, had sent a delegation to New York City to secure money to construct buildings and provide scholarships. The nuns' fund raising was very successful, perhaps because they were not shy about approaching some prominent New Yorkers, among whom the infamous Williams M. "Boss" Tweed of New York City's Tammany Hall was the single-largest contributor.[24]

The Southern Fund not only paid Saidie's one-hundred-dollar tuition but also the $38.60 fee for her piano and singing lessons and rental of a piano. In 1872 Mrs. Dooley also sent her youngest, Josie, to the Mount. The girls attended school year round until 1876, and the Southern Fund paid all their expenses for several years; but later someone in the family—either their mother or their brother—contributed a portion.

On September 26, almost two weeks after Saidie left for West Virginia, Jim Dooley's life entered a new phase. When the Conservative Nominating Convention for the district of Richmond and Henrico met at the Exchange Hotel, Colonel Peyton Wise nominated him to be one of the five Conservative candidates for Richmond seats in the House of Delegates. In an editorial alluding to the well-known corruption of the previous session, the *Dispatch* commented that "the people of Richmond have their ticket before them. . . . They are mostly young and untried men. They have talents and youth, and can do the State service if they show judgment and energy—such invaluable qualities for legislation. . . . No other community in the State has so much depending upon good government—upon wise and faithful legislation—as the people of Richmond."[25]

During the campaign the newspapers occasionally referred to Jim as "Major" Dooley. A front-page announcement in the *Dispatch,* for example, listed the speakers for a political rally as "Judge Ould, Colonels Wynne and Connolly, Captain George D. Wise, Major Dooley . . . and others."[26] The second-to-last paragraph of an account of another political meeting in the same issue of the paper opened with the comment, "Major J. H. Dooley . . . followed Mr. Lovenstein in some graceful remarks, which had the rare fault of being too short. He strikingly discussed the issues . . . and excusing himself on account of the lateness of the hour, promised the attentive audience more at another time." Articles covering events later in the campaign alternated between calling Dooley "Mr." and "Major," but it appears that Richmonders had by then slipped into the habit of thinking of the candidate as "Major Dooley." His physical resemblance to his father and his conduct probably reminded Richmonders of John Dooley, but the fact that he was a lawyer may also have been an element in his "promotion." The later historians of the legal profession W. Hamilton Bryson and Lee Shepard note that many of the leading Virginia lawyers of the 1870s had served as officers in the Confederate army and after the war continued to use their military titles.[27] Since early in Dooley's career his colleagues had recognized him as a rising member of the bar, it is not surprising that they had also allowed him a courtesy title. Then newspapers and the general public began to refer to Jim as "Major" Dooley. From that time on, he was almost always called "Major" Dooley, although he was careful to remind others that he had been only a private.[28]

In the 1870s, Dooley's Irish ancestry was an important asset not just locally but also nationally, when he began advertising his legal services in John Mitchel's New York City newspaper, the *Irish Citizen*.[29] Mitchel's paper was distributed widely: while the younger Dooley had some Irish clients in New York, his advertisements aimed at Irish clientele wherever they lived. The ads, which ran from 1870 through 1872, advised readers that "James H. Dooley Attorney at Law practices in the courts of Richmond, Henrico and Chesterfield. P. O. Box 499, Richmond, VA." Immigrants learned his name almost as soon as they stepped off the boat.

In the fall of 1871, Dooley made frequent appearances at political rallies outdoors and indoors throughout the city. Some were in front of City Hall, some in neighborhoods such as Oregon Hill, where many laborers, mechanics, ironworkers, and their families lived. At a mass meeting held in front of City Hall on October 19, Dooley was the seventh of nine speakers on the schedule. The crowd of several thousand people was the largest during the campaign, and the rally itself must have been colorful: the *Dispatch* reported that the speakers' stand "was illuminated and ornamented by festoons of colored lanterns."[30] A band played a lively accompaniment to the fireworks "on the outskirts of the crowd," and cheers greeted 150 workingmen from Oregon Hill when, during the second speech of the evening, they marched in bringing even more fireworks. During a rally at the Old Market on October 23, the flags of the United States, North Germany, Ireland, and Italy fluttered from ropes strung across the street from buildings on either side.[31] The proceedings were punctuated by skyrockets and the booming of a small cannon, and several blocks were illuminated by blazing tar barrels. A band played lively tunes outside for the first hour, and then everyone—band, spectators, and speakers—thronged into the market hall for the speeches. Dooley reportedly made an excellent speech, "replete with telling hits." A week later another "rousing" meeting at the steamboat shed in Rocketts, at the eastern edge of the city, gave Dooley a chance to repeat his performance.[32] When election day came, the Conservatives made a complete sweep of the seats in the House of Delegates. Of the five winning Conservative candidates for Richmond's seats in the House of Delegates, Jim received the third-highest number of votes, 6,179: 48 fewer than William S. Gilman and 42 fewer than J. Thompson Brown.[33]

A few days later, the *Enquirer* reprinted an editorial from the *Rockbridge*

Citizen on the centrality of Richmond's future in the economy of the state. Apparently, the Chesapeake and Ohio link between the new town of Huntington, West Virginia, and Richmond had caught the attention of investors all across the United States. The *Citizen* article asserted: "The immense trade which is to be attracted by this road will build a colossal city at its eastern terminus. Richmond deserves to be that city. Her associations, her misfortunes, her undespairing enterprise, and her natural advantages, give . . . her the preference. . . . Her growth as a city is our growth as a State."[34]

Naturally, that perspective was shared by Jim Dooley and the rest of the Richmond business community. As one of the newly elected members of the House of Delegates from Richmond, he was well positioned to play a part in making it happen. However, he wasn't only a representative of the business community, and he kept that fact in mind. During his three terms in the House of Delegates, he would propose legislation that represented the concerns and issues of a much wider variety of constituents—the people of Richmond as a whole.

J im Dooley answered his first roll call as a member of the House of Delegates at noon on December 6, 1871. Two days later, when standing committee assignments were announced, he found that he had been appointed to the Courts of Justice Committee.[1] When he submitted the
first motion of his legislative career that day, however, he was concerned not
with judicial matters but with financial issues facing the state. His proposal
was an attempt to ensure that the State of Virginia received fair value at a
scheduled auction of its stock in statewide internal improvement companies,
canals, plank roads, bridges, and railroads.[2] The proposal identified Dooley
with the Funder contingent in the legislature, as did many of his later proposals. Funders advocated paying the state's prewar debts in full, a view they
shared with the business community, which feared that otherwise it would
be impossible to attract investments vital to the state's postwar economy. The
Funders were opposed by the Readjuster contingent of the Conservative
Party, who were to become increasingly vocal during Dooley's six years in the
House. In any event, by the following Monday Dooley's motion had become
House Bill No. 3.[3] He was off to an excellent start as a freshman delegate.

Dooley's proposal was timely. The Board of Public Works had taken almost a year to prepare for the sale. The previous March it had finally determined that selling its shares in its internal improvement companies to private
investors was necessary in light of the deplorable condition of the railroads,
canals, plank roads, and bridges throughout the state.[4] Saddled as it was by
millions of dollars of prewar debts, the State of Virginia had no way of un-
derwriting the necessary repairs to infrastructure. It had to sell its shares, but
there was grave concern that an auction would not yield fair value for its
shares. That was the predicament Dooley hoped to avoid by proposing his
first piece of legislation.

The February 5 auction was successful enough to put the state coffers in
better shape, but even more importantly, as soon as it was over, mending and
extending the railroads within the borders of the Commonwealth could
begin. Private capital poured in from the North. Large interests such as the
Pennsylvania Railroad snapped up the railroad stock formerly owned by the
state.

These were not the only economic issues that confronted Dooley during his first term in the House. His handling of several of them demonstrated his fiscal conservatism, and one of his votes still strikes a responsive chord. He voted "yea" to reduce per diem and mileage allowances for members of the General Assembly.[5] In the following session he attempted to introduce a bill to suspend the pay of members and officers during Christmas recess, a bill that his colleagues unsurprisingly rejected. His commitment to putting the Virginia economy back on its feet prompted his motion against a proposal that would have prevented freight trains from running on Sunday.[6]

During his freshman year in the House of Delegates, Dooley managed to keep up his law practice, invest in some real estate, and tend to family matters. His legal practice was by then bringing in enough income to provide him with some discretionary funds, but there were many calls upon it. For instance, in February his sister Florence and her farmer husband, Willie Lewis, asked him for a loan. He lent them $250 to repair farm equipment and buy seed, but the loan did not end the Lewises' financial troubles.[7] Dooley and, occasionally, his mother would be obliged to help them out again and again in the coming years.

Dooley's real estate ventures included a lot on Franklin Street near Laurel, for which he had paid $2,437.50 in March 1871.[8] In October he paid $150 at a bankruptcy auction for a house on Oregon Hill.[9] His real estate investments did not, however, distract him from his duties in the House of Delegates. In January of his second year in the House, during hearings held by the Courts of Justice Committee, Dooley considered such serious issues as the jurisdiction of county and circuit courts and the pay of county judges. In February 1873 he introduced a bill authorizing the City of Richmond to purchase land within two miles of its corporate limits for a new hospital.[10] His work was interrupted on February 12, 1873, however, by an event that marked a milestone in Virginia's railroad history.

That Thursday was cold and gloomy. Nothing about it suggested that anything exciting might be about to happen in Richmond. In the Capitol, the delegates were in the middle of debating an amendment Dooley had proposed to House Bill No. 116, familiarly known as the Embezzlement Bill, when the Speaker of the House interrupted the proceedings to read aloud a letter that had just been handed to him.[11] The letter invited the delegates to a celebration at the Chesapeake and Ohio Railroad depot. Despite the fact that his amendment was on the floor, Delegate Dooley moved quickly to adjourn.

He and the other delegates walked briskly out of the Capitol toward Bank Street at the foot of the square, where a crowd was waiting for a parade to begin. When McCann's band and drum corps struck up a tune, the First Virginia began to march, and everyone moved forward. At City Hall, the Richmond City Council, escorted by Richmond's Fire Brigade, "in full uniform and with their apparatus," joined the parade, as did members of the Corn and Flour Exchange, the Tobacco Association, and the stonecutters from the Government Works. As a detachment of Richmond police took the lead, the procession marched to the whistles of the Fire Department's steamer engines down Broad Street hill to Seventeenth Street and the Chesapeake and Ohio depot. There, because all business had been suspended, they found a crowd estimated to be about ten thousand strong. After a cannon atop Richmond's Navy Hill boomed a signal that a train had been spotted coming toward the city, the crowd heard the whistle of the train's engine followed by the simultaneous pealing of all the bells of the city and "an almost deafening screeching" from factory steam whistles. When four coal cars pushed by, a little yard engine moved through the crowd, a man on the podium waved his hat, the band played, and thousands of voices roared three cheers for the Chesapeake and Ohio Railroad. Thanks to a rock slide, only the engine and four cars of a longer train had managed to survive the journey from Ohio. Even so, the city's future seemed assured, for, as the *Dispatch* declared in its account, "the great trade with the far west had commenced."

A few weeks after the term ended in April, the Dooley family had to cope with great sadness. Jack had returned to Georgetown College after the war in the hope of realizing his dream of becoming a Jesuit priest, but he had never recovered from the tuberculosis he had contracted while a prisoner of war on Johnson's Island. His mother, brother, and youngest sister were with him at the college infirmary during his last days; he died on May 8 and was buried in the college cemetery. A brief obituary in a Washington, D.C., newspaper mentioned that Jack was a son of Major John Dooley, "whose kindly ministrations to wounded and suffering Union and Confederate soldiers during the late war made his name familiar as a household word in both armies."[12] The *Dispatch* obituary commented that "whilst his death was not unexpected it excites the very deep grief of his family and friends. . . . He was a bright exemplar of the faith in which he had been raised."[13]

The family spent the summer months in deep mourning for Jack, and when the Conservative Party nominating convention opened on August 6, Dooley was notable for his absence. The convention chose Gen. James L. Kemper by acclamation to be the party's nominee for governor, and his enthusiastic supporters formed a new political support group that they called the Kemper Kampaign Klub.[14] Dooley's brother-in-law Tantie Jones became an active member. An outgrowth of a group of Conservatives called the

Swamp Angels organized in 1869, the Klub was often identified by its initials, "KKK."[15] Those initials were also used by the Ku Klux Klan, but there was no relationship whatsoever in philosophy or conduct between the secret and violent Ku Klux Klan and the Kemper Kampaign Klub or its later manifestation, the Konservative Kampaign Klub.[16]

Several days after the convention ended, Governor Gilbert Walker summoned Dooley to his office and appointed him to the board of directors of the Central Lunatic Asylum for the Colored Insane.[17] Among the other men appointed to the board that day was Delegate John W. Daniel, a young lawyer and disabled Confederate veteran from Lynchburg known for his high ethical standards. The two served on the board for the next eight years, through the administrations of two more governors, James L. Kemper and F. W. M. Holliday. They worked well together on the board but years later would publish a series of letters in which they aired serious disagreement on monetary issues.[18]

The brief period during which Virginia seemed to be making slow but steady progress toward financial stability came to an abrupt end that fall. On September 18, financial institutions throughout the United States were rocked by the news that the banking firm J. Cooke and Co. of New York had failed. There was an immediate run on banks across the country, and some people in Richmond began to withdraw their money from the local banks. Even one of Richmond's federal depositories, Merchants National Bank, was thought to be tottering. Nevertheless, it survived, as did the other national banks in the city. The Panic of 1873 had begun, and the depression of the 1870s soon followed.[19] Richmond, which had just begun to feel confident of full recovery from the war and the Evacuation Fire, again found itself slipping into a financial abyss.

October 1873 marked the opening of Dooley's second campaign for a seat in the House of Delegates. His father's friend William English nominated him at the Conservative Party's convention on Friday, October 10, in the old dining room of the Exchange Hotel.[20] Other nominees included Judge Ould and Gen. Joseph R. Anderson. Of the three, only General Anderson gave an acceptance speech that night. Ould was busy in court, and Dooley couldn't be found. It was obvious that this year's campaign was different from the one two years earlier. This time the excitement centered on a hard-fought gubernatorial campaign from which James L. Kemper emerged the winner. His administration, inaugurated during a financial crisis, was marked by his attempts to trim government expenditures.

When the new session of the House of Delegates opened in January 1874, Dooley was again appointed not only to the Courts of Justice Committee but also to the Militia and Police Committee and the Rules Committee.[21] During that term, reduced revenue caused by the Panic of 1873 made it impossible for the State of Virginia to pay the interest due on its prewar debt. Governor Kemper attempted unsuccessfully to negotiate reduced interest payments and struggled with the House over that and other financial issues.[22] Many of Dooley's legislative proposals reflected his attempt to cooperate with the governor's recommendations, such as the bill he introduced in 1875 "to consolidate, establish, and regulate the sinking fund of the state of Virginia."[23] Several of Dooley's proposals to assure fiscal soundness during his second term involved railroads. In one case he proposed a bill "directing the Commissioner of the sinking fund to sell the state's interest in the Richmond Fredericksburg and Potomac railroad." Fattening the state coffers at a time of reduced tax revenues was his primary concern, but the bill did not pass.[24]

Dooley also confronted other issues involving the railroads during that term. Because railroad expansion was key to promoting Richmond's industrial growth, he worked closely with General Anderson, president of Richmond's Tredegar company, to lobby on behalf of the Chesapeake and Ohio Railroad. Anderson had been identified with the interests of the C&O ever since the railroad company had invested fifty thousand dollars in Tredegar stock between 1868 and 1871. That investment had been vital to the financial recovery of Tredegar after the war.[25] It was not just self-interest, however, when in 1875 Anderson lobbied intensely for legislation allowing Richmond to provide $1 million to underwrite the connectors that would link Richmond with the C&O lines in Kentucky and Ohio. The advantage to all Richmond manufacturers who wanted to ship their goods westward was clear, but the heavy indebtedness of the city gave pause to many financial conservatives in Richmond. Some of the business community worried that the C&O itself was teetering financially. When supporters of the proposed legislation met at the Chamber of Commerce on March 15, 1875, Dooley and Anderson were there to hear the merchant Isaac Davenport read a confidential letter from Collis Huntington that the newspaper opaquely characterized as "interesting information on the . . . subject." Whatever it was, the information was persuasive. The men voted to support the legislation.[26]

Two days later, just after the 10:00 a.m. session of the House of Delegates opened, Dooley successfully introduced a bill authorizing the City of Richmond to subscribe to western railroad connections with the Chesapeake and Ohio railroad.[27] In the fall Richmonders would learn just how badly the C&O had needed the money, and how unfortunate the consequences of the Dooley bill would be. In October the bankrupt C&O went into receivership.[28] Unfortunately for General Anderson, because the C&O owed money to Tredegar, the C&O's failure took Tredegar down with it, and Anderson— greatly respected in the business and financial communities—would be appointed receiver of his own company.

Less than a week later, on March 22, an announcement on the front page of the *Dispatch* that John Mitchel had died in Ireland prompted arrangements for what was to be called the "Mitchel Memorial Meeting" on April 22. Many of Richmond's most prominent citizens turned out for it. The governor, two former governors, the mayor, a judge, and Jim Dooley all spoke before a large crowd at the service in Assembly Hall.[29] Dooley paid tribute to Mitchel's role during the wartime battles around Richmond, describing those days as times when "we learned to prize [Mitchel's] heroic spirit which voluntarily cast its lot with ours, teaching us to set honor in one eye and death in the other and look on both indifferently."[30] Governor Wise brought the service to its conclusion by calling for "three cheers for Tipperary."

The next day, recalling the sacrifices of family and friends in service of the Confederacy, Dooley accepted an invitation to be temporary chairman of a gathering of First Virginia regiment veterans who proposed to form an "Old First Association." Almost one hundred members of the regiment came to the Virginia Opera House for the meeting. Introduced as "the son of beloved old Major," Jim Dooley gave a speech that—according to the *Dispatch*—"recalled some of the glorious memories of the regiment in which he served as private in Company C and . . . impressed upon the survivors the necessity of organizing to preserve their history and to maintain the friendly and social relations which existed among members during the war."[31]

From the moment of her arrival in Richmond in 1869, Sallie Dooley had been the wife of an aspiring politician, and Jim's increasing prominence in public life meant that, despite the fact she couldn't vote, she probably went to many political rallies and sat with the other women in the gallery when her husband and other politicians gave speeches. In time, Sallie became well known in her own right through her devotion to charitable works. Of these, one of the most important to her was her position on the Board of Lady Managers of the St. Paul's Episcopal Church Home for Aged and Infirm Women, established in 1875. In the years to come she served on its fundraising committees for events like the one that, according to the *State* newspaper, "featured scenes from *A Midsummer Night's Dream*, Mendelssohn's music and a delicious supper that cost fifty cents extra."[32] Sallie also took a personal interest in the residents of the home, even in later years asking her railroad vice president husband to provide free passes so the ladies might travel on the Richmond and Danville when they wanted to visit their families elsewhere in Virginia.[33]

The senior Mrs. Dooley, Jim's mother, Sarah, now in her early sixties, was also involved in charitable works during these years. For instance, she and several other women had responded to the Panic of 1873 less than a month after it began by organizing a charity at St. Peter's they called the "Ladies Benevolent Society." Sarah Dooley was elected vice president of the forty-four-member society.[34] Her son Jim continued serving as recording secretary of the St. Vincent de Paul Confraternity.

In September 1875, Dooley launched his campaign for a third term in the House of Delegates with a barrage of newspaper ads announcing his candidacy.[35] For Jim, this campaign was neither as exciting as his first one nor as matter-of-fact as his second. Instead, it was marked by discord within the ranks of the Conservative Party, from which well over a hundred Readjusters had broken away and had begun to call themselves Independents.[36] They campaigned particularly against the candidacy of Gen. Bradley T. Johnson, an ardent Funder who was running for a seat in the Virginia Senate. The candidates for the House, however, were not under attack, and at some of the biggest Conservative Party rallies, such as one sponsored by the Konservative Kampaign Klub on October 13, Dooley was one of the featured speakers. It is likely that Sallie attended the rally: ladies were specifically invited, and the Klub's advertisements had assured them that "the most rigid order" would be maintained.[37]

That fall Jim Dooley was, however, the target of a certain amount of negative campaigning that grew out of his service on the House Committee for Constitutional Amendments during his second term. As its chairman, Dooley reported the committee's proposals, and on February 18, 1875, he had moved that Article III of the constitution be amended to add petit larceny to the list of crimes for which a person would be denied the right to vote.[38] The amendment was offensive to many members of the black community, who saw it as a disenfranchisement measure aimed directly at them. On Election Day in November, the animosity generated by the proposed amendment prompted some voters in the predominantly black Jackson Ward to scratch Dooley's name from the ballot.[39] Dooley was reelected anyway, but the incident marred his victory.

He was also elected that month to membership in the Richmond Chamber of Commerce, of which General Anderson was then president.[40] When the new legislative session opened in December, Dooley introduced a bill to charter the Chamber, which, although it had been founded in 1868, had not previously received an official state charter.[41] At the Chamber's annual meeting the following June, the newly elected president, E. Otto Nolting, eager to put Dooley's legal skills to work on its behalf, appointed him to the Chamber's Standing Committee on Arbitration.

Despite the increasing discord within the Conservative Party, when the House of Delegates winter session opened, Dooley's responsiveness to concerns of disparate elements among his local constituents was apparent. In the first week of the new year he presented a petition on behalf of penitentiary guards for an increase of pay. Although the guards did not receive a raise, the petition prompted a compromise measure that provided them with new overcoats.[42] On February 20, he represented a different group of Richmonders when he proposed House Bill No. 246, to incorporate a new gentlemen's club, the "Westmoreland Club of the City of Richmond."[43] The bill was passed in the House on March 8 and in the Senate on March 13. Dooley himself was one of the fourteen original members of the Westmoreland, and he remained a member of the club for the rest of his life.[44]

Matters of importance to the entire state, however, occupied most of Dooley's attention during the term. The future of the James River and Kanawha Canal was a central issue. Competition between the canal and the railroad had begun in John Dooley's day. By 1877 the concern was that the canal could not survive long unless it could be extended to Clifton Forge. On March 1, Dooley presented a petition in the House of Delegates signed by 165 Richmond businessmen asking the legislature to amend the charter of the Buchanan and Clifton Forge Railroad to allow stockholders in the canal company to own stock in the railroad company instead. The petition was an attempt by the business community to support both the railroad and the canal company, which was by then gasping for survival.[45] Dooley was praised by the *Dispatch* for his speech in favor of amending the Buchanan and Clifton Forge charter, but debate on the issue was acrimonious well into the final days of the session in April.[46] After prolonged filibustering, which Dooley tried unsuccessfully to limit, his proposal died late on the night of April 3, and the next day the legislature adjourned.[47] The *Enquirer* lamented that "a dark chapter in the legislative annals of Virginia was brought to a close. The James River Canal is dead."[48] That wasn't entirely accurate, however. The canal company stumbled on for almost four more years.

While the canal debate was still under way on April 3, Dooley and the other members of the legislature left the chamber at two o'clock to attend a Conservative caucus to nominate a candidate for Virginia's first railroad commissioner. Dooley was presiding when Col. Thomas H. Carter of King

William County became the nominee. That evening, before the canal debate resumed, Carter was elected by a joint vote of both houses of the General Assembly. His qualifications included being a graduate of Virginia Military Institute and being "free from railroad entanglements."[49] His election was an important step toward regulating Virginia's railroad industry.

A few hours earlier that day, Dooley's sister Saidie, who had entered the Visitation Monastery on her twenty-second birthday the previous September, received her habit in the chapel of Monte Maria, the Visitation Monastery atop Richmond's Church Hill. Saidie, who eventually served several terms as mother superior of the convent, took the name "Mary Magdalen." The other nuns eventually gave her the nickname "Walking Encyclopedia" in tribute to her intelligence and education.[50]

During the mid-1870s, growth in Dooley's legal practice provided him with the capital to continue investing in real estate, particularly along the western reaches of the city and usually in partnership with one or two other individuals. The Richmond Hustings Deeds Books record a long list of such Dooley purchases. As real estate prices plummeted, his holdings grew, and after the crash of 1873 he even tried his hand at real estate development. In the process, however, he ran up against some of the bureaucratic obstacles that developers routinely encountered, and he was not always successful in his attempts. In 1874, for instance, he petitioned the city's Common Council Committee on the Fire Department for permission to build a frame house or perhaps several frame houses on some of his property. His name appeared in a newspaper list of more than fifty other people who had submitted such petitions.[51] In the end he was one of only four whose petitions were rejected. Instead of being discouraged by the experience, however, he learned from it. A decade later he was president of real estate development companies in three states—Virginia, Minnesota, and Alabama.

Part of the reason Dooley's legal practice continued to grow during the 1870s despite the unfavorable economic circumstances in the United States as a whole was that commercial bankruptcies brought him work. By 1877, businesses were still failing on all sides. Richmond's largest ironworks was one of them, and Dooley was trustee in the bankruptcy case. Readers who opened their Tuesday morning, July 3, 1877, *Dispatch* to the real estate ads couldn't have missed the large one for the "Trustee's Bankrupt Sale of the Entire Outfit of the Richmond Architectural Iron-Works, to be Sold as a Whole. Splendid Opportunity for Investment." The advertisement described the Asa Snyder ironworks at the corner of Eleventh and Cary Streets as "the most complete Iron Foundry in the South."

The deep depression of the late 1870s also fed the continuing disputes in the Conservative Party between the Funders and the Readjusters. In late summer their conflict came to a head. As they arrived at the Richmond Theater for the party convention on August 7, the 1,200 delegates from across Virginia had to thread their way through angry crowds. Once inside the theater, Funders and Readjusters clashed from the outset. Hisses and boos greeted speakers who attempted to articulate the Funders' perspective.[52] Even after the Funders won the contest for leadership of the convention, the contest for the party's candidate for governor was heated. Railroad president and Readjuster William "Billy" Mahone, Funder John Daniel, and Frederick W. Holliday (who kept mum about his preference) endured numerous ballots before Holliday emerged as the winner. Dooley was a prominent figure in these proceedings. He was elected to the Rules Committee and was made chairman of the Resolutions Committee. He and General Anderson drafted the platform adopted by the party.[53]

Dooley's high profile at the convention seemed to indicate that his political career was on track and that he planned to run for another term, but by October 15 he had decided otherwise. The other leading Richmond Conservatives were horrified. An open letter begging him to reconsider and signed by 109 members of the party was published in the "Candidates for Office" column of the next morning's *Dispatch*. Three days later Dooley's response appeared in the same column. In it, he expressed his appreciation for the others' support but declined to run again, citing the pressures of his business. Although Dooley was not specific in his letter about the nature of this "business," he was at that time a thirty-six-year-old lawyer with a successful practice and extensive investments in real estate. In addition, he had begun a new phase of his business career in 1875, when he bought 150 shares in the initial stock offering of the Commercial Fire Insurance Company and agreed to serve as its vice president.[54]

There were also circumstances in his family life that contributed to his decision not to run again. First of all, despite his real estate investments, he and his wife did not have a house of their own. They were still living in a boardinghouse. Even more importantly, he was the head of the extended Dooley family. His mother, several younger sisters, two married sisters with husbands, and several nieces depended on him for financial support. His brother-in-law Willie Lewis had never recovered financially from the destruction of his farm operations during Hunter's Raid by the Union army in 1864. Tantie Jones, his sister Mary's husband, though a hard worker, earned very little. Dooley, like his father before him, had assumed overall responsibility for the family's well-being and may have felt he could no longer afford the distracting and time-consuming demands of public service. He hadn't lost interest in politics, however. Several days after his letter was published, Dooley's name headed a list in the *Dispatch* of 229 Conservatives publicly supporting another candidate for his former seat in the House.[55]

CHAPTER 14 | The Railroad That Got Away

T
he great excitement in Richmond in October 1877 was the arrival of President and Mrs. Rutherford B. Hayes—the first visit of a president of the United States since Virginia's readmission to the Union. Still rebuilding from the Evacuation Fire, the city was eager to put on its best face. The *Dispatch* urged city authorities to ensure "that the streets are swept clean, and that the roadways and pavements are not unnecessarily obstructed by building material."[1] There would be, it noted, "many strangers within our gates, including a battalion of newspaper correspondents from the North, and it is our duty, as it ought to be our pleasure, to make the most presentable appearance possible."

Thousands turned out for the occasion. Special trains brought in spectators from as far away as Danville to hear the president and members of his cabinet speak at a ceremony at the state fair. The governor held an informal reception for Hayes and his wife that Jim and Sallie attended.

Dooley's departure from the legislature allowed him to devote considerably more time to his law practice. Much of his business still came from bankruptcy cases in which he acted as trustee and Chancery Court suits in which he served as special commissioner for property to be sold at public auction. As a whole, his caseload reflected the deep depression of the late 1870s. Dooley also acted as attorney for the firm Seddon and Bruce. One of its partners was Thomas Seddon, a son of James A. Seddon, at one time secretary of war in Jefferson Davis's cabinet.[2] A decade later the younger Seddon would figure prominently in the Alabama iron industry as president of the Sloss Iron and Steel Enterprises, in which Dooley and several other Richmonders invested.

By 1879 Dooley had bought a house for his mother and his unmarried sister Alice at 314 E. Main Street in a quiet, fashionable neighborhood suitable for a genteel widow.[3] At the time, Jim and Sallie still did not have a house of their own but were continuing to share a big house on Grace Street with several other couples. Nonetheless, looking after the older generation and the unmarried women in the family was one of Dooley's responsibilities as the head of the family.

In the fall and early winter of 1879 Dooley invested in several new ventures, among them a partnership with one of the other residents at the Grace

Street house, Stevens M. Taylor, a bookkeeper. Like Dooley, Taylor had an eye for niche business, and they were both attracted to the teamster business, which hauled freight for the railroad industry. In those days teamsters not only hauled cargo to and from trains and businesses in Richmond, but they also transferred cargo from one railroad station to another. Because each of the five short-line railroads serving Richmond had its own depot, hauling cargo between them was a big and, usually, profitable portion of the work for teamsters. In their partnership, Dooley provided the capital, and Taylor, the management. In September Dooley invested the heady sum of $3,785 in "Stevens M. Taylor, & Co. TEAMSTERS," which specialized in hauling "Heavy Machinery, Iron Safes, &c." Their ad in the city directory featured Taylor's name in the upper left-hand corner and Dooley's on the upper right.[4] Dooley was the owner of four spring trucks, two wagons, eleven mules, four horses, nine sets of harness, and all the necessary stable fixtures, as well as some extra wagon bodies that he bought from Taylor, whose part of the bargain it was to keep them busy working.[5]

Dooley's partnership with Taylor, however, seems to have been doomed from the start. In January 1880, Taylor signed the first of a number of ninety-day notes when he borrowed $1,012.41 from Dooley. By June 1882, Dooley, eager to call in all the funds due him, took Taylor to Chancery Court to "enforce collection" of the notes.[6] In an arrangement similar to several worked out by his father to deal with people who owed him money, Dooley agreed to a generous compromise approved by the court. It offered an incentive to Taylor by providing that any payment he made on the principal would be credited for four times its value as long as he paid the interest on the balance on time. Dooley's painfully acquired knowledge of the teamster business served as his personal initiation into the railroad industry and alerted him to the need for "union" stations that would serve more than one railroad company. A few years later he began to advocate publicly for them.

On December 1, 1879, Dooley made another, more significant, investment in the transportation business. This time he bought 298 shares of the Richmond and Danville Railroad from R. H. Maury & Co. at twenty-six and a half, that is, $26.50 per share.[7] Although the receipt indicates that the stock was purchased "for the account of Mr. J. H. Dooley," it also shows that Maury & Co. received two notes in payment. One note was from Dooley; the other was from another young lawyer named Thomas Muldrup Logan. The receipt is the earliest-known record of a James H. Dooley investment in the Richmond and Danville and, perhaps more importantly, of a partnership between the two men that would endure until Logan's death almost thirty years later.

Logan was one of two lawyers who became closely associated with Dooley. The other was Joseph Bryan. Both arrived in Richmond during the early 1870s while Dooley's political career was just beginning. Bryan was a tall, slender man with deep roots in Gloucester County. Only sixteen at the opening of the Civil War in 1861, he spent that year as an undergraduate at the University of Virginia. After that, he served in the Nitre and Mining Bureau of the Confederacy before joining the Confederate army in 1864. He went on to study law at the University of Virginia after the war before settling in Fluvanna County, where he tried unsuccessfully to make a living as a lawyer during the immediate postwar period. By 1870, a discouraged Bryan had left for Richmond, where—thanks to his intelligence and family connections—his law career finally flourished.[8] By 1871 he had fallen in love with and married Isobel Stewart, one of the daughters of a wealthy investor named John Stewart who lived at "Brook Hill" in Henrico County just north of Richmond.

Through his law practice, Bryan became acquainted with Jim Dooley. They soon discovered mutual interests and a shared commitment to helping rebuild not only Richmond and Virginia but eventually the whole South. As in Dooley's case, during the mid-1870s that commitment led to Bryan's active participation in local and state politics. His first step was serving as a supervisor for Henrico County, after which he was an unsuccessful Conservative Party candidate for the House of Delegates in 1873, 1875, and 1877.[9] By the end of the decade, Bryan, too, had become a stockholder in the Richmond and Danville Railroad, at that time only 168 miles long.

Thomas Logan was a South Carolina native and the youngest man to earn the rank of brigadier general in the Confederate army. He had graduated from South Carolina College in 1860 at the top of his class.[10] Like Dooley, he was of medium height and slight, but his hair was as light as Dooley's was dark. He had entered the Confederate army as a private, but—unlike Dooley—had the good fortune to evade capture, although he was wounded twice. He rose quickly through the ranks and was promoted to brigadier general after leading the last charge of the Confederate cavalry in North Carolina.[11]

In 1865 Logan came to live near Richmond, read law on his own, and married Kate Virginia Cox, the daughter of a Chesterfield County judge who owned the Clover Hill coal mine and the Clover Hill Railroad. Logan found favor with his father-in-law, Judge James Henry Cox, who made him president of the Clover Hill Railroad not long after the wedding.[12] While cutting his teeth in the railroad business, Logan also practiced law in the town of Manchester for several years before moving across the James River to Richmond. There, the dash and tactics of the cavalry colored his approach to business and contrasted vividly with Bryan's and Dooley's calmer, quieter approaches.

In spite of, or perhaps because of, their differences, the three men worked well together and established a partnership, first in the railroad business and later in other ventures. As Dooley and Bryan soon learned, Logan was a master at persuading his partners to pay for his shares at the time of purchase, always promising to pay later. His enthusiasm for new ventures chronically outstripped his ability to pay for participating in them. Nevertheless, Logan became one of Dooley's closest colleagues.

For much of 1879, a potato famine in Ireland almost as devastating as its predecessor in the 1840s had been front-page news in Richmond and across the United States. By the end of December, Dooley had taken part in organizing the Irish Relief Society to help allay the suffering that Americans had been reading about. Unfortunately, the weak state of the economy prevented members from initiating a statewide campaign like the one undertaken forty years earlier. This time the effort had to be local, so the Relief Society hired Mozart Hall for a public meeting on January 6 and asked prominent Richmonders and generous friends to sign on as "vice presidents" to guarantee the legitimacy of the relief society and to encourage others to contribute generously. A man didn't have to be Catholic or of Irish descent to be one of the vice presidents: the names of ninety men of every religious and political persuasion and national origin, including Moses Millhiser, who was Jewish, and Anthony Pizzini, who was Italian, appeared on the front page of the January 2 *Dispatch*.

The *New York Times* carried news of the meeting in a front-page column dedicated to "Relief Meetings on Both Sides of the Atlantic." In an article that also mentioned efforts in London, Dublin, Philadelphia, and Wilmington, Delaware, the *Times* devoted half the space to a description of the meeting in Richmond.[13] Dooley's name appeared in the *Times* for the first time on the list of those who had given an address.

Ten days later, the front page of the *Dispatch* carried a somewhat startling headline: "The Irish Agitators Coming to Richmond."[14] The "agitators" were the Irish politician and member of Parliament Charles Stuart Parnell and his friend John Dillon. An enthusiastic group of Richmonders convened to plan a proper reception for the men, and the secretary of the meeting reminded everyone that "there are hundreds of Irish names on Virginia's rolls of honor. Let us, then, do honor to Charles Parnell, and thus maintain the reputation of our good old state at home and abroad."[15] Before the meeting was over, Jim

Dooley and Anthony Keiley were among the fifteen men appointed to the reception committee.

Parnell arrived by train in Ashland, where the reception committee, now boasting twenty men, boarded the train to greet him. Parnell, Dillon, and several members of the committee rode into Richmond in a hired carriage drawn by four white horses and led by a marching band. After being deposited at the Exchange Hotel not far from the Capitol, Parnell and Dillon addressed the crowd assembled there.[16] Then it was on to the Capitol, where, thanks to Dooley's continuing connections in its chamber, the Speaker of the House vacated the chair for ten minutes so that the visitors could be introduced. Parnell's remarks were brief but frankly political. "In Ireland," he announced, "we do not enjoy the blessing of freedom. Our people . . . have to look to the land of the West, which has been a refuge for so many millions, and to the great State of Virginia, which has always welcomed us kindly. If perchance in the near future another wave of emigration sets in, I believe many of our people . . . will turn their face to this State."[17]

Then Dooley escorted Parnell and Dillon to the Senate Chamber, where in welcoming them the lieutenant governor proclaimed, "Our hearts beat with yours, and our warmest sympathies are with the suffering people of Ireland, and in Virginia the people of Ireland will ever find a staunch and faithful friend." That evening, Parnell and Dillon spoke at Mozart Hall. The price of admission was fifty cents, "for the benefit of the suffering Irish." Dooley was one of the listeners who heard Parnell lash into the English government for policies that he said contributed to the problems in Ireland and for its failure to help his country.

Dooley's efforts on behalf of the Irish people did not distract him from pursuing an opportunity just as the depression of the 1870s had begun to lift and the Pennsylvania Railroad decided to sell its stock in the Richmond and Danville. During the depression the Pennsylvania had poured money into the Danville, and by 1879 the latter company was in "excellent order and condition."[18] As stockholders in the Danville, Dooley, Bryan, and Logan were well aware of its improved condition and were eager to buy enough of its stock to bring control of the company into Richmond hands. Despite approaching a number of other Richmonders to join them in the effort, they could not raise enough money. When they learned that a father-son duo in Philadelphia named Thomas and William Clyde had bought a large bloc of the Pennsylvania's Richmond and Danville stock, Dooley, Bryan, and Logan approached them about forming a syndicate to buy even more. They were aware that Thomas Clyde was primarily a steamship company owner, but they also knew that in 1873 he had saved the thirty-eight-mile-long Richmond and York River Railroad, in which Dooley's father had been one of the original investors. After the war the Richmond and York River struggled for years before it could resume business, and even then it teetered on the edge of bankruptcy until Clyde reorganized it as the Richmond, York River and Chesapeake.[19] The Richmond and York River (as it was still called) hauled freight and passengers between Richmond and the Clyde docks at West Point. In a segment of his 1880 annual report for the company, Thomas Clyde had noted, "Much has been done during the past year toward accomplishing the original design [placing] Richmond and all the business materially tributary to this growing city practically at deep water, and in cheap and easy access to all ports, both of our own and foreign countries."[20] His report convinced Dooley and his associates that the Clydes shared their own commitment to bringing prosperity back to Richmond. The pair's next step proved even more convincing. After agreeing to join the syndicate, the Clydes bought twenty-four thousand shares of the Danville from the Southern Railroad Security Company, which held the Pennsylvania's stock. Eight thousand of these were for the Richmonders.

Dooley, Bryan, and Logan hastened to find the money to pay for their shares. Bryan's June 17 letter to "Mssrs. Clyde and Co., New York" enclosed drafts on New York and Baltimore banks in partial payment of $96,875 due two days later for the Richmonders' portion of the eight thousand shares of Danville stock. Bryan assured the Clydes that "Gen. Logan will pay you in New York $4,892."[21] The following day Bryan sent drafts for $8,502.43 more, "which please apply for payment due tomorrow to the Pennsylvania Railroad for purchase of 8,000 shares of Richmond & Danville stock taken by Richmond parties."[22]

Meanwhile, Dooley had been elected to the boards of three financial institutions: Merchants and Mechanics Insurance Company, Petersburg Savings and Insurance Company, and Merchants National Bank. An Irish immigrant named Frederic R. Scott was president of Petersburg Savings and Insurance and a board member of Merchants National Bank. Scott's respect for Dooley's work with Petersburg Savings and Insurance was a factor in Dooley's election to the Merchants National Bank board at its annual meeting on Tuesday, January 13, 1880.[23] His seat on the board meant that, even though he was no longer in the House of Delegates, Dooley had a prominent role in helping to shape Richmond's future. His continuing presence in Conservative Party politics also led in 1880 to his appointment by Governor Frederick Mackey Holliday to the board of the Medical College of Virginia.

Several months later, the competition between the James River and Kanawha Canal and Virginia railroads finally came to a close. It had begun about the time Dooley's father had arrived in Richmond in 1836 and remained an acrimonious issue forty years later, despite attempts by legislators like the younger Dooley to settle it. That important chapter in the history of transportation in Virginia ended at a meeting on March 4, 1880, when the canal company signed a contract to sell its entire works and all of its franchises to the newly organized Richmond and Allegheny Railroad, which when built would give Richmond a two-hundred-mile-long link to the Chesapeake and Ohio Railroad at Clifton Forge. Although the Richmond and Allegheny's first president was Dooley's occasional co-counsel Robert Ould, the *New York Times* pointed out that "the capitalists of the Richmond and Allegheny Railroad Company were chiefly New York bankers."[24]

Four days later, Virginians were deeply involved in opening another new chapter in the history of transportation when the Virginia legislature granted Dooley and his associates a charter for the Richmond and West Point Terminal Railway and Warehouse Company. The Terminal, as it came to be called, was the first railroad holding company in the United States. Its charter permitted the Terminal to link short-line railroads together to make a longer trunk-line system in Virginia and other southern states.[25] The charter of the Richmond and Danville forbade such consolidation. In fact, it prohibited the Danville from operating any railroad that did not connect directly to it, and from extending beyond the borders of Virginia. The Terminal's charter was specifically designed to circumvent those restrictions. Logan has been credited with suggesting it as a means of enabling the Richmond and Danville to expand into the Deep South, but Dooley's legislative experience contributed to their success in obtaining the charter that authorized the Terminal to "unite, consolidate or connect" with any railroad company in Virginia and to subscribe to the stock of any railroad in the state and seven other states: North Carolina, South Carolina, Tennessee, Kentucky, Georgia, Alabama, and Mississippi.[26]

Since most of the railroads in the South were short lines fewer than twenty miles long, of varying width (gauge), and unconnected to any other lines, linking them to each other sped the economic recovery not just of Richmond but of the South as a whole. The resulting interstate system also permitted the growth of industrial might. Dooley, Logan, Bryan, and the other Richmonders who joined the company subscribed to only one hundred shares each in the Terminal, but William Clyde took 250 shares and became its first president.[27]

Investing in the Richmond and Danville and the Terminal propelled Dooley, Bryan, and Logan into the high drama of the railroad business of the early 1880s that swirled around the bankruptcies and reorganization of other railroads in Virginia and elsewhere in the South. Such proceedings offered tantalizing opportunities to acquire railroad stocks at a fraction of their former cost. The scenes pitted Civil War adversaries—and even some former allies—against each other again and again.

One such drama unfolded in the U.S. Circuit Court in Richmond when bankruptcy proceedings against the Atlantic, Mississippi and Ohio Railroad (AM&O) opened on February 8, 1881, after languishing in the court system since 1876. The former Confederate general William "Billy" Mahone was president of the railroad, which ran westward from Norfolk and was therefore an important connector line between the Atlantic seaboard and the Ohio River. Mahone had become a Republican, which made him anathema to Virginia Democrats like Dooley. Although politics was not the issue that morning, it didn't help Mahone's standing with the spectators in the courtroom that counsel for the AM&O was former Union army general Benjamin Butler. On the second day of the trial, the courtroom was jammed with distinguished and prominent men including Dooley and General Anderson. For an hour and a quarter, Butler droned on, pleading for more time to raise the capital needed to stave off the sale of the railroad. According to the *Dispatch,* his proposal to settle the investors' and creditors' claims with one hundred thousand dollars was tantamount to offering a penny on the dollar, and at the suggestion, "the bar smiled . . . the vast crowd laughed, the town laughed."[28] The laughter was not simply the jeering of businessmen over the inadequacy of the sum offered; it was the laughter of sweet revenge over an old enemy. The *Dispatch* reported that shortly after the court adjourned at 3:15 p.m., "General Butler left the city . . . on the northward bound afternoon train." The judge ordered the railroad sold the next day.

When the auction began the next morning on the Custom House steps, crowds filled the sidewalk and carriages lined the Bank Street curbs, but there were only four bidders, one of whom arrived late. According to the *Dispatch:* "The bidding had scarcely [begun] when there was quite a sensation . . . in the crowd. . . . Suddenly a carriage whirled up to the sidewalk, and General . . . Logan, accompanied by a friend stepped out. They represented the Richmond and Danville . . . interest," and they made their bids "with spirit."[29]

The bidding began at $8,078,000, and other bids followed quickly until they reached $8,210,000, when there followed a long pause. The auctioneer asked, "Gentlemen, are you all done?" The pause lasted a few more tense moments before resuming. Logan's final bid was $8,601,000, but he lost the railroad to a stranger in the crowd whose bid topped his by a mere $4,000. The stranger was a dark-haired, bewhiskered forty-year-old in a neat, dark suit. His name was Clarence H. Clark, and he was from Philadelphia. The Confederacy's youngest general had been bested by a civilian from Pennsylvania. More importantly, the control of a Virginia railroad had passed out of Virginian hands. A northern investment firm would control the AM&O and eventually rename it the Norfolk and Western Railroad.[30]

The Richmond and Danville men lost the AM&O, but in early September they acquired its major competitor, the Virginia Midland Railroad. Their February chastening fed their determination even while it brought the realization that they couldn't rely on last-minute tactics if they were to be successful consolidators. They now realized that they needed to secure capital and commitment. Their solution was to form what they called an "Ironclad Pool," to which Dooley, Bryan, Logan, William H. Palmer, John P. Branch, William Clyde, and George W. Perkins subscribed a few months later on June 1, 1881.[31] The members of the Pool promised not to take out their money for ten years, thus giving the Pool a guaranteed sum to call upon whenever opportunity or necessity arose. In mid-July the *Dispatch* caught wind of the Pool agreement and published an article that revealed the reaction of the Richmond business community to its formation: "Under the agreement the stock is to be transferred to a committee of seven a majority of whom are empowered to vote the whole for ten years. Of this committee five are from Richmond . . . and two are from New York . . . this committee will have the power of all the stockholders for ten years, and thus control the whole Danville railroad system of over 1,500 miles. This is indeed gratifying to us as Richmond men. We had feared that . . . [this was] a New York syndicate that might at some future time turn the cold shoulder to this city."[32]

E ven before they formed the Ironclad Pool, the Richmond syndicate created another company they called the Richmond and Danville Extension Company. It was a construction company to build the bridges, tunnels, and tracks required to extend the Danville system in Virginia and well beyond its borders. Significantly, it was not chartered in Virginia but instead in New Jersey, a state friendlier to corporations with national scope.[1] Chartered on May 28, 1881, the Extension Company opened its books on August 3. Logan, Bryan, and Dooley were the first three subscribers, each taking a thousand shares, or one hundred thousand dollars' worth of the fifty thousand shares at a par value of one hundred dollars.[2]

The names of some prominent northern investors appeared on the official list of subscribers to the initial offering, including Emanuel Lehman, who subscribed for five hundred, and George W. Perkins, who subscribed for two thousand.[3] The northern connection was also obvious in the location of the company headquarters at 20 Nassau Street, New York City. The holder of the largest number of shares, however, was neither a southerner nor a northerner. It was not a person at all but a corporation, the Richmond and West Point Terminal Railway and Warehouse Company, which subscribed to 25,500 shares, that is, 51 percent of the stock.

The Extension Company wasted no time in getting to work building the newly organized Georgia Pacific Railroad, a company whose very name encapsulated the ambition of its owners to connect the Deep South with the Far West.[4] A brief announcement in the September 10 issue of the *Dispatch* made it clear, however, that despite the location of its headquarters and its partial ownership by northern investors, the company had a mandate to bring business home to Richmond. The article announced that a Richmond Company named Norvell, Leake & Co. had just "closed a contract to furnish all the cross-ties for the Georgia Pacific railroad between Atlanta, Ga., and Columbus, Miss.—a distance of two hundred and fifty miles."[5]

A week after the Extension Company received its charter, Dooley's role in the affairs of the Richmond and Danville took on a new dimension. When the board met in Richmond on June 4, 1881, Logan nominated him for a seat, and he was elected. He must have been outside in the hall waiting for the news: according to the Directors' Minutes, as soon as he had "been informed of his election [he] came into the meeting and took his seat."[6] During that meeting he was appointed to a committee with Logan, Palmer, and Bryan to negotiate a contract arrangement with the Richmond, York River and Chesapeake Railroad "for the protection of this company's interest therein." Before the next board meeting, the committee hammered out a lease agreement with the York River that brought to fruition the Clyde plan to link the two railroads. It also gave the Richmond and Danville a majority interest in the Baltimore, Chesapeake and Richmond Steamboat Company. As its president, A. S. B. Buford, explained in his annual report the following December, "under this contract this company acquired also a controlling ownership of the steamship lines between West Point and Baltimore and between Richmond and Baltimore via the James river, comprising six steamers in effective working condition."[7]

A year and a half earlier, the Dooleys had finally felt comfortable enough financially to look for a house of their own. They set their hearts on a handsome sixty-year-old house at 212 West Franklin Street in one of Richmond's most fashionable blocks. It was large enough to provide a home not only for the two of them but also for Sallie's father, the retired Lunenburg County physician Henry May, and for her nephew Roger B. Atkinson, who was planning to come from Staunton to read law in Dooley's office. At some point during the depression, the previous owner of 212 West Franklin had borrowed money from a banker named Swepson who boarded at the Exchange Hotel but had his permanent business in Tennessee.[8] When the owner couldn't keep up the payments on the loan, the property fell into Swepson's hands. He put it on the market and returned to Tennessee. On March 11, 1880, Dooley sat down at his law office desk and wrote to Swepson at the Knoxville Gas Light Company, offering to buy the house if Swepson had not yet sold it. Swepson replied the following day that someone else had contacted him about the house. However, "have not heard from the party yet, have been waiting, but will wait no longer. I will sell you my house and lot for $19m [thousand] for house & lot."[9] Shortly thereafter the Dooleys left the house on Grace Street and moved in.

For the first time they had an entire house to furnish and decorate. They made extensive changes to the interior, especially in the library. Several years later, an article in the *State* on "Richmond's Finest Residences" described the house as elegant and comfortable, noting that "one of the special features of this house is the library, the fitting up of which is said to have cost $3,000."[10] The boy who loved books now had a library of his own, but he was still not above buying secondhand books. When the lawyer William Green, with whom Dooley had read law, died and his eight-thousand-volume collection of books was sold at an auction in January 1881, Dooley bought at least thirty-seven books to add to his new library.[11]

Coincidentally, just two months after Swepson accepted Dooley's offer to buy the house, a one-hundred-acre farm that would later become the Dooleys' estate Maymont also came on the market briefly. A real estate company called Grubbs and Williams advertised an auction of the property because its owner had defaulted on a loan of approximately twelve thousand dollars. The ad noted that a plat for dividing the property would be available at the auction.[12] Luckily for the Dooleys, the owner came up with the money to pay off the loan. If he hadn't, the farm would have become a housing development rather than an estate called Maymont. The fates of these two properties in early 1880 are suggestive of positive currents in the economy that year. The depression had bottomed out, and recovery had begun.

That fall, the Danville and the Terminal were listed on the New York Stock Exchange for the first time. Listing them appeared to be an exciting step forward, enabling the companies to attract additional stockholders and generate the funds needed for territorial expansion. However, the listing actually led to a setback for the Ironclad Pool members. The trouble began in October 1881, when two northern members of the Pool, George W. Perkins and W. P. St. John, ignoring the clause requiring that shares remain in the Pool for ten years, asked that some of theirs be "retransferred"—that is, taken out of the Pool and returned to them. Perkins wanted to extract 212 shares.[13] Since he had more than 2,700 shares in the Pool, pulling out less than 10 percent of them should not have rocked the boat, but it did. The Pool was doomed.[14] There was no longer anything "ironclad" about the Pool, and it did not survive the year.

In a February 7, 1882, article on railroads in the South, the *New York Times* reported that the Danville system had been "gridironing" the region and had "bought, leased and secured control of different lines until it now operates two thousand and fifty-eight miles of road." By then the stock of both the Danville and the Terminal companies had become targets of wild speculation in the market, and the price of the stock fluctuated tremendously. In November the Terminal sold for $122 per share; by February, its price had risen to $263.[15] The Richmond and Danville rose from $99.50 to $250 during the same period. Then, in March 1882, the prices of both stocks fell—the Terminal to $100 and the Danville to $110. By September 1882, despite efforts of the men (especially by Logan, who threw every penny he had into trying to keep control of the two companies in Richmond), they had lost control of both to New York financiers.[16] In the melee, Logan lost his house and had to move his family to a small place they had in Buckingham County. At its October 20, 1882, meeting in New York, however, the new board, recognizing Dooley's expertise in railroad law, elected him associate counsel of the company at a salary of $2,400 per annum.[17]

A few days earlier the *Dispatch,* in discussing the last panic in Danville stock, mentioned that "it is now regarded as probable that there was a concerted effort to run the stock down by parties who wanted to buy it up at a low price. Its present price is phenomenally low for a dividend-paying stock, while the business prospects of the road are very bright."[18] An Associated Press item in the paper reported that the officers of the Richmond and Danville "positively" denied "that the Standard Oil company had purchased a controlling interest in the road." Technically the denial was accurate. The Standard Oil Company itself had not bought a controlling interest, but a titan of the national financial world had bought heavily in the stock of the Danville and the Terminal for his own portfolio, and he was the *head* of Standard Oil. His name was John D. Rockefeller. In a front-page story on October 19, the *Dispatch* reported: "Where the ownership of the [Danville] lies is still a mystery. Mr. Rochefellar [*sic*] is looked upon as the mighty man, but whether he is the representative of the Baltimore and Ohio Railroad Company or has bought for investment for himself or others, or for speculation, is not now known. The annual meeting, however, is not far off, and at that time there may be some developments."

The mystery was only partially solved at that meeting in December when Robert Harris, well known as a representative of Rockefeller, joined the board.[19] What the public didn't know was that on September 12 Rockefeller had placed an order with his brokers Jessup & Lamont for stock in both the Danville and the Terminal for his own account. However, he wrote, "I want to feel certain that these orders, as well as all of my business, is kept sacredly confidential and not known excepting to yourselves and a trusted employee if necessary."[20] Rockefeller was well aware that any purchase he made could throw the stock market into a frenzy, so he instructed Jessup & Lamont that they would "find it desirable in these two stocks to move with the greatest caution and select different brokers for you will be very carefully watched."

On December 5, Dooley, badly frightened by the volatility in the stock market, also acted with greatest caution. He drafted a deed conveying his new house on West Franklin and all its belongings to Sallie for the "sum of five dollars, to him in hand paid," even though he had not yet made the final payment of $5,605 due on the mortgage. He was careful to make certain she would be completely protected if he became mired in any future financial disaster. The deed specified that he was conveying all the furniture, silverware, and china as well as "one dark bay horse, called 'Surry,' one Victoria or cabriolet, and one set of carriage harness, now in the stable situated upon the said lot . . . for her sole and separate use . . . free from the debts and control of . . . [her husband] or of any future husband whom she may marry."[21] At the end of the document, Dooley appended a letter to Sallie that clarified that in return for the house and its contents Sallie was giving up her "dower rights" to all the rest of his real estate. The letter began with an eye-opening revelation: "My Dear Wife: My real estate is worth over one hundred thousand dollars." The figure was very likely a low estimate, but even so it revealed just how successful he had been in the real estate business by 1882. The combined property may have been used as collateral for the loans to purchase railroad stock during the recent market frenzy. That in itself was an important reason why Sallie should give up her "dower rights" or face the possibility of being dragged into any financial reverses he might experience.

Dooley did not record the deed until six months later, after he made the last payment on the mortgage. Then, on July 5, he added a paragraph to refine the transaction by specifying a trustee to look after the property for Sallie. He chose Robert Ould's law partner, Isaac H. Carrington, as trustee and conveyed the property and its contents to him, "In trust."

In the interim, Dooley's youngest sister, Josie, married a tall, handsome young doctor named Henry Gibson Houston, who edited a journal published at the Medical College of Virginia.[22] The ceremony took place at 6:30 a.m. at St. Peter's on June 15, 1882, just early enough for the young couple to catch the morning train out of the city to begin their honeymoon.[23] Almost exactly one year later, on June 24, their daughter Eleanora Clare was born. They called her Nora and asked Jim to be her godfather. Sadly, Nora was not yet two when her twenty-nine-year-old father died of tuberculosis on March 16, 1885. From that time on Dooley took an active fatherly interest in Nora, showering her with money for pretty dresses, financing her education, and paying for her art lessons not only in Richmond but also in New York and Paris, where he paid the rent on an elegant apartment for her in a fashionable arrondissement.

The family wedding may have brought Dooley some brief respite from the turmoil in the railroad world in early summer, and recording the deed some relief from his financial worries in July, but even more trouble complicated his life in 1882. In late September, he faced an unexpected upset in the boardroom of the Medical College of Virginia. Governor Frederick W. M. Holliday had appointed Dooley to the MCV board on October 25, 1880. The appointment was among many indications that, although he no longer held an elected office, Dooley was still considered an important figure in the Conservative Party. He had served on the executive committee of the State Conservative Party with Logan and Keiley until May 1881 and remained active in the party on the local level.[24] When William E. Cameron was elected governor in 1881, however, politics no longer favored Conservatives of Dooley's persuasion.

On a cool and rainy September day in 1882, Governor William Cameron made an announcement that caused a legal and political storm that heated up Virginia's capital city for the next six months.[25] The announcement caught Dooley's attention because it was aimed directly at him and nineteen other members of the Board of Visitors of the Medical College of Virginia. He and his colleagues had been "fired" by the governor and replaced by twenty of Cameron's political allies. Dooley and his fellow members were dumbfounded by their elimination from the board. According to the charter granted to the Medical College by the Virginia legislature, there were no term limits to service: indeed, some of the oldest members had been appointed thirty years earlier, when the Medical College first became a state institution.[26]

The member who had served the shortest time on the board was forty-one-year-old Dooley. Prior to his appointment, the Medical College had been struggling financially, in part because its hospital was a city alms hospital serving all Richmonders regardless of ability to pay. Since Dooley was well known for his financial acumen, the appointment was an astute one, but it was also political. Holliday was a Funder, as were Dooley and most of Holliday's other appointees. Cameron, on the other hand, was a Readjuster whose adherents advocated only partial repayment of Virginia's prewar debts. Cameron, who had been in office less than a year, was also a firm believer in the spoils system and felt that his election granted him the power to "readjust" the officeholders and board members throughout the state. Since assuming office he had busied himself with sweeping out Funder officials and appointees. What Cameron failed to consider when he tried to sweep out the Board of Visitors at MCV was the number of lawyers on it. They all knew that firing violated the MCV charter. As a front-page article in the September 23 *Dispatch* noted, "It is understood that the old Board and faculty will resist the appointments made by the Governor yesterday; and it is stated that they are assured by some of the best legal talent in the State that the law plainly sustains them in their proposed action."

Six days after the governor's announcement, the "old" board met to decide how to proceed. The minutes of the meeting reveal that first they consulted with "counsel in the premises," that is, Dooley and John L. Marye, who had previously served as Virginia's lieutenant governor. Both advised them that, despite the governor's action, they still constituted the only legal Board of Visitors of the Medical College. Dooley, known for his skill as a conciliator and consensus builder, then suggested that five members of the board be selected to confer with the attorney general about arbitrating the dispute.[27] Dooley was one of the five who approached Attorney General Frank Blair immediately after the meeting.

When Blair, also a Readjuster, took the governor's side and refused to arbitrate the issue, the board simply carried on with its duties as required by the charter. Short of violence, which the board felt fairly certain the governor would not attempt, the governor's only recourse was the Virginia Supreme Court, the only court in the state empowered to settle such disputes.

The following day, the "new" board appointed by Governor Cameron held its first meeting at Ford's Hotel, across the street from Capitol Square.[28] Cameron urged his appointees to march as a body to the Egyptian Building of the Medical College to assert their right to take charge there, and he persuaded Lieutenant Governor John Lewis to lead them.

Meanwhile the faculty, whose appointments, like those of the Board of Visitors, were essentially permanent, had also met and decided to take a less than conciliatory stance. They assigned two faculty members to bar the door should the new board attempt to enter the college, and to obtain the assistance of police if necessary. In the Keystone Kops–like confrontation that ensued, the Richmond city police arrested the lieutenant governor and led him and the rest of the new board through the crowded city streets to the police station, where the two faculty members were expected to press charges. When the faculty members who blocked the door failed to show up within a reasonable length of time, the lieutenant governor was released and the crowd of new board members dispersed. The next day, in retaliation, the governor suspended payment of the state appropriation for the Medical College, and the new board met again and passed a resolution in support of the governor's action, asking him to "prolong that suspension indefinitely, until Readjuster control of the campus had been established." Fortunately for the college, the state appropriation was so small—at a mere $1,500, a drop in the budgetary bucket even in those days—that it was hardly missed.

A three-month-long stalemate ensued, punctuated by sniping in the press and monthly medical journals. The "old" board met in November and serenely continued to perform its mundane duties. Dooley's committee reported on its unsatisfactory attempt at arbitration with the attorney general. Dooley was also appointed to the auditing committee to check the financial books kept by the faculty.

Meanwhile, the terms of the judges of the Virginia Supreme Court who had been appointed by Governor Cameron's predecessor expired in January, and Cameron appointed judges of the Readjuster persuasion in their places. Shortly thereafter, the "new" board appealed to the Virginia Supreme Court for a writ of mandamus allowing them to seize the college and occupy seats on the Board of Visitors.[29] An unexpectedly heavy workload for the Supreme Court delayed their hearing the case until March. Much to everyone's surprise, in April the Readjuster judges handed down a decision shaped by the code of law rather than politics.[30] Dooley and his colleagues were vindicated, and their seats on the board were saved. Dooley served on the MCV board for another six years before voluntarily retiring. He never lost interest in the Medical College.

Throughout the months consumed by the MCV debacle, the Richmond and Danville Extension Company continued its work on the Georgia Pacific, and its progress alerted the Dooley, Bryan, and Logan partnership to other investment possibilities. Their new railroad would cut through the Black Warrior Coal Fields of northern Alabama on its way from Atlanta through Birmingham to the Texas border. In 1882 the Richmond partners hired William Henry Ruffner, a noted Virginia geologist, to survey the area in Alabama between Atlanta and Birmingham and recommend the best route for the Georgia Pacific through the coal and other mineral resources there.[31] In light of Ruffner's findings, the syndicate asked the Extension Company's general manager, John W. Johnston—formerly of the James River and Kanawha Canal Company and the Buchanan and Clifton Forge Railway—to purchase more than the minimal amount of land needed for the Georgia Pacific right-of-way.[32] The partners planned to create new industries along the railway and build housing for workers in those industries. As the work moved westward from Atlanta to Birmingham through what was essentially wilderness in northern Alabama, Johnston purchased additional land in promising locations. His real estate purchases were astute, and before long he had acquired choice parcels. Other Richmonders began investing in northern Alabama as well. Some, like John Patteson Branch and his father, had previously been members of the syndicate. Among the new investors were James B. Pace (who lived a block away from the Dooleys and was thought to be Richmond's richest man, worth at least $2 million) and E. D. Christian, a tobacco merchant who was president of the Richmond Paper Manufacturing Company.

Meanwhile Joseph Bryan had taken a seat on the Georgia Pacific Board. In April 1883, his wife, two friends, and his brother joined him for a trip to Atlanta, ostensibly to visit cousins in Georgia. They traveled on a private railroad car attached to a Richmond and Danville train. When they arrived in Atlanta, however, Bryan added executives of the railroad company to his party for a side trip along the Georgia Pacific into Alabama.[33] Bryan also spent a day looking over Birmingham and its iron furnaces—especially the Sloss & DeBardeleben. After passing through the city, he and the men took another, shorter side trip along a spur called the Milner Railroad for a look at some of the Milner mines. After surveying another furnace near Anniston and traveling to the farthest reach of the Georgia Pacific to see the workers laying track, they returned to Atlanta. Bryan was so pleased with what he had seen that on his return to Richmond, he made a report of his findings to the Extension Company board and urged them to purchase the Milner Coal and Railroad Company.[34] By June 1883 the board had changed the name of the Milner operation to the Coalburg Coal and Coke Company, and before long Dooley became a member of its board.[35]

The Richmond partners' investments in Alabama coincided with the 1882 bear raid, which precipitated their loss of controlling interest in the Richmond and Danville and the Terminal, and the beginning of a nationwide recession in the mid-1880s that slowed railroad and industrial development in Alabama. The Extension Company kept working on the Georgia Pacific, however, and by November 1883 had completed the work on an 800-foot-long trestle and an 810-foot-long tunnel between Atlanta and Birmingham. Seven months later, however, the work stopped before reaching Coalburg. Mines were shut down, and proposed blast furnaces remained unbuilt.[36]

By the spring of 1884 the hegemony of Richmond in the Richmond and Danville seemed to be over for good, but then a serious financial panic hit Wall Street. As profits and dividends fell, speculators lost interest in the Danville and the Terminal. In Virginia, the Richmond syndicate went to work in an effort to regain control of the Danville and the Terminal. In March 1886, Dooley and Logan were quietly buying back Danville and Terminal stock. For the rest of the year, Logan was in frequent contact with John D. Rockefeller to keep him fully informed of opportunities to buy and the prices he would have to pay, especially for the Richmond and Danville stock, when it was available.[37] On July 7 he wrote to Rockefeller: "Our people continue to buy the R & D stock. . . . You will observe that I have been entirely correct so far about this stock and if you will be guided by my judgment now and take 500 more, you will never have cause to regret it and besides making a hand-some profit on it as a permanent investment you will aid by your co-operation in what we propose doing to make large profits on our Terminal holdings."[38]

In the fall of 1886, Logan and Dooley also enlisted the help of James B. Pace, who had joined them in their Alabama ventures. Pace bought a thousand shares of the Danville. In an October 30 letter to Rockefeller, Logan reported, "In regard to the Richmond and Danville, I am pleased to report that I have increased my Richmond party by the acquisition of Mr. J. B. Pace, who is now the strongest man financially we have in Virginia."[39] A November 16, 1886, Logan memorandum explained what they planned to do once they controlled the Richmond and Danville and the Terminal: "We have organized a party . . . to buy 25,000 shares and then consolidate both of the properties making one stock for the whole system."[40]

Fortunately for the success of the takeover plan, and for the iron industry in Alabama, in late October Dooley, Pace, and Christian took a trip to Alabama together.[41] On October 31, they left on a private railroad car for a trip to Birmingham that lasted almost a week. While there, they inspected the nine hundred acres north of Birmingham targeted for development by their North Birmingham Land Company, for which John W. Johnston had filed incorporation papers on their behalf on October 1.[42] By January 1887, Dooley, Pace, and Christian had organized the North Highland Land Company, the North Birmingham Building Association, and the North Birmingham Street Railway Company to build a connection between the center of Birmingham and the northern edge of the suburb they were planning to develop.

When Dooley, Pace, and Christian arrived in Birmingham, they learned that a new invention for making steel was expected to transform the iron industry in Alabama. The process removed the phosphorus from the kind of iron ore mined in Alabama, which until then had prevented it from being used in making steel. The trio also discovered that the Sloss Furnace Company in Birmingham had just forged an agreement with the inventor, and that John W. Johnston was negotiating an option to buy Sloss Furnace. Within two weeks of Dooley, Pace, and Christian's return to Richmond, Johnston had secured a charter for the company that gave it a new name: Sloss Iron and Steel Company. Pace and Christian each bought 1,500 shares of Sloss Iron and Steel when its books opened.[43] Other Richmonders also bought large blocs of the initial offering of the stock, and a Birmingham newspaper trumpeted the news with the headline "Millions More of Good Hard Cash

Brought to Birmingham."[44] Dooley, however, waited until the following summer before purchasing, and then bought only 268 shares.[45]

Richmonders' investments in Alabama were big news in early 1887. On January 8, identical articles about them appeared in the *Dispatch* and the *Richmond Times*. Only their headlines were different. The *Dispatch* headline stated simply, "Richmond Capital for Alabama," but the *Times* rhapsodized, "Blooming Birmingham: Industrial Companies Organized by Richmond Capitalists." Their articles reported that 25 percent of the stock was owned by Richmond men and 55 percent was controlled by the Richmond syndicate. Both articles wrongly identified Dooley as one of the investors—he wouldn't invest there until the following summer—but the articles were correct in noting that a very small group of Richmond men had succeeded in encouraging one another to make an investment that was central to the industrialization of the Lower South. David Lewis, a later historian of the Sloss companies, notes that only a small number of northern financiers invested in Sloss Iron and Steel; almost all the investors were Virginians.[46]

Dooley's delay before buying Sloss Iron and Steel Company stock seems to have been prompted, at least in part, by devotion to his wife. No matter how busy he was, giving Sallie whatever she wanted was one of the prime motivations in his life. Three days before he left for Alabama with Pace and Christian, he had signed a deed to buy a farm in Henrico County just west of Richmond's city limits. Years later Dooley recalled that he and Sallie had found the farm while out horseback riding and "were greatly struck with the beauty of the views of the River and the beautiful oaks that were on the slope of that hill. Mrs. Dooley fell in love with the place, and begged me to buy it and give it to her for a home."[47] The property encompassed large orchards, vineyards, gardens, a house, a number of farm buildings, a pure water spring, and, next to the canal and the railroad tracks, three quarries, one still working. It had been described as "one of the most beautiful" farms "in the vicinity of the city."[48] Dooley paid $31,335 for the farm, making a down payment of $6,424 and taking out a mortgage for $24,911 to be paid in three installments six, twelve, and eighteen months later.[49]

A month after Dooley's purchase of the property, the Richmond syndicate succeeded in reacquiring the Richmond and Danville. On November 20 the *Dispatch* reported that "the movement in Richmond and West Point Terminal which has engrossed the attention of Wall [S]treet throughout the week, developed into a genuine sensation to-day." The paper noted that the purchase of the Danville by the Terminal also guaranteed "the unification of the entire system 2,700 miles of track and avoids the disintegration, which was feared and about which there was some danger." The Richmond business community was overjoyed, for as the paper put it, "the system penetrates a territory the trade of which is of inestimable value to Richmond and the knowledge that men having the interest of the city deeply at heart are . . . in position to influence the policy of the company is a source of great gratification to our merchants especially."[50]

That day the New York correspondent for the *Dispatch* reported: "The Richmond Terminal combination still continues to be an engrossing subject of conversation in railroad and financial circles here. . . . [A]n insider in the deal said to your correspondent to-day that this was but the beginning of a gigantic scheme, the effects of which would be felt widely in southern transportation matters."[51] Not surprisingly, the Terminal stock began to attract speculators once again. The *Dispatch* picked up the story from an article in the *New York Mail and Express* and reprinted it: "The chief interest in the stock market almost up to Thanksgiving-day was the strange and uninterrupted rise in the Richmond and Terminal stock. There is no doubt that during the last two weeks thousands of people have been dealing in Richmond Terminal stock without even knowing whether it is a trunk line or a branch line. . . . To the few initiated stock speculators the real situation is of course known."[52] In the following weeks the work of consolidating the two systems continued unabated and undisturbed by the speculative frenzy spinning around it.

On December 16, the day after a general bear raid in the stock market, the *Dispatch* reported that the Terminal stock suffered a "hammering . . . the preceding afternoon. . . . Richmond and West Point Terminal were not specially singled out, but went the downward way of all the rest. . . . The tremendous decline is credited to Jay Gould and Addison Cammack. . . . Wall [S]treet had not had such a violent shaking up in or out in many years."

Three days before Christmas 1886, a journalist from Atlanta named Henry Grady spoke at the New England Society of New York. He was the first southerner to speak before the society, and his speech would make him famous throughout the country as the spokesman for the New South. Among the themes he touched upon that evening were the necessity for the end of sectional bitterness, the development of mutual understanding between the North and the South, the loyalty of both sections to the nation as a whole, and the growth in the New South of a "diversified industry that meets the complex need of this complex age."[53] Grady was not, however, the only spokesman for the New South on the national scene at that time. A close Dooley friend, who, ironically, was a former general in the Confederate cavalry, was one of the most popular spokesmen of the New South movement.

He was also now the governor of the Virginia, and his name was Fitzhugh Lee. The nephew of Robert E. Lee, he was a graduate of West Point who had served under his uncle as a brigadier general in the Confederate army. After the war he had resolutely turned his eyes toward the future and had become the political embodiment of the ambitions of the New South and the voice of reconciliation with the North. A warm and genial man, he was immensely popular on both sides of the Mason-Dixon Line—so much so that Grover Cleveland was considering him as a possible running mate in his race for a second term in the White House.[54] Lee was also a man of action who participated in building the "diversified industry" in the South of which Grady so eloquently spoke. In January 1887, however, well aware of the political implications of his doing so, he led a group of Virginia businessmen on an investment trip to territory not in the South but in the North. Dooley had planned to go on that trip.

G overnor Lee and his companions were scheduled to depart for Washington on January 23, but when the group gathered at the railroad depot early that morning, two of the men were missing. One of them was the governor himself, who had spent the previous evening having dinner at the White House with President and Mrs. Cleveland. He would join the group in Washington when they changed trains for Chicago. The other missing man was Dooley. He and Sallie were in deep mourning for her father, the retired Lunenberg County physician Henry May, who had died suddenly the day after Christmas. Dooley sent Sallie's nephew Roger Atkinson in his place. Traveling with Roger were the banker and financier John Patteson Branch and his son Blythe; the lawyers Joseph Bryan and Thomas Nelson Page, the latter of whom was just beginning to gain renown as the author of nostalgic Lost Cause tales of the Old South; and the former lieutenant governor John Marye. Also in the party was George J. Rogers, a new addition to Dooley's office staff and a cousin of Sallie's from Petersburg. Rogers, a Confederate veteran who had been disabled by a wound to his throat during the war, was to serve as Dooley's secretary and bookkeeper for many years.[1]

Their final destination was St. Paul, Minnesota, where one of Dooley's newest businesses, the Richmond and St. Paul Land and Improvement Company, was to be chartered. The company had been featured in the "Local Brevities" column of the Sunday, January 7, *Richmond Times,* which reported: "The last share of stock in the Richmond and St. Paul Land Company was yesterday subscribed for, making a total subscription of $500,000. . . . [T]he company is principally organized to purchase St. Paul real estate." St. Paul was a growing metropolis that for some time had been jockeying with Chicago to become the center of commercial life in what was then called the Northwest and the nexus for all railroad travel in that region and westward. By December 1886, St. Paul claimed to have outdistanced its Illinois rival. According to a Christmas Day article in the *St. Paul Globe:* "The railroad center is fast building up at St. Paul. There is not a prominent road in the West that is not headed for St. Paul or will be eventually."[2]

Since developing railroad connections from Richmond to the Pacific was one of their goals, Dooley and his associates had begun to look at St. Paul as the place for such a connection. Dooley, perhaps more than the others, was also interested in real estate investment there. He had seen Chicago develop as his father had predicted it would, and he had absorbed his father's lessons on what to look for when analyzing potential for commercial and residential growth. St. Paul seemed to measure up under his scrutiny, so he persuaded his associates to invest in real estate there on a large scale. Their success in Alabama may have colored their judgment. Nevertheless, they decided the time was right to move northward.

Governor Lee and the Richmonders boarded a train for Chicago, where they spent the night and then transferred to a train for St. Paul. Their arrival—in the midst of the city's Winter Carnival—had been eagerly anticipated. An article in the *St. Paul Globe* hailed Governor Lee as the epitome of the New South and the rest of the men as "Richmond excursionists," reporting that they were in town for the purpose of "enjoying the carnival and looking after their investments."[3] It marveled at the "wealth and energy" that was coming from the South, "a section which is popularly supposed to be lacking in both," and added that the "gentlemen who accompany the governor . . . are . . . the embodiment of as much enterprise, as can be found [in] any city in the Union."[4] Somehow the *Globe* missed the fact that one of the "Richmond excursionists" was not from Richmond. He was Maj. Richard Venable, a keen-eyed but quiet man from Baltimore with whom the Richmonders often consulted when investment opportunities arose.

During their weeklong visit, Lee and his companions took in the Winter Carnival, where they went tobogganing and rode in a great boat-shaped sleigh called the Nightingale. They attended a performance at the St. Paul opera house and were guests at numerous dinners, as well as a banquet for a hundred given by two of the city's most prominent men's clubs—the Magnolia Club, comprised of expatriate southerners, and the Possum Club, a group of railroad executives who really did eat possum at their annual banquets. Among the railroad men at the banquet that night was the railroad titan J. J. Hill, who lent the visitors his private railroad car for side trips to Minneapolis and Duluth.[5] In Minneapolis an expatriate Virginian named P. B. Winston hosted a dinner in their honor, at which other guests included the three Pillsburys (Charles; his father, John; and his uncle, George), whose flour mills were already famous. They also attended a meeting of the St. Paul Chamber of Commerce, where Governor Lee spoke. None of these events, however, prevented them from carrying out their main mission. On Monday, January 24, 1887, they filed the incorporation papers for the Richmond and

St. Paul Land and Improvement Company, whose president and treasurer was their missing partner, James Henry Dooley.[6]

The coverage in the Minnesota press suggested that the Virginians' visit was a political success, and the courtesy J. J. Hill extended to them seemed a possible first step in developing a northern railroad connection between Richmond manufacturers and markets in the Far West that would parallel the Richmond and West Point Terminal system's southern route. That had already reached the Texas border, and the Richmonders had begun working toward connecting it with railroad systems farther west.

In Minnesota, however, they ran into problems. Their investment approach there differed from the one they had adopted in Alabama, where Bryan had taken a trip to visit his cousins in Georgia and entered the state quietly. He and the other Richmonders were building bridges and tunnels for their railroad before the real estate boom began; in fact, they helped create it. In Minnesota they had arrived with great fanfare and also invested in real estate long after the boom had begun. As Major Venable told a reporter for the *Baltimore Sun* after the group returned, there were warning signs. Real estate prices had risen between 300 and 400 percent in the previous two or three years, and it was impossible to predict whether the boom was over. Nonetheless he felt certain that St. Paul and Minneapolis were so close together that they were destined eventually to "become one of the greatest aggregations of city population in the west."[7]

It didn't take long for the Richmond men to realize that other problems would impede the success of their company as well. One of their first hints that trouble might lie ahead came from Fred Scott's son John, who went to work on a commission basis selling parcels of their property for the McClung, McMurran, & Curry firm in St. Paul, which acted as their agent there. John wrote to his father in late 1887 complaining that McMurran was not paying the commissions due him from the sales he made.[8] Other problems continued to pop up. Sales were slow. In the summer of 1888, Joseph Bryan wrote to Dooley that the lackluster performance of the Richmond and St. Paul Land and Improvement Company was of serious concern. As he put it in that letter, "There has been great restlessness and suspicion on the part of some of these stockholders, the latter, course, unmerited and the former uncontrolled."[9] Dissatisfaction with the return on investment was still apparent two years later, when an editorial in the *State* noted: "There never was a summer perhaps when the Richmond . . . real estate market was stronger than now. . . . [I]f the big money sent from Richmond to St. Paul, Minneapolis, and Birmingham had been invested at home, better profits should have been realized."[10]

In the summer of 1888, the Dooleys decided to take their vacation in the Far West. Sallie, who had always loved mountain scenery, was eager to visit the areas around Yosemite in California and Yellowstone in Wyoming, the latter of which had become the first national park in 1872. As always, their vacation was destined to be a working vacation. Dooley was eager to visit San Francisco, where connections for shipping Richmond manufacturing goods to the Far East were readily available.

They crossed the country by train and by mid-June were staying at the Palace Hotel in San Francisco.[11] Along the way Dooley and Bryan corresponded, with Bryan's letters full of details about progress in their real estate business in Richmond and Dooley's full of accounts of the adventures and misadventures he and Sallie were having out west. The couple traveled from San Francisco to Yosemite by train and stagecoach—a strenuous journey over rocky and perilous terrain. Sallie, Jim reported, had been thrilled by their visit to Yosemite Valley but also apparently frightened by some of the geological wonders they had to cross. Bryan replied that he was "glad that Mrs. Dooley's prayers were answered amid the perils of Yosemite. I shall await with much pleasure a personal recital from both of you of your experiences."

From Yosemite the Dooleys traveled to Yellowstone and visited the geysers before starting their return trip, with a stop in St. Paul in late July. Bryan was particularly interested in the work Dooley planned to do there. On July 12 he wrote, "While in St. Paul please do not fail to look closely into all our interests; not merely the Richmond and S. [sic] Paul Land Co. of which you are *facile princeps* as far as the Richmond parties are concerned, but into our St. Anthony Park, Lake Park, Excelsior Park interests." Bryan was now eagerly awaiting Dooley's return to the world of business and, in a July 23 letter, expressed the wish that "you are refreshed, as a giant from his sleep, and ready to tackle the real estate business in St. Paul."

Apparently real estate was not the only business Dooley conducted while in St. Paul. He also seems to have investigated the Seattle, Lake Shore and Eastern Construction Company, created to build a railroad that would run eastward from Seattle along the border between Canada and the United States and connect with one of the railroads running westward from St. Paul. In 1885 a group of Seattle businessmen had pooled their funds and started the company, but by 1888 they faced bankruptcy and were willing to sell. Acquiring the business seemed to Dooley an essential step toward a transcontinental connection for Richmond.

Dooley, Logan, and Bryan bought thirty thousand shares of the construction company, with the intention of completing the road and developing industries along its path. Once again, as they had in Alabama, they commissioned W. H. Ruffner to do a geological survey of the region through which the railroad would run. By 1889 Ruffner had produced *A Report on Washington Territory,* a book more than 238 pages long. The Seattle and Lake Shore Railway published it in New York, where its new owners hoped it would attract investors to finance the coal mines, quarries, and lumber companies needed to exploit the rich natural resources Ruffner found while completing his survey.[12] Dooley's copy remains on a shelf in his Maymont mansion library.

The bold but risky move out of the South into the real estate and railroad construction businesses in the Northwest was not the only new venture Dooley undertook that summer. His next one catapulted him into the exciting and completely unfamiliar field of communications. Even before Dooley had arrived in St. Paul, Logan had contacted him about investing in a newly invented device called the telautograph. It was the prototype of what later generations would call the fax machine. Logan wanted to organize a corporation to manufacture and market the new invention, and by mid-July he had contacted not only Dooley but several other potential investors as well. This time most of them were not southerners. Instead, some of them were from the West—places like Chicago and St. Louis—others from New England, several from Washington, D.C., and a couple from New York.[13] In fact, at this early stage Dooley and Logan were the only Virginians.

The new venture had its beginning in a laboratory in Highland Park, Illinois, not far from Chicago. While the Dooleys were on their way home from their western vacation, they apparently stopped for a day or two in Highland Park so Dooley could visit the laboratory and discuss business opportunities with Elisha Gray, a well-known inventor with many patents to his credit. A month earlier, Gray had submitted a patent application for the telautograph, which was granted by the U.S. Patent Office on July 31.[14] Ten days before Dooley's visit, Gray and most of the other men Logan had contacted appeared before notaries in their own locales and signed the documents required to apply for a charter for a joint-stock company.

On Monday, August 6, 1888, Dooley, who had barely arrived home, submitted the request for a charter for the Gray National Telautograph Company to Richmond judge B. R. Wellford Jr. of the Circuit Court of Richmond, "*in vacation.*" The urgency felt by the men chartering the company was clear from that phrasing. Judge Wellford's court had been called for special duty. Wellford granted their request, and the *State* reported the news the next day, describing the telautograph's unprecedented ability to transmit "messages or other communications" written out in "ordinary script" as well as drawings and codes over electric, telephone, or telegraph lines. The paper noted that the company's principal office was to be in Richmond.[15]

The next day's *New York Times* essentially reprinted the *State*'s article but added an opening comment that the new invention, "it is believed, will create a stir in the electric and telegraphic world," and an intriguing final remark: "Some of the largest capitalists in the country are said to be interested in the enterprise." That was an understatement. A wealthy New Yorker with a well-deserved reputation as a knowledgeable and sophisticated investor was very interested in Gray National Telautograph. At the time of his death in 1913, J. P. Morgan owned five thousand shares of the company.[16]

Dooley spent very little time at home before heading north again. Two days after he had succeeded in obtaining the charter for the telautograph company, he was in New York City. Before long a reporter for the *New York Star* approached him for an interview that appeared in its "Comment of the Street" column on August 9 under the headline "What a Southern Capitalist Thinks of the Results of Grover Cleveland's Administration."[17] Dooley was introduced as one of "the prominent Southern men on Wall [S]treet [and] one of the leading lawyers and capitalists of Richmond, Va." The ostensible subject of the article was Dooley's opinion of the Cleveland administration, but the interview also enlarged upon the "general prosperity of the South" and the business health of Richmond in particular. Dooley told the interviewer that although Richmond "for many years had a hard struggle for a bare existence," it was "for the first time since 1865 . . . enjoying something that might be called a boom." He proudly alluded to the city's "fourteen miles of electric street railway . . . the finest street car service in the whole world" and added that real estate values in the suburbs had jumped "100 to 300 per cent during the past two years." Mentioning business opportunities in Durham, Atlanta, Birmingham, Bessemer, Anniston, Asheville, and Chattanooga, he stated categorically that "if there is any depression of business in any part of the United States it certainly does not exist in the South." In speaking of the growing industrialization of the South, Dooley declared that it was "revolutionizing our economic and, to some extent, our social conditions." News of the Dooley interview may have reached Richmond before he did. The day after it appeared in New York, the *Richmond Times* quoted it in full on its front page.[18]

Investments in railroads in the Far Northwest, real estate in Minnesota, and manufacturing in Illinois were not to be Dooley's only business forays in the year that followed. He and Joseph Bryan, who for some time had been pooling funds to purchase scattered pieces of property on the western edge of Richmond, decided the time was right to ask some of their associates in the railroad and technology spheres to join them in establishing a local real estate company. They named this venture the West-End Land and Improvement Company. The day after it was granted a charter on February 26, 1889, the front page of the *Dispatch* announced the news under the headline "A Million Dollar Improvement Company Organized," reporting that "one of the directors intimated yesterday afternoon that the company will erect small houses as homes for families of small means. . . . The organization is probably the largest and most wealthy one of its kind in the state."

Sometime in the spring, the Dooleys—now entering their late forties—took a step Jim's parents had taken at approximately the same age. They decided to have their portraits painted. They commissioned the painter William Garl Brown Jr., who was well known throughout the South for his portraits, to do the work. Brown had opened a studio in Richmond in 1880, and not only the Dooleys but many of the city's business leaders and members of prominent families commissioned him to paint their portraits.[19] Both Dooley portraits now hang in the Maymont mansion front hall.

In the second half of the 1880s, Dooley took under his wing a promising young man in his early twenties named John Skelton Williams. The oldest son of the banker and broker John L. Williams, he was the compiler of guides to southern investments called *A Manual of Investments: Important Facts and Figures Regarding Southern Investment Securities,* published by his father's firm. Over six feet tall, thin, and very hardworking, Williams, according to the historian Douglas Southall Freeman, could be found day and night "on a high stool in a basement office on Main street . . . patiently . . . [making] his way through hundreds of financial reports issued by Southern corporations. . . . [He] seldom left his desk in daylight-hours and at night he came back to it and stayed, till Main street was silent and he could hear the police signal to one another, from Seventh street to the Old Market, by beating on the pavement with their night-sticks."[20] He was just the kind of young man Dooley liked to encourage.

Among the companies Williams noted with special interest in the 1888 *Manual* were the railroads of the Seaboard Air Line System and a construction firm called the Maritime Canal Company of Nicaragua. The Seaboard System at that time included a growing number of small, independent railroad companies loosely connected by friendly agreements to cooperate in transporting passengers and shipping freight. Of the Seaboard, Williams wrote, "Upon the completion, this System will, with its direct line from Chesapeake Bay to Atlanta, in the heart of the South, become one of the most valuable and important of the Southern Trunk Lines."[21] Within a year Dooley and John Skelton Williams had begun investing in the Seaboard.

Williams devoted four pages of the 1888 *Manual of Investments* to commentary on the proposed Nicaragua Canal Company, then under consideration by Congress. The bill had passed the Senate by the time the *Manual* was published but had not yet come up for a vote in the House. In his final paragraph on the topic, Williams commented that "should the bill become a law . . . it is possible to see, even now that . . . the Canal when opened will have a value immeasurably beyond that of the average business enterprise, with a future of steady and certain growth."[22]

By the time Williams was writing about the Nicaragua Canal Company in the 1889–90 *Manual,* a number of Richmonders, including his father, had already begun investing in its construction arm. Among them were Joseph Bryan, Col. William H. Palmer, and Robert A. Lancaster Sr., all Dooley business associates.[23] Richmond newspapers featured articles on Nicaragua, and the *Richmond Times* deemed the canal's construction to be of "immense importance . . . to the South."[24]

Meanwhile, John Skelton Williams and Dooley continued to acquire stock in the Seaboard and other railroads that fed into it. By 1892 the Seaboard had reached Atlanta, and by 1893 Dooley and Williams and their associates were well on their way to acquiring enough stock to control the company. They hoped to extend its reach to the Gulf coast of Florida and from there by water to the Nicaragua Canal.

In the background during those years, pursuit of the capital needed to build the manufacturing headquarters for the Gray National Telautograph Company also occupied the efforts of the company's founders, Dooley and Logan, and their board of directors. Finding investors was increasingly difficult. Although the United States economy was flourishing in 1888, by 1892 first the South and then the rest of the country had slipped into an economic downturn and what would become the Panic of 1893.

Meanwhile, the telautograph made its first appearance in Richmond at the Logan household, and probably at the Dooleys' as well. One of the Logans' daughters later wrote that she and her siblings "were delighted when two test machines were set up in their home and they could write from room to room."[25]

In late November 1889, notices in the *Dispatch* announced that the first annual meeting of the Telautograph stockholders was to be held at noon on December 3, in one of the rooms of Dooley's office on the second floor of 1103 East Main.[26] There is no public record of what transpired at the meeting, but the company was preparing to face not only financial but also legal hurdles in the near future.

CHAPTER 17 | More New Ventures

W hile her husband and his partners were deeply involved in their enterprises in Alabama, Minnesota, and the Far West, Sallie Dooley was becoming active in the historic preservation movement then sweeping the country. In 1889 she joined the newly organized Association for the Preservation of Virginia Antiquities, familiarly known as the APVA, and served on committees for its fund-raising balls.[1] Before long she would be invited to be a founder of two more organization dedicated to historic preservation.

In 1891 Sallie accepted an invitation to become the founding regent of Virginia's first chapter of the Daughters of the American Revolution (DAR). It was only the seventh chapter in the nation, and Sallie was invited to choose a name for it. She decided to call it the Old Dominion Chapter.[2] Membership was restricted to women who could provide proof that an ancestor had fought in the American Revolution. According to an 1891 article in the *Richmond Times,* the purpose of the organization was to honor the memory of those who had fought in the Revolution by acquiring and protecting historic places; erecting monuments; encouraging and publishing research about the Revolutionary period; preserving documents, relics, and service records of Revolutionary soldiers; and promoting celebrations of patriotic anniversaries.[3] On January 25, 1892, Sallie presided over the inaugural meeting of the Old Dominion Chapter in her parlor at 212 West Franklin Street. She appointed the officers and board members and must have been gratified when Jim agreed to serve as legal advisor.[4] She appointed a committee to draft bylaws for the chapter and announced the names of twenty-one women applying for membership. Eighteen-year-old Ellen Glasgow, a debutante who would go on to become a Pulitzer Prize–winning novelist, was among the applicants. Among the other "charter and organizing" members of the Old Dominion Chapter was Mary Virginia Hawes Terhune, a prolific writer well known throughout the country by her pen name, Marion Harland. Terhune had been living in New Jersey since her marriage in 1856, but her roots were in Virginia. She still had family in Richmond and visited often. A third literary personage at the meeting that day was Mary Newton Stanard, who several decades later would publish a social history of the city, *Richmond: Its People and Story,* as well as a number of other works.[5] By the end of that first meeting the women had agreed on their first project: raising funds for the Virginia Historical Society, which was then in the process of transforming a Franklin Street house into its headquarters. By April, membership in the Old Dominion Chapter of the DAR had reached fifty-one.[6]

A year later Sallie became one of the thirteen founding members of another exclusive women's organization, this one restricting membership to descent from a "worthy" ancestor who had lived in an American colony prior to 1750.[7] Sallie agreed to serve on its board of managers and also proposed other women for membership—among them her friend and distant relative Sally Nelson Robins, who, like Sallie, descended from the colonial governor Sir Dudley Diggs. Thanks in part to her efforts, by the end of its first year there were forty-five members in the Virginia Society of the Colonial Dames.

Sallie was not the only member of the family to be involved in the founding of new social organizations. In 1890, Dooley and Joseph Bryan were among the 130 men who attended an organizational meeting for a new gentlemen's club in the city. Another such club hardly seemed necessary: there were already two well-established ones, the Richmond Club and the Westmoreland Club. Barely thirteen years earlier, Dooley, a founder of the latter, had introduced the legislation to charter it. The proposal for a new club sprang largely from the economic boom Richmond was then enjoying, and served as a gauge of just how prosperous the city had become during the twenty-five years since the Evacuation Fire. Many younger, newly well-to-do business and professional men in the city aspired to the comforts only a gentlemen's club could provide, but the clubhouses of the older clubs were too small to accommodate a large number of new members.

Bryan and Dooley were elected to serve on the fifteen-member board of directors for the new club. Dooley was named chair of the finance committee,[8] and the first meeting of the board was held on January 5 in his office.[9] Among several names proposed for the new organization were the "West-End Club" and the "Lee Club," but in the end the "Commonwealth Club" was chosen and remains the name today, well into the twenty-first century.

During the winter of 1890, the Dooleys conferred frequently with the young architect Edgerton Rogers about what he referred to as their "suburban villa," the fashionable Richardson Romanesque mansion he was designing for the top of the hill on their property in Henrico County. According to their ledger book, they broke ground for the dwelling in June.[10] They spent the next three years watching it being built. Even before the excavation began, Dooley had overseen the layout of the double roadways of the driveway. He had magnolia trees planted between them and elm trees planted along each side. The trees were the first new trees of what would become a renowned private arboretum.

Dooley's business connections in New York led that year to his being elected to another gentlemen's club, this one the Manhattan Club in New York City. He was not the only nonresident member of the club from Richmond.[11] Thomas Logan had been elected to membership in 1886; Joseph Bryan, the previous December; and several other Richmonders, in 1890. Membership in the Manhattan Club gave the Virginians additional opportunities to promote Richmond's interests while socializing with both New York resident members and nonresidents from other parts of the country. Years later Dooley would also join New York's University Club, to which he would be elected in 1911.[12]

In addition to promoting Richmond in distant places, Dooley continued to play a prominent part in local efforts to promote the city. He was, for instance, one of the speakers in a series of monthly public meetings organized in 1890 by the Richmond Chamber of Commerce to encourage "more concentrated effort in developing and building up the city." In his talk Dooley pointed out that Richmond would benefit if the railroads serving the city built new passenger depots and if the city appropriated more money for necessary street repairs.[13] He asserted that poorly maintained streets prevented the city from growing. Dooley felt so strongly about the need for street improvements that a year and a half later, in the midst of pressing financial problems in the Terminal system, he took time to submit a proposal to the city council for a way to fund them. Called the "Dooley Bill," it advocated authorizing "the city of Richmond to Impose Special Taxes for Street Improvements and to issue 4 Per Cent Bonds."[14] To his dismay, despite strong support on the editorial page of the *Richmond Times* and from some members of the city council, adding new taxes was not popular with most of the councilmen or their constituents, and his proposal was not adopted.[15]

In his speech at the Chamber of Commerce that evening in 1890, Dooley was also frank in his criticism of the city government for not annexing territory from the surrounding counties. He accused the city government of surrounding Richmond with what he referred to as a "Chinese wall." Years later Dooley came to rue the day he advocated annexation, but at the time he was vehemently in its favor, declaring: "I was always a 'bull' on Richmond. The first money I ever made I invested, as they say out west, 'in Richmond dirt.' I have been investing in it ever since, and I have never had cause to repent of my judgment."

By 1890, he was also investing in the "dirt" of another place in Virginia.

He had begun buying large pieces of property near the little resort town of West Point sometime around 1887, when he became the president of the Richmond and West Point Land, Navigation, and Improvement Company.[16] Some of Dooley's purchases there provided the land needed for extending the Richmond and West Point Terminal Railway and Warehouse Company's buildings and docks; some of it was slated to be divided into residential lots; and several parcels on the eastern end of the peninsula were designated for a hotel.

On July 19, 1890, Dooley and several of his associates were the subject of front-page articles in both the *New York Times* and the *Washington Post.* Under the headline "At a Million Profit Several Richmond Gentlemen Enriched by a Railroad Venture," the *Post* reported that "the most successful railroad deal ever made by Richmond men has just been consummated, and Gen. T. M. Logan and Messrs. James B. Pace, E. D. Christian, and James H. Dooley are thereby much the richer." The *Times* article (alluringly entitled "A Fortune without Effort: Virginia Capitalists Said to Have Cleared a Million") attributed the Richmonders' coup to their 1888 investment in the Seattle, Lake Shore and Eastern Railway. The dramatic tone of the *Post* and *Times* articles contrasted with the matter-of-fact coverage given by the *Richmond State,* which had been following the story ever since they had bought their Seattle and Lake Shore stock. Under the title "Richmond Capitalists: They Build and Sell a Railroad and Make a Fine Profit," the *State* commented mildly, "This Richmond capital coming back home with big results cannot but be beneficial to the city."[17]

All three papers missed or ignored at least two dimensions of the story. The men had sold the Seattle and Lake Shore because their attempt to connect their city with the Pacific coast had become too costly. Despite publishing Ruffner's *Report on Washington Territory* in New York, they had apparently not yet attracted the investors they needed to continue building the railroad. They had also underestimated the effort and expense imposed by the inhospitable climate and mountainous terrain. By 1890, they had built only 140 miles of railroad from Seattle and were under contract to build only 84 more.[18] That was far short of what was necessary to connect the Seattle and Lake Shore with a railroad coming toward it from the east. In the end, they sold their thirty thousand shares to the Oregon Trans-continental Company, an arm of the Northern Pacific.

Six months after their supposed triumph out west was announced, the 1891 New Year's Day issue of the *Dispatch* featured an article on Virginia's railroads by John Skelton Williams entitled "A Fine Showing[,] Wonderful Development of Virginia by Her Railroads." Williams reported admiringly that the Richmond Terminal, which controlled 8,053 miles of railroad and 500 miles of "water lines," was the second-largest system in the United States—411 miles shorter than the Atchison, Topeka, and Santa Fe and 525 miles longer than the Union Pacific. Apparently he wasn't aware at the time that in spite of, or perhaps because of, its great size, the Terminal was having financial and management problems. By then, the Terminal system controlled more than thirty railroads in the southern states as well as a number of steamship lines. The management of those companies was left mostly in local hands, which meant costly overlap of management structures. Signs of the trouble became obvious the following August when the Terminal had to borrow money to meet its obligations to bondholders. One of the banks lending the necessary money was Drexel, Morgan & Company, which was said to have furnished somewhere between one hundred thousand and five hundred thousand dollars.[19]

The Terminal problems suggest that Dooley could not have enjoyed much of 1891 or most of the year that followed. As the *State* noted in its December 8 account of the annual meeting of the Terminal, there was an "organized attack" on the company during 1891. Jay Gould, thought to have been behind the attack, and his son George J. had come on the board. Terminal stock was at its lowest in the history of the company.[20] Bankruptcy seemed to be hovering on the horizon.[21]

At about the same time, Dooley was asked to serve on a committee investigating a possible scandal in the insurance industry. The president of the New York Life Insurance Company, who was at the time the highest-paid corporation executive in the country, had been charged with gross mismanagement and illegal financial dealing. Dooley had a hefty life insurance policy with New York Life, a mutual insurance company with an excellent reputation nationally. Its policyholders viewed their policies and annual dividends as important parts of their financial portfolios. Many, however, if not most of them, including Dooley, had noticed over the preceding two or three years that although the company's annual reports claimed a vigorous increase in value, policyholders' dividends had been shrinking alarmingly. Then, in June 1891, the *New York Times* published the first story of a series exposing a scandal in the New York Life executive suite. The *Times* reported that, three years earlier, the cashier of the company, a twenty-year employee named Theodore Banta, had charged the president and several trustees with gross mismanagement and illegal financial dealings and had asked the board of trustees of the company to investigate. The trustees had formed a committee to do so, but instead of acting to clean up the matter, they had tried to force Banta to with-draw his charges.[22] They did not, however, fire him or ask him to resign, and the matter was hushed up.

By the summer of 1891, Banta felt compelled by fiduciary responsibility to make his charges public and wrote a letter to the editor of the *New York Times* outlining his charges. On August 28 the *Times* published the letter on its front page, and New York Life president William H. Beers fired Banta. Policyholders and insurance agents across the United States called for an in-vestigation of Banta's charges, and newspapers and insurance journals picked up the story. By mid-September policyholders across the nation had met and appointed committees to investigate.[23]

Early that fall, Dooley was invited by a New York lawyer, the former Union army general and three-term congressional veteran Henry Slocum, to join a committee of seventy policyholders from around the country to try to clean up the problem at New York Life. Dooley accepted and on November 5 attended the first meeting of the committee at the Windsor Hotel in New York. At the meeting he was appointed to an executive committee charged with examining the issues and protecting the interests of both policyhold-ers and company. By early January the committee found itself the target of mudslinging by New York Life president William Beers, who furiously con-tested the charges in insurance journal articles and advertisements, accusing the committee of representing only their own self-interest and trying to re-organize the company.[24] The *New York Times* defended them, noting that in forming the committee, "great care" had been "exercised in selecting influ-ential men in various parts of the country." After the committee asked for a report from the New York State Insurance Department and the report con-firmed Banta's charge, in February the committee forced Beers to resign and picked his successor.[25]

Even before the New York Life scandal erupted, Dooley was seriously con-cerned with an economic issue facing the entire country, and his concern led to his first-known publication. In July 1890 the U.S. Congress had passed the Sherman Silver Purchase Act, which required the U.S. government to purchase enough silver each year to join gold in backing up its currency, at a rate of sixteen ounces of silver to each ounce of gold. The act grew out of attempts begun in the 1870s to end the post–Civil War currency deflation. The sixteen-to-one ratio caused inflation, a result that especially appealed to farmers in the middle section of the country who borrowed money to buy seed. Inflation enabled borrowers to pay back their loans with cheaper money, but Dooley could see only disaster in the devaluation of American currency in a world where other countries were on the gold standard. He felt strongly enough about the matter in August 1891 to write what was then called an "open letter" to Virginia senator John Daniel, with whom he had worked closely in the past, and send it to the *Richmond Dispatch*. The letter found favor with the editor, who published it on August 30, 1891, but not with Senator Daniel.[26]

Almost a month passed before Daniel responded to Dooley in a letter also published in the *Dispatch* under the long title "Hon. John W. Daniel: He Discusses Major Dooley's Letter on the Currency Question: Legal Tender for Debts, Congress Has Full and Complete Power to Control the Subject; No Surplus of Silver; No Known Accumulated Stock of It in the World."[27] Dooley then replied to Daniel with another letter in the *Times* ("Gold Contracts in Silver: Major Dooley Offers Further Reflections on the Subject; Results from Free Coinage of Silver; Disappointment Awaiting Those Who Rely on Free Silver to Afford Sufficient Currency").[28] Daniel, however, was not convinced by Dooley's arguments and remained firmly in the silver camp. Nevertheless, their exchange generated enough interest to be reprinted in 1892 in a widely distributed twenty-two-page pamphlet entitled *Payment of Gold Contracts in Silver: Correspondence between James H. Dooley and U.S. Senator John W. Daniel.*[29] When Dooley's insistence that adopting the silver standard would have deleterious consequences for the economy of the United States proved prophetic and the country confronted the Panic of 1893, Dooley would be asked to write other essays on economic issues.

Before that, however, Dooley's correspondence with Daniel led to a December 1891 interview in the "Richmond Short Talk" column of the *State*. The interviewer described Dooley as "one of the best financial prognosticators in this country," who could "tell you with almost absolute certainty when business is going to be dull, and he nearly always hits it in predicting flush times."[30] The interviewer quoted Dooley as saying that "next year would be marked by wonderful prosperity [and] people would be free to spend money." If Dooley did make such a rosy prediction, the events of the following year demonstrated just how wrong he could be. Only two months later, a *Richmond Times* article from its New York Bureau reported interstate commerce throughout the South to be "at about as low an ebb as has been known since the war." The writer expressed the hope that a reaction would come soon, opining that "with improved business conditions the value of railroad properties and securities will naturally rise."[31] But they didn't. By 1892 the Terminal was still in serious trouble. All hopes for rising values in railroad properties and securities were quashed when not just the Terminal but even other such behemoths as the C&O and the Atchison, Topeka and Santa Fe went into receivership.

At a Terminal bondholders meeting in Baltimore in mid-May, Dooley was elected one of eight members of a bondholders committee.[32] Rumors circulated on Wall Street that Drexel, Morgan & Company was to be "induced to take hold of the Terminal Company and some of its constituent companies and reorganize them." But the "office" at Drexel, Morgan "said that nothing was known of any such scheme."[33]

Several months earlier, Dooley—worried about imminent financial disaster as he faced the downward spiral of the Terminal and mounting expenses from the construction of his new house in Henrico—had decided to put the house on Franklin Street on the market and to hasten the process by selling it at auction. On February 21 the *Dispatch* reported that Dooleys' "Splendid . . . residence and grounds" at 212 West Franklin had been sold. The new owners paid thirty-five thousand dollars for it, all of which went to Sallie, who had been the sole owner ever since Dooley deeded the property to her in 1884. The Dooleys agreed to grant the new owners possession on May 1, even though their new house wouldn't be ready and they would have to move elsewhere. They decided to go back to a suite in the Ballard House Hotel where they had lived for a while after their wedding, but eventually they moved to the big house on Grace Street owned by the T. G. Peytons and settled in with their old friends for a stay that would last for more than a year.

Meanwhile, Dooley concentrated his efforts on the troubled Richmond and Danville and Terminal systems. Although there was steady buying of Terminal stock, the buyers were not friendly to Richmond interests. A major purchaser was a man named Thomas Fortune Ryan. Originally from Virginia, he had been a speculator on Wall Street for many years. He bought enough stock to take a seat on the Terminal board. From then on, he was Dooley's nemesis.

A week and a half after the sale of the Franklin Street house was announced, and more than a year before the crash that is now remembered as the Panic of 1893, Dooley took a step similar to, but slightly different from, the one he had taken in the 1880s to protect Sallie by deeding that house to her. This time he executed a deed transferring ownership of their new house in Henrico County, still under construction, and the acreage around it to her "in consideration of the sum of Ten thousand Dollars."[34] From that time on, despite maps and articles in the newspapers that identified her husband as its owner, Maymont actually belonged to Sallie. Thanks to the proceeds from the sale of their first house, she would also have the wherewithal to finish the house at Maymont, and perhaps even to furnish it, no matter what happened to her husband. Most importantly, if he failed financially, creditors would have to look elsewhere. The ten thousand dollars from Sallie came at a particularly auspicious time for Dooley, enabling him to cover a purchase he had made at an auction in West Point a little earlier in February. Apparently, despite the gathering financial clouds, he had not been able to resist a bargain.

On Saturday, February 13, he had taken the Richmond and York River train to West Point. He arrived in time for the noon auction of the Terminal Hotel, the town's most glamorous hostelry, which stood on the banks of the York River at the eastern edge of town. The Richmond and West Point Land Navigation and Improvement Company had built, furnished, and sold it a number of years earlier. Since then, the hotel had passed through the hands of two owners, the second of whom, Thomas Henley, was now bankrupt.[35] Henley had bought the two-hundred-room hotel three years earlier for twenty-eight thousand dollars and had lavished money on it.

The auction began promptly, but bidding was slow and did not go on for very long. Henley's debts amounted to more than twelve thousand dollars, but the bidding went no farther than Dooley's offer of nine thousand dollars.[36] By April he had rented the hotel to a management company, and the four-story building's high Victorian towers were soon welcoming tourists who came to West Point by train and steamboat.[37] Conveniently, both conveyances unloaded their passengers at a boardwalk leading directly to the hotel's lobby.

In the midst of all the demands on his time and finances during the early 1890s, Dooley's local real estate ventures must have provided some consolation even though they were not immune to the malaise of 1892. At first, the West-End Land and Improvement Company he and Bryan had established in 1889 had flourished. When the first annual meeting of the company took place at noon on April 2, 1890, in Dooley's office in the Shafer Building at 1103 East Main, the success of its first year prompted the board to resolve "to purchase one thousand shares of the stock from the lowest bidder," in effect increasing the value of the remaining shares.[38]

By May 3, 1891, when their ad appeared in the real estate column of the Sunday paper, they had finished building four ten-room "Queen Anne *cottages.*"[39] A year later, in his April 1892 annual report to stockholders, however, Dooley admitted that the intervening year had been "one of great dullness in the real estate market, not only in and around Richmond, but generally throughout the country. In the South especially we have felt since our last annual meeting the depressing effects of the panic of November, 1890, the

consequent collapse of the land booms and the low price of cotton, resulting from the production of two successive crops unparalleled in the history
of that staple."[40] Despite the general slump in the economy, however, Dooley
could report that the company had on hand assets worth a little over a half
million dollars.

Meanwhile, construction on the house at Maymont continued through
1892, with the Dooleys hoping to move in by November.[41] The house created
such interest in Richmond that the newspapers periodically published bulletins on its progress. In February 1892, the *Times* predicted the house would
be "one of the handsomest in the South."[42] Seven months later, when its elegant stained-glass Tiffany window was installed, an item on the front page
of the October 4 *Times* described the house as "palatial" and the window as
a cathedral window, "one of the finest and most exquisite pieces of art ever
seen in the South." Delays of the sort familiar to anyone who has ever tried
to build a new house, however, made it increasingly clear that the workmen
would not meet the November deadline.

While work on the house continued in 1892, Dooley and his associates confronted the potential loss of their railroad empire, but that was not
Dooley's only problem. Raising the necessary capital to develop their telautograph was another hurdle that he and the officers and board of Gray
National Telautograph Company had to surmount as the economy began its
decline. Even before then, the young company had faced unanticipated expenses that sprang from technological glitches. Elisha Gray filed patent applications for improvements on the telautograph in 1889, 1890, 1892, 1893, and
1894. Not until 1894 did an employee of the company, George S. Tiffany, "as-
signor to the Gray National Telautograph Company, Richmond, Va.," receive
a patent for a commercially viable version.[43]

In addition, by early 1892 the board had realized that their 1888 Richmond
Circuit Court charter could be challenged on the grounds that granting corporate charters was a task reserved for the state legislature. In February 1892
they moved quickly to fend off challenges and succeeded in persuading both
houses of the Virginia legislature to "ratify, confirm, and adopt" the company's 1888 Richmond Circuit Court charter. Virginia Senate Bill No. 299
to that effect was introduced on February 3 and passed on February 8. The
General Assembly concurred on February 15.[44]

Other legal work required on the local level included seeking a city ordinance permitting the establishment of a telautograph exchange in Richmond. Finally, on November 19, 1892, the Richmond City Council approved
an ordinance granting "the right of way along and through the streets of the

city to A. S. Buford and others for the purpose of telautographic and tele-phonic communication."[45] The new names in the long list of Richmonders to whom the ordinance was granted provided evidence that the company had finally managed to meet the charter's requirement of six hundred thousand dollars in stock subscriptions before it could open for business. The ordi-nance gave the company permission "to erect poles in the streets and alleys" of Richmond and to "run wires under James River." In return, the company was required "to furnish telautographic and . . . telephonic exchange service to the city at a special reduction of $10 per annum for each municipal station." Three weeks after the ordinance was published, the Gray National Telauto-graph Company once again held its annual meeting in Richmond.[46] Plans went forward for public demonstrations of the new invention in Richmond, New York, and Chicago, and for transmitting telautograph signals at the 1893 World's Fair.[47]

JOHN DOOLEY,
HAT MANUFACTURER,
AND DEALER IN
CAPS, LADIES' FANCY FURS,
HATTERS' PLUSHES,
TRIMMINGS, MANUFACTURING MATERIALS,
AND ALL GOODS BELONGING TO THE TRADE.

Public attention is called to this SOUTHERN MANUFACTURING ESTABLISHMENT.

In no house, North or South, is there a greater variety or larger stock of GOODS constantly on hand.

This advertisement for John Dooley's company appeared in *Butter's Richmond Directory, 1855*. (The Valentine)

This oil portrait of John Dooley in his office was painted by the artist Peter Baumgras in 1859. (Maymont Mansion, Richmond, Va.)

This 1859 oil portrait of Sarah Dooley and child by Peter Baumgras is a companion to the John Dooley portrait. (Maymont Mansion, Richmond, Va.)

THE AMBULANCE COMMITTEE

The artist William Ludwell Sheppard depicted the Ambulance Committee at work on this Civil War–era carte de visite. (Virginia Historical Society)

Thomas Muldrup Logan and James Dooley were partners for many years in railroad and technology ventures. (Courtesy of Elizabeth P. Scott)

For more than thirty years Joseph Bryan and James Dooley were partners in various enterprises. (Virginia Historical Society)

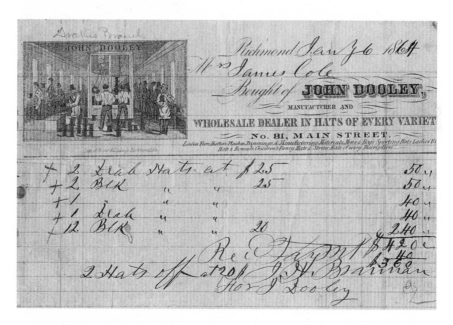

This bill from "John Dooley Manufacturer" for hats purchased in January 1864 features a drawing by an unknown artist of the interior of Dooley's manufacturing building and his employees. (Virginia Historical Society)

Sallie May Dooley was a young married woman in this ca. 1870 photograph. (The Valentine)

James Dooley was a young lawyer when this ca. 1870 photograph was taken. (The Valentine)

James Dooley, who served as president of the Art Club of Richmond for more than thirteen years, gave the building in this photograph to the club in 1908. (Special Collections and Archives, James Branch Cabell Library, VCU Libraries)

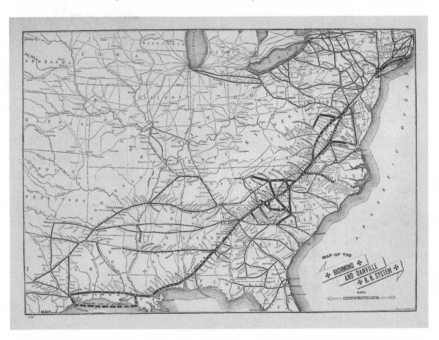

An 1882 map of the Richmond and Danville Railroad. At various times James Dooley served as associate legal counsel, head of the law department, member of the board, and vice president of the company. (Virginia Historical Society)

This sketch of Maymont Mansion by the architect Edgerton S. Rogers was published in the Richmond Chamber of Commerce 1893 booklet *Richmond: The City on the James*. (The Valentine)

An aerial view of Maymont was taken ca. 1930, when the estate was surrounded by open land. (Dementi Studio)

Sallie Dooley gave her friend Mary Newton Stanard permission to publish this photograph of a portion of the Maymont Italian garden in Stanard's 1923 book *Richmond: Its People and Its Story*.

A 1926 photograph of Swannanoa shortly after Sallie Dooley's death. (Library of Virginia)

Dooley's niece Nora Houston is sitting on the far left of the center-row car seat in this 1915 photograph of Equal Suffrage League members demonstrating on Capitol Square. (Virginia Historical Society)

James Dooley's oil portrait painted in 1889 by William Garl Brown Jr. hangs in the front hall of Richmond's Maymont Mansion. (Maymont Mansion, Richmond, Va.)

This 1889 oil portrait of Sallie Dooley by William Garl Brown Jr. hangs across the hall from her husband's in Maymont Mansion. (Maymont Mansion, Richmond, Va.)

Richmond welcomed 1893 with a flurry of parties that seemed to suggest it was blissfully unaware of the economic clouds that had been gathering in the South and the nation as a whole. The mood was buoyant, and the crowning event of January was political. Grover Cleveland had been elected in November to his second term as president of the United States, and Virginia's Democrats, especially the members of Richmond's Cleveland Club, were planning to celebrate by giving a splendid banquet in his honor at the end of the month.

Dooley served on the Reception Committee, headed by the tobacco magnate Lewis Ginter. Joseph Bryan, chairman of the Invitations Committee, sent invitations to Democrats all over the country as well as Virginia. Although President and Mrs. Cleveland were expected almost to the last moment, they did not make the trip down from Washington.

Even so, huge photographs of President Cleveland and Vice President Adlai Stevenson—bedecked with red, white, and blue bunting—greeted the 250 men who did come. The eight o'clock banquet, which the *Dispatch* called a "Virginia Thanksgiving dinner" and featured only Virginia-grown food, took two hours to consume, but the speeches lasted until 1:00 a.m.[1] They touched on issues of concern to Dooley such as tariff reform, the need for a sound currency, and the effect of the Democratic triumph on commerce. A theme that ran through the speeches was the end of sectionalism and the uniting of the country as a whole now that twenty-three years had passed since Virginia had been readmitted to the Union. Nevertheless, everyone at the banquet jumped to their feet and roared when the band played "Dixie."[2]

Dooley may have taken the opportunity that night to discuss the silver question with a number of the Democratic faithful, because an article he wrote on the topic—"Dooley on Finance"—was published in the *State* just five days later.[3] The essay was typical Dooley, who by this time was well known, both locally and nationally, for his cogent explanations of the vicissitudes of the economy. He explained in terms simple enough for the least financially sophisticated reader to understand why he advocated repeal of the Sherman Silver Purchase Act. He asserted that "the effort to restore silver to parity with gold by bulling it against the whole world is a dead failure" and predicted, "If the Sherman law is not repealed . . . we are threatened with a financial revolution which will cast down the United States from the lofty position which she now occupies . . . [to] a monetary level with the second class nations of the world."

The rest of the winter passed swiftly. In addition to overseeing the construction of her new house, Sallie Dooley worked with other members of the Old Dominion Chapter of the Daughters of the American Revolution to raise funds for the new headquarters of the Virginia Historical Society. In February, the chapter produced a play called *Our Boys* that was already a financial success when it opened to a full house at the Academy of Music, with Irene Langhorne (later famous as the Gibson Girl) one of the stars. In March Sallie wrote a letter to Joseph Bryan, president of the Virginia Historical Society, enclosing a check for $821.30—about twenty thousand dollars in today's money. In gratitude, Bryan published her entire letter in his newspaper, the *Times*.[4]

Across the United States, 1893 would be remembered as the year of the Grand Columbian Exposition (as the World's Fair in Chicago was called) and a year of disastrous economic upheaval that would later be called the Panic of 1893. For the Dooleys, it was also the year they finally moved into their splendid new home in Henrico County on the southwestern edge of Richmond. In March 1893, the *State's* "Newsy Notes" columnist reported that workmen were putting the finishing touches on the house,[5] while the *Dispatch* reported in early April that it was "rapidly approaching completion."[6]

The exact date of the move is unknown, but before 1893 was over Sallie declined reelection as regent of the Old Dominion Chapter of the DAR to concentrate her efforts on furnishing the house and working in her new garden. The couple loved the natural beauty spots throughout their hundred acres, and before long Jim hired masons to put in concrete walkways to four especially beautiful places where he had gazebos built, each different from the others. Although the Dooleys were renowned for the parties they gave at their old house on Franklin Street, they held no large affairs at their new one for several years. They did, however, have a steady stream of visitors.

For Dooley, the early months of 1893 were crammed with meetings at which he confronted pressing financial concerns, especially the troubles of the Terminal and the Richmond and Danville Railroad. Just before the Democratic banquet, Virginia-born Thomas Seddon, president of the Sloss Iron and Steel Company in Birmingham, Alabama, arrived in Richmond to consult with Bryan, Dooley, and other Richmonders who had invested heavily in his company.[7] Because the Sloss Steel enterprise was entangled with the

Richmond and Danville and the Terminal, Seddon needed advice on weathering the economic turbulence.

In January a bill of great interest to Dooley and Bryan came up before the House Committee on Interstate and Foreign Commerce. It was the Nicaraguan Canal Bill, upon which the railroads were depending in their quest to extend their reach to the Pacific.[8] Seven years later, in a speech at the banquet celebrating the completion of the Seaboard Air Line, Dooley would characterize the Nicaragua Canal as essential to Richmond's efforts to become a center for international commerce. Meanwhile the French were struggling with a canal they were trying to build in Panama.

On February 2, Dooley and Bryan turned their attention to their current financial challenges when the *Dispatch* published a letter from William Clyde and Thomas Fortune Ryan to Drexel, Morgan & Company, asking them to reorganize the Terminal. The answer didn't come for more than two months, when Drexel, Morgan finally agreed to undertake the reorganization, and the Terminal board announced that the company would begin to receive deposits of stocks and bonds at Drexel, Morgan's office immediately but "in no event later than May 1, 1893."[9] In reorganizing the Terminal, Drexel, Morgan created a new, much shorter railroad system called the Southern Railway, which incorporated the profitable subsidiaries of the Terminal system, appointed as president Samuel Spencer, a well-respected railroad man originally from the South, and spent millions on improvements.[10]

On April 5, Dooley's attention shifted from railroad business to local real estate when he gave his annual report to the stockholders of the West-End Land and Improvement Company. They had gathered for the annual meeting in his comfortable office at 1103 East Main. The year 1892 had been particularly successful for the company, which had sunk almost a half million dollars into its holdings west of Richmond's Boulevard. At the meeting Dooley was reelected president.[11] The report the stockholders heard was printed in full in the *State* the following day, perhaps because Dooley placed his remarks on the health of the company within the context of state and regional economics.[12] He noted that the "general depression of business in the South during the year 1892" had affected Richmond but that banking and manufacturing in the city had done well the previous year. He was "pleased to be able to say that all signs indicate improvement and increased activity in real estate during the current year."

Only two weeks later, when the *State* asked Dooley to submit another article, his tone had changed. He characterized the country's financial situation as one of "suspense and some anxiety."[13] As he saw it, the United States was in temporary difficulties mainly caused by the Sherman law, and he rec-ommended that the country "make a large sale of bonds for gold" to restore confidence. By the date the article appeared, however, U.S. gold reserves had fallen below their statutory limit. The Panic of 1893 was sweeping through the stock market and the banking world.

Although the banks in Richmond remained open, more than a hundred banks failed elsewhere across the country. The value of silver, which had been declining ever since the Sherman Silver Purchase Act became law, fell even more quickly. The result was that in June, when the British closed the mints in India from which the United States had been buying at least half the silver it needed to fulfill the requirements of the Sherman Act, the nation's silver mining industry collapsed as well.

Despite the deteriorating financial situation, there were hopeful develop-ments in Richmond when a new invention appeared in public for the first time. On a Monday morning in May, a large crowd gathered by the window of John L. Williams and Son, the bank at the corner of Tenth and Main Streets, as soon as it opened, and lingered there all day long. Peering in the window, people could see two desks placed a few feet from one another. On each desk were boxes holding rolls of paper. The boxes were connected by a wire. As the crowd watched, a man sitting at the first desk wrote with an or-dinary pencil on the paper on the roller of the box in front of him. Near the point of the pencil were two silk threads that connected with the box. Every so often the man at the desk would push on a lever on the left side of the box to move along the paper he was writing on. Meanwhile, at the box on the other desk, a pen attached to an arm extending from that box was producing an exact copy of the original message. Every time the demonstrator pushed the lever to move his paper, the paper at the second desk moved as well. The people closest to the window could see what was being written and also what was being produced by the pen on the desk opposite.[14] Although they didn't realize it, they were witnessing the first public demonstration of a telauto-graph in Richmond.

Two days later, a front-page article in the *State* was full of enthusiasm for the "amazing new machine."[15] The reporter assured readers that "when it is understood that the physician may sit in his office and write his prescription at the very desk of the druggist, and the train dispatcher his orders at the desk of every station agent along his line, and that the telegraph messenger service will be conducted direct from the central office by written orders from the subscriber, it will be seen at once that the revolution in electrical intercom-munication is universal." The article went on to boast: "The Gray National

Telautograph Company is establishing local exchanges . . . and it is said that in a very short time one will be instituted in Richmond, which will probably be among the first, if not the first, in operation in the United States. . . . Richmond was one of the first cities to take hold of the telephone. She had the first electric railway, and she will now complete the record by establishing the first Telautograph Exchange."

When the Columbian Exposition opened in Chicago later that spring, Elisha Gray himself demonstrated his telautograph in the Electricity Building.[16] He created something of a sensation there by transmitting facsimiles over 250 miles of electric wire. Within a few years the telautograph was widely used in banks and railway stations and adapted to a variety of industrial uses.

Despite the excitement over the telautograph, the national economic situation remained a central concern for Dooley, as an interview he had in July demonstrated. He and Sallie were in Staunton visiting her family when a local correspondent for the *Richmond Dispatch* caught up with him to ask for his opinion on the probable effect Britain's closing of the mints in India would have on the U.S. financial system.[17] In his response, Dooley observed that "in attempting single-handed to restore silver to its former position as a money metal we are playing the role of a Don Quixote amongst the nations." As he saw it, the ultimate consequence of the closing of the mints in India would be that "the Sherman law will be repealed when Congress meets." It was repealed, but not as quickly as Dooley predicted.

Dooley's concern about the economy prompted him to try yet again to influence public policy and encourage new legislation, this time by appealing directly to President Cleveland. In a strongly worded open letter to the president published July 30 on page 2 of the *Dispatch* under the headline "Dooley's Diagnosis," he described himself as a "life-long Democrat" but declared that "it is right for me to say to you respectfully what I know to be the sentiment of a very great number of mechanics, manufacturers, and businessmen in every walk of life. . . . When our country is in danger it is time to act and speak truth." The brunt of his attack was aimed at the "free-trade features [of] the McKinley law," which he thought had "precipitated and aggravated the financial crisis" by doing away with a number of protective tariffs. In the body of the letter Dooley marshaled statistical facts and figures to illustrate the error in the free-trade lobby's claim that "lowering or removing tariffs on imports from foreign countries" would enable those countries to purchase more goods from the United States. He demonstrated that "our experience proves the very reverse" and predicted economic disaster if the president advised Congress "to let down the bars and flood the country with additional importations." As Dooley saw it, "capitalists will continue to withdraw from every enterprise, bankers will . . . curtail their loans, manufacturers will discharge their employees, the land will swarm with tramps, while the women and children will be turned out of their happy homes to beg, starve, or worse." The deep depression of the following four years bore out his prediction.

In the summer of 1893, Dooley's sisters and their mother followed reports of the nation's worsening financial situation with growing concern. They couldn't avoid reading about the reorganization of the Terminal system and probably read all of the newspaper interviews with Jim, as well as his published essays. They may well have presumed the worst about his finances and become concerned for the welfare of the family, dependent as they all were on him. A decision his youngest sister made suggests as much. Josephine Houston, now a thirty-six-year-old widow, seems to have decided that letting her brother continue to pay the tuition for her nine-year-old daughter, Nora, to attend St. Joseph's Female Academy was too much to ask under the circumstances. She also must have been aware that other parents were feeling the pinch of the deepening depression. Bright, able, and a well-educated woman by the standards of her time, Josephine saw an opportunity in the convergence of those facts. In the fall of 1893 she opened a primary school in her house at 314 E. Main Street. To make it an attractive option for the parents of other children approximately Nora's age, she set the cost of the tuition for her school well below that of St. Joseph's and opened its doors to boys as well as girls.[18] The school was successful enough to last through the 1897 school year. By that time Nora was old enough to enter the upper school at St. Joseph's, and her uncle's financial life was considerably more settled.

The fight in the United States Congress to repeal the Sherman Act continued well into the fall of 1893. On Thursday, September 14, Senator John W. Daniel, with whom Dooley had battled on the issue in 1891, gave one of the great speeches of his career on the floor of the Senate. It was a four-hour-long tour de force that showed just how ineffective Dooley's attempt to change Daniel's mind had been.[19]

At the end of the first week of December, Dooley was approached by a *Dispatch* reporter eager to hear his views on Grover Cleveland's message to Congress, in which the president had come out firmly for repeal of the Silver Purchase Act. Although Dooley took a very diplomatic stance at the beginning of the interview, his answers to the reporter's questions grew increasingly acid. In the subsequent article, published on December 10, Dooley sharply criticized Cleveland for endorsing a tariff proposal Dooley characterized as "sectional and unwise."[20] He pointed out that the bill proposed dropping the protective tariff on raw materials produced in the South while retaining the tariff on goods manufactured in the North. He attacked the North in language reminiscent of diatribes on tariff issues heard in Richmond during the decade before the Civil War. "For nearly one hundred years New England has been laying tribute upon the South through the machinery of the tariff. She has grown fat and rich at our expense," he fumed. "Thus it has been ever since the foundation of the government. We have been the hewers of wood and drawers of water, while New England has waxed fat, rich, and insolent by using the machinery of government taxation to levy tribute on the South."

The new year 1894 had hardly begun when Dooley felt compelled to write a letter to the editor of the *Dispatch*. In it, he returned to attacking the tariff proposal as unfair and reminded readers that "the chief cost of production is labor, whether in the finished and polished cutlery of New England or in the coal and iron of the South." He closed his letter with a call for reform that demonstrated just how dire the economic situation was in the nascent industries of South: "Labor is no more entitled to protection amongst the educated and trained artisans of the North than it is when found ragged, dirty, and ignorant in the mines of the South."[21]

CHAPTER 19 | Highways and Railways

Despite the demise of the Richmond Terminal system, Dooley continued to invest in the railroad industry throughout the 1890s. He and John Skelton Williams were leaders of a group of Richmond investors intent on consolidating a number of independent railroads into a new trunk line system between Richmond and the Gulf of Mexico they called the Seaboard Air Line. In the 1888 edition of the *Manual of Investments,* Williams had stated that the line would provide direct connection from the Chesapeake Bay to Atlanta, but by 1895 Tampa had become the goal. From there, they planned to reach the Nicaragua Canal. That connection would give Richmond access to markets not only along the Pacific coast of North and South America but of the Far East as well. Realizing that they had to seek additional investors to finance the new system, and determined to keep their enterprise in southern hands, the Richmond group joined forces with J. W. Middendorf, Oliver and Company, a banking and investment firm in Baltimore. With Middendorf's help, the Richmond syndicate seemed well on its way to positioning Richmond as a center in the global economy.

In the depression of the mid-1890s, a number of the small railroads in the Lower South found themselves in financial trouble and were sold, often at less than their full worth. This situation gave Williams, Dooley and their associates the opportunity to buy large blocs of stock in a number of those troubled lines, and also to acquire some of them outright. The scenario was similar to the one Dooley, Bryan, and Logan encountered in the late 1870s and early 1880s, when they began to invest in the short-line railroads they added to the Richmond and Danville. There was, however, one major difference. This time the Richmonders faced relentless opposition from an investor determined to prevent them from controlling the Seaboard. They had come up against him before, during the period in which the Terminal had begun to fail. He had taken advantage of the very low prices of its stock to buy enough to take a seat on the Terminal board. Their opponent was Thomas Fortune Ryan, and he was ready to fight for control of the Seaboard. Dooley's membership on the boards of many of the twenty railroad companies slated for consolidation gave him front-row seats for Ryan's battles to stymie the consolidation process.

For a few days in October 1895, however, Dooley was occupied with a battle of a different sort. The Virginia State Fair was in progress on the outskirts of Richmond, and the city was teeming with farmers and their families. A convention organized by Virginia's Good Roads Association was being held at the same time, and Dooley was a delegate to its proceedings. Virginia was only one of many states holding such conventions, which were manifestations of a movement for road improvement that was sweeping the country in the 1890s. The conventions were backed by an arm of the United States Department of Agriculture called the Office of Road Inquiry.

The Virginia convention was being held during the state fair because most of its delegates were farmers. Some, however, were like Dooley—businessmen active in the railroad industry. Their interest grew out of their awareness of problems faced by farmers wanting to ship produce and livestock to market by rail. To get from their farms to railroad junctions, most farmers had to travel by wagon over badly constructed, poorly maintained rural roads. The general public also had a strong interest in road improvement because although most people traveling long distances went by rail or boat, they were often forced to make connections by stagecoach. Years later, historians of the Virginia State Highway Department noted that in the 1890s, Virginia's roads were in such poor condition that out-of-state travelers were cautioned to avoid the state entirely.[1] There was no state highway system in the Virginia of the 1890s. Instead, the roads were built and maintained by the residents of the cities and counties through which they ran, and their quality varied depending on the wealth and commitment of each locality. Road conditions were distressingly unpredictable. Crossing a county line might mean shifting from a well-maintained road to one in terrible condition. Broken axles and overturned vehicles were common. There were almost no automobiles in those days: most of the vehicles were those drawn by horses, mules, oxen, or donkeys that negotiated with greater or lesser success a network of hard-packed dirt, oyster shell, gravel, or cobblestone roads.

Dooley's interest in the problem grew partly out of his role in the railroad industry, but it was also personal. By 1895, he had been living in Henrico County for approximately two years. Although improving city streets had long been one of his concerns as a city dweller, he asserted that he had learned "the necessity for good roads" after he moved to the county because of "the very bad roads he had to travel over in every direction."[2]

In the business meeting that took place at the opening of the convention, Dooley was elected vice president and appointed chairman of the Legislative Committee.[3] Throughout the rest of the two-day Good Roads Convention there were speeches and committee meetings that explored the problems Virginia faced in attempting to improve its roads. First among these was identifying ways to raise the necessary capital for road construction and improvement. Dooley's committee met at three in the afternoon on the first day and worked for several hours on legislative proposals. The next morning's session opened at ten o'clock. Dooley arrived with the Legislative Committee's report in hand and read its recommendations into the record. The committee recommended the enactment of a single statewide road law and the repeal of all existing laws then on Virginia's statute books. (Up until then, each county had been permitted to have its own road laws.) It condemned the common practice of using enforced labor of ordinary "able-bodied" citizens on roads as "unjust and ineffective" and recommended that instead counties be allowed to hire convicts for the work.[4]

In recommending "state aid to permanent improvement of the main highways," the Legislative Committee addressed the unpopular issue of taxation as a source of revenue for roads by recommending that real estate and personal property be taxed at a rate of five cents on every one hundred dollars of the assessed value of such property, and that the monies collected be earmarked for a state roads fund. It also recommended that county residents be allowed to vote to authorize bond issues for road improvement in their own county. To oversee road-related developments, the committee suggested that Virginia establish the post of state highway commissioner and hire an expert to fill the position for a term of four years. Its final recommendation was that counties be required to hire engineers to supervise road projects.

At the final meeting of the convention Dooley gave detailed explanations of each section of the report in a question-and-answer session that lasted for three hours. (The *Dispatch* described his explanations as "masterly" and printed the report in full in its next day's edition.)[5] The Legislative Committee's report was accepted by the "almost unanimous" vote of the convention, and the committee was asked to frame its recommendations in appropriate form for presentation to the Virginia legislature for action in the next session. Its report was also reprinted and distributed throughout the nation by the U.S. Department of Agriculture in its *Office of Public Roads Circular Number 18*.

Regrettably, the progressive reforms it recommended faced stern opposition. Many years passed before the need for changes recommended by the Legislative Committee of the 1895 Good Roads Convention became obvious to Virginia legislators.[6] The State Highway Commission wasn't established until 1906, eleven years later. State financial support for roads wasn't approved until 1916, when the General Assembly voted to use vehicle registration fees for road maintenance. It was 1918 before federal funds were available for roads in Virginia, and 1923 before a tax on gasoline was enacted to pay for road construction.

At this point in his career Dooley had good reason to feel comfortable financially. Sloss Iron and Steel in Alabama was doing well. It had begun to ship pig iron not only to places like the Richmond Locomotive Works, which depended on it to build its engines, but to such distant states as Oregon and California, and to foreign markets as far away as Australia, India, and Japan.[7] In 1896 Sloss also had contracts from the U.S. Navy, and some of its pig iron was used in building two battleships, the *Oregon* and the *Texas*. The Richmond Locomotive Works, too, had found success in international markets and was shipping its engines as far away as Chile, Finland, and Sweden. Richmond's economy seemed to be on the upswing. Only Dooley's real estate in Minnesota was still problematical.

The year 1895 ended on a dark note. A tremor of near-earthquake proportions shook the city when Richmonders opened their Sunday papers on December 15 to learn that James B. Pace, president of Planters National Bank, who was thought to be the city's richest man, had declared bankruptcy. The *Times* published the news on its front page, but the *Dispatch* buried its article on page 16. According to the *Times,* Pace's was "the largest assignment . . . ever . . . recorded in the Chancery court of the city of Richmond."

The news must have hit Dooley and Bryan particularly hard. For more than a decade Pace had been an integral member of their investment syndicates, not only in Virginia but also in Alabama, Minnesota, and the Washington Territory. In 1886 he had been the only man in the city able to make a significant enough investment to return control of the Richmond and Danville and the Terminal to Richmond hands, and he had taken a seat on the Terminal board. His investments in Virginia included the West-End Land and Improvement Company, and the Richmond and West Point Land, Navigation and Improvement Company. He had joined in the telautograph venture and taken a seat on its board. He and Dooley jointly owned various pieces of real estate in the city.

Fortunately for Richmond, although Pace's bankruptcy came as a great shock because he was the president of one of its biggest banks, his was a personal bankruptcy rather than a financial disaster for the bank or the city. It did put pressure, however, on those like Dooley who had joint ventures with him. They had to scramble to prevent the loss of their portion of joint investments.

Pace's failure was not the only upset that week for Dooley and Bryan. On Thursday they learned that E. D. Christian had also failed. His failure was said to have been the result of Pace's. Once again, the bankruptcy was personal and did not bring down the Richmond Paper Manufacturing Company, of which Christian was president. Even so, the news must have been highly disconcerting for Dooley and Bryan, who had to struggle to avoid being pulled into the morass. The result for Pace and Christian was that from then on they had to live more modestly. Even so, they remained highly regarded. In 1905, Pace was even elected treasurer of the City of Richmond—a post in which he served until his death in 1920.[8]

During the years when her husband had been preoccupied with the massive problems of the Terminal and working on developing a new trunk line in the South, Sallie had continued her charity work. She was still deeply devoted to helping the residents of St. Paul's Home for Aged and Infirm Women. During the 1880s she had assisted with fund-raising for the construction of a building for the home and its infirmary, which offered even nonresident elderly women free treatment.[9] During the Panic she served as a patron for the only ball held that year, a much-reduced version of the city's annual Charity Ball.[10]

In 1895 Sallie also became a member of a new club, the first she joined that was devoted neither to charity nor historical preservation. Called simply "The Woman's Club," it was, like the Colonial Dames and the DAR, the local manifestation of a national movement, but unlike those groups, it had no organizational connection to other clubs of its kind throughout the country.[11] The Woman's Club was, and still is in the twenty-first century, specifically dedicated to the educational and cultural development of its members. Not surprisingly, several of its founders were heads of local schools and eager to expand the intellectual horizons of club members. During its first year, the club established two lecture series, a Monday series devoted to literary topics and a Thursday series that explored a variety of cultural issues. Among the lecturers that year were professors from Columbia University and the University of the South.[12] Although Sallie was not one of the founders of the organization, she was among 125 women who joined during its first year. She had to pay a five-dollar initiation fee and annual dues of ten dollars. One of its leaders was a much younger woman, twenty-eight-year-old Mary Cooke Branch Munford, whom Major Dooley had known since her birth at her grandparents' home across from the Dooley family home on Broad Street. Her husband, the lawyer Beverley Munford, had served as counsel for the Richmond and Danville, and recently had presided at the Good Roads Convention. Mary Munford was one of the brightest and most intellectual of the founders of the Woman's Club. According to a later history of the club, she had "yearned for higher education and spent several years trying to convince her mother to allow her to attend college. Disappointed in the end, she creatively sought less formal alternatives that would provide the intellectual stimulation and development she craved."[13]

The founding of another club in 1895 was a milestone in the cultural history of the city. On November 30, a group of the city's better-known professional and amateur artists met at the Grace Street home of Dr. George Ben Johnston and his wife, Helen, to form "an Artists Club."[14] Among the artists present were the architect Edgerton Rogers, whom the Dooleys had hired to design their house at Maymont; the sculptor (and Dooley childhood friend) Edward Valentine; and the painter Adele Williams, recently returned from Paris, where she had exhibited at the Salon and won the Prix Concours medal at the Académie Julian. That night they launched what they would call the Richmond Art Club, or, alternately, the Art Club of Richmond. Dooley took great interest in the fledgling organization and soon became a nonartist member, a guarantor of its exhibitions, and, a decade later, its president.

On New Year's Day 1896, the *Richmond Times* published an article that undoubtedly caught Dooley's eye. Written by John Skelton Williams's younger brother, Robert Lancaster Williams, now a partner in John L. Williams and Sons, it reviewed the financial operations of railroads important to Richmond.[15] Lancaster mentioned the reports on the earnings and expenses of the Petersburg Railroad, the Richmond, Fredericksburg and Potomac, the Southern, the Norfolk and Western, and even the Farmville and Powhatan, but he did not mention the Seaboard. Or at least so it seemed. Lancaster's article did mention one other railroad, however, the Georgia and Alabama, and he noted it had been "organized in August, 1895" and was the "successor to the old Savannah, Americus, and Montgomery Railway." He also mentioned that it was a "railroad, in which a large amount of Richmond capital has been invested," but he failed to mention that his brother John Skelton had been elected its president. The Georgia and Alabama was only 140 miles long at the time, but as a later historian of the Seaboard pointed out, it was the "first major step" toward the formation of the Greater Seaboard Air Line Railway.[16] Clearly Dooley and the other Richmond investors were working quietly as well as carefully while they acquired railroad companies for their future trunk line.

Despite their caution, Thomas Fortune Ryan was watching every step of the way. He wanted the Seaboard and was willing to fight relentlessly for it.

He chose the courtroom for his battles. Exactly when he started trying to throw up legal barriers to the consolidation process is unclear, but he used injunctions as one of his weapons. There were many battles that took years to win.[17] As a result, the cost to the Virginians of building the Seaboard included not only the expense of building bridges and laying new track but of arguing in court.

Despite the Ryan problem, in 1897 and 1898 Dooley and Williams continued their efforts to consolidate the Seaboard. Perhaps their most significant business accomplishment in 1898, however, was to establish a new banking institution in Richmond, which they named the Richmond Trust and Safe Deposit Company. Williams was its president; Dooley, the vice president; and Henry Landon Cabell, the secretary and treasurer. According to the newspaper advertisements published before its opening on June 1, 1898, its functions included acting in the usual trust capacities as guardian, receiver, trustee, or executor charged with managing estates and collecting incomes. Its charter also granted it the right to lend money on approved collateral, and to act as fiscal agent for cities and corporations.[18] The company, which had three hundred thousand dollars in capital stock when it opened, grew so quickly that its capital rose to seven hundred thousand dollars by the following February and to $1 million by April 1899.

Throughout 1899, news of the work on the Nicaragua Canal often competed with the Seaboard for space on the front page of Richmond newspapers. For example, the January 15 front page of the *Times*—featuring a sketch captioned "At Work on the Nicaragua Canal"—reported that "Nicaragua will be the busiest spot in the Western Hemisphere this year . . . and as soon as the question of control is settled the work will be vigorously pushed. It is to be a broad, beautiful canal that will accommodate our war cruisers, and it will run through the finest portion of Central America." On January 29 the *Times* printed a map showing the route of the canal from the Atlantic Ocean through Lake Nicaragua to the Pacific. Unmentioned but obvious were the hopes of the canal project's Richmond backers, who had invested heavily in the company and shared a dream that the canal would make the city a center of the global economy.

Meanwhile the fight over the consolidation of small southern railroads into the new Seaboard trunk line continued throughout 1899. Thomas Fortune Ryan's efforts to prevent Williams, Dooley, and their associates from cobbling together the Great Seaboard Air Line culminated in three circuit courtrooms in three different states: Maryland, Georgia, and North Carolina.[19] In January Ryan filed suit in Baltimore against the Williams syndicate.

Ryan's claim was that he represented "large interests in the Seaboard," and he asked for an injunction to prevent the sale of thousands of shares of pooled stock to Williams and his associates. The *Dispatch* conjectured that the Williams syndicate's purchase would "beyond a reasonable doubt be effected, but not without a good deal of litigation. Mr. Thomas F. Ryan [who contends he] represents the holders of large interests in the Seaboard has been fighting the controlling faction with great bitterness for several years with a view to ousting the present management." When the Circuit Court in Baltimore decided against Ryan and ordered him to pay court costs, he announced that he would appeal.[20]

A little over two weeks later, Dooley was present at the meeting in Baltimore at which control of the Seaboard was formally transferred to the Williams syndicate. John Skelton Williams was elected president of the companies constituting the system, and Dooley was elected to the board of the Seaboard and Roanoke.[21] The changes were later confirmed by a vote of the stockholders at the November 11 annual meeting in Norfolk. The *Richmond Times* characterized this as the first sign of harmony "since the struggle for the control of the Seaboard Air line between opposing capitalists began."[22]

On December 9 stockholders of the Raleigh and Gaston Railroad met in Raleigh to vote on preliminary steps toward joining the Seaboard. In the vote, "99.8 per cent of the entire stock had voted in favor of the plan" when word came from Norfolk of "the unexpected opposition of Thomas F. Ryan" and another Ryan attempt to obtain an injunction.[23]

Nonetheless, by the end of the year Williams and his Richmond and Baltimore associates had acquired the Florida Central and Peninsular Railroad, which ran from Columbia, South Carolina, to Tampa, a purchase that gave them access to markets in the Gulf of Mexico, South America, and (when and if the Nicaragua Canal was built) the Pacific. Thomas Ryan took note and laid plans for yet another injunction.

The twentieth century opened on a high note in Richmond. Encouraged by the prosperity of 1899, businessmen were optimistic about prospects for the new year. The future of the Seaboard Air Line seemed assured as well. Although the company still faced a number of challenges, fortunately the Richmond Chamber of Commerce was a strong ally. On January 4 it adopted a resolution "earnestly commending the completion and consolidation of the Seaboard Airline system" and condemning "as inimical to our best interests every effort that has been or may be made by individuals or combinations to delay, hinder, or defeat the consolidation." Clearly aimed directly at Thomas Fortune Ryan, the resolution was offered by Col. John B. Purcell "in behalf of our city and State, and the whole South."[1]

As the resolution indicated, Ryan's specter was still hovering over Dooley and Williams's ambitious plans to consolidate twenty smaller railroad companies into the Seaboard Air Line. During a New Year's Eve interview Williams had told a *Dispatch* reporter that "he had nothing to say regarding his controversy with Mr. Ryan" but that "the consolidation schemes were progressing in the most satisfactory manner."[2] On January 24, however, Ryan managed to interrupt the process yet again by seeking an injunction in federal court in Macon, Georgia, to prevent the consolidation of the Georgia and Alabama, Central, and Peninsular Railways with the Great Seaboard Air Line system.[3] The judge in the case, aware of Ryan's many requests for injunctions in other jurisdictions, made certain that everyone in the courtroom knew he intended to observe judicial impartiality, announcing: "It is not the purpose of the Court to allow its powers to be used to arrest a legitimate enterprise . . . nor is it our purpose to deny to the complainant the opportunity of a fair and full inquiry." Four days later, when he handed down his decision refusing the injunction, the judge noted that similar cases were pending in North Carolina and Virginia and cautioned that the "gravest consequences" might result if judges passed "conflicting decisions on the same facts and in the same controversy, producing endless confusion and distrust in the administration of the law." Such results, he stated, would reward "parties who are stubbornly litig[i]ous, who are endowed with great resources for litigation, and who not infrequently seek to use the courts as pawns in the game they play on the gigantic chessboard marked by the transportation lines of the country."[4]

The judge's comments seemed intended to forestall another legal foray by Ryan, who nevertheless came back for one more try. In February he made a last-ditch effort in the U.S. Circuit Court in Richmond to obtain an injunction. There he was finally defeated in his efforts to prevent the consolidation of the Richmond, Petersburg and Carolina Railroad with the Seaboard and Roanoke.[5]

The Ryan court cases finally behind it, the Seaboard faced another hurdle, this one in the legislature. The problem was that the Seaboard had forged ahead with construction on the last piece of its planned system—a railway link running northward out of Richmond called the Richmond and Washington Air Line—before the proposed subsidiary had been granted a charter. The Seaboard's attempt to secure legislative approval for the connector ran headlong into the vested interests of the Richmond, Fredericksburg and Potomac (RF&P) Railroad, which at the time had what amounted to a stranglehold on the northbound rail business out of Richmond. The company had favored status in the legislature because the State of Virginia still owned RF&P stock, having held on to it after selling its interests in other railroads during the 1870s. The state quite understandably wanted to protect the revenue accruing from its holdings.

In an attempt to obtain the charter for his new company, Williams launched an intense lobbying effort that included publishing interviews with members of the U.S. Congress who were in favor of the charter.[6] Meanwhile Dooley worked behind the scenes, only occasionally surfacing in local lobbying efforts. One of these rare appearances came on February 2, 1900. That evening he spoke at a general meeting of the Richmond Chamber of Commerce in the hope of persuading it to adopt a resolution urging the General Assembly to pass the charter bill. "Are we returning to the dark ages when monopolies are sold by the governments?" he demanded. Answering his own rhetorical question, he identified himself as "a business-man and a citizen of Richmond always having at heart the interest of this dear old city" and continued that he did not "believe that the Legislature could confer a greater boon upon this great and progressive community than by chartering a competing line from Richmond to the North."[7] The next morning the *Dispatch* noted that attendance at the meeting "was exceptionally large, and the reaction was hearty and enthusiastic."

Months later the charter Dooley and Williams had pursued was granted, but it did not permit quite what they had envisioned. Instead of being the sole owner, the Seaboard had only a one-sixth interest in the line. It would have to share with the Pennsylvania, the C&O, the Southern, the Atlantic Coast Line, and the Baltimore and Ohio.[8]

While Dooley was devoting much of his time to the Seaboard that winter, his wife was doing her own lobbying in the legislature. She and other members of the Colonial Dames had joined a growing movement that advocated repairing, painting, and fireproofing the Capitol Building in Richmond. As a member of a Dames committee charged with "ascertain[ing] the cost and necessary details" of the project, Sallie had a small but important role in lobbying for an appropriation in the state budget. Such tasks were typical ones for the Colonial Dames, whose mandate was the preservation and protection of the memory and artifacts of the nation's history. The Dames were also working to save the State Library's books and manuscripts, which at that time were stored in the rooms inside the Capitol dome. The task was very much to Sallie Dooley's taste. Not only was she a historic preservation enthusiast, but, thanks to her husband's three terms in the House of Delegates and his continued prominence in Democratic Party circles, she was extremely well connected. Many members of the legislature had been guests at Maymont. When she appeared in the halls of the Virginia legislature, its members were likely to listen politely. She and the other members of the committee, including its chairwoman, Catherine Claiborne, and Betsie Montague, wife of Virginia's attorney general, simply made an appointment to meet with the chairman of the Appropriations Committee.[9]

Although in this instance Sallie Dooley was willing to lend her powers of persuasion to the cause, she was ardently opposed to women having the right to vote and a decade later became a member of the executive committee of the Virginia Association Opposed to Women's Suffrage. Marching down to the legislature to lobby on any issue seemed quite out of character for her. In doing so, however, she was merely acting within the tradition of the "southern lady" of an earlier time, when custom allowed and even encouraged women to express their views and cajole the men of their circle to act accordingly.[10]

Sallie also took an active part in celebrating the new epoch. The City of Richmond, eager to do something unique to mark the opening of the twentieth century, decided to hold a three-day-long street fair in mid-May. When a special feature, the Floral Carriage Parade, took place on Wednesday, May 16, an estimated seventy-five thousand spectators lined the parade route on Franklin Street to watch. Two lines of carriages festooned with flowers passed the Jefferson Hotel, where judges viewed them from the upper porch, on their way to Capitol Square, where the judges viewed them again as they passed the Executive Mansion.[11] Sallie was among the women invited to drive or ride in one of the carriages.[12] Although there are no photographs of her in the parade, she was a participant, and it is likely that her carriage was decorated with roses from some of the spring bloomers among the hundreds of rose bushes she had planted at Maymont.

The crowning events of the first year of the new century for her husband began with the ceremonial driving of a gold spike that connected the final Seaboard rails. It took place when the first train from Richmond to Tampa returned to the city on June 2. It was pulled by locomotives manufactured at Richmond Locomotive Works and had stopped at towns and cities along the way to pick up close to a hundred passengers who were board members of the railroad companies amalgamated into the Seaboard system. Pulling into Richmond, the train was greeted by cheering crowds waving hats and handkerchiefs, brass bands, a twenty-one-gun Howitzer salute, and a tiny boy holding a silver-headed mallet. John Skelton Williams Jr., nestled securely in the arms of his grandfather, John L. Williams, was to drive in the gold spike. The noise of the locomotive, the Howitzers, the brass bands, and the cheering was deafening as the little boy hammered. The spike was halfway in when he spotted his mother on the platform and, overcome by the noise, leaned in her direction and tried to run. She walked quickly toward him instead, and together they hammered it in the rest of the way. Afterward, the trainload of passengers piled into horse-drawn carriages and, escorted by the Richmond Blues and their brass band with banners waving, rode to Capitol Square. There they heard speeches by the governor, the mayor, and the president of the Chamber of Commerce.[13]

That night Dooley gave one of the toasts at the celebratory banquet at the Jefferson Hotel. Ninety-seven of the men there that evening were directors of the system's twenty constituent companies. The banquet, described as "surpassing magnificence," began at nine o'clock and was accompanied by the reading of congratulatory telegrams from such luminaries as President William McKinley and former president Grover Cleveland.[14] By the time the plates were cleared and cigars lighted, the presentation of three-handled, sterling silver "loving cups" to the directors of all the companies in the system had begun.

It was almost midnight when John Skelton Williams rose to speak. His speech traced the growth of the system from its beginnings as the forty-eight-mile-long Seaboard and Roanoke to the two-thousand-mile-long behemoth it had become. Then the traditional round of toasts and their responses began, each toast introduced by music appropriate to its theme. Dooley had the last word that evening. He raised his glass to the global ambitions of the company and the South, emphasizing that the South now had its *own* industries and railroad and no longer had to depend on other regions and foreign countries for manufactured goods. The South should look now, he suggested, to "the great Pacific Ocean, with its dense populations" for customers for its products. "The South wants the Nicaraguan Canal," he proclaimed. "The other world powers are training for the race for business; let us not be laggards in the race."[15]

The fall brought a somber duty for Dooley, who served as an honorary pallbearer at the funeral for his old friend Dr. Hunter Holmes McGuire. Several months later, Dooley and a group of other McGuire friends formed the McGuire Monument Association to raise funds and choose the sculptor for a statue in his honor. They selected William Couper to execute the work, and the resultant bronze sculpture of a seated McGuire was unveiled on the north lawn in Capitol Square in January 1904.[16]

By December 1900 a rumor began to circulate that the Seaboard and the Southern Railroad were planning to consolidate. When a *Dispatch* reporter asked John Skelton Williams to comment on the possibility of consolidation, Williams dodged, just awkwardly enough to add fuel to the fire.[17] He also mentioned with a smile that the Seaboard was hauling a large portion of the orange crop from Florida, a crop that previously had traveled via the Southern, and commented that despite this, the two railroads "were living in harmony," were not cutting rates, and, "so far as he knew, there was no likelihood of their entering into a rate war."

On another front, activity in Congress had important ramifications for the Seaboard and the Nicaragua Canal Construction Company. On December 4, President McKinley submitted to Congress the Isthmian Canal Commission report unanimously recommending that the canal be located in Nicaragua rather than Panama.[18] After the commission's recommendation was announced, Dooley's vision of Richmond as a center of world trade took on the aura of a fait accompli.

Other gratifying developments in 1900 for Dooley and Williams included the growth of the Richmond Trust and Safe Deposit Company. A Richmond Chamber of Commerce publication for 1900 described the company's growth as an "unprecedented success" and added that the company had "the largest capital of any bank or trust company in the South Atlantic States and as large as any in the entire South."[19] An article in the January 1, 1901, edition of the *Dispatch* commented that the company was being managed by the "leading financiers of our town, and has inaugurated some of the most colossal enterprises the Old Dominion capital has ever known."[20]

In June a Virginia constitutional convention met at the Capitol. Dooley wasn't happy about one of the issues before the convention: the proposal to establish a state corporation commission with the power to regulate railroad rates. The business community across the Commonwealth shared this concern, as did a few of the delegates, but regulating railroad rates was popular with many Virginians who felt that the railroad companies dominated the political and economic life of the state, and a majority of the delegates at the convention seemed to favor a commission.[21] By early December the *Norfolk Ledger* was reporting that the "question of the corporation commission [possessed] more interest for the people of the State than anything that has hitherto been before the convention.[22] By then the Corporations Committee of the convention had made significant progress toward producing a document favoring the creation of a corporation commission. The committee had also responded to the urgent entreaties of several Richmond businessmen who had written to request that the committee "give a hearing" to them and a "delegation present from all sections of the State with a view to securing a modification" of that document. Among those who had signed the letter were Dooley, John Patteson Branch, H. L. Cabell, William R. Trigg, E. L. Bemiss, and John L. Williams.[23] The petitioners appeared before the Corporations Committee in the Supreme Court room of the Capitol at 3:30 p.m. on December 19 and were joined there by businessmen from Norfolk, Christiansburg, Roanoke, Petersburg, and Lynchburg. Dooley was the first and John Patteson Branch the last of six men who spoke that afternoon in opposition to the creation of a corporation commission.[24] The hearing lasted until past seven o'clock, but the committee did not reach a conclusion. Instead, it set January 3, 1902, as the date for continuation of the hearing and requested that "representatives of the railroads of the State . . . be present and speak in behalf of the roads." Dooley attended both the hearing on January 3 and another session the following day but didn't speak.[25] Several weeks later, however, he did something else in an attempt to influence the Corporations Committee.

On a cold evening later in January, Dooley welcomed eighteen guests for a stag dinner in honor of the Commonwealth's new governor, thirty-nine-year-old Andrew Jackson Montague, who had been inaugurated three weeks earlier. A number of the guests were delegates to the convention, and even those who were not delegates were committed to one side or the other of the proposal to establish a state corporation commission. Two of the guests,

Eppa Hunton Jr. and A. Caperton Braxton, were members of the Corporations Committee.

That evening the young governor, whom friends called "Jack," was on comfortable turf, surrounded by old friends and associates. He had known Dooley at least since 1889, when he began to work for the Richmond and Danville Railroad as its counsel in Danville, and he had lived in Richmond since 1898, when he was elected Virginia's attorney general in the administration of Governor J. Hoge Tyler. His wife, Betsie, a Colonial Dame, had been welcomed to Richmond by Sallie and her friends as one of their own.

Among Major Dooley's other guests that evening were William A. Anderson, a director of the Valley Railroad from Rockbridge County who by then was the newly elected attorney general of Virginia; Seaboard president John Skelton Williams; Judge L. L. Lewis; Richmond businessmen Thomas Rutherfoord, Col. Archer Anderson, John A. Coke, and James Alston Cabell; Dooley's close friend John Patteson Branch; and Branch's son John Kerr Branch.

That night there were so many kinds of roses artfully arranged amid palms and potted plants throughout the house that the society column of the *Dispatch* declared that it had been transformed "into a garden."[26] The arrangement of American Beauty roses on the dinner table, "which reached almost to the chandelier and held a drooping shower of crimson blossoms," made dignified across-the-table conversation virtually impossible, but that in itself hinted at Dooley's skill as a consensus builder. At dinner at least, contentious issues could not easily be discussed and so ruin the digestion of gentlemen of opposite persuasions. After dinner, however, over brandy and cigars in the library, the men on each side could have the ear of the governor.

Ten days later, Braxton came before the convention to present the committee report proposing the establishment of the State Corporation Commission. A few days after that, Hunton presented the minority report against the proposal. Ultimately Braxton's position prevailed, and the State Corporation Commission was established. Of the three men Montague appointed to that first commission, two of them, Beverley Crump of Richmond and the Hon. Henry Tennant Fairfax of Loudon County, were friends of Major Dooley. It is possible that the elegant stag dinner at Maymont on January 24 played a role in those appointments.

Creating state corporation commissions was only one of many reforms that grew out of the Progressive movement then sweeping the entire country. In the South, however, progressivism primarily manifested itself as an educational reform movement aimed at remedying serious deficiencies in the public school systems throughout the region. Just three days after his inauguration on January 3, Montague established the Southern Educational Conference Committee to plan a public relations campaign that would inform the public of the deficiencies in the public schools of the Commonwealth. Montague became nationally known as a leader among a number of southern governors elected in the early years of the new century who spearheaded the educational reform movement.[27] They were aided in their efforts by the Southern Education Board—organized by the northern businessman Robert C. Ogden and funded by a group of northern philanthropists—and by its successor, the General Education Board, funded by John D. Rockefeller. In Dooley, Montague found a firm local ally who not only shared his ideals but also joined in the campaign to improve educational opportunities for all Virginians.

In 1902, Dooley's name appeared in the *World Almanac and Encyclopedia* list of "American Millionaires," along with those of five other Richmond men: John Patteson Branch, Joseph Bryan, Thomas M. Logan, Lewis Ginter, and Moses Millhiser, the last two deceased.[28] This list was much shorter than the tally of reputed millionaires published ten years earlier in the *New York Tribune Monthly,* where sixteen Richmond names appeared, but, as in the earlier list, the kind of business in which each individual made his millions was included beside his name. In 1892 Dooley's listing had mentioned "law, and building, and management of railroads. Is an officer in many Southern roads."[29] Beside Dooley's name this time was a single abbreviation: "capt." for "Capitalist."

In late June 1902, when the delegates of the constitutional convention finally finished their deliberations and prepared to leave Richmond, a number of prominent businessmen in the city decided to honor them with a banquet on Thursday, June 26. Joseph Bryan was chosen toastmaster for the evening. Governor Montague was to give welcoming remarks, and prominent politicians and delegates were to give speeches. The *Times* reported that the banquet committee "had great difficulty in selecting the speakers, so many brilliant orators did they find."[30] But they eventually settled on nine men, of whom Dooley was one. As was so often the case, he was to be the final speaker, to have, as usual, the last word. Each speaker was assigned a topic, and Dooley's was "Richmond."

In contrast to many of his previous speeches, on this occasion Dooley spoke not about the Richmond of the present or the future but about the Virginia of the postwar years, of Reconstruction and the painful climb to the prosperity of 1902. His speech that night was an emotional tribute to the men who helped Virginia rise from the devastation wrought by the Civil War: "At this banquet . . . I see . . . those boys in faded gray who 37 years ago . . . turned their sad faces from the ruined past, and . . . took up the peaceful task of restoring their desolated Commonwealth. . . . [T]housands of her sons . . . fled to other . . . lands. Not so did you. . . . All through the dark and stormy days of reconstruction . . . all through the long, dreary years of poverty and distress which followed . . . you toiled unremittingly in her behalf. . . . And Richmond . . . proud metropolis of the New Industrial South . . . tenders you her congratulations."[31] Dooley's speech was greeted with prolonged applause as everyone rose to drink to his health.

Even as Virginia moved toward the future with its new constitution, the state and the South as a whole seemed to spend more and more time looking backward to the Civil War and focusing its energies on building monuments to Confederate heroes. This tendency was obvious in Dooley's personal life as well as his speeches. Just a week before he gave his speech at the banquet, he applied for "active" membership in R. E. Lee Camp No. 1, an old soldiers' home for Confederate veterans.[32] Some members lived in the cottages of the camp; others, like Dooley, only participated in its activities.[33] Before the year was over he donated what must have been a family treasure, a portrait of his father, Maj. John Dooley, to the camp's portrait gallery.[34]

That summer Dooley demonstrated his emotional attachment to the Confederate past in another way: by taking an active role in the continuing effort to raise money for the Jefferson Davis memorial to be erected on Richmond's Monument Avenue. Years before, a national effort by the Jefferson Davis Association had failed, and by 1902 there still weren't sufficient funds to build the elaborate many-columned backdrop designed by the Richmond architect William C. Noland or pay for the sculpture by Edward Valentine.[35] The fund-raising campaign revived, however, in July 1902, when Dooley received a letter appealing for donations to help erect the statue. His interest in sculpture and his friendship with Valentine prompted his favorable response and a challenge published in the newspaper: "In the hope of raising the sum of $10,000 for the purpose, I offer to be one of ten to give $1,000 each, or one of twenty to give $500 each."[36] Nevertheless, funds grew very slowly, and the Valentine statue of Davis was not erected until 1907.

During the first week of August 1902, the Virginia Bar Association held its annual meeting in Hot Springs, and Sallie's brother-in-law T. C. Elder, who had been elected president for the 1901–2 term, gave the opening address. Somewhat surprisingly, Dooley did not go. The topic of Elder's speech, "Private Business Corporations in Virginia," may have been the reason.[37] In it Elder not only revealed that he was a staunch advocate of the newly established State Corporation Commission but also attacked land and improvement companies, which he accused of being purely "speculative schemes" doomed to failure.[38] As president of four such companies, Dooley would have had a hard time sitting through Elder's address, especially since one of the companies, the Richmond and St. Paul Land and Improvement Company, had been a problem almost since its founding.

At a November 1902 meeting of the Richmond Education Association, Dooley introduced a speaker he knew well, William H. Baldwin. The president of the Long Island Railroad, Baldwin was a leading figure in the Ogden movement.[39] He was also the first president of the General Education Board, which had been established the previous January by a $1 million pledge from John D. Rockefeller to help "promote education in the United States of America without distinction of sex, race, or creed . . . [and] to promote the educational needs of the people of our Southern States."[40] Baldwin was a trustee of Tuskegee Institute in Alabama and a good friend of Booker T. Washington.[41] In essence, the two men on the stage that evening represented the commitment of the corporate world in both the North and the South to improve educational opportunities in the South.

Baldwin's speech was entitled "Why Business Men Should Be Interested in Public Education."[42] In it, he called for "attention to the problem of how best to help the sixteen million people who live in the sparsely settled rural districts of the South" and shared his vision for the manual training to be offered by rural schools.[43] "We must find at the start some form of education that can be helpful to every human being, poor or rich, white or black," he declared. Baldwin also underscored the need for tax support for public schools, a concept that met with great resistance at that time. He also emphasized that "where the public school flourishes economic development follows," adding that "the public school is the first solvent to be used in the analysis of human possibilities." Baldwin's seventy-minute speech was the opening salvo of a campaign for rural education in Virginia that Baldwin predicted accurately would be long and hard.

Education was not the only contemporary issue that occupied Dooley's time in 1902. He also kept a sharp eye on economic issues. Earlier in November a speech on the financial condition of the United States by Frank A. Vanderlip, the newly appointed vice president of National City Bank in New York, received wide coverage in the national press. In his speech, Vanderlip, who had previously served as assistant secretary of the Treasury under President McKinley, sounded a note of warning about the state of the nation's economy, admonishing his audience not to assume that the commercial growth and prosperity of recent years would continue. Vanderlip focused particularly on foreign trade and swings in the United States' gold reserves as indicators of trouble ahead. When the stock market lurched into a slump less than two weeks later, Vanderlip's speech was said to be one of two precipitating causes, the other being a rumor that J. P. Morgan was suffering from a serious illness.[44]

A week or so after Vanderlip spoke, Dooley and John Skelton Williams attended the meeting of the American Bankers Association in New Orleans. Vanderlip's speech, which had been published in pamphlet form, was likely the source of considerable discussion at the meeting. When the two men returned to Richmond, Dooley published a sharply critical reply to Vanderlip in the November 16 *Dispatch* and then republished his essay as a pamphlet.[45] In it he refuted Vanderlip's arguments point by point and made his own far more optimistic predictions for the future. In his concluding paragraph, however, he admitted, "it is scarcely possible to form a reliable opinion" about whether "this country has reached its climax of prosperity and must now retrograde."[46] As Dooley put it succinctly, "too much depends on the weather."

CHAPTER 21 | A Steep Decline

A
s 1903 began, the financial weather was not promising. Economic conditions worsened as Vanderlip warned they might, and the stock market experienced a steep decline, as Dooley hoped it wouldn't. Seven years later, in an essay about trends in the economy of the United States published on the front page of the *Times-Dispatch*, Dooley looked back at 1903 and labeled it the year of the "great depression."[1]

An early hint of trouble surfaced in February, when John L. Williams and Sons informed the board of the Seaboard Air Line that they had decided to sell their interest in the Savannah and Statesboro Railroad, which they had bought jointly with Middendorf and Associates several years earlier. According to John Skelton Williams, that purchase "was only one of the many instances in which we invested large sums of our own money in our effort to provide branch lines and feeders for the Seaboard without requiring the Seaboard to provide the funds for securing the business."[2] Dooley, then chairman of the Seaboard executive committee; W. W. Mackall of Savannah; and James M. Barr, vice president and general manager of the Seaboard Air Line, were appointed to a committee to look into the consequences of the sale.

A second hint of trouble brewing in the economy hit Richmond in May, when an abrupt change occurred in the transportation business. With only a week's warning, the Clyde Company broke the last tenuous thread of the business connection between William Clyde and the Dooley, Bryan, and Logan syndicate when its ships departed permanently from the city docks.[3] Their departure meant the loss of three hundred jobs in Richmond, a serious blow to the business community.

Further financial difficulties became apparent throughout the country in the summer. When, in August, R. G. Dun & Co. reported the number of business failures in the United States for the month of July, the *Times-Dispatch* commented that "the sum of liabilities is the largest of any July in a decade, exceeding the record [set] in 1896. The increase comes from all classes of bankruptcies [including] the collapse of three Wall-Street houses."[4]

The strains caused by the weakness in the stock market complicated the financial problems of the Seaboard and prompted Dooley to resign as chairman of its executive committee, although he retained his seat on the board.

187

He later explained that the engineers had underestimated the cost of building the Atlanta & Birmingham extension while the growing depression had prevented the Seaboard from borrowing money or selling bonds. Experienced railroad men and financiers were appointed to the executive committee after Dooley resigned as chairman, but their approach worried Dooley as the Seaboard's situation deteriorated. As Dooley noted in a speech the following year: "These gentlemen were talking about raising a million dollar loan and were going to pledge for it all of the available assets of the railroad company. The President . . . and I knew . . . that we needed at least two and a half millions. If we allowed them to take our best assets as they proposed to do it meant certain and irretrievable bankruptcy."[5]

All during August, problems on Wall Street grew. The editorial writer for the August 8 issue of the new *Richmond Times-Dispatch*—created by a merger of the *Times* with the *Dispatch*—recognized the crisis, but developments in southern railroads made him optimistic.[6] Clearly unaware that the Seaboard had overreached itself, the writer mentioned not only the Southern; the Louisville and Nashville; the Chesapeake and Ohio; and the Norfolk and Western; but also the Seaboard Air Line as evidence that the future of the South was bright.

The Seaboard's financial situation was, however, increasingly precarious. Just five days after that editorial appeared, its problems became public knowledge across the country when a western firm, the Rock Island–Frisco Railroad, bought a "substantial share" of the Seaboard, and the *New York Times* covered the story. The *Times* declared that "in financial circles the announcement aroused the greatest interest" because it showed that "the depression had extended at least as far as Baltimore, and the belief being generally expressed that this acquisition would never have been brought about had it not been that some of the financiers who had backed the Seaboard Air Line had found it necessary to seek relief somewhere."[7]

The Rock Island–Frisco purchase was of great interest in Richmond but for a different reason. It provided a transcontinental trunk line for the Seaboard. The Seaboard's extension from Atlanta to Birmingham, intended originally to provide access to the iron and steel industry in Birmingham and to the iron and coal fields north of that city, now became the connector in a cross-continental system with the access to the Pacific that Richmond had been seeking for many years. The Frisco also benefited. Before the purchase, it could ship freight eastward only as far as Birmingham before being forced to transfer it to other carriers. Buying into the Seaboard gave it its own company line to the Atlantic.

The financial problems behind the deal were, however, as dire as the *New York Times* had suggested. John Skelton Williams and several other Seaboard officials, perhaps including Dooley, toured the work being done on the Atlanta-Birmingham link in early September. According to the *Times-Dispatch*, "The chief object of their trip was to inspect the work being done . . . and to hurry" it.[8] But hurrying the work wasn't all they were worried about.

On October 1, John Skelton Williams was in Baltimore for the announcement by John L. Williams & Sons and J. William Middendorf and Co. that the firms must "ask the temporary indulgence of their creditors."[9] When Richmonders picked up the *Times-Dispatch* the next day, they found the headline "Firms in Temporary Financial Straits" on the front page. The *New York Times* reported, "Southern Firms Are Embarrassed." Both papers printed in full the letter sent the previous night to all the creditors of the firms. The letter blamed the current predicament on "the extraordinary and unexpected financial situation now existing in New York" and assured the public that "the Seaboard Air Line Railway will be in no wise affected by the action of their respective firms in this matter." Nevertheless, the Seaboard Air Line took "an unexplained and striking decline" on the stock exchange that day.[10]

The shocked reaction in Richmond as a whole was immediate but also somewhat softened by sympathy for the firm. As an editorial in the *Times-Dispatch* observed, the news would be "received in this community and throughout the South with universal regret. Both concerns have shown commendable enterprise and public spirit in developing the Seaboard Air Line Railway, numerous street car enterprises, and various financial and industrial institutions." The editorial writer joined in blaming the "embarrassment" on "the abnormal depression in the price of securities and the stringency in the money market."[11]

Such sympathetic commentary likely helped prevent a run on Richmond Trust and Safe Deposit, as did a front-page headline in the next morning's edition that reassuringly noted, "City's Banks Undisturbed."[12] The *Financial Chronicle* commented later:

> The two concerns . . . had done so much towards the up building of the South, the enterprises in which their funds were tied up were of such importance that the hope was universal that they might be able to extricate themselves from their difficulties. The fact that they had become embarrassed did not reflect in the slightest degree upon their good judgment of the stability or profitable character of the enterprises in which they had

engaged. The truth is, conditions were exceptional and peculiar. Security values on the stock exchanges had been steadily declining all through 1903 and confidence in the future of even the best of investment properties seemed to be almost completely gone.[13]

For the next several weeks, the stock market continued to fluctuate severely, and by the end of October the Seaboard was on the brink of bankruptcy. At a regularly scheduled meeting of its board, John Skelton Williams announced that the firm required three hundred thousand dollars for a payment due the first of November.[14] Dooley later described what happened next at that meeting: "We looked at the financiers and the financiers looked at us. . . . Only five days until the first of November and no apparent way to relieve the situation. Then the President spoke up: 'I will get this money.' We looked at him in amazement! 'Where will you get it, how will you get it?' He said 'I will go to my friends. . . .' He, a broken man! He went to his friends and he did get it. . . . Of course we knew that that was only a temporary expedient . . . that we must have two and a half million dollars in two months." At that juncture Dooley was appointed to help Williams find the two and a half million more. When none of the financiers they approached "would consider such a proposition at such a time," as Dooley later revealed, Williams "went to his bitterest enemy; the man who had fought him for four years . . . and the Seaboard Air Line was saved."[15]

The "enemy" was Thomas Fortune Ryan, who bought $2.5 million in Seaboard bonds. In December Williams resigned as president of the company but stayed on as chairman of the board, and Dooley remained on the board as well. Ryan formed a Seaboard syndicate with the Blair & Company railroad conglomerate and financier T. Jefferson Coolidge Jr. of Boston to handle the financial exigencies of the company. The first post–Civil War railroad in the South to be financed totally by southern money had been forced to capitulate to a syndicate from the North and the West.

During the first week of January, when the Seaboard Railway board met in New York to work out the details of the Ryan-Blair agreement, Dooley stayed at home. The syndicate formed by Thomas Fortune Ryan, the Blairs, and Coolidge of Boston had agreed to supply another $2.5 million to the ailing Seaboard, take over the company, and pay themselves a bonus of 5 percent on the $5 million for doing so. On January 12 the center of the front page of the *Times-Dispatch* featured a cartoon—reprinted from the *Baltimore News*—in which two men, one labeled "New York," the other, "Boston," were seated at a table with knives and forks in hand, ready to carve up a turkey on the table labeled "Seaboard" and pour from a gravy boat labeled "stock bonus." The caption under the cartoon read, "A Toothsome Turkey from the South."

At the end of March 1904, Dooley was returning home by train after a meeting in New York when he learned that John B. Dennis, a member of the firm of Blair & Company who was chairman of the Seaboard syndicate, was also on board. Dennis, as Dooley later recounted, "had his officer's car on the train and invited me to go back and see him. I went in and spent an hour talking with him freely and confidentially."[16] When Dooley asked Dennis for assurance that "Blair & Company's Syndicate meant to take care of this property and not have it reorganized," Dennis replied that Blair & Company "went into properties to stand by them and to build them up."

A few days later, Dooley was in Baltimore for the April 6, 1904, meeting of the Williams and Middendorf companies' creditors, who were eager to collect the payments due on the Seaboard mortgages and other loans. That day Dooley made a compelling speech on behalf of the two companies. In it, Dooley asserted that the men of both firms were as eager "to pay you as you are to receive pay!" Dooley also revealed his motivation for speaking: "I have thought of all the turns of the Seaboard with the calm and the intensity of a man not only having one fourth of his fortune invested in its securities, but of a man who had been identified with the enterprise since its inception, and who does not, in his latter days, desire to have his name connected with ignominious disaster." In his conclusion, Dooley offered a bit of philosophy in support of the Williams firm:

> If you want to know how a man stands, go to his home! Ask the people with whom he has lived; ask the people who have seen him in poverty and . . . in prosperity. . . . Gentlemen . . . the people of Richmond endorse John L. Williams & Sons . . . the citizens of that community, of all classes and conditions, from the mechanic to the Chamber of Commerce. . . . This firm has the confidence of that community.

By the end of the meeting the creditors had agreed to continue extending credit to Williams and Middendorf. The wisdom of their decision to take Dooley's advice was clear. By May 1, 1905, the two firms had liquidated their liabilities, and an advisory committee dissolved after declaring the firms once again "on their feet."[17]

Although the precarious situation of the Seaboard dominated much of Dooley's working life from early 1903 through 1904, he also found time to contribute to the cultural life of Richmond. When in March 1903 Dooley was asked to serve as president of the Richmond Art Club, he accepted happily and was elected unanimously by the membership.[18] The club members hoped his election would assure financial viability for its school, and for more than a dozen years it did.

The Art Club's original aim was to provide studio space where artists could critique each other's work and encourage one another.[19] The professional members also taught classes in painting and sculpture that provided them with a small but relatively steady income. A series of annual exhibitions featured the work not only of members but of artists from all over the nation. In 1902, the Art Club decided to establish a school "for the promotion and advancement of those in Richmond who have talent, and have not yet had the opportunity to find a place here where they can study and work," and it hired a New York artist, Anne C. Fletcher, as instructor and director.[20] Her mandate was to build up the school while Richmond's own professional painters and sculptors pursued their careers.

Shortly after Dooley became president of the Art Club, Anne Fletcher began work on his portrait, which was to be hung in the spring exhibition.[21] While Dooley sat for her, she discussed not only her goals for the art school but her experiences as an art student both in this country and in France. Talking at length with a woman who worked for a living may have helped Dooley see his niece Nora in a new light. Nora and a number of other Richmond girls had been studying painting and drawing with Lily Logan, Thomas Logan's sister. For most of the pupils, these lessons were simply contributions to the "finish" young ladies were expected to acquire. One of Anne Fletcher's goals for the art school, however, was to provide the basis for a career in art. Nora, whose talent had been encouraged by Lily Logan, began to study at the Art Club School within the year. Not long after, her uncle Jim provided the funds for her to study further—first in New York and later in Paris—and to have a career as a professional artist.

Throughout the years her husband was president, Sallie supported his efforts to build the Art Club and was a hospitable presence in numerous receiving lines there. She even contributed financially as a guarantor for several of its exhibitions.[22] Her primary interests, however, still lay elsewhere.

Dooley's Art Club presidency coincided for a number of years with his efforts to help improve public schools. It began in the late afternoon of February 7, 1905, when he entered the parlor of the John Marshall House to attend a meeting presided over by Joseph Bryan. The twenty-two people who came that day, including Mary Munford and her husband, the lawyer B. B. Munford, were all ardent advocates of public education. Governor Montague had invited them to help him raise public awareness of the need to reform the state's public schools by establishing an organization to be called the Co-operative Education Association.[23] The meeting had been prompted in part by professional educators who had issued a call for a public relations campaign to carry the message that there should be "a chance for every child, whether living in the city or the country, whether white or black" to be educated, not simply for the child's sake, but for the community's.[24] At the time only half the children in Virginia were enrolled in public schools, and only one-third actually attended regularly. There was no law requiring attendance, and most children went to school only five and a half months per year.[25]

Before the meeting was over, everyone had made a monetary pledge to launch the so-called "May Campaign." Dr. S. C. Mitchell of Richmond College pronounced it "the strongest single impulse in Virginia for 'educational' progress in our day." In addition to pledging financial support at that February meeting, Dooley was for many years the single most faithful financial backer of the Co-operative Education Association.[26] He also served for years as its vice president while Mary Munford was president, and he published several essays on educational issues.

A month after the John Marshall House meeting, Joseph Bryan came into Dooley's office on a different mission. This time he was concerned about the future of Richmond's most glamorous hotel, the Jefferson, which had opened in 1895 only to burn in 1901. It had limped along for three years after reopening in 1902 with only 110 of its original 340 rooms still standing. As Dooley later explained: "When we had almost given up hope of seeing its walls arise again from the unsightly ruins, Mr. Bryan came to me one day and said quietly, 'Dooley, we are going to rebuild the Jefferson, I want you to help.' . . . [U]nder his personal supervision, there arose a grander, more imposing, more majestic structure than the original."[27] On April 17, 1905, Bryan filed a certificate of incorporation with the State Corporation Commission for the Jefferson Realty Company, and he received the charter from the Chancery Court two days later.[28] An architect designed a 430-room, fireproof hotel with private baths in all the rooms and a pool in the Palm Court where alligators swam. Two years later, on May 6, 1907, the Jefferson reopened just in time to welcome the influx of tourists coming through Richmond on their way to and from the Jamestown Tricentennial Exposition, as well as delegates to the Triennial Convention of the Episcopal Church. From that day forward, the Jefferson was Richmond's most elegant hostelry and remains so into the twenty-first century.

CHAPTER 22 | Sallie's Book and Another Railroad

hile construction work on the Jefferson Hotel was progressing, Richmonders learned that their city was to be President Theodore Roosevelt's first stop on his tour of the South. The news upset Dooley for several reasons. The first was the president's decision in January 1902 to buy the unfinished Panama Canal works from the bankrupt French construction company and to finish the canal there instead of building the one in Nicaragua as recommended by the Isthmian Canal Commission during the McKinley administration. Roosevelt's decision had put an end to the Richmond business community's effort to make the city a center of the global economy by connecting its railroad and shipping lines to the canal in Nicaragua, where it had invested a great deal of capital. Roosevelt's populist, antibusiness policies also irritated Dooley. His distaste had intensified in December 1904, when in his message to Congress Roosevelt had proposed that the Interstate Commerce Commission be given the power to set the rates charged by the nation's railroads for shipping freight.

When President and Mrs. Roosevelt arrived in Richmond on October 18, 1905, factory whistles blew, church bells clanged, and cannon boomed as the president's train pulled into Main Street Station drawn by a Seaboard Air Line engine.[1] Thousands of cheering spectators lined the streets to watch as the horse-drawn carriage carrying the Roosevelts and Governor and Mrs. Montague passed by on its way to Capitol Square, where Roosevelt was scheduled to speak. When the carriage finally arrived at the Bank Street gate of Capitol Square, a band played "Dixie" as President Roosevelt and Governor Montague mounted the speakers' platform. The prominent Richmonders and Virginia politicians who had been waiting there stood while the crowd roared with enthusiasm. Among the men on the speakers' platform were some of the usual luminaries: Joseph Bryan, Thomas Nelson Page, Mayor Carlton McCarthy, Senators Thomas Martin and John Daniel, but not James H. Dooley. His absence was glaringly obvious.[2]

Dooley did, however, appear several hours later among the four hundred Richmond men in frock coats and silk top hats who lunched with the president at the Masonic Temple in midafternoon. Undoubtedly he stood with the rest of them when they cheered a proposal to make Roosevelt an "adopted Virginian." Only an editorial in the October 15 issue of the *Times-Dispatch* hinted at something other than general enthusiasm for the visit. In it, Richmonders were admonished that although "Mr. Theodore Roosevelt has said and done some things which Richmond does not approve . . . that has nothing to do one way or the other with our conduct in receiving him. Our president is coming as our invited guest and we are going to entertain him as becomes the dignity of the guest and the hospitality and patriotism of the host."[3]

Whether Sallie Dooley held the same view of Roosevelt as her husband is not known, but at two o'clock that afternoon she was among several hundred Richmond women who attended Mrs. Montague's reception for Mrs. Roosevelt at the Executive Mansion. They found her "most gracious and responsive, unaffected and sincere."[4]

Months later, in his December 1905 message to Congress, Roosevelt took up the rate regulation issue again. After reading the president's comments, Dooley responded with an article that appeared on the front page of the *Times-Dispatch* on January 6, 1906.[5] Dooley's intense dislike for Roosevelt's policies was evident in the essay, which began: "Will you walk into my pa[r]lor, said the spider to the fly? It is the prettiest little parlor that ever you did spy." Dooley cautioned his readers, "Before we hasten to avail ourselves of this polite invitation extended to us, by Mr. Roosevelt, I would like to place before my fellow citizens of the South . . . some very grave reasons why I think it ought to be rejected." He proceeded to attack not only Roosevelt but lawmakers of the North and West, pointing out that in the forty-one years since the Civil War ended, all U.S. presidents had come from those regions. Therefore, he fumed, "the government has been substantially, and for all practical purposes, government by the North and the West. Rate regulation by the government then means that the prices at which the South may sell her goods in competitive markets, shall be fixed by the North and West, through a Commission, of whose members the North and West will have a very large majority, to be appointed . . . by the President." He insisted that "the North and West . . . have systematically made use of the government to enrich themselves, regardless of our interests," and asserted that the proposal to regulate railroad rates was an "insidious proposition . . . [that] comes before us in the guise of a patriotic effort to protect the people against the impositions and exactions of the railroad companies. That is not the real object . . . [but] an attractive veneering, put on to popularize the movement. . . . The North and West have taken alarm at the rapid strides which the South has been making in manufactures and commerce. The great and important design which underlies the rate proposition, is to control the trade and commerce, which now flow in an ever-rising tide to Southern ports and cities."

The essay created quite a stir not only in Richmond but in Washington and New York. The day after it appeared, the *Times-Dispatch* published a retort by a U.S. congressman from Virginia, John Lamb, attacking Dooley, and several days after, a response to Lamb by Samuel Spencer, president of the Southern Railroad, who agreed with Dooley.[6] Dooley's reaction was to reprint his essay in an eight-page pamphlet so it could be circulated more widely.[7] Dooley's efforts, however, had no effect on Roosevelt's populist policy. Seven months after the president's visit, the Hepburn Act was passed in Congress, and rate regulation was imposed on the railroads of the nation.

Meanwhile, Dooley was preparing to face a problem closer to home that had begun to boil the previous August, when he had learned that the City of Richmond had decided to annex a large portion of Henrico County that included Maymont. His reaction was similar to the reaction of many other property owners then and now: he was ready to fight. Dooley's eagerness to do so was ironic, since sixteen years earlier, in an 1890 speech at the Chamber of Commerce, he had firmly advocated extending the city limits and insisted that doing so was essential to Richmond's future. That speech came back to haunt him, but he lost no time hiring lawyers to prevent the annexation of his estate.

In February 1906, the Richmond newspapers carried detailed accounts of two weeks of testimony in the case.[8] Feeling in the city and county ran so high that a judge, J. E. Nicol, had to be imported from Alexandria to hear the case. Henrico County witnesses pleaded that "Henrico [would] . . . greatly suffer if any part of its territory [were] . . . taken away." Dooley was represented by Henry Anderson and Frank Christian of Munford, Hunton, Williams & Anderson, Richmond's first full-service corporate law firm.[9]

Among the witnesses on Dooley's side were several city councilmen, including A. Beirne Blair, who declared the proposed annexation of Maymont "unjust."[10] Dooley's friend John Patteson Branch observed that the Dooley property was so "hilly and rocky [it] could not be used for city purposes." When Dooley himself took the stand, he spent more than an hour explaining what he and his wife had been doing at Maymont for the thirteen years they had lived there. Sallie, he announced, had "been devoting her time and energies and her studies to making this place beautiful." Specifically, she had "put out six hundred rose bushes and thousands of other flowers, and purchased the most costly evergreens from all parts of the world, and all of those beautiful cherry trees they have in Japan, at great cost." He also noted that Sallie had done much of the planting with "her own hands," assisted by "twenty men" hired to help her. As to his own contribution, he had "made cement walks to all points of interest and beauty, put up summer houses four in number, and made various other improvements to beautify the place." In sum, he contended that "altogether we have made the place . . . an ornament and a credit to the city of Richmond, as well as the county of Henrico; strangers that come to Richmond from all parts of the country are brought there to see it and really I think it is a most valuable addition to the city of Richmond."[11]

During his testimony, Dooley called attention to a point of law governing annexation: "The law says that the judge shall see that no property is taken into the city that is not adapted to city improvements."[12] He then explained that since he made his own gas to light the house and got his water "from one of the finest springs in the country," tying in with city utilities would not be an improvement. "I not only don't want city improvements," he asserted, "but I would not have any that they can give me."[13]

When Dooley's lawyer, Henry Anderson, reminded him that one of the reasons the city wanted to annex his property was its need to control the creek in its northern section for storm "drainage purposes," Dooley responded by addressing Judge Nicol: "I would like to say to your honor, that if my property were needed in the development and growth of the city of Richmond . . . I would not stand in the way of the progress of Richmond. In regard to this sewer, as soon as I found what the gist of the matter was, I stated that if the city needed my creek, it should have it."[14] He then submitted a fully drawn set of options for using the creek in question without annexing the bulk of the property.

In the end Judge Nicol accepted Major Dooley's compromise and left the main portion of Maymont outside the city limits. The *Richmond News-Leader* noted that, as he left the courtroom, Major Dooley was "warmly congratulated for the victory" he had won.[15]

Meanwhile, for most of 1906, Sallie was very busy with a book she had written. Called *Dem Good Ole Times,* it was typical of a popular genre of the period: nostalgic, idealized accounts of life on southern plantations before the Civil War that later generations would find distressing for their complacent depiction of slavery and the relationships between the white and black races. Nonetheless, works in the genre by the Dooleys' friend Thomas Nelson Page had been best sellers throughout the country ever since the 1887 publication of a collection of his short stories called *In Ole Virginia.* Lectures and musical performances depicting happy slaves and Negro dialect were a widely popular counterpoint to the injustice of the Jim Crow laws then being enacted throughout the South.

Sallie's version of the genre was a fictional narrative in dialect by a former slave, now a free man and a grandfather, who described life on the plantation to an inquisitive grandchild. Sallie dedicated it, "In Memory of the Dear Old Southern Mammies Whose Love and Fidelity Were the Inspiration of This Book." Her sentiment seems condescending now, but it would not have seemed so to white contemporaries of Sallie's class, many of whom had fond memories of those stalwart black women.

Doubleday, Page & Company, a New York publisher with a large stable of best-selling authors, scheduled it for a fall release and gave the book widespread prepublication publicity. In September 1906, the *New York Times*'s "Saturday Review of Books" carried a notice that included a brief summary of its contents and included it in the "Autumn Book List Number 1906."[16] Doubleday, Page sent review copies of it to newspapers and magazines across the United States and even across the Atlantic to the British edition of *Country Life*.[17] Readers and reviewers in faraway places greeted the book warmly. Perfectly timed for the Christmas market and packaged in a decorative presentation box, it sold for the heady price of two dollars in bookstores throughout the United States and for $4.80 in England.[18] In a letter to Major Dooley, Sallie's Staunton friend Armistead Gordon, a leading figure in Virginia literary circles, wrote that he had seen favorable reviews of *Dem Good Ole Times* in several northern papers.[19]

In Richmond, both the *Times-Dispatch* and the *News-Leader* reviewed *Dem Good Ole Times*. The *Times-Dispatch* review was as flowery as the illustrations and decorations in the book. The reviewer commented approvingly, "We catch the perfume of tea-roses, the rich glory of old gardens, the clear notes of fresh young voices, the beautiful white light of love, which permeates the one hundred and fifty pages of this interesting book."[20] The initials "S. N. R." at the end of the review provided the only clue that it was written by Sallie's close friend Sally Nelson Robins. That didn't bother the publishers one bit. They reprinted the sentence about tea roses, young voices, and the "beautiful white light of love" in their newspaper and magazine advertisements for the book from then on.

The *News-Leader*'s anonymous reviewer, armed with a sharper pen, was not impressed. The reviewer declared that "Mrs. Dooley gives us . . . a picture of the patriarchal southern life of ante-bellum days with the inherent kindness and serenity that was so truly a part of it all, together with the further glamour of beauty and romance which forty years of separation have thrown over what faults or defects its nearer presence might once have disclosed."[21]

Dem Good Ole Times sold well enough to go through two editions in Sallie's lifetime, the second one appearing in 1916. The book was also republished in 1972, almost fifty years after her death, as part of the Black Heritage Library Collection by Books for Libraries Press in Freeport, New York.

By the time Sallie's book appeared, the Dooleys had transformed much of what had been pastureland at Maymont into an elegant landscape. In 1904 they also built a fine granite carriage house that was centrally heated, lighted by gas, and so advanced it was featured in an article in the *News-Leader.*[22] By 1907 the couple was considering what to do with the barren and treacherous spot not far from the house at the top edge of the abandoned quarry where the land dropped forty-five or more feet to the bottom of the quarry. The Dooleys decided to consult the engineer Henry Baskervill of Noland and Baskervill, a Richmond architectural and engineering firm, about the hazardous site. Baskervill's solution to the problem was a design for a formal Italian garden to be built on the spot.[23] The retaining wall he proposed to build along one side of the garden had a dual function. It not only enclosed that side of the garden but also prevented anyone from falling over the top edge of the old quarry.

Planning for the garden was interrupted in May 1907, when Dooley's mother died at the house she shared with her daughters Alice and Josephine at 314 East Main Street. Her funeral at St. Peter's was large and included nine active pallbearers along with fifteen honorary ones, John L. Williams among them. Sarah Dooley was buried beside her husband; oldest son, George; and baby daughter Alice Irina in Shockoe Cemetery. Her obituary in the *News-Leader* was oddly full of errors and gave incorrect figures for both her age and the length of her residency in the United States.[24] The writer, who described her late husband only as a "well known Confederate soldier," did not appear to know much about the family. There was no mention of the years Sarah Dooley had served as a leader in charitable organizations of her church and city or of her advocacy of women's suffrage—an ideal she shared with her five daughters. Sarah was in her late eighties when she died, but unfortunately she did not live to see her daughters Alice and Josephine—and her granddaughter Nora—become leaders of the women's suffrage movement.

Perhaps because of his mother's death and the nationwide Panic of 1907 in the financial realm, Dooley did not authorize the actual construction work that transformed the remains of the quarry into the Italian garden until 1908. That September, as she often had before, Sallie spent most of a month in

Staunton with family and friends. She returned at the end of the first week in October to discover what the *Times-Dispatch* described as a "surprise" for her: "Italian gardens of a style comparing favorably with anything of this kind in the South have been laid off . . . at 'Maymont' [which] . . . give every promise of showing under Virginia skies the same effects as in the palatial estates of Southern Europe."[25] Since the Dooleys had been talking with Baskervill about putting in the Italian garden since 1907, the report's spin was obviously inaccurate. The "surprise" was probably only that the actual work had finally begun. Be that as it may, the Dooleys' enthusiasm for formally organizing part of the Maymont estate grounds in this way led eventually to their trip to Italy in 1910.

Almost two months later, on the evening of November 20, 1908, Dooley's close friend and partner for more than thirty years, Joseph Bryan, died at his home, "Laburnum." A vigorous and strong man during his early years, Bryan had never quite recovered from the typhoid he contracted eight years before his death. It had seriously weakened his heart, but he had refused to spare himself, continuing, as his son John Stewart Bryan wrote, to throw himself "wholly and unreservedly into all that he undertook."[26] After Bryan's funeral, Dooley, as he had after Dr. Hunter Holmes McGuire's death, joined a group to raise funds for a statue of their friend. The Joseph Bryan Memorial Association chose William Couper, who had created the McGuire statue, to sculpt a seven-and-a half-foot bronze statue of their friend, which was unveiled on June 10, 1911, in Monroe Park, where it still stands. Inscribed on its base were two sentences that Dooley had helped phrase: "To exalted citizenship in private walks of life, as illustrated by the career of Joseph Bryan, this statue is dedicated by the people of Richmond. The character of the citizen is the strength of the state."

Bryan's death meant some changes in several businesses in which he and Dooley had been principals. Of special importance was the opportunity it provided for the Richmond and St. Paul Land and Improvement Association to wind up the business entirely. Such, at least, was the hope of ten stockholders whose investments constituted more than one-tenth of the stock in the company. On April 22, 1909, they asked Dooley and P. H. Mayo, as the surviving trustees of the company, to call a meeting to consider closing the association, either in whole or in part.[27] After the meeting took place on June 15, Dooley wrote to William McMurran, the association's attorney in St. Paul, for advice on selling the company's property there. McMurran advised holding on to the property for a year or two more.[28]

The stockholders met again in November to determine how much Dooley should be paid for performing his duty as president and treasurer of the company. He had served in that capacity for almost twenty-three years without any compensation.[29] In a letter to shareholders, the committee noted frankly: "As this real estate venture has been a most disastrous failure . . . it becomes embarrassing to determine what is a reasonable and fair compensation to Major Dooley for the . . . faithful and intelligent service he has given." In the end, they decided to pay him the equivalent of twenty-five dollars per month. They still did not close their books but instead took McMurran's advice to hold on, although not for one or two years but for nine. Finally, in 1918, Dooley sent a letter to shareholders notifying them that a final distribution would be made on July 2, when all shares in the company were to be surrendered at his office.[30] The books of the Richmond and St. Paul Land and Improvement Company were finally closed.

Several months after Bryan's funeral, a new chapter in the railroad business opened for Dooley when he traveled to New York City to attend a February 23, 1909, meeting of the board of directors of the Chesapeake and Ohio Railway Company. Although the C&O had its general offices in Richmond, it had recently rented an office in the Empire Building. Several other Richmonders, including Decatur Axtell, Frederic W. Scott, and Henry T. Wickham, were at the meeting. Scott had only recently been elected to the board at its February 11 meeting, as had two other board members present that day: Henry E. Huntington, nephew of Collis Huntington (the late, longtime president of the C&O); and Frank Vanderlip, then president of National City Bank in New York, with whom Dooley had differed about the health of the U.S. economy back in 1902.[31] At the meeting Wickham, then general counsel for the railroad, tendered his resignation, and Dooley was elected to take his place.[32] Dooley was then sixty-eight years old and well known for both his legal expertise and his experience in railroad matters. He also had a long history as an advocate for the C&O that went as far back as his work on its behalf in the House of Delegates. In addition, as chairman of the executive committee of the Seaboard Air Line, he had encouraged the two railroads to cooperate in an important venture for Richmond, the building of the city's Main Street Station. For the following nine years, except when he was on vacation, Dooley traveled once a month to New York City for a meeting of the C&O board, usually traveling with the C&O's president, George Stevens, in his private car. During those years, Dooley worked closely with Frank Vanderlip on financial and legal matters facing the C&O. In 1915, for instance, they served as a committee of two on legal and financial aspects of the sale of C&O stock in the Kanawha & Michigan Railway Company.[33]

Dooley and Huntington both attended most of the board meetings during those years and undoubtedly discovered their mutual interests in art and books. Interestingly, they both added Italian and Japanese gardens to their estates during that time, projects that may have given them a great deal to talk about before and after the meetings.[34]

CHAPTER 23 | Travel Abroad and a Mountain Palace

I n January 1910, Dooley celebrated his sixty-ninth birthday. By then he and Sallie had lived at Maymont for almost seventeen years, and like most homeowners, they had continually made improvements, especially to their gardens and grounds. They had added a new water tower and a stone barn in 1908, and the Italian garden was still under construction. He had taken frequent trips out of state looking after his business interests, and he and Sallie had traveled throughout the country during long vacations. Instead of slowing down, however, they took on more projects—adding the Japanese garden at Maymont, searching for mountain land on which to build a vacation house, and making plans for a trip abroad.

Dooley remained active in the Democratic Party and had supported William Hodges Mann for governor in 1909. Mann's attraction for Dooley was his strong support of educational reform, but they had both been railroad lawyers, and that shared experience made it easy for the two to develop a friendship despite their differences on such issues as Mann's support of Prohibition.

In 1906, two years after the Co-operative Education Association was founded, Mann, then a state senator, had introduced the "Mann High School Act," intended to provide the first financial support by the state for public high schools. The Virginia legislature had authorized the establishment of public high schools in the Commonwealth in 1903 but had failed to provide any funding for them.[1] As a result, there were still very few high schools in Virginia, and only 5 percent of the qualified students were actually enrolled. Mann's proposal had a salubrious effect, and by 1909 there were 345 public high schools in the state, nearly half of them four-year institutions.

Despite such progress, compulsory school attendance was a controversial political issue, tantamount to political suicide for politicians speaking out in its favor. Resistance was especially strong in rural areas, where farmers depended on their children to provide necessary labor. In his crusade for reform of the educational system, Mann found an ally in Dooley, whose essay "How May State Receive Return for Money Spent on Education," published in June 1909, had focused on issues about the curriculum offered in rural schools.[2] Later, during Mann's administration, Dooley also wrote an essay on compulsory education that was so well received when it was published in the newspaper that it was distributed to all of the state's school districts and republished in 1911 in an official document of the Commonwealth of Virginia by the Virginia Department of Public Instruction and the Co-operative Education Association.[3] Despite Dooley's essay and the efforts of Mann's administration, compulsory education did not become law in Virginia until 1922.[4]

A few weeks before Mann's inauguration, Dooley left Richmond by train to explore a piece of land on the southern ridge of Afton Mountain not far from Frederic W. Scott's vacation home, "Royal Orchard." Dooley and a real estate agent looked over the property, called "Carrie's Rest," which was just west of Rockfish Gap and had beautiful mountain views.[5] The location appealed especially to Sallie, who loved the mountains and was happy with the prospect of being close to her family in Staunton. Although Dooley was eager to please her by buying the property, negotiations with the current owner, a farmer named Yount, dragged on. Nothing was settled by late May, when he and Sallie boarded ship for a trip to Europe.

By June 10 they were staying at the Hotel Regina in Rome, visiting gardens at such places as the Villa Medici and the Villa Torlonia and shopping at the city's art galleries.[6] From Rome the Dooleys traveled to Florence and then Venice, where they stayed at Le Grand Hotel. Writing to his niece Nora Houston, Dooley told of their plans to go on to Milan, Como, and Lucerne, adding, "We will have a number of objects of art, to put up at Maymont after we return: all of them, I think very beautiful." One of the "objects of art" was a marble temple with columns topped by a filigreed iron dome. The Dooleys bought it in Venice and shipped it home to Maymont, where it still stands on a grassy knoll near the Italian garden.[7]

When the *Lusitania* docked in New York on September 2, the Dooleys were among the 563 first-class passengers who disembarked.[8] They did not return to hot and muggy Richmond immediately but instead went to Staunton to spend a few weeks in the cool Shenandoah Valley. Sallie had been spending part of September there for most of their married lives, surrounded by her brothers and sisters and their children.

While they were in Staunton, Dooley responded to a letter he had received from Henry Evans, president of the Continental Fire Insurance Company in New York, on whose board Dooley sat. Evans had written to ask for Dooley's "views 'in extenso' upon the business outlook." Evans's letter and Dooley's response were subsequently published on the front page of the Sunday *Richmond Times-Dispatch* on September 25, 1910. In his reply Dooley predicted another depression or perhaps even another panic within the next twelve months, apportioning blame to a "boom in stocks . . . hurried on and carried too far by the great capitalists and speculators," President William Howard Taft's "program for regulating the railroads," and Taft's "backing of a low tariff bill."

At the end of his letter, Dooley shared his theory about economic trends: "I have a theory which I think is supported by experience, that once in every three or four years circumstance, conditions, or manipulation will bring about a great boom, on which to sell, and a correspondingly great depression, on which to buy." He then listed numerous three- to four-year fluctuations in the economy beginning with 1878 before he ominously noted: "In 1907 came what I may call Roosevelt's panic. Next year will be 1911." He concluded that although he thought a depression was imminent, "I hope I may be disappointed." In fact, he was. The depression he anticipated did not happen, but his letter created some understandable unease in Richmond and New York.

The following Tuesday, in a note thanking him for the present he had brought back for her from Italy, his sister Josephine wrote that his letter "seems to have made quite an impression. Several people have spoken to me about it, and I have been told that people generally were talking of it."[9] She ended her letter with a comment that suggested that the trip to Italy was, at least in part, an attempt to improve Sallie's health: "I hope Sister Sallie has benefited very much by her trip, and that she will come back ready and able to see all her pretty things unpacked." By then Sallie may have begun to suffer from the diabetes that would plague her later years, and for which in the early years of the twentieth century there was no known remedy. As the decade progressed there were other signs of health problems. She apparently suffered from leg ulcers, which often afflict victims of diabetes.[10] Some years later, apparently because of Sallie's health problems, Dooley began to accompany his wife to St. Paul's Episcopal Church. His sister Sarah—now Mother Mary Magdalene up at Monte Maria—was scandalized, presuming that he had left the Catholic Church.[11] A more likely explanation was that he was simply helping Sallie into church and staying with her after their chauffeur deposited them at the church door.

In November 1910, Dooley and Sallie's nephew, the lawyer Fitzhugh Elder, exchanged a series of letters about the purchase of the mountain land Dooley had explored back in February.[12] Eager to purchase it, and inspired by the Italian Renaissance architecture they had seen, the Dooleys had asked Noland and Baskervill to draw up preliminary plans for a palazzo big enough to entertain large numbers of friends and family. They also asked the firm to create a fountain for Maymont modeled after one they had seen at Villa Torlonia and to add a grotto near the canal.

Negotiations for the mountain property dragged on for months, and Dooley was frustrated and impatient with the delays. In one of his November letters to Fitzhugh Elder he complained: "Your aunt is exceedingly desirous that I should buy . . . the property and I want to gratify her. I am able to pay for it and, it would seem, I ought to be able to buy it." By spring, he had done so.

Meanwhile, on November 4, 1910, Dooley was reelected president of Richmond Art Club. During his tenure he encouraged joint programs with the Co-operative Education Association, presided at many receptions and exhibitions openings, and introduced numerous speakers.[13] In 1908 he had offered to give two thousand dollars toward the purchase of a new building for the Art Club's school if his gift were matched by other donors. In 1910, his challenge having remained unmet, he bought a building and paid to have the interior transformed to house the studios and meeting rooms the club needed.[14] He also funded "Dooley Scholarships" for children whose families couldn't afford to pay for lessons at the school.[15]

On November 16, Nora Houston's first one-woman exhibition opened at the Richmond Art Club, where she was now instructor in "Oils and Still Life." Her portrait *Uncle Jim* was No. 22 in the catalogue, and a landscape, *The Lawn at Maymont,* was No. 25.[16] Nora would contribute work to Art Club exhibitions and remain on its faculty until it closed in 1918.

Dooley had planned to inspect his new mountain property in January 1911, but he didn't manage to make the trip there until the week after Easter. On April 21 a small item in the *Valley Virginian* noted that "Major Dooley and twenty of his friends and a surveyor from Richmond spent most of the past week at his recently purchased farm near Afton, having the roads, walks, flower gardens surveyed and a situation for a very large residence."[17] And large it was. As planned, the dwelling's thirty-nine rooms covered twenty-two thousand square feet on what was eventually 761 acres. The Dooleys called their new estate Swannanoa.

A month before the surveying trip, Dooley read an article in the March 1911 issue of the *North American Review* by Walker K. Tuller, who advocated that a convention be held to amend the U.S. Constitution.[18] In response, the seventy-year-old Dooley wrote his last-known essay, a nine-page pamphlet with the title "A National Constitutional Convention and Its Possible Consequences: What Limitations Can Be Imposed upon the Powers of a Convention Called to Amend the Constitution of the United States?"[19] Highly critical of Tuller's article, Dooley's work showed that although its author had given up his law practice, he was still deeply interested in legal issues and constitutional history. As usual, the essay was published as a pamphlet, a copy of which still survives in the University of Michigan Law School Library.

In June 1911, Dooley arrived at the Empire Building in New York City for the regularly scheduled meeting of the C&O board. On the agenda was a vote on the sale of a piece of swampland adjoining Maymont.[20] Dooley had wanted to buy it ever since he purchased the ninety-six acres next to it in 1886, but despite repeated efforts, he had been unable to acquire it. The difficulty was its clouded title. The site had been a turning basin for the James River and Kanawha Canal until 1880, when the Richmond and Allegheny Railroad bought the right-of-way and laid its new tracks along what had been the towpath. After the Richmond and Allegheny failed, the C&O apparently acquired the title to the former turning basin, although no written document existed to confirm the change of ownership. During the meeting President George W. Stevens announced that "he had agreed to sell to Mrs. Sallie M. Dooley . . . about 5 acres [between] the canal and grounds of Major Dooley's suburban residence. . . . [The site] is entirely cut off and inaccessible to others, and no other disposition of the property is practicable. . . . [T]he price offered, Seven Hundred and Fifty 00/100 Dollars ($750.00) is, in the judgment of a disinterested real estate agent, in excess of its value." Dooley left the room during the discussion, returning only after a vote was taken and recorded. A few moments later, the sale was approved by vote. Sallie finally owned the five acres on which a traditional Japanese garden would later be created. Payment of a sum in excess of its assessed value was undoubtedly motivated by her husband's wish to make what is sometimes called a "clean hands transaction" so that he could not be accused of taking advantage of his position on the board to enrich his wife at the railroad's expense.

The Dooleys then engaged a renowned Japanese gardener, Y Muto, to design the garden. By 1912 he had transformed the stone outcropping of the old quarry near their Italian garden into a stunning version of the waterfall that was a classic feature of traditional Japanese gardens. Water cascaded down forty-five feet into a pond before flowing under an arched footbridge into the garden.[21]

Meanwhile, construction was beginning on the new summer retreat on Afton Mountain just west of Rockfish Gap. The Dooleys, eager to watch the house being built, spent a good deal of time in Staunton that summer since it was a very short ride from there to Afton by train. They even hosted picnics at the building site for Staunton relatives and friends while the house was under construction. Over the years of its construction, their guests watched as mule and horse teams hauled marble up the mountain from the Afton railroad station to the house site. They also heard what must have seemed a babble of languages spoken by the foreign craftsmen working there who knew very little English.[22]

In late November Dooley was among the delegates from across the United States who attended the First Annual Road Congress of the American Association for Highway Improvement, held in Richmond. He was a substitute for President Joseph Himmel, S.J., of Georgetown College, who was too ill to attend.[23] President Taft was scheduled to give the opening address but sent his regrets at the last minute. Dooley must have been disappointed when Taft didn't appear, but he found it gratifying nonetheless that issues he had confronted fourteen years earlier at the state level were now considered important enough to have attracted the attention of the president.

On Saturday, December 9, Sallie slipped away from her duties at Maymont to go into Richmond. According to an entry in the diary of her friend Catherine Claiborne Cox, at four thirty that afternoon there was a "meeting of a few ladies at the home of Mrs. Henry Taylor to form some plan to urge the legislature to take no steps toward granting equal suffrage until the views of the majority of the Virginia women was known."[24] Unlike Dooley's sisters, who were supporters of the women's suffrage movement, the women who attended the meeting at the Taylor home were opposed to it. That day they established the Virginia Association Opposed to Woman's Suffrage, and by early 1912 the group was very active. At its organizational meeting on March 16, Sallie was elected to its executive board.[25] The fledgling organization burst forth with pamphlets and published by-laws stating their many reasons for being against voting rights for women.[26] In one of its pamphlets, *Why Women Should Oppose Equal Suffrage,* the association asserted that because "the methods of a political campaign are repugnant . . . and the personal notoriety connected with such a campaign impossible," the women of the association would do their work "quietly; their aim being to prove that the large majority of Virginia women are opposed to Equal suffrage." The association posed a number of questions in their pamphlet, among them: "Shall women be forced to vote?," "Is the right to vote inherent?," and "Should women enter politics?" To each question, the pamphlet answered an emphatic "No," followed by a brief explanation defending that answer. Although the twenty-three founders of the association were prominent in Richmond, in the years that followed they discovered they were outnumbered by the women in favor of women's suffrage. The "quiet" work of the antisuffrage women faded into the background in 1919, when the U.S. Congress passed the Nineteenth Amendment granting suffrage to women. Virginia women were allowed to vote for the first time in 1920, when the amendment became law, but the influence of the antisuffrage movement prevailed in the Virginia legislature until 1952, when the General Assembly finally ratified the amendment.

History doesn't record whether Sallie ever knew about a meeting of the Art Club at which her husband confronted, or was confronted by, the issue of women's suffrage. It happened just as he sat down to begin the meeting. His niece Nora and her friend, the art teacher Adele Clark, both officers of the Equal Suffrage League, approached him with a petition in support of women's right to vote.[27] The women were confident that Dooley would sign the petition. Not only Nora but his sisters Alice and Josephine were ardent advocates who had demonstrated on behalf of the movement. Soon-to-be-famous photographs of suffragettes on the steps of Capitol Square featured them, as well as Lila Meade Valentine and other leaders of the movement.[28] Although Sallie Dooley wasn't at the Art Club board meeting herself, her influence was clearly felt. Dooley refused to sign.

The Dooleys sailed to Europe again in 1912, this time on the *Lusitania*'s sister ship, the *Mauretania*. Their arrival in London was reported in the *New York Times,* which noted that the couple had stayed at Claridges before leaving for a leisurely, two-month-long, chauffeur-driven motor car trip through Europe.[29] They made a long stop in Munich, where Dooley immersed himself in the art of the Alte Pinakothek museum and the 1912 Annual Exhibition at the Kgl. Glaspalast (Royal Glass Palace). The following November he shared his enthusiasm for what he saw there with members of the Richmond Art Club in a lecture entitled "Munich as an Art Center."[30] The *New York Times* made note of their activities again just before their return: "James H. Dooley, who spent the last week-end motoring in the chateau district, with Mrs. Dooley, left the Hôtel de Crillon on Tuesday for London, where they will make a stay previous to returning to America."[31]

The Dooleys returned to Maymont in time to follow Woodrow Wilson's campaign for the presidency. Although Virginia-born, Wilson was then governor of New Jersey. That December, when Richmond hosted the National Governors' Conference, he was probably expected to come. The inhabitants of Richmond extended themselves mightily on the governors' behalf, outdoing themselves to entertain them. The society column of the *Times-Dispatch* declared that "affairs given in honor of the visiting Governors and their wives are the most important events taking place here this week."[32] One of the highlights of the conference week was lunch at Maymont, where the Dooleys entertained 250 people including the governors of forty-six of the forty-eight states, along with their wives and staffs. The guests came at half past one to find the house, as the *Times-Dispatch* gushed, "a perfect bower of lovely flowers."[33] The only two governors not present were the governor of Colorado, who had had a death in the family, and the governor of New Jersey, now president-elect, who was in Bermuda recovering from the rigors of the presidential campaign.

Sometime in late 1912 several young women artists, including the Dooleys' niece Nora, decided to create and sell a calendar for 1913 that they called "A Year in Richmond." They illustrated the pages of the calendar with drawings by local women artists and quotations from literary works by local women authors. Sallie received a letter from Adele Clark asking if she would allow them to use a quotation from *Dem Good Ole Times*.[34] She readily agreed, replying that she was "very much flattered that you . . . consider anything in my book worthy of a place in your calendar."[35] The quotation appeared on the page for February and March below a drawing by Edith Anne Pemberton Ragland.

A year later, on December 23, 1913, Woodrow Wilson signed the Federal Reserve Act. Initially sponsored by Carter Glass, the congressman from Lynchburg, Virginia, the act established twelve banks in the Federal Reserve System whose location was to be chosen by a committee appointed by the president. Fortunately for Richmond, Wilson appointed Glass, then secretary of the Treasury, and John Skelton Williams, comptroller of the currency, to the committee to designate the sites for the Federal Reserve System. Any city interested in becoming home to a Federal Reserve bank was to prepare documents enumerating the reasons it should be selected. On January 21, 1914, Dooley, well aware that Baltimore was vying with Richmond to become the bank site for the southern region, wrote to Williams explaining why he thought Richmond should be selected instead. In the letter Dooley was dismissive of Baltimore's claims, maintaining that Baltimore could not "compare with Richmond in what the two cities have done for the development of the Southern States since the conclusion of hostilities." In support of Richmond, he reviewed the city's central role in banking and business since the war ended and reminded Williams that Richmond "is still to all intents and purposes the capital of . . . [the southern states]. She is the capital city of their business, the capital city of their banking. . . . You know as well as I do . . . how vehemently they are opposed to being compelled to do their banking with any other city."[36] In conclusion, he advised Williams not to be restrained by "delicacy in urging . . . the interests of your own city."

Months passed as the selection committee worked to divide the country into districts and choose the cities for the banks. By the beginning of April,

Richmond's business community was in a state of restless anticipation over the outcome. When someone heard that the choices were to be announced on April 2, a group of men gathered in an office to hear the news.[37] The sudden ringing of the telephone interrupted their conversation. John Skelton Williams was on the line. He prolonged his announcement by describing the parameters of the newly established Federal Reserve districts. Only after that did he reveal that Richmond had indeed been selected as headquarters of the fifth district. He couldn't miss hearing the cheer that filled the air when the men heard the news. Most Richmonders learned the news the next morning when they awoke to read the headlines in the *Times-Dispatch*. On page five they found Major Dooley's January 21 letter to Williams reprinted in full.

During 1914 Dooley lost another friend and business associate when, on August 11, Thomas Muldrup Logan died in New York City. Although he maintained a home in Buckingham County, he had spent most of his time in New York since the early 1890s. The family brought Logan's body to Richmond for burial in Hollywood Cemetery.

Dooley turned seventy-four in January 1915. He was still an active member of several corporate boards, including that of Birmingham's Sloss-Sheffield Iron and Steel Company, and made frequent long-distance trips by train. His financial situation was not as healthy as he wished, however. As he explained in a May 7 letter to his sister Florence, the Sloss-Sheffield Company had stopped paying dividends, and he had lost heavily in the last several years.[38] In March 1915, when the number of seats on the Sloss-Sheffield board was reduced from twelve to ten members, he gladly dropped off the board, only to be persuaded to return two days later.[39] Why he did so is unclear, but the war in Europe, instead of being a drain on the economy of the United States, had "become a bonanza" for heavy industry by then, and the company's financial condition was beginning to improve.[40] Dooley may have heard that it was likely the company would resume paying dividends by the end of the year, a possibility he mentioned in a letter to his sister Alice the following July.[41] In the end, he remained on the Sloss-Sheffield board until the annual meeting in 1918, when his resignation was announced and Melville Branch of Richmond took his seat.[42] By then, despite Branch's appointment to the executive committee, Virginian impact on the growth of north Alabama was coming to a close.

May 1915 brought bad news on two fronts—one international and the other personal. On May 7, a German U-boat attacked and sank the *Lusitania,* the largest and most luxurious ship afloat, and the ship on which, almost exactly five years earlier, the Dooleys had sailed to England. More than a thousand passengers died, and outrage spread throughout the United States, which had not yet entered the First World War.

At about the same time, Dooley was attempting to rescue his sister Florence from impending financial ruin. Although each of his sisters had a small income from their mother's estate, Dooley had been their primary support for a number of years. He had been giving them monthly allowances, extra money for clothing, and generous financial gifts. During his mother's lifetime both she and he had lent considerable sums to Florence and her husband, William Lewis, who needed financial help running their farm, "Lynnside."[43] In May 1915, Florence, who had been widowed for years and was badly in debt despite the money Dooley sent her, wrote to say she was planning to borrow even more to pay off a five-year loan for which she had put up her farm as collateral. Dooley sent her a frank response describing his own financial situation: "I do not wish to discourage you from making an effort to borrow the money you need. It would be quite a relief to me if you could do so, because besides having sunk a tremendous amount of money in Swannanoa (far more than I had expected to) I have lost heavily in the years that succeeded the Wilson election, and feel very reluctant to assume other people's obligations."[44] Despite his obvious irritation, he suggested a plan to help her. He noted that he was supporting her sisters in two different houses, each of which was large enough to accommodate all of them, and proposed that they live together under one roof, in Sweet Springs, where they had been spending their summers together for years. In his view it was "sensible" under the circumstances. He explained that he would make some improvements to the beautiful columned colonial mansion, such as putting in a furnace and—if Florence could get "water-pressure"—a bathroom. He included an itemized list of Florence's current and future income and noted that by selling his Sloss-Sheffield stock he could give her more. He even agreed to pay for the fuel for the furnace and to pay all Florence's debts "if you will all come together and aid each other." Just as he feared, however, his sisters in Richmond were not happy with his proposal. Letters flew back and forth. His niece Nora wrote that she objected to his proposal because "I am now, thanks to your investment in my training, a painter and instructor in good standing, with an esteemed profession, and a position of honor in the community. . . . I hope that you will not press this matter, and insist upon my abandoning my work, just as it is becoming a dependable certainty."[45] After a deluge of such letters, on July 4 he withdrew his proposition "entirely and unconditionally."

He did not, however, withdraw his promise to "take care of" Florence's debts even though they were probably much larger than he first realized. On August 27 Dooley bought the 147 acres of the Lynnside tract from Florence for five dollars in cash and paid her $7,800 debt to her creditors.[46] Dooley's effort to help his sister and her children did not end there. Seven months later, on April Fool's Day, he gave Florence a "life estate" in Lynnside. In the deed he also made provision for her children to inherit the property.

CHAPTER 24 | Extraordinary Gifts

I n 1916 the Medical College of Virginia was facing a crisis. The facilities
of its Memorial Hospital were no longer adequate to provide clinical
training for its students or to carry the burgeoning patient load. The hospital was so overcrowded that some of its would-be patients were either
shifted to the City Home, a charitable institution, or, in the case of those who
were better-off, sent to Baltimore or quarantined, along with their families,
in their own homes.[1] Two new hospitals and a residence hall for nurses were
badly needed. If the hospital for treatment of contagious diseases were to be
built, its beds would be the only ones in the whole city for patients suffering
from serious diseases such as diphtheria.

In the spring, the board of trustees decided to launch a capital campaign
to raise the $250,000 needed, and to approach Dooley for a leadership gift
they could announce at a banquet opening the campaign. John Kerr Branch,
who was described as a fund-raising "human dynamo," and Dooley's friend
Dr. Stuart McGuire agreed to call on him. They hoped he might give enough
to endow a room or at least a bed in the public or the children's ward.

Branch made the appointment for June 5. Shortly after he and McGuire
arrived at Dooley's office, the two men outlined their mission and handed
him a pledge card. Dooley asked several thoughtful questions, especially
about the cost of building and equipping the hospital for contagious diseases.
They explained that the estimated cost for the whole facility, fully furnished,
was forty thousand dollars and were pleased to see Dooley sign the pledge
card. When they looked at it after the interview, they discovered that he
had pledged to give the entire forty thousand dollars. According to Branch,
McGuire later said "in private" that he felt as though "he had thrown away
$10,000 because he was confident that if he had asked for that much more
he would have gotten it."[2]

Meanwhile, the First World War was raging in Europe, and on the night of
April 2, 1917, Woodrow Wilson addressed a special session of Congress and
declared that the United States must enter the war to "make the world safe
for democracy." On April 6, Congress voted to declare war. A few days later,
the president announced a bond campaign to raise the funds needed for the
war effort. It was the first of four successful "Liberty Loan" campaigns. These
featured appearances by prominent personalities, including movie stars and

sports heroes, at big rallies in major cities. A little over a month after Wilson's announcement, a well-known international figure arrived in Richmond on May 19 to encourage bond purchases by whipping up patriotic enthusiasm.

The Rt. Hon. Arthur James Balfour, the British foreign secretary and head of the British High Commission to the United States, had accepted an invitation to visit "the capital of the Confederacy."[3] Cheering crowds lined the sidewalks when the foreign secretary, the British ambassador to the United States, a British army general, and a Royal Navy admiral arrived.[4] From the first moment, Balfour's skill as a diplomat was obvious. He achieved his objective by stirring memories of the Civil War. After lunch at the Governor's Mansion, the British military contingent emerged from the building to place a wreath at the base of the Stonewall Jackson statue on Capitol Square. On the way toward the City Auditorium, where Balfour was to make a speech at three thirty, the military men placed wreaths at the Monument Avenue statues of Robert E. Lee and J. E. B. Stuart.

The $2 billion Liberty Loan campaign opened in every bank in the United States the following Monday. Richmond's bankers felt the campaign opened auspiciously, and although the first-day total was not announced, it was described as "entirely satisfactory."[5] A number of bonds "for fairly large amounts, ranging up to $1,000," were sold that day. There were plans for house-to-house canvassing by Boy Scouts delivering circulars that provided information about the bonds. Several of the banks positioned young women at tables in their lobbies to sell bonds—mostly in fifty-dollar denominations—to be paid for in weekly installments. On Wednesday the board of First National Bank itself bought five hundred thousand dollars in bonds.[6] The board felt that it was "important that every one who is able to do so, subscribe promptly to show to the world that the American people are solidly behind their government."

The next morning, May 24, Dooley made his regular weekly visit to Merchants National Bank, where he was still on the board of directors. While he was there, he matched the purchase of the entire First National Bank board by buying a five-hundred-thousand-dollar Liberty Loan bond. His munificence made the front-page headlines of the *News-Leader* that evening.[7]

The Dooleys spent most of the summer and all of September 1917 at Swannanoa. Although Sallie apparently did not write any other long narratives after the publication of *Dem Good Ole Times,* she did continue to write poetry, and her sojourns at Swannanoa often provided her inspiration. In September 1917, for instance, she sent a copy of a poem called "Autumn" to an old friend, the Staunton lawyer Armistead C. Gordon, also a novelist and poet.[8]

In a letter to her on September 12, Gordon, who apparently was not above flattering friends, responded: "Thank you very much for sending me your poem . . . which I have read with pleasure and admiration, and shall preserve among my library treasures. Some of the lines are Tennysonian: and the descriptions of nature in its autumnal moods are lovely. If you will pardon me for saying so, I think that one who wields so graceful a pen as yourself ought to write more."[9]

Sometime during World War I, the servants who worked for the Dooleys began whispering among themselves that Major Dooley might be a spy and that "the downstairs was wired up to do wire tapping."[10] The rumor may have started with a telautograph machine that had been in Dooley's study since the 1890s. At some point before the United States entered World War I, Dooley and his Richmond friends who had invested in the Gray National Telautograph Company were rewarded handsomely when its machine was selected by the U.S. Army for fire-control communication in the Coastal Defense System. Telautographs were installed in the most important forts on the Atlantic and Pacific coasts, which provided the only on-land defense in the United States against offshore enemy attack.[11] The soundless telautograph was chosen instead of the telephone or telegraph for these secret installations because when their guns were fired it would have been impossible to hear the ringing of a telephone or the clicking of a telegraph transmission.

Toward the end of the winter of 1919, the seventy-eight-year-old Dooley caught a heavy cold that apparently turned into pneumonia. His doctor forbade him to leave the house, and his sisters, mindful that their father had died of a similar ailment, became nervous. Dooley spent much of February confined to his bed. By March 5, the date of a dinner celebrating the fifteenth anniversary of the Co-operative Education Association, of which he continued to be vice president and a member of the finance committee, Dooley was still under doctor's orders not to go out. He sent a letter of regret to Mary Munford, which she read to the large crowd at the dinner at the Westmoreland Club. In it he announced that he had decided to double his annual donation to the association for the next three years "to aid the development of our most important work and more widely extend its influence" and added, "Please assure your co-laborers I am with them heart and soul."[12] The letter had an immediate impact on the other members of the finance committee. They joined him in doubling their subscriptions for the next three years.

By the spring of 1920, construction of the Dooley Hospital for Contagious Diseases was coming to an end, but there were cost overruns, in this case amounting to eleven thousand dollars—more than 25 percent of the original estimated cost. Predictably, in mid-April emissaries approached Dooley. First they asked if he would donate the eleven thousand dollars necessary to finish building the hospital. Without hesitation, Dooley agreed to give the additional money.[13] Then they explained that MCV had no place to treat the local children who had been crippled during the recent polio epidemic, asking if he would agree to allow the hospital he had endowed to become a hospital for crippled children.[14] Once again, he agreed.

At about the same time in April, John M. Miller, president of the First National Bank of Richmond, wrote to invite Dooley to a meeting in the bank's boardroom. Two other bankers, E. L. Bemiss and Oliver Jackson Sands, joined Miller in signing the letter. In it they explained that the meeting concerned "a situation [that] has just developed in Richmond which we feel requires the best thought and co-operation of those who have the interests of the city at heart."[15] Although just what the situation facing the city was is now unknown, what is known is that Dooley did not attend the meeting. A few days later, Dooley was partially paralyzed by a serious stroke from which it took him months to recover. Not long afterward, he received a letter from President J. B. Creeden of Georgetown College conveying the news that the college was awarding him an honorary doctor of laws degree. Dooley was too weak to respond, but on May 6 Sallie wrote to thank him, adding that "Mr. Dooley . . . has been confined to the bed for several weeks, and as soon as he is sufficiently strong he will write and express his appreciation of the honor you intend to confer."[16] Dooley did not regain his strength in time to attend the commencement exercises. His honorary degree was conferred in absentia during the graduation ceremony on June 8. He missed hearing himself described as a "brilliant member of the class of 1860 . . . who has won from the days of his youth the boundless admiration of all who have examined his remarkable career."

When the new three-story hospital—with Dooley's name over the door—opened on October 29, 1920, twenty-nine young orthopedic patients, all wards of the state, were transferred to the hospital, which had the capacity to care for fifty children.[17] A plaque under the big clock on the wall in the front hall read: "This Building Was Erected and Equipped by James H. Dooley as a Token of the Affection He Bears to His Native City and Her People." What Dooley apparently never knew, however, was that the hospital was already too small to serve the many children stricken by the polio epidemic. As early as 1917, a group headed by the orthopedic surgeon Dr. William T. Graham had begun to work toward the creation of a "crippled children's hospital" in Richmond. They had formed a board of trustees and, on May 1, 1920, six months before Dooley Hospital opened, secured a charter from the State Corporation Commission.[18] They had also organized a women's auxiliary to help with their efforts, including fund-raising. In November 1920, its board met several times to consider ways to raise funds but decided that the time was not right for a capital campaign.

The following summer, while the Dooleys spent five months at Swannanoa, Dooley and his secretary, William Bentley, kept in touch by letter. One of Dooley's letters from that time reveals that his stroke had impaired his memory. In it, he wrote to Bentley: "Never fear to express your opinion about any of my investments. I have so many, and was sick so long, that I cannot now carry them all in my mind, as I used to, of course."[19]

In the fall, back in Richmond again and still not completely recovered, Dooley felt well enough to go to his office regularly. Perhaps with the thought of closing it, he began to go through his papers. Among them were some relating to the settlement of his father's estate more than fifty years earlier. He found records of at least two debts incurred by his father that he had never settled, and he promptly undertook to do so. On December 6, he wrote to S. P. Cowardin enclosing a check for $884.06, "being principal and interest" of his father's debt to Cowardin's father, and asking him to distribute the money to his father's heirs.[20] Dooley also paid a much smaller sum to J. J. English, owner of the Bell Book and Stationery Company, enclosing a check for $34.79 due to its predecessor firm, the booksellers Randolph and English.

Although Dooley was failing physically, sometime in December 1921 he managed to respond to blandishments from Georgetown College for a contribution to its building fund by asking Bentley to send a check to the college. Bentley tucked it into a letter explaining Dooley's intention and mentioning that Dooley's health had improved in the "past few months." Georgetown president J. B. Creeden responded on December 22, thanking him and expressing the hope "that you may be able to visit Washington and see the College. During the next term we shall have a Dinner for the Honorary Degree Men of the College, and I hope that you may be able to attend."[21]

After spending the summer of 1922 at Swannanoa, the Dooleys returned to Maymont in late October. A little more than a week after arriving home, Dooley was paralyzed by a second stroke and taken to Grace Hospital in Richmond. This time his condition did not improve. He lingered in the hospital until his death just before midnight on November 16, 1922.

He was the last of the three young Richmond lawyers who forty-two years earlier laid the groundwork for the industrialization of the South when they joined together to borrow enough money to buy eight thousand shares of stock in the Richmond and Danville Railroad, then only 168 miles long. Their success in that endeavor prompted their creation of the first railroad holding company in U.S. history and the transformation of the Danville into an interstate system that by the mid-1880s had become the fastest-growing and second-longest railroad in the United States. They created railroad construction companies to build their system and searched for rail links not only in the South but also in the Midwest, Far Northwest and even Nicaragua. Their loyalties were local, but their vision was global. The three gathered around them a small network of Richmond men who encouraged one another to participate in long-distance investments. They commissioned geological research and used its results as a guide to investments in businesses and real estate along their rail lines. Their efforts were closely chronicled by regional and national newspapers that called them "The Virginians." After they lost control of the Richmond and Danville system in the depression of the 1890s, Dooley joined John Skelton Williams in developing another trunk line, this one from Richmond to the Gulf of Mexico as a step toward an international trade route through the Nicaragua Canal. The work of Dooley and his associates had lasting impact. Passengers and freight in the twenty-first century still travel railroad routes built under their auspices. Dooley, who articulated their vision, became a respected and often-published commentator on economic, financial, and political matters.

Each of the men grew wealthy, even though their rise to wealth was not linear. Dooley's partners, Bryan and Logan, had roots in the antebellum plantation world, but Dooley was a first-generation American from the urban South. His understanding of the exigencies of corporate business was cultivated early by the necessity of running his immigrant father's interstate manufacturing company during the Civil War.

All of the partners were intelligent, but James Dooley's publications suggest that he was the most intellectually inclined. Early in his career his excellence as a lawyer was recognized by the leading figures in his profession, and his dedication to public and community service earned him the devotion of Richmond residents at every level of society. His business colleagues respected and sought his opinions on financial and political matters.

The day after his death, Dooley's picture and lengthy articles about him appeared on the front page of both the *Times-Dispatch* and the *News-Leader.* The *Times-Dispatch* account stuck to facts about his personal life and his wealth. The *News-Leader,* on the other hand, emphasized his leadership in rebuilding Richmond and industrializing the South after the Civil War. In an editorial, Douglas Southall Freeman summed up James Dooley's importance to the Richmond—and the South—of his time:

> His life and its early comfort, followed by harsh vicissitudes and later successes mirrored the life of Richmond and the South. Today Richmond owes a large part of its wealth and its commercial importance and widespread manufacturing to the foresight and the labors of the generation to which Major Dooley belonged. Some of the men of that generation made fortunes—among them was Major Dooley—but the money they gained from their labors was insignificant compared with the prosperity and opportunities that they brought to others. . . . It was not by chance that Richmond retained supremacy; it was by labor and effort and forethought and sacrifice, and in all that patriotic work Major Dooley played a large and conspicuous part.[22]

Dooley was, Freeman concluded, a "sagacious, kindly, brave and unflinching patriot in peace or war, blessed in an idyllic home life, honored and respected."

Sallie had her husband's body brought back to Maymont for a funeral in the drawing room at 3:30 p.m. on Saturday, November 18. Much to the distress of Dooley's sister, Mother Mary Magdalen of Monte Maria, Sallie asked her minister at St. Paul's Episcopal Church, the Rev. Dr. Walter Russell Bowie, to conduct the funeral service. Sallie did not overlook Dooley's lifelong connection to St. Peter's Catholic Church, across the street from St. Paul's, however. She asked the Catholic bishop, the Rt. Rev. Denis J. O'Connell, a good friend of the family, to be one of the honorary pallbearers.[23] Attending were family, numerous close friends and business associates, and a detail of four Confederate veterans from the R. E. Lee Camp No. 1.

Sallie commissioned Henry Baskervill to design a mausoleum to be built on the gently sloping west lawn beyond the house, and both Dooleys were eventually interred there. Baskervill designed a small structure very like an ancient Greek temple with olive leaf wreaths symbolizing "heroic achievement" at each corner of the frieze just below the roofline.[24] Construction of the North Carolina white granite building began in the spring of 1923 and was finished the following October.

There was a great stir in Richmond when Dooley's will was published and the public learned that he had recommended that Sallie leave to the City of Richmond "all of the land known as Maymont . . . to be used as a Public Park and a museum and that she bequeath also to said city all of the Bric a brac, pictures, furnishings, ornaments and household effects in the resi-dence ... to be used as a museum for the benefit and pleasure of the people of Richmond."[25] The Sisters of Charity at St. Joseph's Female Academy and Orphan Asylum rejoiced when they learned that he had left them land across the street from Maymont's gates, along with instructions to construct there three "handsome brick" buildings for their orphanage and school. The will went into some detail regarding the architecture and purpose of the build-ings, reflecting not only his concern for crippled children and orphans but also his understanding that the education of women in the twentieth century should "enable them ... to go into the world to make an honest living." He left $3 million to the Sisters of Charity to enable them to fulfill his instruc-tions. It was said to be the largest monetary gift to a Catholic charity in the United States up to that time.[26]

A rumble of disapproval traveled through the households of Dooley friends sometime later, when the Sisters of Charity approached the Chan-cery Court for permission to disregard Dooley's wishes for the location of buildings and to build them instead on a one-hundred-acre property north of Richmond owned by their Order.[27] The court granted their request.

The will also generated considerable dissatisfaction among the Dooley relatives. Three of his sisters felt they had been slighted in the will. Mother Mary Magdalen was especially upset to learn that she had been left only five thousand dollars, while in her opinion her sisters had been remembered "lib-erally."[28] Alice Dooley, Mother Mary Magdalen, and Josephine Houston sued the estate in the Chancery Court and won their case. The result was that they and all the relations on both the Dooley and the May sides of the family within a specified degree of consanguinity were granted large settlements.[29]

By January 1923, two months after Major Dooley's death, the members of the women's auxiliary of the as-yet-unbuilt and unfunded Crippled Chil-dren's Hospital had grown impatient, and they approached the board "for approval of a building fund drive."[30] Once again the board turned the ladies down, "advising them to delay any campaign." Although the women didn't know it, the funds necessary to build the Crippled Children's Hospital had already been promised by a donor who had sworn the board's executive com-mittee to secrecy. The impatience of the auxiliary members grew to a fever pitch until a little over six months after James Dooley's death, when the chair-man of the board announced at a June 19, 1923, meeting of the auxiliary "that a bequest of $500,000 to build a hospital for crippled children had been made by a wealthy citizen, and that this sum was expected to be available before many years.[31]

The mystery about the identity of the donor deepened for more than two years, until September 1925, when Sallie Dooley died and her will was read. It revealed that she was "the wealthy citizen" mentioned at that ladies' auxiliary meeting so long before. She left a half million dollars to the Crippled Children's Hospital, of which half was to buy the land and "to construct and equip" the hospital; the other half was to be invested as an endowment.[32] Once again, thanks to a Dooley gift, a capital campaign for a Richmond hospital was over before it had begun. The name of the institution was subsequently changed to Children's Hospital, but it is still helping disabled children. According to a history of the hospital published on its fiftieth anniversary, Sallie Dooley's bequest was "the most liberal sum ever given to a private charity in the state of Virginia" up to that time.[33]

Sallie's will also revealed that she had left Maymont—the land, the house, and its contents—to the City of Richmond, as her husband had recommended. In addition to bequests to members of her family and employees, she left the proceeds of the sale of her "jewelry and precious stones" to the Rev. Dr. Walter Russell Bowie "to be disposed of by him in my name . . . to such foreign missions as he may select." She also left a quarter of a million dollars to the "Protestant Episcopal Church in the Diocese of Virginia" to be invested and its income devoted to the bishop's discretionary fund. Her final bequest was a half million dollars to the City of Richmond to buy land on which to construct and furnish a public library "as a memorial" to her husband "to be known as 'The Dooley Public Library.'"

Six months after Sallie's death, on Easter Sunday 1926, the City of Richmond opened the gates of Maymont to the public. That day thousands of visitors entered its gates to enjoy one of the Dooleys' extraordinary gifts.

NOTES

I. A YOUNG FAMILY

1 Parish Record Book, Part II: Record of Marriages: 1812–March 1855, St. Mary's Roman Catholic Church, Alexandria, Va.

2 Marriage Bond, August 24, 1836, Arlington County (Alexandria County) Marriage Bonds, 1834–1839, Misc. microfilm reel 38, Library of Virginia, Richmond (hereafter cited as LVA).

3 Miller, *Emigrants and Exiles,* 34.

4 Thanks to Jean Murray of Limerick Archives and Limerick Ancestry, Limerick, Ireland, for locating Dooley Family Records in the National Archives of Ireland and forwarding them to me.

5 *Richmond Courier and Daily Compiler,* Sept. 19, 1836, 3.

6 A listing for "James Dooley, Hatmaker" on Mary Street, Limerick, appears in the 1824 "Trades Directory" for Limerick.

7 Thanks to Linda Singleton-Driscoll for finding their names on the ship's manifest for the *Helen Mar* in "New York Passenger Lists, 1820–1857," at Ancestry.com. John Dooley's "Alien Report" was previously the only available printed source for the date of John Dooley's immigration (see Richmond City Virginia Hustings Court Minute Book no. 13, [1837–40], Nov. 15, 1838, p. 293, microfilm reel 89, LVA). Interestingly, "Sally," the seventeen-year-old girl listed on the ship's manifest under the Dooley name, may not have been John Dooley's sister. He did have a sister named Sally, but she immigrated with her husband, Denis Heaton, and children in 1856. The Sally "Dooley" on the manifest may actually have been a cousin on his mother's side named Sarah McNamara who was listed erroneously as a "Dooley" simply because she was traveling under the care of John's mother. Several accounts of the Dooleys' marriage state that the bride and groom were cousins. In *Commonwealth Catholicism: A History of the Catholic Church in Virginia,* Gerald P. Fogarty, S.J., states that John and Sarah obtained a "dispensation from close kinship" before they were married (68). Charles M. Caravati, M.D., in his 1978 biography *Major Dooley,* states that they met on board the ship.

8 Christian, *Richmond, Her Past and Present,* 140.

9 [Terhune], *Marion Harland's Autobiography,* 227.

10 Christian, *Richmond, Her Past and Present,* 128.

11 Ibid., 134.

12 Dooley also owned stock in the Richmond and Danville, the Richmond and York River, and the Virginia Central.

13 *Richmond Courier and Daily Compiler,* Sept. 19, 1836, 3.

14 Christian, *Richmond, Her Past and Present,* 138.

15 Parish Baptismal Register for 1837, St. Peter's Roman Catholic Church, Richmond City, Va., microfilm reel 1081, LVA.

16 Interment Card, "Richmond City Bureau of Cemeteries: Shockoe Cemetery 1822–1892," Misc. microfilm reel 927, LVA.

17 "John Dooley Report as Alien," Richmond City Virginia Hustings Court Minute Book no. 13 (1837–1840), Nov. 15, 1838, p. 293, microfilm reel 89, LVA.

18 One woman was between thirty-six to fifty-four years old, and the other one was younger, between ten and twenty-three years old. The male slave was said to be between ten and twenty-three years old. See U.S. Census Records, 1840, "Virginia: Richmond-Henrico, Slave Inhabitants Richmond Ward 1," Record Group 29, microfilm 704, National Archives and Records Administration, Washington, D.C. (hereafter cited as NARA); Film 0029687, Family History Library, Salt Lake City, Utah.

19 Dabney, *Richmond: The Story of a City,* 136.

20 Varon, *We Mean to Be Counted,* 77.

21 Ibid., 76–79.

22 Christian, *Richmond, Her Past and Present,* 142.

23 Gibson, *Cabell's Canal,* 195.

24 Meagher, *History of Education in Richmond,* 76.

25 "Cash Book, 1841–1854," Records of the Richmond Library Company, 1841–61, Virginia Historical Society (hereafter cited as VHS).

26 Dabney, *Virginia Commonwealth University: A Sesquicentennial History,* 4; Christian, *Richmond, Her Past and Present,* 151.

27 Richmond City Hustings Deeds Book no. 46 (1844), pp. 469–71, microfilm reel 24, LVA.

28 Henrico County Minute Book, 1844–45, p. 192, microfilm reel 83, LVA.

29 Christian, *Richmond, Her Past and Present,* 149.

30 Varon, *We Mean to Be Counted,* 88–89; see also Daniel, "Richmond's Memorial to Henry Clay."

31 "Henrico County" list, Subscription Book, Virginia Association of Ladies for Erecting a Statue of Henry Clay, VHS; see also Emily Rusk, "Mothers and Grandmothers," *GRIVA [Genealogical Research Institute of Virginia] News & Notes* 23, no. 3 (March 2003): 41, 44–46, 52. Thanks to Emily Rusk, who found Sarah Dooley's name on the list of subscribers and called it to my attention.

32 Varon, *We Mean to Be Counted,* 87.

33 Richmond City Hustings Deeds Book no. 47 (1845), pp. 353–55, microfilm reel 24, LVA.

34 Richmond City Hustings Deeds Book no. 53 (1847), pp. 81–85, microfilm reel 27, LVA.

35 Virginia, vol. 43, p. 25, R. G. Dun & Co. Credit Report Volumes, Baker Library, Harvard Business School.

36 Christian, *Richmond, Her Past and Present,* 155–56.

37 For an example of Dooley supplying military caps for the Mexican War, see "Adjutant General Report," *Times and Compiler,* Jan. 5, 1847, 2.

38 See, for example, the description of the Virginia Rifles, a "new" company, in "Celebration of the Fourth," *Enquirer,* July 6, 1850.

39 Board of Public Works, entry 144, folder "List of Stockholders of the Richmond and Danville Rail Road Company," in Richmond and Danville Railroad, Correspondence, Reports etc. 1847–49, 1853, 1854, 1855; (September 22, 1866), Special Collections, LVA.

40 Virginia, vol. 43, p. 25, R. G. Dun & Co. Credit Report Volumes, Baker Library, Harvard Business School.

2. RICHMOND RESPONDS TO THE GREAT FAMINE AND
POLITICS IN IRELAND

 1 *Times and Compiler,* Jan. 15, 1847, 3.

 2 Crawford, "Great Famine," 239.

 3 See the report of forwarding gifts to be shipped on "our national vessels ordered by Congress," *Whig,* March 27, 1847, 2.

 4 *Whig,* April 6, 1847, 2.

 5 Ibid.; Crawford, "Great Famine," 239.

 6 Thanks to Norma Marshall, staff member of St. Joseph's Villa, for sending me a handwritten copy of "An Act to Incorporate St. Joseph's Female Academy and Orphan Asylum, in the City of Richmond, passed, March 27, 1848," on file at St. Joseph's Villa.

 7 Inflation calculator, www.westegg.com/inflation/.

 8 Christian, *Richmond, Her Past and Present,* 158.

 9 Virginia, vol. 43, p. 25, R. G. Dun & Co. Credit Report Volumes, Baker Library, Harvard Business School.

10 See Gleeson, *The Irish in the South, 1815–1870,* 67–70, for discussion of these groups elsewhere in the South.

11 *Enquirer,* Aug. 22, 1848, 2.

12 Miller, *Emigrants and Exiles,* 335.

13 There is some dispute about the exact date of its founding (see Kimball, *American City, Southern Place,* 202; and Manarin and Wallace, *Richmond Volunteers,* 169).

14 *Whig,* March 23, 1849, 2.

15 Personal Property Tax Books, City of Richmond, 1852, p. 24, Auditor of Public Accounts, microfilm reel 823, LVA.

16 Personal Property Tax Books, City of Richmond, 1855, p. 29, Auditor of Public Accounts, microfilm reel 824, LVA.

17 Meagher, *History of Education in Richmond,* 62.

18 For an account of President James K. Polk's two-hour visit, for example, see Christian, *Richmond, Her Past and Present,* 157.

19 A number of those books are now in the Maymont Mansion library in Richmond (see Bayliss, "The Dooleys: A View from Their Library").

20 Richmond City Hustings Deeds Book no. 57 (1849–50), pp. 308–10, microfilm reel 29, LVA.

21 Blanton, *Medicine in Virginia in the Nineteenth Century,* 43–44.

22 Christian, *Richmond, Her Past and Present,* 172, 211.

23 Board of Public Works, entry 156, "Virginia Central Rail Road Co. List of Stockholders," folder "Virginia Central Railroad, Correspondence, Reports, etc. 1848, 1850–53," Special Collections, LVA.

24 Virginia, vol. 43, p. 251, R. G. Dun & Co. Credit Report Volumes, Baker Library, Harvard Business School.

25 Virginia, vol. 43, p. 288, R. G. Dun & Co. Credit Report Volumes, Baker Library, Harvard Business School.

26 Christian, *Richmond, Her Past and Present,* 171.

27 Ibid., 179.

28 Ibid., 176.

29 Board of Public Works, entry 145, box 239, "Private Stockholders of the Richmond and York River Rail Road Company, 30 Sept. 1854," Special Collections, LVA.

30 Board of Public Works, entry 145, box 238; also in the same box, "List of Stockholders of the Richmond & Petersburg Rail Road Company 1st October, 1854," folder "BPW Richmond & Petersburg Railroad Correspondence' Reports etc. 1850–1855 . . . ," Special Collections, LVA.

31 "Non-Intercourse Meeting," *Enquirer,* Dec. 13, 1850, 2; "Articles of Association . . ." list appeared in *Enquirer* Nov. 27, 1850, 2.

32 See, for example, "To the People of the Southern and South-Western States," *Richmond Dispatch* (hereafter cited as *RD*), April 6, 1858, 1.

33 *RD,* Jan. 1, 1853, 3.

34 Ibid., Jan. 13, 1853, 2.

35 Ibid., March 4, 1853, 2.

36 See, for example, the front-page article "Eloquent Extract," *RD,* Jan. 31, 1853.

37 See ad in the "Amusements" column, "Thomas Francis Meagher," *RD,* March 3, 1853, 3.

38 *RD,* March 7, 1853, 2.

39 See Michael Byrne to John Dooley, Sept. 19, 1857, and Nov. 29, 1857.

40 B. Weatherley, Archives Manager, Daughters of Charity, St. Joseph's Provincial House, Emmitsburg, Md., to author, Dec. 14, 2001.

41 *Enquirer,* Aug. 18, 1853, 3.

42 *RD,* Sept. 24, 1853, 4.

3. FAMILY MATTERS

1 *Enquirer,* Feb. 4, 1854, 3.

2 Obituary, *RD,* Feb. 13, 1854, 2; Interment Card no. 157–41, 1848–70, Richmond City Bureau of Cemeteries: Shockoe Cemetery 1822–1982 Interment Blair-Flohr, microfilm reel 927, LVA.

3 *RD,* Feb. 14, 1854, 2.

4 The *Pacific* manifest lists Byrne as an "agriculturist."

5 Dillon, *Life of John Mitchel,* 2:29–39.

6 "Distinguished Arrival," *RD,* May 27, 1854, 2.

7 "The Mitchel Dinner," *RD,* May 29, 1854, 2.

8 *Southern Citizen,* Oct. 31, 1857, 3; see also Gleeson, *The Irish in the South, 1815–1870,* 71.

9 *RD,* March 6, 1854, 2.

10 Meagher, *History of Education in Richmond,* 76. See also John Dooley's name on the list of the board of managers for the Mechanics' Institute in the "Local Matters" column, *RD,* April 11, 1855, 2.

11 Bruce, *Virginia Iron Manufacture in the Slave Era,* 316.

12 Baptismal Register, St. Peter's Roman Catholic Church, Richmond.

13 For an account of his campaign, see Bladek, "Virginia Is Middle Ground"; see also Fogarty, *Commonwealth Catholicism,* 122.

14 Christian, *Richmond, Her Past and Present,* 184.

15 *RD,* March 19, 1855, 6.

16 "Speech of Senator Douglas," *RD,* March 28, 1855, 2.

17 Christian, *Richmond, Her Past and Present,* 184–85.

18 Only fragments of Michael Byrne's half of their correspondence survive. They can all be found in the Maymont Mansion Archives (hereafter cited as MMA).

19 Byrne to John Dooley, Nov. 10, 1855.

20 Byrne to John Dooley, Sept. 6, 1855, and April 29, 1856.

21 *The Richmond Directory and Business Advertiser for 1856,* comp. M. Ellyson (Richmond: H. K. Ellyson Printer, 1856), 103.

22 The book is Thomas Morrell's *An Abridgment of Ainsworth's Dictionary of English and Latin,* published in Philadelphia.

23 Minute Book, Young Catholic Friend Society, Diocese of Richmond Archives.

24 Byrne to John Dooley, April 29, 1856.

25 Byrne letters, April 29, May 14, and July 29, 1856.

26 Freedley, *United States Mercantile Guide,* 459. With thanks to Evelyn Zak for alerting me to the existence of this book.

27 As Ron Chernow has pointed out, at this point in business history such an arrangement was not uncommon (see Chernow's *Death of the Banker,* 9).

28 Richmond City Hustings Deeds Book no. 70a (1856), pp. 114–16, microfilm reel 38, LVA.

29 O'Byrne to John Dooley, Sept. 11, 1856, MMA.

30 Geo. T. Browne to John Dooley, May 7, 1857, MMA.

31 Copy of stock certificate, MMA; list of directors, *Second Annual Directory for the City of Richmond to Which Is Added a Business Directory for 1860,* comp. W. Eugene Ferslew (Richmond: W. Eugene Ferslew, 1860), 49.

32 For a complete list of the officers and board, see *Butters' Richmond Directory* (Richmond: Ellyson's Steam Power Presses, 1855), 195.

4. GEORGETOWN: PRELUDE TO WAR

1 Georgetown College, Entrance Book 1850–95, list for the academic year 1856–57, Special Collections, Georgetown University Library. In *The Bicentennial History of Georgetown University,* Robert Curran states that Jim was enrolled in "Third Humanities" (1:167), but the *Catalogue of Georgetown College, 1856–57,* lists Jim in First Humanities and Jackie in Third (17).

2 *Catalogue of Georgetown College, 1856–57,* 7.

3 Ibid., 8.

4 Ledger Book, Georgetown College, 1856–57, 86–87.

5 *Catalogue of Georgetown College, 1856–57,* 9.

6 Curran, *Bicentennial History of Georgetown University,* 1:167.

7 List of awards given at the "Annual Commencement of Georgetown College . . . 7th of July, 1857," *Catalogue of Georgetown College, 1856–57,* 34–42.

8 *Catalogue of Georgetown College, 1856–57,* 29; *1857–58,* 29; *1858–59,* 29; *1859–60,* 28.

9 Dramatic Association "Secretaries Book," Special Collections, Georgetown University Library.

10 "Hibernian Society," *RD,* June 8, 1857, 1; "Hibernian Society," *RD,* June 22, 1857, 1.

11 John Dooley to Sarah Dooley, MMA.

12 Christian, *Richmond, Her Past and Present,* 189.

13 *RD,* Sept. 14, 1857, 1.

14 Byrne to John Dooley, April 11, 1858, MMA.

15 Undated fragment of letter, Byrne to Dooley, apparently written between May 25 and June 1, 1858, MMA.

16 *Catalogue of Georgetown College, 1857–58,* 37–38.

17 Christian, *Richmond, Her Past and Present*, 194.

18 Byrne to John Dooley, Sept. 15, 1858, MMA.

19 Byrne to John Dooley, Aug. 23, 1858, MMA.

20 Christian, *Richmond, Her Past and Present*, 198.

21 Meagher, *History of Education in Richmond*, 16.

22 *RD,* May 25, 1859, 2.

23 *Ferslew's Richmond City Directory, 1860,* 110.

24 "Annual Commencement" program, *Catalogue of Georgetown College, 1858–59,* 33–36.

25 Byrne to John Dooley, Sept. 30, 1859, MMA.

26 U.S. Census Bureau, Eighth Census, [Henrico County, Va.], vol. 12; Gleeson, *The Irish in the South, 1815–1870,* 40–41.

27 Virginia, vol. 43, p. 288, R. G. Dun & Co. Credit Report Volumes, Baker Library, Harvard Business School.

28 *RD,* Nov. 21, 1859, 1.

29 Ibid., Dec. 7, 1859, 1.

30 Ibid.

31 See, for example, the item in *RD,* Dec. 5, 1859, 1, suggesting that anyone thinking of buying a pianoforte should check with Richmond's own piano builders, Dorr & Rade, before sending an order up north.

32 *RD,* Sept. 3, 1860, 2.

33 McLaughlin, *College Days at Georgetown and Other Papers,* 97–98.

5. ECONOMIC SLOWDOWN

1 *RD,* Dec. 6, 1859, 4. See Catherine B. Hollan, *Virginia Silversmiths, Jewelers, Watch- and Clockmakers 1607–1860: Their Lives and Marks* (McLean, Va.: Hollan, 2010), 37–38, for a thumbnail sketch of Bartholomew's career in Richmond.

2 "Letter from His Father," John E. Dooley, S.J., Papers, Special Collections, Georgetown University Library.

3 *Journal of the House of Delegates of the State of Virginia* (hereafter cited as *JofH*) *for the Session 1859–60,* 182, 239.

4 For a complete list of board members, see *RD,* April 10, 1860, 2.

5 *RD,* June 15, 1860, 3.

6 See *JofH* 6 (1859–60): 140, for motion "that the committee on banks enquire into the expediency of incorporating the Old Dominion Savings Bank of the City of Richmond." See also *JofH* 6 (1859–60): 472; *RD,* Jan. 22, 1860, 4; ibid., April 10, 1860, 2.

7 *RD,* Jan. 18, 1860, 1.

8 Varon, *We Mean to Be Counted,* 93.

9 Christian, *Richmond, Her Past and Present,* 208.

10 *RD,* July 4, 1860, 1.

11 *Catalogue of Georgetown College, 1859–60,* 33–34.

12 *Evening Star* (Washington, D.C.), July 10, 1860, 2, and July 11, 1860, 3; see also *Daily National Intelligencer* (Washington, D.C.), July 11, 1860, 3.

13 Christian, *Richmond, Her Past and Present,* 212.

14 *RD,* Sept. 1, 1860, 1.

15 "Presidential Movements: Douglas in Virginia . . . ," *New York Times,* Sept. 5, 1860, 1.

16 See, for example, *RD,* Sept. 3, 1860, 2.

17 "Breckinridge Meeting," *RD,* Nov. 3, 1860, 2.

18 "Died," *RD,* Oct. 1, 1860, 1.

19 Slaughter, *A Brief Sketch of the Life of William Green, LLD,* 16.

20 Bryson, *Legal Education in Virginia 1779–1979,* 265.

21 Ibid., 267.

22 For the address, see Bryson, ed., *Essays in Legal Education in Nineteenth Century Virginia,* 185–202.

23 "Political Notices," *RD,* Nov. 3, 1860.

24 *RD,* Dec. 29, 1860, 1.

25 Ibid., Nov. 21, 1860, 1.

26 "Special Notices," *RD,* Dec. 4, 1860, 1.

27 *RD,* Jan. 29. 1861, 1.

28 Ibid., Dec. 31, 1860, 1.

29 Ibid., Jan. 9, 1861, 1.

30 Ibid., March 25, 1861, 4.

31 See Lankford, *Cry Havoc,* 100–101.

32 *Alexandria Gazette,* April 1, 1861, qtd. at www.virginiamemory.com, Education and Outreach Division, LVA.

33 Jones, *A Rebel War Clerk's Diary,* 1:20; "Southern Rights Convention," *RD,* April 16, 1861, 2.

34 *RD,* April 16, 1861, 4.

35 Christian, *Richmond, Her Past and Present,* 215.

36 [Terhune], *Marion Harland's Autobiogrpahy,* 370–71.

37 *RD,* April 15, 1861, 1.

38 List of Richmond delegates, *RD,* April 16, 1861, 2.

39 *RD,* April 18, 1861, 1.

40 Jones, *A Rebel War Clerk's Diary,* 1:21.

41 Ibid., 1:22.

42 Caravati mistakenly states that Jim took part in the student demonstration (see Caravati, *Major Dooley,* 6). For Cowardin's participation, see his obituary, *RD,* Oct. 17, 1877, 1.

43 Ledger Book, Georgetown College, May 1861, Special Collections, Georgetown University Library.

6. WAR

1 Loehr, *War History of the Old First Virginia Infantry Regiment*, 7.

2 "Local Matters," *RD*, May 4, 1861, 1.

3 John Keiley to his mother, July 23, 1861, Keiley Family Papers, VHS.

4 Rebel Archives, War Department Record Division, NARA.

5 *RD*, March 17, 1862, 4.

6 Loehr, *War History of the Old First Virginia Infantry Regiment*, 9.

7 Will Book no. 4, p. 363, Circuit Court of the City of Richmond.

8 *RD*, July 19, 1861, 1.

9 Confederate States War Department, voucher no. 64, on form no. 12, Rebel Archives, Record Division, NARA.

10 Entry for July 27, 1861, in Frank Potts, Diary, Personal Papers Collection, LVA. The "Major" in this excerpt was Maj. Frederick Skinner. Thanks to Bill Rose for calling this diary to my attention.

11 Loehr, *War History of the Old First Virginia Infantry Regiment*, 10.

12 Entry for July 29, 1861, in Frank Potts, Diary.

13 Loehr, *War History of the Old First Virginia Infantry Regiment*, 11.

14 "Local Matters," *RD*, July 30, 1861, 2.

15 Manarin, *Richmond at War*, 26–27.

16 Service Record, "Dooley John, Co. C First Virginia Inf'y, Williams Rifles, Register," *Compiled Service Records*, microfilm reel 354, LVA.

17 *RD*, Dec. 13, 1861, 1.

18 Loehr, *War History of the Old First Virginia Infantry Regiment*, 15.

19 Kimball, *American City, Southern Place*, 235; Dew, *Ironmaker to the Confederacy*, 92–93.

20 See, for example, *RD*, April 8, 1862, 1.

21 "Muster Roll," microfilm 109, LVA. Some of his papers say he enlisted April 1; others give the date as April 5.

22 Loehr, *War History of the Old First Virginia Infantry Regiment*, 16.

23 Ibid., 17.

24 Sneden, *Eye of the Storm*, 64.

25 Loehr, "Was Not Captured," *RD*, Aug. 18, 1895, 11. I am grateful to Bill Rose for calling my attention to this article. The rest of this account is based heavily on Loehr's article.

26 *Enquirer*, May 15, 1862, 1. In *Defend This Old Town: Williamsburg during the Civil War*, Carol K. Dubbs gives a slightly different version of the episode (see 182 and 230).

27 *RD,* May 8, 1862.

28 *Enquirer,* May 9, 1862, 2; *RD,* May 9, 1862, 3.

29 Dubbs, *Defend This Old Town,* 41.

30 Ibid., 54.

31 Ibid., 234.

32 *Enquirer,* May 10, 1862, 2.

33 *RD,* May 12, 1862, 1.

34 "The Infirmary Corps," *RD,* March 15, 1862, 2.

35 See, for example, "Military Notices," *RD,* Sept. 11, 1862.

7. THE AMBULANCE COMMITTEE

1 For an account of the meeting at which Mayor Mayo formed the committee and a list of his appointees, see "Our Wounded Soldiers," *RD,* April 21, 1862, 4; for a brief biographical sketch of Enders, see *Richmond Portraits in an Exhibition of Makers of Richmond, 1737–1860* (Richmond: Valentine Museum, 1949), 64.

2 *Examiner,* June 5, 1862, 2.

3 Putnam, *Richmond during the War,* 135.

4 "The Lines—Incidents and Scenes of Late," *RD,* June 4, 1862, 3.

5 "The First Virginia Regiment," *RD,* June 10, 1862, 2.

6 *RD,* June 3, 1862, 2.

7 Blanton, *Medicine in Virginia in the Nineteenth Century,* 280–83.

8 *Examiner,* May 30, 1862, 1.

9 Ibid., March 3, 1864, 1.

10 Putnam, *Richmond during the War,* 133.

11 "The Hospitals," *Examiner,* June 28, 1862, 1; "Our Wounded," *Examiner,* June 28, 1862, 2.

12 Dr. William Allen Carrington to Adaline Mayo Carrington, July 9, 1862, Carrington Family Papers, VHS; see also Calcutt, *Richmond's Wartime Hospitals,* 186.

13 *RD,* July 12, 1862, 2. I am grateful to Emily Rusk for pointing out this ad to me.

14 "Prison Journal," *Irish Citizen* 3, no. 138 (June 4, 1870): 270.

15 They were not the only women in Richmond doing men's work during the Civil War. Others made cartridges in the powder works. Some women worked in government offices. The Confederate Treasury office employed a large number of women to sign the newly minted Confederate currency. See, for example, Loughborough and Johnston, *The Recollections of Margaret Cabell Brown Loughborough,* 73, 75. Some, like one of John Mitchel's daughters, worked in the Quartermaster's Department (ibid., 75).

16 "Roll of Confederate Prisoners of War," Aug. 2, 1862, microfilm 109, reel 354, LVA.

17 "Confederate Register," No. 274, pt. 708, p. 24, microfilm 109, reel 354, LVA; *Enquirer,* Aug. 7, 1862, 2.

18 *Enquirer,* Aug. 7, 1862, 2.

19 John E. Dooley, *John Dooley's Civil War,* 17.

20 Ibid.

21 Ibid., 35.

22 "Army of the Confederate States Certificate of Disability for Discharge," JHD, microfilm 109, reel 354, LVA.

23 Dabney, *Richmond: The Story of a City,* 248.

24 Although Jim's exam and his subsequent position as "Lieutenant of Ordnance" is mentioned in biographical sketches of his career as early as R. A. Brock's 1888 account in *Virginia and Virginians: Eminent Virginians* (2:779–80); and later in Lyon Gardiner Tyler's *Men of Mark in Virginia: Ideals of American Life* (3:246); as well as later in Caravati's *Major Dooley* (7), I have been unable to find supportive primary-source evidence to verify it. Possible reasons include the burning of Ordnance headquarters and its contents in Richmond's April 3, 1865, Evacuation Fire.

25 *Irish Citizen* 3, no. 133 (April 30, 1870): 230.

26 Ibid., 3, no. 136 (May 21, 1870): 254.

27 Ibid., 3, no. 137 (May 28, 1870): 262.

8. NEW DUTIES

1 Loehr, *War History of the Old First Virginia Infantry Regiment,* 32; see also John E. Dooley, *John Dooley's Civil War,* 90.

2 John E. Dooley, *John Dooley's Civil War,* 90.

3 *Irish Citizen* 3, no. 137 (May 28, 1870): 262.

4 *RD,* Dec. 15, 1862, 1.

5 Ibid., Dec. 17, 1862, 1.

6 John E. Dooley, *John Dooley's Civil War,* 123.

7 Ibid., 125.

8 Ibid., 127.

9 Ibid., 128.

10 Furguson, *Ashes of Glory,* 207.

11 "The Situation—A Yankee Raid," *RD,* May 4, 1863, 1.

12 "The Enemy at Ashland," *RD,* May 5, 1863, 1.

13 *RD,* May 4, 1863, 1.

14 Furguson, *Ashes of Glory,* 204.

15 *Irish Citizen* 3, no. 138 (June 4, 1870): 270.

16 Manarin, *Richmond at War,* 331.

17 "Headq'rs City Volunteers," *RD,* May 21, 1863, 1.

18 See, for example, "Military Notices," *RD,* August 2, 1863; and *Irish Citizen* 3, no. 138 (June 4, 1870): 270.

19 "Returns of Licenses 1863, Danville-Richmond" folder, p. 1, box 1261, Record Group 454, Auditor of Public Accounts, Special Collections, LVA.

20 "Returns of Licenses 1862, Danville-Richmond" folder, p. 1, box 1260, Record Group 454, Auditor of Public Accounts.

21 Stock certificate (photocopy from private collection), MMA.

22 As qtd. in *War of the Rebellion: Official Records,* ser. 1, vol. 27, pt. 3, 873; and *Southern Historical Society Papers,* 25:113.

23 *Irish Citizen* 3, no. 138 (June 4, 1870): 270.

24 John E. Dooley, *John Dooley's Civil War,* 169–70.

25 Ibid., 179.

26 "Local Matters," *RD,* July 13, 1863, 1.

27 Calcutt, *Richmond's Wartime Hospitals,* 82; see also *RD,* July 13, 1863, and July 25, 1863.

28 *Irish Citizen* 3, no. 138 (June 4, 1870): 270; Dillon, *Life of John Mitchel,* 2:180.

29 Ibid., 2:181.

30 Ibid., 2:182.

9. FAME

1 John E. Dooley, *John Dooley's Civil War,* 229.

2 *New York Times,* Nov. 8, 1863, originally published in the *Richmond Enquirer,* Oct. 29, 1863.

3 In his May 17, 1864, diary entry, Jack mentions reading about his father's work with the Ambulance Committee in an extract from the "New York News." John E. Dooley, *John Dooley's Civil War,* 264.

4 See the advertisement for Ambulance Committee Tobacco, *Whig,* Jan. 11, 1865, 1.

5 *RD,* Jan. 23, 1864.

6 *Irish Citizen* 3, no. 140 (June 18, 1870): 286.

7 Ibid.

8 *RD,* March 4, 1864, 2.

9 Ibid., March 19, 1864, 1.

10 *Examiner,* March 19, 1864, 1.

11 Ibid., March 31, 1864, 1.

12 "Robberies," *RD,* May 16, 1864, 2.

13 Marriage Register 1856–1954, p. 40, St. Peter's Roman Catholic Church, Richmond, microfilm reel 1081, LVA.

14 *RD,* June 24, 1864, 1.

15 "Change of Schedule," *Enquirer,* Nov. 4, 1864, 3.

16 See *New York Times,* Nov. 19, 1864, article on the arrival of the Ambulance Committee in Savannah; and the *New York Times,* Dec. 18, 1864, account of their work in Charleston.

17 John E. Dooley, *John Dooley Confederate Soldier,* 161n26.

18 Richmond City Hustings Deeds Book no. 81b (1864–65), p. 141, microfilm reel 49, LVA.

19 Richmond City Hustings Deeds Book no. 81b (1864–65), p. 154; and no. 81a (1864–65), p. 343, microfilm reel 49, LVA.

20 *RD,* Jan. 2, 1865, 4.

21 "Public Meeting at the African Church," *RD,* Feb. 7, 1865, 4.

22 John E. Dooley, *John Dooley's Civil War,* 340.

23 *Irish Citizen* 3, no. 143 (July 9, 1870): 310.

24 John E. Dooley, *John Dooley's Civil War,* 340–41.

25 Ibid., 342.

26 Richmond City Hustings Deeds Book no. 81b (1864–65), p. 203, microfilm reel 49, LVA.

27 *Irish Citizen* 3, no. 143 (July 9, 1870): 310.

10. THE EVACUATION FIRE: MILITARY OCCUPATION

1 For discussion in city council meetings between May 3, 1862, and February 25, 1865, of other options for destroying the tobacco, see Manarin, *Richmond at War,* 169–86, 544, 570–72; for appointment of the committee to destroy the liquor, see the April 2, 1865, minutes, ibid., 592–94.

2 Handy, "The Fall of Richmond in 1865," 11–14. The quotations in this account are taken from this eyewitness report.

3 Putnam, *Richmond during the War,* 367.

4 See *Whig,* April 6, 1865, for a contemporary account of the looting and fire; see also Lankford, *Richmond Burning,* chaps. 8–10, for a detailed description of the night of April 2–3 and its aftermath.

5 *Whig,* April 7, 1865, 1

6 Lankford, *Richmond Burning,* 190.

7 Ledger Books, Georgetown College, 1856–65, Special Collections, Georgetown University Library.

8 Qtd. in Dillon, *Life of John Mitchel,* 2:213–14.

9 *Whig,* April 6, 1865, 2; and April 14, 1865, 5.

10 Ibid., April 12, 1865, 5. Special thanks to Nelson Lankford for calling John Dooley's service on the committee to my attention.

11 *Whig,* "Sufferers by the Late Fire," April 15, 1865, 7.

12 Ibid., April 21, 1865, 5.

13 Dabney, *Richmond,* 201.

14 See, for example, accounts of bank vaults being recovered from the ruins in the *Whig,* April 18, 1865, 5; and April 24, 1865, 5.

15 See, for example, *Whig,* May 2, 1865, 4.

16 Ibid., May 8, 1865, 2.

17 Putnam, *Richmond during the War,* 386.

18 *Richmond Times* (hereafter cited as *RT*), May 19, 1865, 5.

19 Paragraph no. 2 of President Johnson's May 29, 1865, Amnesty Proclamation granted "amnesty and pardon . . . with restoration of all rights of property, except as to slaves, and except in cases where legal proceedings, under the laws of the United States providing for the confiscation of property of persons engaged in rebellion, have been instituted . . . " (see *Whig,* June 29, 1865, 2, for letters from several banking and investment firms that discuss the impact of the confiscation issue).

20 "The Meeting Tonight," *Whig,* June 24, 1865, 3.

21 O'Hara to John Dooley, MMA.

22 Richmond City Hustings Deeds Book no. 81b (1864–65), p. 154, microfilm reel 49, LVA; Richmond City Hustings Deeds Book no. 81a (1864–65), p. 343, microfilm reel 49, LVA.

23 See, for example, "John Dooley of Ambulance Committee Par. June 24, 1865," Case Files of Applications from Former Confederates for Presidential Pardons ("Amnesty Papers") 1864–67, Group I, Pardon Applications Submitted by Persons from the South: Virginia, Cr–Ea, microfilm reel 4, "U.S. Office of the Adjutant General, Va. Case Files for Presidential Pardons . . . ," LVA.

24 "Meeting of Citizens," *Whig,* June 23, 1865, 2.

25 "An Important Meeting," editorial, *Whig,* June 23, 1865, 3.

26 "Pardoned," *Whig,* June 26, 1865, 2.

27 *New York Herald* qtd. in *Whig,* June 26, 1865, 2; "Recommended for Pardon," *New York Times,* June 26, 1865, 5.

28 *Whig,* June 26, 1865, 2.

29 *Norfolk Post,* June 30, 1865, 2.

30 *Catalogue of Georgetown College,* vol. 2 (1860–70), [1864–65], p. 32; *Evening Star* (Washington, D.C.), July 5, 1865, 1.

31 "Building in the Burnt District of Richmond," *Norfolk Post,* July 13, 1865, 2. Thanks to Evelyn Zak for calling this article to my attention.

32 *Whig,* June 21, 1865, 2.

33 Ibid., June 28 1865, 2.

34 *Second Annual Directory for the City of Richmond, to Which Is Added a Business Directory for 1860,* comp. W. Eugene Ferslew, 49.

35 *RD,* Dec. 9, 1865, 4.

36 *Irish Citizen* 3, no. 148 (Aug. 13, 1870): 350.

37 Dillon, *Life of John Mitchel,* 2:253.

38 For an account of such an exam given approximately twenty years later that suggests just how informal such judicial interviews must have been in Dooley's day, see Cutchins, *Memories of Old Richmond,* 130.

39 Henrico County Court Minutes, 1864–67, Sept. 4, 1865, p. 319, microfilm reel 88, LVA.

40 Henrico County Court Minutes, 1864–67, Nov. 7, 1865 p. 343, microfilm reel 88, LVA.

41 Richmond City Virginia Hustings Court Minute Book no. 29 (1863–66), Nov. 13, 1865, p. 495, microfilm reel 97, LVA.

42 Richmond City Orders No. 21, Jan. 7, 1861–Nov. 14, 1868, Virginia Supreme Court of Appeals, Oct. 9, 1866, p. 375, microfilm reel 8, LVA. The following note appeared on the front page of the October 10, 1866, *Richmond Dispatch* under the heading "Supreme Court": "In the Supreme Court of Virginia, in session in the capitol yesterday, James H. Dooley qualified as counsel."

43 *The City of Richmond Business Directory and City Guide 1866,* 79.

44 "Death of A. Judson Crane, Esq.," *Whig,* Jan. 5, 1867, 3; see also Shepard, "Sketches of the Old Richmond Bar: A. Judson Crane," *Richmond Quarterly* 6, no. 2 (Fall 1983): 14.

45 Ibid., 12–15.

46 *RT,* Nov. 29, 1865, 20.

47 *RD,* Dec. 22, 1865, 1.

48 Minute Book, Society of St. Vincent de Paul, 1865–71, Archives, Diocese of Richmond.

49 *RD,* March 13, 1866, 3.

50 Ibid., July 21, 1866, 3.

51 *Whig,* Jan. 7, 1867, 1.

52 Ibid., May 1, 1866.

53 *1866 Richmond City Directory,* comp. William J. Divine & Co., 205.

54 *RD,* May 7, 1866, 1.

55 Mitchell, *Hollywood Cemetery,* 64.

56 "Hollywood Memorial Association," *RD,* May 15, 1866, 1. The list of ladies' names in the paper that day differs from the list published in Mitchell, *Hollywood Cemetery,* 169–70n9.

57 *RD,* May 26, 1866, 1.

58 Mitchell, *Hollywood Cemetery,* 66.

59 Ibid., 71.

1 "At a Meeting of the Bar of the City," *RD,* Oct. 10, 1866, 1.

2 Officers elected were James Lyons, president; William McFarland, first vice president; and Gustavus Myers, second vice president.

3 "Circuit Court of Henrico," *RD,* Oct. 30, 1866, 1.

4 Crane and Dooley Papers, MMA. The receipts for the other cases mentioned here are also at Maymont.

5 Receipt, Crane and Dooley Papers, MMA.

6 *RD,* Jan. 2, 1868, 2.

7 See, for example, *Boyd's Directory of Richmond City and a Business Directory for 1866,* 132, for the Southern Land, Emigration and Product Company ad.

8 "Report of the Commissioner of Immigration," *Journal of the Senate of Virginia 1866,* 503.

9 *Acts of the General Assembly of the State of Virginia Passed in 1866–67 in the Ninety-First Year of the Commonwealth* (Richmond, 1867), 677.

10 Christian, *Richmond, Her Past and Present,* 281.

11 Salmon and Campbell, *Hornbook of Virginia History,* 52.

12 "Conservative Convention of Virginia," *RD,* Dec. 12, 1867, 2.

13 "February 18, 1868," Parish Register, St. Peter's Roman Catholic Church, microfilm reel 1081, LVA.

14 *Whig,* Feb. 21, 1868, 1.

15 *RD,* Feb. 25, 1868, 1.

16 See Judge John A. Meredith to Gen. R. S. Granger, dated June 4, 1868, in *RD,* June 6, 1868, 1.

17 *RD,* June 5, 1868, 1.

18 "The Impeachment Trial—of Judge Meredith," *Whig,* June 16, 1868, 1.

19 "Investigation of the Charges against Judge Meredith," *RD,* June 6, 1868, 1.

20 Testimony of James Lyons, *RD,* June 15, 1868, 1.

21 "Investigation of the Charges against Judge Meredith," *RD,* June 12, 1868, 1. For slightly different versions of JHD's testimony, see also the *Whig* and the *Enquirer and Examiner,* June 12, 1868.

22 *RD,* June 13, 1868, 2.

23 Ibid.

24 *Whig,* June 13, 1868, 1.

25 *RD,* July 1, 1868, 1.

26 "Seymour and Blair Club," *RD,* Aug. 1, 1868, 1.

27 "Meeting" column, "Seymour and Blair Ratification Meeting," *RD,* July 30, 1868, 2.

28 John Dooley Jr. to JHD, June 14, 1869, MMA.

29 "City and Suburban," *Whig,* Sept. 30, 1868, 1.

30 "The Wise Meeting," *RD,* Nov. 16, 1868, 1.

31 JHD to his mother, May 14, 1869, MMA.

32 "Row at the First Ward Polls," *RD,* June 25, 1869, 1; see also "The Murder of Joseph Kelly, Particulars of the Death," *RD,* June 28, 1869, 1.

33 "The Murder of Joseph Kelly, the Jury of Inquest Continued Session," *RD,* June 29, 1869, 1.

34 "The Murder of Joseph Kelly, Particulars of the Death," *RD,* June 28, 1869, 1.

35 "Callahan Discharged from Custody," *RD,* Aug. 17, 1869.

36 "Handing around the Hat," *RD,* Sept. 2, 1869, 1.

37 "An Awful Calamity," *RD,* July 3, 1869, 1.

38 "Funeral of Colonel James R. Branch Accidents and Incidents," *RD,* July 6, 1869, 1.

39 Saidie May to JHD, Aug. 27, 1869, MMA.

40 "Dooley, Sept. 11, 1869," Staunton City Hall Index to Register of Marriage, vol. 1 (1802–1928), no. 161, p. 4.

41 *New York Tablet* 2, no. 8 (July 24, 1858): 5; *New York Tablet* 2, no. 9 (July 31, 1859): 5.

42 JHD to his mother, Sept. 11, 1869, and Sept. 27, 1869, MMA.

12. A YOUNG POLITICIAN

1 *RD,* March 7, 1870, 1.

2 Ibid., March 10, 1870, 1.

3 *Whig,* March 18, 1870, 3.

4 "Conservative Meeting," *RD,* May 16, 1870, 1.

5 "Local Matters," *RD,* May 25, 1870, 1.

6 "Rome: Mass Meeting of Catholics at St. Peters," *RD,* Jan. 13, 1871, 3.

7 "Mass Meeting in Sympathy with the Pope," *RD,* Jan. 12, 1870, 1.

8 Qtd. in Fogarty, *Commonwealth Catholicism,* 163.

9 Bailey, "Anthony M. Keiley and 'The Keiley Incident.'"

10 *Enquirer,* March 3, 1871, 3.

11 "St. Patrick's Day Celebration Yesterday," "Local Matters," *Enquirer,* March 18, 1871, 1. Keiley's speech was also printed in full.

12 *Richmond Directory, Dean Dudley & Co., 1870,* 46.

13 Personal Property Tax Books, City of Richmond, book 2, p. 18, no. 9, Auditor of Public Accounts, microfilm reel 834, LVA.

14 See, for example, the record for Tuesday, October 17, 1871, in Richmond's Chancery Court. Dooley, Christian, and Lyons were counsel in the case "Cottrell and others, vs. Lyon's administrator, &c."

15 *Enquirer,* March 4, 1871, 2.

16 "The Alleged Christie Murder," *Whig,* March 11, 1871, 4.

17 "Commonwealth vs. John Smith," "Ended Causes 1871," box 52, Richmond City Hustings Court Records; *Whig*, April 20, 1871, 4.

18 *Proceedings of the Bar of the City of Richmond on Occasion of the Death of Hon. Robert Ould, Held at Richmond, Virginia, February 24, 1883*, 8–9.

19 See accounts of the trial in the *Whig, Enquirer*, and *Dispatch*, April 21–24, 1871.

20 *RD*, June 6, 1890, 1; *Enquirer*, March 8, 1871, 1.

21 See entries for "Dooley, James H. and W." and "Hibernia Building Fund," General index to Deeds, Richmond City Hustings and Chancery Court Deeds 1782–1917, book 6.

22 *RD*, Aug. 29, 1876, 4.

23 Mount de Chantal Bill Books, "Mrs. Sarah Dooley," entries 1871–1876, Archives, Mount de Chantal Visitation Academy. I am grateful to Sister Joanne Gonter, school historian, for giving me access to the records.

24 "Subscriptions for the Academy of the Visitation, Mount de Chantal near Wheeling West VA," Archives, Mount de Chantal Visitation Academy.

25 *RD*, Sept. 27, 1871, 2. For a discussion of the corruption rampant in the earlier session, see Moger, *Virginia: Bourbonism to Byrd*, 14–15.

26 *RD*, Oct. 20, 1871, 1, 2.

27 Bryson and Shepard, "The Virginia Bar, 1870–1900," 172.

28 In the twenty-first century, James H. Dooley is still called "Major Dooley," and the title of a 1978 biography by Charles M. Caravati is *Major Dooley*.

29 *Irish Citizen* 4, no. 157 (Oct. 15, 1870): 1.

30 *RD*, Oct. 19, 1871, 1.

31 Ibid., Oct. 24, 1871, 1.

32 Ibid., Nov. 1, 1871, 2.

33 Ibid., Nov. 10, 1871, 1.

34 *Enquirer*, Nov. 18, 1871, 2.

13. IN THE HOUSE OF DELEGATES

1 *JofH, 1870–71*, 32.

2 Ibid., 35.

3 Ibid., 41.

4 For an example of the state's advertisements for the auction, see *RD*, Jan. 21, 1872, 4.

5 *JofH, 1871–72*, 156.

6 Ibid., 64, 117.

7 IOU, "W.Va. Lynnside, February, 1872," MMA.

8 "Transfers of Real Estate," *RD*, April 2, 1871, 1.

9 Receipt, Crane and Dooley Papers, MMA.

10 *JofH, 1872–73*, 190, 201.

11 Ibid., 247. See also "Proceedings of the General Assembly of Virginia" and "Through from Cincinnati: The Arrival of the Huntington Train," *RD,* Feb. 14, 1873, 2.

12 "Dooley, John E.," Georgetown Alumni Directory Card, Special Collections, Georgetown University Library.

13 *RD,* May 10, 1873, 1.

14 "Kemper Kampaign Klub," *Enquirer,* Aug. 23, 1873, 1.

15 "Konservative Kampaign Klub," *RD,* Jan. 1, 1877, 1.

16 *Chataigne's City Directory, 1879–1880,* 31.

17 *RD,* Aug. 13, 1873, 1.

18 Reports of the Board of Directors and Medical Superintendent of the Central Lunatic Asylum, Virginia, 1873–81.

19 For a fuller account of the Panic and the depression's impact in Richmond, see Christian, *Richmond, Her Past and Present,* 341–42; and Chesson, *Richmond after the War,* 161–62.

20 *RD,* Oct. 11, 1873, 1.

21 *JofH, 1874,* 40–41.

22 R. B. Jones, "James Lawson Kemper: Native-Son Redeemer," in Younger and Moore, eds., *The Governors of Virginia,* 69–79.

23 *JofH, 1875–76,* 100.

24 Ibid., Jan. 6, 1875, 102.

25 Dew, *Ironmaker to the Confederacy,* 310–16.

26 Ibid., 316.

27 "House of Delegates," *RD,* March 18, 1875, 2.

28 Christian, *Richmond, Her Past and Present,* 350.

29 "Tributes to the Memory of John Mitchel," *Enquirer,* April 23, 1875, 1; "Mitchel Memorial Meeting: Richmond's Tribute to the Irish Hero," *RD,* April 23, 1875, 1.

30 *Enquirer,* April 23, 1875, 1.

31 "The Old First Regiment," *RD,* April 24, 1875, 1.

32 "Entertainment and Supper," *State,* April 5, 1877, 4.

33 JHD to Maj. J. B. McPhail, June 29, 1885, VHS.

34 "Benevolent Orders," *RD,* Jan. 1, 1877, 7.

35 See, for example, *RD,* Sept. 1, 1875, 1.

36 "The Meeting at Monticello Hall Last Night," *Enquirer,* Oct. 13, 1875, 4.

37 "Grand Rally and Ratification Meeting: The First Gun of the Campaign to Be Fired: The K.K.K.'s to the Front," *Enquirer,* Oct. 13, 1875, 4.

38 *JofH, 1874–75,* 204, 330–31.

39 *RD,* Nov. 5, 1875, 1.

40 Minute Book 31, Chamber of Commerce, p. 360; list of new members, *RD,* Dec. 9, 1875, 1.

41 *JofH, 1875,* 57.

42 "House of Delegates," *RD,* Jan. 9, 1877, 2.

43 *JofH, 1876–77,* 311, 334, 355–56.

44 Caravati, *Major Dooley,* 25; Cutchins, *Memories of Old Richmond,* 156.

45 "From the Capitol," *State,* March 1, 1877; "House of Delegates," *RD,* March 2, 1877, 2.

46 *RD,* Feb. 8 1877, 1.

47 *JofH, 1876–77,* 503–5.

48 *Enquirer,* April 4, 1877, 1.

49 "Railroad Commissioner Nominated," *RD,* April 4, 1877, 1.

50 Visitation Monastery biographical essay, Dooley-Houston Papers, VHS.

51 "Wooden Buildings," *RD,* Sept. 22, 1874, 1.

52 "The Great Convention," *RD,* Aug. 8, 1877, 1.

53 For further brief discussions of the turmoil at the convention and beyond, see Moger, *Virginia: Bourbonism to Byrd, 1870–1925,* 32; and Maddex, *The Virginia Conservatives, 1867–1879,* 251–53.

54 Stock certificates (photocopies from private collection), MMA. See also "State Corporation Commission Index to Corporation Charter Books, 1887–1981," Misc. microfilm reel 4010, LVA.

55 *RD,* Oct. 22, 1877, 1.

14. THE RAILROAD THAT GOT AWAY

1 "The Decorative Art," *RD,* Oct. 29, 1877, 1.

2 See 1879 receipt assigning interest to Dooley as "atty for Seddon & Bruce," MMA.

3 *Chataigne's City Directory for the Years 1879–80,* comp. J. H. Chataigne, listed the address as "317," but that was a misprint (118).

4 Ibid., 238.

5 Richmond City Circuit Court Deed Book no. 117b (1880–81), microfilm reel 191, LVA.

6 Crane and Dooley Papers, MMA.

7 R. H. Maury & Co. receipt, MMA.

8 McCabe, "Joseph Bryan: A Brief Memoir," iii–xxix.

9 James L. Lindgren, "Bryan, Joseph," in *Dictionary of Virginia Biography,* 2:200, LVA. See also "Conservative Ticket Henrico County, Virginia, November 6, 1877," in Bryan, *Joseph Bryan, His Times, His Family, His Friends,* 208.

10 Tyler, *Men of Mark in Virginia,* 257.

11 Morrill, *A Builder of the New South,* 30–66.

12 *Gillis' Richmond City Directory, 1871–72,* 9.

13 "The Destitute Irish People: Relief Meetings on Both Sides of the Atlantic," *New York Times,* Jan. 7, 1880, 1.

14 *RD,* Jan. 17, 1880, 1.

15 Ibid.

16 Ibid., Feb. 5, 1880, 1.

17 Ibid., Feb. 7, 1880, 1.

18 Ibid., April 3, 1880.

19 Klein, *Great Richmond Terminal,* 87.

20 "Local Matters: York River Railroad, Annual Meeting of the Stockholders," *RD,* Jan. 15, 1880, 1.

21 Joseph Bryan Letter Book, Joseph Bryan Papers, 1869–1910, sec. 6, p. 251, VHS.

22 Joseph Bryan Letter Book, Joseph Bryan Papers, 1869–1910, sec. 6, p. 253, VHS.

23 "Merchants National Bank," *RD,* Jan. 14, 1880, 1.

24 *New York Times,* March 5, 1880, 2.

25 Klein, *Great Richmond Terminal,* 89.

26 "An Act to Incorporate the Richmond and West Point Terminal Railway and Warehouse Company," *Acts and Joint Resolutions Passed by the General Assembly of the State of Virginia During the Session of 1879–80* (Richmond, 1880), 231–32.

27 Klein, *Great Richmond Terminal,* 90.

28 *RD,* Feb. 10, 1881, 1.

29 Ibid., Feb. 11, 1881, 1.

30 Clark represented the Enoch W. Clark firm in Philadelphia (see Rand Dotson, "New South Boomtown: Roanoke, Virginia 1882–1884," *Virginia Magazine of History and Biography* 116, no. 2 [2008]: 151–90).

31 "Pool Agreement of Syndicate of Richmond and Danville Stockholders," "R&D.R.R. Co. Pool Committee Minutes, 1881–1882," pp. 1–2, Norfolk Southern Historical Collections, Norfolk, Virginia (hereafter cited as NSHC).

32 *RD,* July 21, 1881, 2.

15. NEW VENTURES

1 Klein, *Great Richmond Terminal,* 92.

2 Folder "Stock Subscriptions 1881," Richmond and Danville Extension Company Contracts, Correspondence etc. 1881–92, NSHC.

3 Others who subscribed included John Patteson Branch, 250 shares; Moses Millhiser, 125 shares; General Anderson 1,428½ shares; Col. A. S. Buford, 500 shares; Thomas Seddon, 200 shares; John Stewart and his brother Daniel Stewart, 1,000 shares each (NSHC).

4 Poor, *Manual of the Railroads of the United States for 1882,* 389.

5 *RD,* Sept. 10, 1881, 1.

6 "Directors' Minutes, 1869–1883," "R-2b," p. 467, Richmond and Danville Railroad Records, NSHC.

7 Qtd. in *RD,* Dec. 15, 1881, 1.

8 *Richmond City Directory, 1880–81.*

9 Richmond Chancery Court Deed Book 116c, p. 276, March 29, 1880.

10 *State,* Jan. 31, 1886, 4.

11 See "Catalogue of the Choice and Extensive Law and Miscellaneous Library of the Late Hon. William Green, LL.D.," VHS; and the books still in the Maymont Mansion library.

12 *RD,* May 10, 1880, 4.

13 "Pool Committee Minutes," Oct. 7, 1881, 3, NSHC.

14 *Railroad Gazette* 13 (1881): 610, 641; *State,* Oct. 24, 1881, and Nov. 5, 1881; Klein, *Great Richmond Terminal,* 28, 96.

15 Klein, *Great Richmond Terminal,* 96.

16 *RD,* Oct. 15, 1882, 1.

17 "Board of Directors Minutes," Richmond and Danville Railroad Records, p. 208, NSHC.

18 *RD,* Oct. 15, 1882, 1.

19 Ibid., Dec. 14, 1882, 1.

20 Part 2, "Business Investments, Correspondence ... 1881–1893," Papers of John D. Rockefeller, Sr., microfilm reel 5; University of Houston microfilm 2173, reel 18.

21 Richmond City Deed Book no. 124a, pp. 80–81. He did not convey his books!

22 *Virginia: Rebirth of the Old Dominion: Virginia Biography,* vol. 3 (Chicago: Lewis, 1929), 403–4. See also "Death of Dr. H. G. Houston," *State,* March 17, 1885, 4.

23 Dooley Family Papers, MMA.

24 "The State Convention," *RD,* May 19, 1880; "The Conservative Democracy," *RD,* July 29, 1881, 1.

25 "Weather Report" and "The Medical College Board," *RD,* Sept. 2, 1882, 1.

26 "The Medical Muddle," *RD,* Sept. 24, 1882, 1.

27 "Minutes of the Board of Visitors of the Medical College of Virginia," Sept. 28, 1882, Archives, Tompkins-McCaw Library, Medical College of Virginia.

28 The following account is based on James Tice Moore's "Battle for the Medical College: Physicians, Politicians and the Courts, 1882–1883," 164.

29 "Lewis & Als vs. Whittle & Als, On a Petition for Mandamus," Briefs, Supreme Court of Appeals of Virginia, VHS.

30 Hansbrough, *Reports of Cases Decided,* vol. 77, *January 1, 1883–November 1, 1883,* 415–24.

31 Lewis, *Sloss Furnaces and the Rise of the Birmingham District,* 117–19.

32 Ibid., 109–10.

33 Joseph Bryan, Diary of 1883 trip to Alabama and Georgia, "Commonplace Book, 1877–1893," pp. 294–95, VHS. The three executives were Joseph Johnston, Major R. H. Temple, and Colonel Foreacre.

34 Lewis, *Sloss Furnaces and the Rise of the Birmingham District,* 119.

35 Ibid., 125.

36 Ibid., 121–22.

37 T. M. Logan letters to John D. Rockefeller, "Business Investments Correspondence, 1881–1893," microfilm reel 6, John D. Rockefeller, Sr., Papers, Rockefeller Archive Center.

38 Logan to John D. Rockefeller, reel 6, frame 00944.

39 Logan to John D. Rockefeller, reel 6, frame 00948.

40 Logan to John D. Rockefeller, memo, reel 6, frame 00951.

41 *RT,* Oct. 30, 1886, 4.

42 Lewis, *Sloss Furnaces and the Rise of the Birmingham District,* 124–25.

43 Ibid., 136.

44 Ibid., 128.

45 Ibid., 136.

46 "Richmond Capital for Alabama," *RD,* Jan. 8, 1887; Lewis, *Sloss Furnaces and the Rise of the Birmingham District,* 136–37.

47 "The City of Richmond VS the County of Henrico, S.M. Dooley, and others," Annexation Records, vol. 2, p. 1813, Circuit Court, County of Henrico, Va.

48 "Trustees Sale of Very Valuable Farm," *RD,* May 10, 1880, 4.

49 Henrico County Va., Deed Book no. 119, pp. 47–49, 119.

50 "The Danville Road," *RD,* Nov. 21, 1886, 4.

51 "The Terminal Combination," *RD,* Nov. 24, 1886, 3.

52 "The Danville and Terminal Deal," *RD,* Nov. 30, 1886, 2.

53 Henry W. Grady, *The New South: Writings and Speeches of Henry Grady* (Savannah: Beehive, 1971).

54 Henry Warren Readnour, "Fitzhugh Lee: Confederate Cavalryman in the New South," in Younger and Moore, eds., *The Governors of Virginia,* 11–120.

16. THE NEW SOUTH ON THE MARCH

1 "St. Paul Matters," *St. Paul Globe,* Jan. 24, 1887, 2; George J. Rogers obituary, *RT,* Oct. 20, 1912, 2.

2 "A Young Giant: St. Paul's Phenomenal Growth and Great Future," *St. Paul Daily Globe,* Dec. 25, 1886, 3.

3 *St. Paul Globe,* Jan. 23, 1887, 1.

4 Ibid., Jan. 24, 1887, 4.

5 Ibid., Jan. 26, 1887, 3.

6   Ibid., Jan. 26, 1887, 4.

7   *Baltimore Sun,* "Supplement," Feb. 2, 1887, 1.

8   Gibson, *The Major,* 37.

9   Joseph Bryan to JHD, July 23, 1888, "Letterbook 1888," Papers of Joseph Bryan, VHS.

10 "The Strong Real Estate Market," *State,* Aug. 8, 1890, 2.

11 Joseph Bryan to JHD, June 19, 1888.

12 Ruffner, *A Report on Washington Territory.*

13 Charter Book no. 7, pp. 232–38, State Corporation Commission, Commonwealth of Virginia, LVA.

14 "Alphabetical List of Patentees to Whom Patents Were Issued on the 31st Day of July, 1888"; "386.815. Telautograph," *Official Gazette of the United States Patent and Trademark Office* 44 (1888): iii, 459 (on microfilm at the James Branch Cabell Library, VCU). I have been unable to locate correspondence or any other records of a Dooley visit in Elisha Gray records despite prolonged attempts to do so. Nonetheless, the events of the next few weeks suggest that the two men met at this time and worked out a business agreement before Dooley returned to Richmond.

15 "A Telautograph Company Chartered," *State,* Aug. 7, 1888, 4.

16 "Varied Stocks Held by Morgan," *New York Times,* July 12, 1913.

17 *New York Star,* Aug. 9, 1888, 7, Library of Congress Bound Volume no. 9054 (July–September 1888).

18 "Richmond's Boom, Also the General Prosperity of the South as Presented by Major James H. Dooley," *RT,* Aug. 10, 1888, 1.

19 For several examples of portraits by Brown, see Virginius Cornick Hall's *Portraits in the Collection of the Virginia Historical Society.*

20 Douglas Southall Freeman, "John Skelton Williams," *Richmond News-Leader,* Nov. 4, 1926.

21 Williams, *A Manual of Investments,* 1888, 39.

22 Ibid., 89.

23 "Stock Here in the Big Canal," *Richmond News,* Dec. 19, 1901, 1.

24 "Nicaragua Canal Convention," *RT,* Nov. 26, 1892, 5.

25 Morrill, *A Builder of the New South,* 183.

26 See, for example, *RD,* Nov. 27, 1889, 2.

17. MORE NEW VENTURES

1   Munford Jr., *Richmond Homes and Memories,* 227–28; *RD,* Jan. 1890, for accounts of the "Colonial Assembly."

2   Old Dominion Chapter, DAR website.

3   "The Richmond Chapter," *RT,* April 10, 1891, 6.

4 "Old Dominion Chapter," *RT,* Jan. 31, 1892, 2.

5 Morse et al., *History of the Virginia Daughters of the American Revolution, 1891–1987,* 398; see also *RT,* Jan. 31, 1892, 2.

6 *RT,* April 16, 1892, 1.

7 "Article III—Eligibility of Members," in Society of the Colonial Dames of America in the State of Virginia, *History and Register of Ancestors and Members of the Society of the Colonial Dames of America in the State of Virginia 1892–1930,* lxxxi.

8 "The West-End Club . . . ," *RD,* Jan. 3, 1890, 1; Gibson, *This Splendid House,* 22–25.

9 Gibson, *This Splendid House,* 22.

10 MMA.

11 Manhattan Club membership roster, New York, 1920, Maymont Mansion library.

12 With thanks to Maureen Manning, assistant librarian, University Club library.

13 "Richmond's Wants," *RD,* June 6, 1890, 1.

14 "To Better the Streets: A Discussion of the Dooley Bill," *RT,* Jan, 8, 1892, 5; see also "Maj. Dooley Bill," *State,* Jan. 7, 1890, 4; and Jan. 8, 1890, 1.

15 "Dooley Bill Rejected," *RT,* Jan. 15, 1892, 2.

16 The King William County Deed Book has a long list of such purchases.

17 *State,* July 18, 1890, 4.

18 Ibid.

19 *RD,* Aug. 22, 1891, 3.

20 *RT,* Nov. 29, 1891, 10.

21 Ibid., Dec. 2, 1891, 6.

22 *New York Times,* June 17, 1891.

23 "Manhattan Island," *RD,* Sept. 20, 1891, 2; "The New York Life Insurance Co," *RD,* Sept. 20, 1891, 3.

24 "Beers as Mudslinger," *New York Times,* Jan. 4, 1892, 3.

25 *New York Times,* Feb. 27, 1892, 8.

26 "An Open Letter to Senator Daniel from Major James H. Dooley," *RD,* Aug. 30, 1891, 7.

27 "Hon. John W. Daniel: He Discusses Major Dooley's Letter on the Currency Question," *RD,* Sept. 20, 1891, 6.

28 *RT,* Oct. 4, 1891, 10.

29 Special Collections, Georgetown University Library.

30 *State,* Dec. 11, 1891, 4.

31 "Insiders Buy Freely of Richmond Terminal Stock," *RT,* Feb. 25, 1892, 6.

32 "A New Terminal Plan," *RT,* May 19, 1892, 6.

33 "Another Terminal Change," *RT,* May 18, 1892, 6.

34 Henrico County Deed Book, # 139a, pp. 204–5, microfilm, Henrico County Courthouse.

35 Advertisement, "Commissioner Sale of the Terminal Hotel," *RT,* Feb. 4, 1892, 5.

36 "The Terminal Hotel Sold," *RD,* Feb. 14, 1892, 7; "Major Dooley the Purchaser," *RT,* Feb. 14, 1892, 1.

37 "West Point's Hotel and Bars," *RD,* April 8, 1892, 4.

38 *RT,* April 4, 1890, 2.

39 Ibid., May 3, 1891, 12.

40 Ibid., April 7, 1892, 5.

41 Ibid., Feb. 28, 1892, 4.

42 Ibid.

43 To locate the patent paper for each improvement, see page listing in the alphabetical Index of Inventions in the *Official Gazette of the Patent and Trademark Office,* vols. 57, 62, 63, 68, 73.

44 *Journal of the Senate of Virginia, 1892,* p. 289; *JofH, 1892,* 389.

45 *RT,* Nov. 22, 1892, 3.

46 Ibid., Dec. 15, 1892, 5.

47 Coe, *The Telephone and Its Several Inventors,* 72.

18. THE PANIC AND BEYOND

1 *RD,* Jan. 26, 1893.

2 *State,* Jan. 26, 1893.

3 "Dooley on Finance," *State,* Jan. 31, 1893, 2.

4 "The Historical Society," *RT,* March 17, 1893, 5.

5 *State,* March 23, 1893.

6 *RD,* April 7, 1893.

7 *State,* Jan. 26, 1893.

8 *RD,* Jan. 11, 1893.

9 "Richmond Terminal . . . Mssrs. Drexel, Morgan & Co. Acquiesce in the Wish of the Directors—Their Plan," *RD,* April 14, 1893, 3.

10 See Strouse, *Morgan: American Financier,* 321–22.

11 "West-End Land and Improvement Company," *RD,* April 6, 1893, 4.

12 "Our Progress: What Maj. Dooley Says about Improvements in Richmond," *State,* April 6, 1893, 4.

13 "Dooley on Money," *State,* April 22, 1893, 4.

14 *RT,* May 9, 1893, 6.

15 "The Telautograph: A Richmond Company to be Organized Soon," *State,* May 10, 1893, 1.

16 "Gray, Elisha," in *Dictionary of American Biography,* ed. Allen Johnson and

Dumas Malone (New York: Scribner's Sons, 1931), 514; Coe, *The Telephone and Its Several Inventors,* 72.

17 "Silver Question: Major Dooley Discusses the Close of the Indian Mints," *RD,* July 2, 1893, 11.

18 Meagher, *History of Education in Richmond,* 125.

19 *RT,* Sept. 15, 1983.

20 "Tariff and Finance: Major Dooley Carefully Discusses These Great Questions," *RD,* Dec. 10, 1893, 2.

21 "Tariff Theories: The Effect of 'Free Raw Materials' on Foreign Trade," *RD,* Jan. 9, 1894, 4.

19. HIGHWAYS AND RAILWAYS

1 Ronald L. Heinemann, "The 1923 Highway Bond Referendum," in *Encyclopedia Virginia,* ed. Brendan Wolfe (Virginia Foundation for the Humanities, 2010), encyclopediavirginia.org.

2 "Good Roads for Virginia," *RT,* Oct 11, 1895, 5.

3 "For Better Roads, *RD,* Oct. 11, 1895, 3.

4 "Agree on Road Law: The Convention Adopts a Number of Recommendations to Legislature," *RD,* Oct. 12, 1895, 2.

5 "The Good Roads Convention," *RD,* Oct. 15, 1895, 7.

6 VDOT History Highlights, online at www.virginiadot.org/about/vdot_history .asp.

7 Lewis, *Sloss Furnaces and the Rise of the Birmingham District,* 201.

8 Pace obituaries, *Richmond News-Leader* (hereafter cited as *RNL*), Aug. 5, 1920, 1, and *Richmond Times-Dispatch* (hereafter cited as *RTD*), Aug. 6, 1920, 1.

9 "Bazaar Association," 1881 flier, Albert Small Special Collections Library, University of Virginia; "Home Matters," *Richmond Standard,* Jan. 29, 1881, 1; "Quite a Full Week," *RD,* Feb. 17, 1895, 1.

10 *RD,* Jan. 7, 1894, 2.

11 Treadway, *Women of Mark,* 3–26.

12 "The Woman's Club," *RD,* Oct. 6, 1895, 9.

13 Treadway, *Women of Mark,* 5.

14 Bayliss, "Exhibitions of Talents," 174.

15 "Richmond's Railroads," *RT,* Jan. 1, 1896.

16 Prince, *Seaboard Air Line Railway,* 81.

17 K. Richmond Temple, "John Skelton Williams," 39. Temple asserts that Ryan initiated twenty suits in his attempt to stop the Williams/Dooley plan.

18 Richmond Trust and Safe Deposit advertisement, *RD,* June 1, 1898, 6.

19 "Seaboard Wins Again," *RD,* Jan. 28, 1900, 4.

20 "Ryan Puts in a Plea," *RD,* Jan. 6, 1899, 1.

21 "Seaboard Air Line Transfer: Williams Syndicate in Control," *New York Times*, Feb. 7, 1899, p. 1; *RT*, Feb. 7, 1899, 1.

22 "Harmony in the S.A.L.," *RT*, Nov. 12, 1899, 15.

23 "Seaboard Air Line Combine," *RT*, Dec. 10, 1899, 1.

20. THE NEW CENTURY

1 *RD*, Jan. 5, 1900, 1.

2 Ibid., Jan. 2, 1900, 3.

3 "The Greater S.A.L. in Georgia," *RD*, Jan. 25, 1900, 1.

4 "Dady Is Downed," *RD*, Jan. 28, 1900, 13.

5 "Argue the Ryan Case: Judge Waddill Hears argument on application for Injunction," *RD*, Feb. 3, 1900, 1.

6 See, for example, the account of the visit of three U.S. congressmen in "The Seaboard Bill," *RT*, Feb. 6, 1900, 1.

7 "The Resolution Adopted," *RD*, Feb. 3, 1900, 1.

8 Prince, *Seaboard Air Line Railway*, 85–86.

9 *RT*, Feb. 1, 1900, 7; *RD*, Feb. 1, 1900, 8.

10 For a thorough treatment of this approach, see Varon, *We Mean to Be Counted*.

11 "The Flower Festival," *RD*, May 17, 1900, 1.

12 "The Flower Parade," *RD*, May 13, 1900, 8.

13 "Grand Opening of the S.A.L," *RD*, June 3, 1900, 1.

14 "The Seaboard Feast . . . ," *RD*, June 3, 1900, 1.

15 Excerpts from a transcript of Major Dooley's speech at the banquet in honor of the completion of the Seaboard Air Line Railway System, June 2, 1900, at the Jefferson Hotel, in "Speeches Delivered at Tampa, Jacksonville, Columbia, Savannah, Raleigh, Petersburg, and Richmond on the Occasion of the Ceremonies Attending the Passage of the First Through Train from Richmond, Virginia, to Tampa, Florida over the Seaboard Air Line Railway May 31st to June 2nd, 1900," sec. 4, Williams Family Papers, VHS.

16 *RTD*, Jan. 8, 1904, 1.

17 "S.A.L. and Southern, Mr. Williams Neither Denies nor Confirms Rumors," *RD*, Dec. 8, 1900, 3.

18 *RD*, Dec. 5, 1900, 1.

19 *Richmond, the Pride of Virginia* (Philadelphia: Progress, 1900), 49.

20 "Our Banking World," *RD*, Jan. 1, 1901, 5.

21 Gay, "Creating the Virginia State Corporation Commission," 465.

22 Qtd. in *RD*, Feb. 8, 1902.

23 *RD*, Dec. 8, 1901, 25.

24 "Business-men Argue," *RD*, Dec. 20, 1901, 2.

25 "Keep Out Capital . . . Mr. Branch Is Emphatic, Will Vote Against New Constitution If . . . ," *RD,* Jan. 4, 1902; *Washington Post,* "Hot Shot for Solons, Financier Branch Arraigns the Convention," Jan. 4, 1902, 1.

26 *RD,* Sunday, Jan. 26, 1902, 20.

27 Larsen, *Montague of Virginia,* 156.

28 *The World Almanac and Encyclopedia 1902,* 146.

29 *New York Tribune Monthly* 4, no. 6 (June 1892): 55. Thanks to Beth O'Leary for sharing this citation with me.

30 "Will Adjourn to a Given Date," *RT,* June 22, 1902, 12.

31 Combined selections from his speech as qtd. in *RD* and *RT.*

32 Minutes of June 20, 1902, Minute Book, p. 146, R. E. Lee Camp No. 1, VHS.

33 Minutes of June 27, 1902, Minute Book, p. 147, R. E. Lee Camp No. 1, VHS.

34 The minutes of the January 9, 1903, meeting reported that it was then hanging on the headquarters wall (Minute Book, p. 200, R. E. Lee Camp No. 1). Sometime after that notation, the portrait disappeared from the collection.

35 "The Davis Monument," *RT,* June 2, 1895, 3.

36 *RD,* July 5, 1902, 4.

37 *Report of the Fourteenth Annual Meeting of the Virginia State Bar Association, August 5, 6, 7, 1902,* 189–219.

38 Ibid., 203.

39 See Underhill, "The Virginia Phase of the Ogden Movement."

40 *The General Education Board: An Account of Its Activities, 1902–1914* (New York, 1917), 3.

41 Deutsch, *Booker T. Washington, Julius Rosenwald, and the Building of Schools for the Segregated South,* 72–73.

42 *RD,* Nov. 23, 1902, 21.

43 "Manual Training the South's Hope," *RT,* Nov. 23, 1902, 18.

44 *RD,* Nov. 11, 1902, 6.

45 The headline of the article was "Maj. Jas. H. Dooley, Some Financial Questions Calmly Considered by Him. Vanderlip's Late Address. Has This Country Reached Its Climax of Prosperity, and Must It Now Retrograde:—That Proposition Reviewed by the Major." The title of the pamphlet is *Has Our Country Passed the Climax of Its Prosperity? A Reply to the Address of Mr. F.A. Vanderlip. . . .* The only known copy of the pamphlet is housed in the Albert and Shirley Small Special Collections Library, University of Virginia. Dooley referred to specific pages of the Vanderlip work in his reply. See, for example, Dooley's reference to page 13 of Vanderlip's speech on page 6 of his own pamphlet.

46 Dooley, *Has Our Country?* 8.

1 "Predicts Great Fall in Stocks: In Open Letter Major Dooley Gives Views of Financial Outlook. Business Men Drawing in Horns," *RTD*, Sept. 25, 1910, 1.

2 *RNL*, Feb. 8, 1905, 6; see also *RTD*, Feb. 9, 1905, 3.

3 *RTD*, May 26, 1903, 1.

4 "The South's Progress," *RTD*, Aug. 8, 1903, 4.

5 "Speech of Mr. James H. Dooley at Creditors Meeting. . . . Baltimore, April 6, 1904," sec. 61, Williams Family Papers, VHS.

6 *RTD*, Aug. 8, 1903, 4.

7 "Rock Island Gets Seaboard Air Line," *New York Times*, Aug. 13, 1903, 2.

8 "Hurrying the Work," *RTD*, Sept. 10, 1903, 3.

9 *RTD*, Oct. 2, 1903, 1; see also "Rehabilitation of Banking Firms," *RTD*, May 10, 1905, 8.

10 "New York Transactions," *RTD*, Oct. 2, 1903, 2.

11 "The Banks of Richmond," *RTD*, Oct. 2, 1903, 2.

12 "City's Banks Undisturbed," *RTD*, Oct. 3, 1903, 1.

13 *Financial Chronicle* qtd. in *RTD*, May 10, 1905, 8.

14 Dooley speech at creditors' meeting, April 6, 1904.

15 Ibid.

16 Ibid.

17 *RTD*, May 10, 1905, 8.

18 Minutes of the Board, March 6, 1903, p. 63, Richmond Art Club.

19 Bayliss, "Exhibitions of Talents," 174.

20 *RD*, Nov. 18, 1902, 12.

21 *Eighth Annual Exhibition of the Art Club of Richmond, VA. and Pictures by Professional Artists May 18th to 30th MCMIII*, exhibition catalogue, p. 9, Richmond Art Club.

22 See, for example, the list of guarators in Richmond Art Club catalogues for the ninth and tenth exhibitions.

23 *Annual Report of the Co-operative Educational Association of Va. for the Year Ending November 20, 1911*, Department of Public Instruction, 6.

24 Ibid., 5.

25 Co-operative Education Commission, "An Appeal to the People of Virginia," April 15, 1904.

26 Correspondence: "Dooley, Mary Munford and Henry Anderson about Dooley's Financial Support"; see also Correspondence: "Dooley with William Bentley, 1920–1921," Branch & Co. Records, VHS.

27 Transcript of Dooley speech at the first meeting of the Joseph Bryan Memorial Association at the Jefferson Hotel, Dec. 3, 1908, microfilm, VHS.

28 State Corporation Commission Charter Book, vol. 202, bk. 56, 397–405.

1 *RTD,* Oct. 19, 1905, 1.

2 Ibid., 5.

3 Ibid., Oct. 15, 1905, 4.

4 "Richmond's Fair Women Meet Mrs. Roosevelt," *RTD,* Oct. 19, 1905, 7.

5 "Rate Regulation by Government," *RTD,* Jan. 6, 1906, 1.

6 "Shipper Ought to Have a Show," *RTD,* Jan. 7, 1906, 1; "Major Dooley and His Critics," *RTD,* Jan. 17, 1906, 5.

7 *Rate Regulation by the Government: What It Means to the South,* pamphlet.

8 *RTD,* Feb. 5, 1906, 5.

9 Freeman, *The Style of a Law Firm,* 1–5.

10 *RTD,* Feb. 7, 1906, 12.

11 Transcript: "Direct Examination of Major Dooley 1906 Annexation Suit, City of Richmond vs. Henrico County, S. M. Dooley and Others," 1814–15, LVA.

12 Ibid., 1817.

13 Ibid., 1818.

14 Ibid., 1825.

15 *RNL,* Feb. 16, 1906, 6

16 "Saturday Review of Books," *New York Times,* Sept. 1, 1906, 543; "Autumn Book List Number 1906," *New York Times,* 654.

17 *Country Life* 11 (Dec. 1906): 127.

18 *American Monthly Review of Reviews* 34, no. 203 (Dec. 1906): 14.

19 A. Gordon to JHD, Dec. 4, 1906, MMA.

20 *RTD,* Oct. 28, 1906, 7.

21 *RNL,* Nov. 3, 1906, 7.

22 Ibid., Sept. 20, 1904, 5; see also Jurgens, "One of the Finest and Most Commodious."

23 Wheary, *The Italian Garden at Maymont,* booklet.

24 "Funeral of Mrs. Sarah Dooley," *RNL,* May 24, 1907, 10; see also "Obituary," ibid., 5.

25 "Italian Gardens at Home of Maj. J. H. Dooley," *RTD,* Oct. 12, 1908, 8.

26 Bryan, *Joseph Bryan,* 273.

27 Proxy for Thomas M. Logan, MMA.

28 McMurran to JHD, June 29, 1909, MMA.

29 Proxy for John P. Branch; Notice "To the Shareholders of the Richmond & St. Paul Real Estate & Improvement Company," Dec. 1, 1909, MMA.

30 JHD to stockholders, MMA.

31 C&O Board Minutes, Feb. 11, 1909, Corporate Records Collection, Chesapeake and Ohio Railway, pp. 245–46, Misc. microfilm reel 1677, LVA.

32 C&O Board Minutes, Feb. 23, 1909, p. 255, Misc. microfilm reel 1677; *RTD,* Feb. 25, 1909, 1.

33 C&O Board Minutes, June 17, 1915, p. 144, Misc. microfilm reel 1677.

34 In *Henry Edwards Huntington: A Biography,* James Thorpe asserts that although Huntington belonged to many corporate boards, at this point in his career he no longer attended their meetings. The attendance records in the minutes of the C&O board, however, reveal that Huntington attended most of the meetings during the years he and Dooley served together on that board.

23. TRAVEL ABROAD AND A MOUNTAIN PALACE

1 William A. Rhodes, "William Hodges Mann: Last of the Boys in Gray," in Younger and Moore, eds., *The Governors of Virginia,* 87.

2 *RTD,* June 13, 1909, 9; *How May State Receive Return for Money Spent on Education,* pamphlet (Richmond: Richmond Press, 1909).

3 "Annual Report of the Co-operative Education Association of Va. for the Year Ending November 20, 1911," 31–33.

4 Gunter, "A History of Public Education in Virginia," 12.

5 JHD to Fitzhugh Elder, November 21 1910, MMA.

6 JHD to Nora Houston, June 10, 1910, MMA.

7 JHD to Florence Lewis, April 11, 1913, MMA.

8 "Returned from Abroad," *RTD,* Sept. 2, 1910, 5; see also Ellisisland.com for a partial list of passengers, including the Dooleys, on that voyage.

9 Josephine Dooley Houston to JHD, "Family Letters" file, box 3, Adele Goodman Clark Papers, Special Collections and Archives, James Branch Cabell Library, VCU.

10 According to her death certificate, Sallie died of gangrene of the left leg.

11 *Sentinel on the Hill: Monte Maria and One Hundred Years,* Monastery of the Visitation (Richmond, 1966), 76.

12 JHD to Fitzhugh Elder, Nov. 21, 1910, MMA.

13 See, for example, "Art Exhibits for Rural Schools," "Co-operative Education Association of Virginia Annual Report, Year Ending November 1, 1915," 5.

14 "Art Club Holds Annual Meeting," *RNL,* Nov. 5, 1910, 1.

15 Richmond Art Club School brochure, 1912–13.

16 See review, *RTD,* Nov. 20, 1910, B2.

17 Wheary, "Swannanoa: Summer Home of James and Sallie Dooley, 1913–1925," *Augusta [County] Historical Bulletin* 50 (2013): 25.

18 "A Convention to Amend the Constitution. Why Needed. How It May Be Obtained," *North American Review* 193, no. 664 (March 1911): 369–87.

19 The University of Michigan Law School Library copy of the essay has been digitized and is available online. Walker K. Tuller's essay is also available online in the digital archives of the *North American Review.*

20 C&O Board Minutes, June 15, 1911, pp. 301–2, Corporate Records Collection, Chesapeake and Ohio Railway, microfilm reel 1678, LVA.

21 This description is based on Maymont's present Japanese garden designed by Barry Starke, who based his rendering on traditional Japanese garden design. No record of Mr. Muto's actual design has been found.

22 Wheary, "Swannanoa," 26.

23 JHD to Rev. Joseph Himmel, S.J., Oct. 24, 1911, Special Collections, Georgetown University Library.

24 Diary, Mrs. William R. Cox, VHS.

25 List of officers of the Association Opposed to Woman's Suffrage, in *Why Women Should Oppose Equal Suffrage,* pamphlet, Equal Suffrage League Collection 1909–1938, LVA. See also Brent Witt, "Toilers in the Sun: Wonderful World of Women," *Everywoman's Magazine* 1, no. 12 (Nov. 1917): 51–71.

26 *Virginia Association Opposed to Woman Suffrage By-Laws,* booklet (Richmond: Whittet & Shepperson Printers, undated), Equal Suffrage League Collection, LVA.

27 Minutes of the Richmond Art Club Board, Adele Goodman Clark Papers, VCU.

28 Photograph, Special Collections and Archives, James Branch Cabell Library, VCU.

29 *New York Times,* June 23, 1912.

30 "Social and Personal," *RTD,* Nov. 15, 1912, 5.

31 "Homeward Tide Affecting Paris," *New York Times,* Sept. 1, 1912.

32 "Social and Personal," *RTD,* Dec. 4, 1912, 5.

33 *RTD,* Dec. 7, 1912, 5.

34 The other women authors they chose were Kate Langley Bosher, Ellen Glasgow, Mary Newton Stanard, Mary Johnston, and Sally Nelson Robins.

35 "Art Club of Richmond" folder, Adele Goodman Clark Papers, VCU.

36 "History and Tradition Favored Richmond Bank, Major Dooley's Letter to Comptroller Williams Dwelt on Strong Bond between South, and One-Time Capital of the Confederacy," *RTD,* April 3, 1914, 5.

37 "John Skelton Williams," *RNL,* Nov. 5, 1926.

38 JHD to Florence Lewis, May 7, 1915, Adele Goodman Clark Papers. VCU.

39 Lewis, *Sloss Furnaces and the Rise of the Birmingham District,* 336–37.

40 Ibid., 338.

41 JHD to Alice Dooley, July 4, 1915, Adele Goodman Clark Papers. VCU.

42 Lewis, *Sloss Furnaces and the Rise of the Birmingham District,* 349.

43 See, for example, letters and receipts from Florence and William for loans, 1870, 1872, 1873, MMA.

44 JHD to Florence Lewis, May 7, 1915, Adele Goodman Clark Papers. VCU.

45 Nora Houston to JHD, n.d., Adele Goodman Clark Papers. VCU.

46 Deed, August 27, 1915; Deed, April 1, 1916, MMA.

24. EXTRAORDINARY GIFTS

1 "Memorial Campaign Is Being Supported by Leading Citizens," *RTD*, May 28, 1916, 1.

2 "Dooley Gives $40,000 for Hospital Building," *RTD*, June 7, 1916, 1; "Fund of $100,000 Starts Campaign," *RTD*, June 14, 1816, 1.

3 "Balfour Will Visit Us Next Saturday," *RNL*, May 16, 1917, 1.

4 "Cheering Throngs Welcome Balfour, Britishers Pay Visit of Greeting to Entire South," *RTD*, May 20, 1917, 1.

5 "Sale of Liberty Loan Opens Auspiciously," *RTD*, May 23, 1917, 12.

6 "Liberty Loan Sales Here Increase Daily," *RNL*, May 23, 1917, 1.

7 "Major Dooley Has $500,000 of Loan: Largest Individual Subscription in Virginia Made by Richmond Man," *RNL*, May 24, 1917, 1.

8 MMA.

9 A. C. Gordon to Sallie May Dooley, Sept 12, 1917, MMA.

10 Mrs. Ruby Childs, oral history project interview by Lauranett Lee, Jan. 8, 1999, "Oral History" files, MMA.

11 Coe, *The Telegraph,* 21.

12 *Community League News* 2, no. 3 (March 28, 1919): 1. Although Dooley mentions giving only five hundred dollars each year, others reported that he had been giving one thousand dollars per year for a long time.

13 "Major Dooley Gives $11,000 to Hospital, Augments Previous Donation," *RTD*, June 2, 1920, 1.

14 Chairman of the MCV executive committee to JHD, April 30, 1920, MMA.

15 J. M. Miller to JHD, April 12, 1920, Branch & Company Records, VHS.

16 Sallie May Dooley to Georgetown president (May 6, 1920), "Georgetown Presidents: Creeden," box 7, Special Collections, Georgetown University Library.

17 "Open Gift of Major Dooley to Richmond," *RNL*, Oct. 29, 1920. With thanks to Andrew Bain, special collections assistant, Tompkins-McCaw Library, Medical College of Virginia, for sending me a copy of this article.

18 "Ask Charter for $300,000 Hospital for Deformed Children," *RTD*, May 2, 1920, 1.

19 JHD to William Bentley, Aug. 29, 1921, MMA.

20 JHD to S. P. Cowardin and J. J. English, Branch & Company Records, VHS.

21 President J. B. Creeden to JHD, Dec. 22, 1921, Branch & Company Records, VHS.

22 "Major James H. Dooley," *RNL*, Nov. 17, 1922, 10.

23 "Men of Thin Gray Line Will Attend Maj. Dooley's Funeral," *RTD*, Nov. 18, 1922, 12.

24 Loth, "The Dooley Mausoleum at Maymont."

25 Copy of Dooley's will, MMA.

26 "James H. Dooley," *Catholic Virginian* 7, no. 1 (Nov. 1931): 15, 38–39.

27 Author interview with former Virginia Supreme Court justice Thomas C. Gordon Jr., grandson of Sallie's friend Sally Nelson Robins, November 2000.

28 *Sentinel on the Hill,* 76.

29 Records of bequests in James Henry Dooley Papers, Trust Department, First and Merchants Bank.

30 Adams, *Crippled Children's Hospital, Richmond, Virginia,* 27.

31 Ibid., 31.

32 Copy of Sallie May Dooley's will, MMA.

33 Adams, *Crippled Children's Hospital, Richmond, Virginia,* 41.

BIBLIOGRAPHY

NEWSPAPERS AND PERIODICALS
Commercial and Financial Chronicle (New York City)
New York Tribune Monthly 4, no. 6 (June 1892)
North American Review

Library of Virginia
Richmond Newspapers
Courier and Daily Compiler
Dispatch
Enquirer (both semi-weekly and daily editions)
Evening Leader
Examiner
News-Leader
Standard
State
Times
Times-Dispatch
Whig and Public Advertiser

Other Newspapers
Appeal (Memphis, Tenn.)
Gazette (Alexandria, Va.)
Globe (St. Paul, Minn.)
New York Times
Plain Dealer (West Point, Va.)
Post (Norfolk, Va.)
Southern Citizen (Knoxville, Tenn.)
Star (Washington, D.C.)
Valley Virginia (Waynesboro, Va.)

Cornell University
Irish Citizen (New York)

Library of Congress
Star (New York)

Online Resources
Chronicling America. Digital Newspapers. Library of Congress.
Richmond Civil War Newspapers. Digital Project, University of Richmond.
Robert Kinzer, director.

OTHER PRIMARY SOURCES

Alexandria & Alexandria (Arlington) County Virginia Minister Returns & Marriage Bonds 1801–1852. Transcribed by T. Michael Miller. Bowie, Md.: Heritage, 1987.

Algoma Log Book: September 9, 1890–September 8, 1893. Transcribed and edited by Elizabeth P. Scott. Richmond: privately published, 2003.

Arlington County (Alexandria County) Marriage Bonds, 1834–39. Microfilm reel 38. Library of Virginia, Richmond.

Art Club of Richmond Exhibition Catalogues, 1896–1905. Virginia Historical Society, Richmond.

Art Club of Richmond School Prospectus[es], 1908–16. Virginia Historical Society, Richmond.

Auditor of Public Accounts. Personal Property Tax Books, City of Richmond. Microfilm reels 823–827. Library of Virginia, Richmond.

———. Record Group 454. Special Collections. Library of Virginia, Richmond.

Baist, G. W. *Atlas of the City of Richmond, 1889*.

Benton, Harmon. *A Successful Southern Hay Farm*. Farmers' Bulletin No. 312. Washington, D.C.: U.S. Dept. of Agriculture, 1907.

Bill Books, 1875–85. Archives. Mount de Chantal Academy of the Visitation, Wheeling, W.Va.

Black, May Gardner. "Confederate Surgeons and Hospitals." *Confederate Veteran* 36, no. 5 (May 1928): 183–85.

Board of Public Works [Virginia]. Records. Library of Virginia, Richmond.

Branch & Company Records (Richmond, Va.), 1837–1976. Virginia Historical Society, Richmond.

Brodie, D. A. *Building Up a Run-Down Cotton Plantation*. Farmers' Bulletin No. 326. Washington, D.C.: U.S. Dept. of Agriculture, 1908.

Bryan Family Papers. Library of Virginia, Richmond.

Bryan Family Papers. Virginia Historical Society, Richmond.

Bryan, John Stewart. "James H. Dooley." *Proceedings of the Thirty-Fourth Annual Meeting. The Virginia State Bar Association*. July 1923.

———. *Joseph Bryan: His Times, His Family, His Friends: A Memoir*. Richmond: privately published, 1935.

Joseph Bryan Commonplace Book 1877–1893. Virginia Historical Society, Richmond.

Joseph Bryan Papers. Virginia Historical Society, Richmond.

"By-Laws of the Montgomery Guard, Second Company, First Regiment Virginia Volunteers, adopted July 17, 1850 and Revised May, 1858." Richmond, 1858. Library of Virginia, Richmond.

Byrne, Michael. Letters to John Dooley. Maymont Mansion Archives. Richmond.

Carrington Family Papers. Virginia Historical Society, Richmond.

Case Files of Applications from Former Confederates for Presidential Pardons ("Amnesty Papers"), 1864–67. Group I, Pardon Applications Submitted by Persons from the South: the National Archives and Records Service, General Services Admnistration, 1976: "U.S. Office of the Adjutant General, Va. Case Files for Presidential Pardons 1864–1867." Misc. microfilm 3930, reel 4. Library of Virginia, Richmond.

Catalogues of Georgetown College, 1856–68. Special Collections. Georgetown University Library, Washington, D.C.

Chamberlayne, E. H., Jr., comp. *Record of the Richmond City and Henrico Co. Virginia Troops, Confederate States Army*. Series No. 1. Richmond: W. E. Jones, Printer, 1879.

The Chesapeake and Ohio Railway Company Records, 1888–1948: The Chesapeake & Ohio Railway Corporate Records Collection. Misc. microfilms, 1677-168. Library of Virginia, Richmond.

Christian, George L. "Reminiscences of Some of the Dead of the Bench and Bar of Richmond." *Virginia Law Register* 14, nos. 9, 10, 11 (1909).

"City of Richmond vs. S. M. Dooley and Others." Vols. I and II. Henrico Circuit Court. Jan. 29–Feb. 17, 1906. Henrico County Virginia Circuit Court Records, Library of Virginia, Richmond.

Adele Clark Papers. Virginia Historical Society, Richmond.

Adele Goodman Clark Papers. Special Collections and Archives. James Branch Cabell Library, Virginia Commonwealth University, Richmond.

Coke, Ben H. *John May, Jr. of Virginia: His Descendants and Their Land*. Baltimore: Gateway, 1975.

Colonial Dames of America in the State of Virginia. *History and Register of Ancestors and Members of the Society of the Colonial Dames of America in the State of Virginia, 1892–1930*. Richmond: privately published, 1930.

Commissioner of Revenue, City of Richmond. "Business License Records 1842–1863." Auditor of Public Accounts Record Group 454, "Returns of Licenses." Special Collections. Library of Virginia, Richmond.

Community League News. Cooperative Education Association of Virginia.

Compiled Service Records of Confederate Soldiers Who Served in Organizations from the State of Virginia. War Department Collection of Confederate

Records. Record Group 109. National Archives and Records Administration, Washington, D.C. Microfilm 354. Library of Virginia, Richmond.

Cox, Catherine Cabell Claiborne. Diaries. Virginia Historical Society, Richmond.

Crane and Dooley Papers. Maymont Mansion Archives, Richmond.

Daniel, John W. "Hon. John W. Daniel: He Discusses Major Dooley's Letter on the Currency Question." *Richmond Dispatch,* Sept. 20, 1861, 6.

Deed Books. City of Richmond, Virginia. John Marshall Courthouse, Richmond.

Deed Books. County of Henrico. Henrico County Courthouse, Richmond.

Deed Books. King William County. Microfilm. Library of Virginia, Richmond.

Dooley, James H. *Compulsory Education.* Pamphlet. N.d. Reprinted in *Annual Report of the Co-operative Education Association of Va. for the Year Ending November 20, 1911,* 31–33. Richmond: Department of Public Instruction and the Co-operative Education Association, 1912.

———. "Dooley on Finance." *State,* Jan. 31, 1893, 2.

———. "Dooley on Money." *State,* April 22, 1893, 4.

———. "Dooley's Diagnosis." *Richmond Dispatch,* July 30, 1893, 2.

———. "Gold Contracts in Silver: Major Dooley Offers Further Reflections on the Subject." *Richmond Times,* Oct. 4, 1891, 10.

———. *Has Our Country Passed the Climax of Its Prosperity? A Reply to the Address of Mr. F.A. Vanderlip.* Pamphlet. 1902. Special Collections, University of Virginia Library.

———. "History and Tradition Favored Richmond Bank: Major Dooley's Letter to Comptroller Williams." *Richmond Times-Dispatch,* April 3, 1914, 5.

———. "How May State Receive Return for Money Spent on Education." *Richmond Times-Dispatch,* June 13, 1909, 9. The Richmond Press published a pamphlet with the same title in 1909.

———. "How to Make Richmond Grow as a Manufacturing Center, the Necessary Steps." *Richmond Times-Dispatch,* Jan. 10, 1904, 4.

———. *A National Constitutional Convention and Its Possible Consequences.* Pamphlet. 1911. University of Michigan Law Library.

———. "Open Letter to Senator Daniel from Major James H. Dooley." *Richmond Dispatch,* Aug. 30, 1891, 7.

———. "Predicts Great Fall in Stocks." *Richmond Times-Dispatch,* Sept. 25, 1910, 1.

———. "Rate Regulation by the Government: What It Means to the South." *Richmond Times-Dispatch,* Jan. 6, 1906, 1. Also published as a pamphlet in 1906.

———. "Silver Question: Maj. Dooley Discusses the Close of the Indian Mints." Interview. *Richmond Dispatch,* July 2, 1893, 11.

———. Student essays. Georgetown College class exercise booklets. Maymont Mansion Archives, Richmond.

———. "Tariff and Finance: Major Dooley Carefully Discusses These Great Questions." Interview. *Richmond Dispatch,* Dec. 10, 1893, 2.

———. "Tariff Theories: Effect of 'Free Raw Materials' on Foreign Trade." *Richmond Dispatch,* Jan. 9, 1894, 2.

Dooley, James H., and John W. Daniel. *Payment of Gold Contracts in Silver: Correspondence between James H. Dooley and U.S. Senator John W. Daniel.* Pamphlet. Richmond: Hill Printing Co., 1891. Special Collections, Georgetown University Library.

Dooley, Mrs. James H. *Dem Good Ole Times.* Garden City, N.Y.: Doubleday Page, 1906.

Dooley, John E. Civil War Journal. Manuscript. Special Collections, Georgetown University Library.

———. *John Dooley, Confederate Soldier: His War Journal.* Edited by Joseph T. Durkin, S.J. Washington, D.C.: Georgetown University Press, 1945.

———. *John Dooley's Civil War: An Irish American's Journey in the First Virginia Infantry Regiment.* Edited by Robert Emmett Curran. Knoxville: University of Tennessee Press, 2012.

———. S.J. Papers. Special Collections. Georgetown University Library.

Dooley Family Letters. Maymont Mansion Archives, Richmond.

Doswell Family Papers. Virginia Historical Society, Richmond.

Thomas Claybrook Elder Papers. Virginia Historical Society, Richmond.

Files for Presidential Pardons, 1865–67. U.S. Office of the Adjutant General. Microcopy 1003, roll 59. National Archives and Records Administration, Washington, D.C.

"Finance Book 1859–1875." Mount de Chantal Academy of the Visitation, Wheeling, W. Va.

Frazier, Irvin, comp. *The Family of John Lewis, Pioneer.* San Antonio, Tex.: Fisher, 1985.

Freedley, Edwin T., ed. *United States Mercantile Guide. Leading Pursuits and Leading Men: A Treatise on the Principal Trades and Manufactures of the United States. Showing the Progress, State and Prospects of Business: and Illustrated by Sketches of Distinguished Mercantile and Manufacturing Firms.* Philadelphia: Edward Young, 1856.

The General Education Board: An Account of Its Activities 1902–1914. New York: General Education Board, 1915.

Georgetown College. Entrance Book 1850–95. Special Collections. Georgetown University Library.

———. *Georgetown College Journal* 48 (1919–20). Special Collections. Georgetown University Library.

———. Ledger Books, 1856–65. Special Collections. Georgetown University Library.

Georgetown University. Diploma: Doctor of Laws Degree, "Jacobus H. Dooley."
Translated by H. Lee Perkins. Maymont Mansion Archives, Richmond.
————. "Official Greetings of the President of the University." At presentation
of honorary doctor of laws degree to James Henry Dooley. June 8, 1920. Special
Collections, Georgetown University Library.
————. "One Hundred and Twenty-First Annual Commencement." Program.
June 8, 1920. Special Collections, Georgetown University.
Handy, Moses Purnell. "From His Journal." Pt. 1. *Watchman* 1, no. 4–16 (Feb. 3–
April 28, 1866). Reprinted as "The Fall of Richmond in 1865." *American Maga-
zine and Historical Chronicle* 1, no. 2 (Autumn–Fall 1985–86): 2–21.
Hansbrough, George W. *Reports of Cases Decided in the Supreme Court of Appeals
of Virginia.* Charlottesville, Va.: Michie, 1921.
Henrico County Circuit Court Records. Microfilm.
Henrico County Court Minutes, 1864–67. Microfilm.
Hobson Family Papers. Virginia Historical Society, Richmond.
Houston Family Papers, 1850–1943. Virginia Historical Society, Richmond.
Jones, J. B. *A Rebel War Clerk's Diary at the Confederate States Capital.* Phila-
delphia, 1866. Reprint, 2 vols. New York: Time-Life Books, 1982.
Journals of the House of Delegates and the Senate of the Commonwealth of Virginia,
1871–77. Library of Virginia, Richmond.
Keiley, Anthony M. *In Vinculis; Or the Prisoner of War Being the Experience of a
Rebel in Two Federal Pens Interspersed with Reminiscences of the Late War, Anec-
dotes of Southern Generals, Etc.* New York, 1866.
Keiley, Anthony M. Letterbook 1885. Virginia Historical Society, Richmond.
Keiley Family Papers. Virginia Historical Society, Richmond.
*Lewis & Als v. Whittle & Als, In the Matter of the Medical College of Virginia: Brief
of Messsrs. Joseph Christian, William Wirt Henry, and Guy & Gilliam.* Rich-
mond, Va.: Wm. Ellis Jones, Book and Job Printer, 1883. Virginia Historical
Society, Richmond.
*Lewis & Als v. Whittle & Als, On a Petition for Mandamus: Brief of John W. John-
ston, for Whittle and Others.* Richmond, Va. Wm. Ellis Jones, Book and Job
Printer, 1883. Virginia Historical Society, Richmond.
Loehr, Charles T. *War History of the First Virginia Infantry Regiment, Army of
Northern Virginia.* 1884. Reprint, Dayton, Ohio: Morningside Bookshop, 1970.
————. "Was Not Captured." *Richmond Dispatch,* Aug. 18, 1895, 11.
Loughborough, Margaret, and James H. Johnston. *The Recollections of Margaret
Cabell Brown Loughborough: A Southern Woman's Memories of Richmond, VA,
and Washington, D.C. in the Civil War.* Lanham, Md.: Hamilton, 2010.
"Major James H. Dooley Resolution Adopted by the Board of Directors." Nov. 27,
1922. Merchants National Bank, Richmond.

Manarin, Louis H., ed. *Richmond at War: The Minutes of the City Council, 1861–1865*. Official Publication No. 17. Richmond Civil War Centennial Committee. Chapel Hill: University of North Carolina Press, 1966.

Manhattan Club membership roster. New York: Clubhouse, 1905. Maymont Mansion library, Richmond.

Manhattan Club membership roster. New York: Clubhouse, 1920. Maymont Mansion library, Richmond.

Mann, Etta Donnan. *Four Years in the Governor's Mansion of Virginia: 1910–1914*. Richmond: Dietz, 1937.

Maupin Family Papers. Albert H. Small Special Collections Library, University of Virginia.

McLaughlin, J. Fairfax. *College Days at Georgetown and Other Papers*. Philadelphia: Lippincott, 1899.

Medical College of Virginia Board of Visitors Minutes. Archives, Tompkins-McCaw Library, Medical College of Virginia, Virginia Commonwealth University, Richmond.

Meyer, Virginia M., and John Frederick Dorman, eds. *Adventures of Purse and Person Virginia 1607–1624/5*. Alexandria, Va.: Order of First Families of Virginia, 1607–1624/25, 1987.

Mitchel, John. "Journal: Being Continuation of Jail Journal." Series. *Irish Citizen* (New York), 1868–72.

Mordecai, Samuel. *Richmond in By-Gone Days*. 1860. Reprint, Richmond: Dietz, 1946.

Morrison, Andrew, ed. *City on the James: Richmond, Virginia: The Chamber of Commerce Book*. Richmond: G. W. Engelhardt, 1893.

———, comp. *Richmond Virginia and the New South*. Richmond: G. W. Engelhardt, 1888.

Morse, Genevieve F., et al. *History of the Virginia Daughters of the American Revolution 1891–1987*. Privately published, 1993.

Munford, Beverley Bland. *Random Recollections*. Privately published, 1905.

Mary Munford Papers. Library of Virginia, Richmond.

Official Gazette of the United States Patent and Trademark Office, 1885–95.

Old Military and Civil Records. Record Group 109. Microfilm. National Archives and Records Administration, Washington, D.C.

Personal Property Tax Records. City of Richmond, Virginia, and County of Henrico. Microfilm. Library of Virginia, Richmond.

———. County of Lunenburg, Virginia. Microfilm. Library of Virginia, Richmond.

Poor, Henry Varnum. *Manual of the Railroads of the United States*. New York and London. [Various nineteenth-century editions]. New York: H. V. & H. W. Poor. Virginia Historical Society, Richmond.

————. *Poor's Directory of Railway Officials* [a nineteenth-century series]. New York: Poor's Railroad Manual. Library of Virginia, Richmond.

Potts, Frank. Diary. 1861. Personal Papers Collection. Library of Virginia, Richmond.

Proceedings of the Bar of the City of Richmond on Occasion of the Death of Hon. Robert Ould, Held at Richmond, Virginia. Feb. 24, 1883. Booklet. Richmond, 1883. VHS.

Prospectus of Mt. de Chantal, near Wheeling, W. Va., Incorporated under the Title of Wheeling Female Academy, Academic year 1875–'76. Richmond: Dispatch Steam Printing House, 1876.

Prospectus of Mt. de Chantal, (near Wheeling, West Virginia,) Incorporated under the Title of Wheeling Female Academy, Academic Year 1876–'77. Richmond: Dispatch Steam Printing House, 1877.

Putnam, Sallie Brock. *Richmond during the War: Four Years of Personal Observation.* 1867. Reprint, Lincoln: University of Nebraska Press, 1996.

Records of Constitutional Convention, 1901–2. Record Group 97. Library of Virginia, Richmond.

Records of the Portrait Committee of R. E. Lee Camp No. 1. Virginia Historical Society, Richmond.

Records of the Richmond Library Company, 1841–61. Virginia Historical Society, Richmond.

Register of Marriages, Staunton, Virginia. Vol. 1, 1802–1928. Augusta County Courthouse, Staunton.

R. E. Lee Camp No. 1. Minute Book. Confederate Veterans Association. Virginia Historical Society, Richmond.

R. G. Dun & Co. Early Handwritten Credit Reporting Ledgers of the Mercantile Agency. Baker Library Historical Collections, Harvard Business School.

Report of the Fourteenth Annual Meeting of the Virginia State Bar Association. Edited by Eugene C. Massie. Richmond: Everett Waddy, 1902. Virginia Historical Society, Richmond.

Reports of the Board of Directors and Medical Superintendent of the Central Lunatic Asylum for the Colored Insane. Richmond: Superintendent Public Printing. Library of Virginia, 1873–81.

Richmond and Danville Extension Company Records. Norfolk Southern Historical Collection, Norfolk, Virginia.

Richmond and Danville Railroad Company Records. Norfolk Southern Historical Collection, Norfolk, Virginia.

Richmond and West Point Terminal and Warehouse Company Records. Norfolk Southern Historical Collection, Norfolk, Virginia.

Richmond City and Henrico County, Virginia 1850 United States Census. Compiled by Virginia Genealogical Society. Special Publication No. 6, 1977. Library of Virginia, Richmond.

Richmond City Directories [various publishers], 1855–1924. Archives, The Valentine [Museum], Richmond.

Richmond City Hustings Deeds. Richmond Chancery Court. Microfilm, Library of Virginia, Richmond.

Richmond City Virginia Hustings Court Minutes. Microfilm. Library of Virginia, Richmond.

Richmond City Virginia Hustings Court Records. "Ended Causes." Library of Virginia, Richmond.

Richmond, The Pride of Virginia: An Historical City. Philadelphia: Progress, 1900.

Rockefeller, John D., Sr. Papers. Rockefeller Archive Center, Pocantico Hills, N.Y. Also available online; and through interlibrary loan (microfilm 2173) at University of Houston.

Ruffner, William H. *A Report on Washington Territory.* New York: Seattle, Lake Shore and Eastern Railway, 1889.

St. Mary's Roman Catholic Church. Alexandria, Va. Parish Record Book. Part II: Record of Marriages 1812–March 1855.

St. Mary's: 2000 Years for Christ: 1795–1995. Alexandria, Va.: St. Mary's Catholic Church, 1995.

St. Paul's Episcopal Church, Richmond. Records. Virginia Historical Society, Richmond.

St. Peter's Roman Catholic Church, Richmond. Marriage and Baptismal Records. Microfilm 1081. Library of Virginia, Richmond.

Sanger Historical Files. Archives, Tompkins-McCaw Library, Medical College of Virginia, Virginia Commonwealth University, Richmond.

Slaughter, Philip. *A Brief Sketch of the Life of William Green, LLD: Jurist and Scholar, with Some Personal Reminiscences of Him.* Richmond: Wm. Ellis Jones Book and Job Printer, 1883.

"Slave Inhabitants, City of Richmond." Schedule 2. Population Schedules of the Seventh Census of the United States, 1850: Virginia, vol. 12. Microfilm 121. Library of Virginia, Richmond.

"Slave Inhabitants in 2nd Ward City of Richmond." Schedule 2. Virginia Slave Schedules. Population Schedules of the Eighth Census of the United States, 1860; vol. 3. Microfilm 226e. Library of Virginia, Richmond.

"Slave Inhabitants, Richmond Ward 1." Population Schedules of the Sixth Census of the United States, 1840. Record Group 29, Microfilm 704, Family History Library Film 0029687. National Archives Records Administration, Washington, D.C.

Sneden, Private Robert Knox. *Eye of the Storm: A Civil War Odyssey.* Edited by
   Charles F. Bryan Jr. and Nelson D. Lankford. New York: Free Press, 2000.
Society of the Colonial Dames of America in the State of Virginia. *History and
   Register of Ancestors and Members 1892–1930.* Richmond: William Byrd, 1930.
Society of St. Vincent de Paul. Minute Book. Archives, Diocese of Richmond, Vir-
   ginia.
Southern Historical Society Papers, 1876–1959. Richmond: Virginia Historical
   Society.
"Subscriptions for the Academy of the Visitation. Mount de Chantal. Near Wheel-
   ing West VA." [1865]. Archives, Mount de Chantal Academy of the Visitation,
   Wheeling, W.Va.
[Terhune, M. V.] *Marion Harland's Autoiography: The Story of a Long Life.* New
   York: Harper and Brothers, 1910.
Tuller, Walker K. "A Convention to Amend the Constitution: Why Needed.
   How It May Be Obtained." *North American Review* 193, no. 664 (March 1911):
   369–87.
U.S. City Directories. Microfilm 229. Library of Virginia.
Valentine, Edward V. "My Recollections circa 1890–1899." Library, The Valentine
   [Museum], Richmond.
Virginia State Corporation Commission Charter Books. State Government Records
   Collection. Library of Virginia, Richmond.
Virginia Supreme Court of Appeals. Order Books. Library of Virginia, Richmond.
*War of the Rebellion: A Compilation of Official Records of the Union and Confederate
   Armies.* Washington, D.C.: U.S. Congress, 1880–1901. Microfilm. National Ar-
   chives and Records Administration, Washington, D.C.
Will Books. Circuit Court of the City of Richmond. John Marshall Courthouse,
   Richmond.
Williams, John L. *A Manual of Investments: Important Facts and Figures Regarding
   Southern Investment Securities.* Richmond: John L. Williams, Banker and Bro-
   ker, 1886.
———. "Money and Its Uses." *Richmond Dispatch,* Jan. 14, 1894, 2.
Williams, John Skelton. "A Fine Showing: Wonderful Development of Virginia by
   Her Railroads." *Richmond Dispatch,* Jan. 1, 1891, 1.
———. *A Manual of Investments: Important Facts & Figures Regarding Southern
   Investment Securities.* Richmond: John L. Williams & Son, Bankers, 1888.
———. *A Manual of Investments: Important Facts & Figures Regarding Southern
   Investment Securities.* Richmond: John L. Williams & Son, Bankers, 1889–90.
———. Papers. Albert H. Small Special Collections Library, University of Vir-
   ginia.
Williams Family Papers. Virginia Historical Society, Richmond.

The World Almanac and Encyclopedia 1902. Buffalo, N.Y.: A. J. H. Smith, 1902.

Young Catholic Friend Society. Minute Book. Diocese of Richmond Archives. Richmond.

SECONDARY SOURCES

Adams, Marjorie Branner. *Crippled Children's Hospital, Richmond, Virginia: The First Sixty Years.* Richmond: The Hospital, 1979.

Ayres, Edward L. *The Promise of the New South: Life after Reconstruction.* New York: Oxford University Press, 1992.

Bailey, James H., II. "Anthony M. Keiley and 'The Keiley Incident.'" *Virginia Magazine of History and Biography* (Jan. 1956): 65–81.

———. *A History of the Diocese of Richmond: The Formative Years.* Richmond: Diocese of Richmond, 1956.

Bayliss, Mary Lynn. "Almost at Home at Maymont." *Maymont Notes,* no. 2 (Fall 2002): 11–16.

———. "At Home at Maymont: The Beginning." *Maymont Notes,* no. 1 (Fall 2001): 5–8.

———. "The Dooleys: A View from Their Library." *Richmond Quarterly* 9, no. 1 (Summer 1986): 1–8.

———. "Exhibitions of Talents: Adele Williams and the Richmond Art Scene." *Virginia Cavalcade* 44, no. 4 (Spring 1992): 166–77.

———. "Major Dooley and the Richmond and Danville Railroad." *Maymont Notes,* no. 3 (2003–4): 12–17.

———. "Will the Real Major Dooley Please Stand Up." *Richmond Quarterly* 14, no. 2 (Fall 1991): 31–34.

———. *Will the Real Major Dooley Please Stand Up? and Other "Maymont Moments."* Booklet. Richmond: Capital One Financial, 2005.

Bell, Landon C. *Cumberland Parish: Lunenburg County, Virginia, 1746–1816, Vestry Book 1746–1816.* Richmond: William Byrd, 1930.

———. *The Old Free State: A Contribution to the History of Lunenburg County and Southside Virginia.* Richmond: William Byrd, 1927.

Bladek, John David. "'Virginia Is Middle Ground': The Know-Nothing Party and the Virginia Gubernatorial Election of 1855." *Virginia Magazine of History and Biography* 106, no. 1 (Winter 1998): 35–70.

Blanton, Wyndham B., M.D. *Medicine in Virginia in the Nineteenth Century.* Richmond: Garrett and Massie, 1933.

Bowie, Walter Russell. *Sunrise in the South: The Life of Mary-Cooke Branch Munford.* Richmond: William Byrd, 1942.

Brock, R. A. *Virginia and Virginians: Eminent Virginians.* 2 vols. Richmond and Toledo: H. H. Hardesty, 1888.

Bruce, Kathleen. *Virginia Iron Manufacture in the Slave Era.* 1930. Reprint, New York, A. M. Kelley, 1968.

Bryson, W. Hamilton, ed. *Essays on Legal Education in Nineteenth Century Virginia.* Buffalo, N.Y.: W. S. Hein, 1998.

———. *Legal Education in Virginia 1779–1979: A Biographical Approach.* Charlottesville: University Press of Virginia, 1982.

Bryson, W. Hamilton, and E. Lee Shepard. "The Virginia Bar, 1870–1900." In *The New High Priests: Lawyers in Post–Civil War America,* edited by Gerard Gawalt. Contributions in Legal Studies No. 29. Westport, Conn.: Greenwood, 1984.

Burns, Bryan. *Lewis Ginter: Richmond's Gilded Age Icon.* Charleston, S.C.: History Press, 2011.

Byrd, Odell R., Jr. *Richmond, VA: A City of Monuments and Statues: Historical Highlights Recorded in Metal and Stone.* Richmond: Tambuzi, 1989.

Calcutt, Rebecca Barbour. *Richmond's Wartime Hospitals.* Gretna, La.: Pelican, 2005.

Campbell, E. G. *The Reorganization of the American Railroad System, 1893–1900: A Study of the Effects of the Panic of 1893, the Ensuing Depression, and the First Years of Recovery on Railroad Organization and Financing.* New York: Columbia University Press, 1938.

Caravati, Charles M., M.D. *Major Dooley.* Richmond: privately published, 1978.

———. *Medicine in Richmond: 1900–1975.* Richmond: Richmond Academy of Medicine, 1975.

Cash, W. J. *The Mind of the South.* Introduction by Bertram Wyatt-Brown. 1941. New York: Vintage, 1991.

Censer, Jane Turner. *The Reconstruction of White Southern Womanhood: 1865–1895.* Baton Rouge: Louisiana State University Press, 2003.

Chernow, Ron. *The Death of the Banker: The Decline and Fall of the Great Financial Dynasties and the Triumph of the Small Investor.* New York: Vintage, 1997.

———. *Titan: The Life of John D. Rockefeller, Sr.* New York: Random House, 1998.

Chesson, Michael B. *Richmond after the War: 1865–1890.* Richmond: Virginia State Library, 1981.

Christian, W. Ashbury. *Richmond, Her Past and Present.* Richmond: L. H. Jenkins, 1912.

Claiborne, John Herbert. *Seventy-Five Years in Old Virginia.* New York: Neale, 1904.

Clark, John E. *Railroads in the Civil War: The Impact of Management on Victory and Defeat.* Baton Rouge: Louisiana State University Press, 2001.

Coe, Lewis. *The Telegraph: A History of Morse's Invention and Its Predecessors in the United States.* Jefferson, N.C.: McFarland, 1993.

———. *The Telephone and Its Several Inventors: A History.* Jefferson, N.C.: McFarland, 1995.

Coke, Ben H. *John May, Jr. of Virginia: His Descendants and Their Land.* Baltimore: Gateway, 1975.

Cooper, John Milton. *Pivotal Decades: The United States 1900–1920.* New York: Norton, 1990.

Cowell, Mark W., et al. *The Family of John Lewis, Pioneer.* San Antonio, Tex.: Fishere, 1985.

Crawford, E. Margaret. "Great Famine." In *Oxford Companion to Irish History,* edited by S. J. Connolly. Oxford: Oxford University Press, 2007.

Curran, Robert Emmett. *The Bicentennial History of Georgetown University.* Vol. 1, *From Academy to University 1789–1889.* Washington, D.C.: Georgetown University Press, 1993.

Cutchins, John A. *A Famous Command: The Richmond Light Infantry Blues.* Richmond: Garrett and Massie, 1934.

———. *Memories of Old Richmond (1881–1944).* Verona, Va.: McClure, 1973.

Dabney, Virginius. *Richmond: The Story of a City.* Garden City, N.Y.: Doubleday, 1976.

———. *Virginia: The New Dominion: A History from 1607 to the Present.* Charlottesville: University Press of Virginia, 1971.

———. *Virginia Commonwealth University: A Sesquicentennial History.* Charlottesville: University Press of Virginia, 1987.

Daniel, W. Harrison. "Richmond's Memorial to Henry Clay: The Whig Women of Virginia and the Clay Statue." *Richmond Quarterly* 8 (Spring 1986): 39–44.

Davenport Insurance Corporation. *The Experience of a Century: A Narrative Report of the Century 1848–1948 as It Has Dealt with the Davenport Insurance Corporation and a Pictorial Record of Various Contemporary Events in the Period.* Richmond, 1948.

Deutsch, Stephanie. *Booker T. Washington, Julius Rosenwald, and the Building of Schools for the Segregated South.* Evanston, Ill.: Northwestern University Press, 2011.

Dew, Charles B. *Ironmaker to the Confederacy: Joseph R. Anderson and the Tredegar Iron Works.* Richmond: Library of Virginia, 1999.

Dillon, William. *Life of John Mitchel.* 2 vols. London: Kegan Paul, Trench and Co., 1888.

Dubbs, Carol Kellenburg. *Defend This Old Town: Williamsburg during the Civil War.* Baton Rouge: Louisiana State University Press, 2002.

"The First Hundred Years of the Medical College of Virginia: 1838–1964." Special issue, *Medical College of Virginia Bulletin* 61, no. 1 (Fall 1963). Virginia Historical Society, Richmond.

Fogarty, Gerald P. *Commonwealth Catholicism: A History of the Catholic Church in Virginia.* Notre Dame, Ind.: University of Notre Dame Press, 2001.

———. "Virginia." In *The Encyclopedia of the Irish in America,* edited by Michael Glazier, 928–31. Notre Dame, Ind.: University of Notre Dame Press, 1999.

Freeman, Anne Hobson. *The Style of a Law Firm: Eight Gentlemen from Virginia.* Chapel Hill, N.C.: Algonquin Books of Chapel Hill, 1989.

Friedman, S. Morgan. "Inflation Calculator." www.westegg.com/inflation/.

Furguson, Ernest. *Ashes of Glory: Richmond at War.* New York: Knopf, 1996.

———. *Freedom Rising: Washington in the Civil War.* New York: Knopf, 2004.

Gay, Thomas Edward, Jr. "Creating the Virginia State Corporation Commission." *Virginia Magazine of History and Biography* 78, no. 4 (Oct. 1970): 464–80.

Gibson, Langhorne, Jr. *Cabell's Canal: The Story of the James River and Kanawha.* Richmond: Commodore, 2000.

———. *The Major: Frederic Robert Scott, 1830–1898.* Privately published, 2006.

———. *My Precious Husband: The Story of Elise & Fred Scott.* Royal Orchard Land Corporation, 1994.

———. *This Splendid House: One Hundred Ten Years at the Commonwealth Club.* Richmond: Commonwealth Club, 2001.

Gilliam, George H. "Making Virginia Progressive: Courts and Parties, Railroads and Regulators, 1890–1910." *Virginia Magazine of History and Biography* 107, no. 2 (Spring 1999): 189–222.

Gleeson, David T. *The Irish in the South, 1815–1877.* Chapel Hill: University of North Carolina Press, 2001.

Gordon, Armistead C. *Virginian Portraits: Essays in Biography.* Staunton, Va.: McClure, 1924.

Gorman, Michael D. "A Conqueror or a Peacemaker? Abraham Lincoln in Richmond." *Virginia Magazine of History and Biography* 123, no. 1 (2015): 2–88.

Gunter, Margaret B. "A History of Public Education in Virginia." Commonwealth of Virginia Department of Education, 2003. www.cteresource.org.

Gwathmey, John H. *Legends of Virginia Lawyers: Anecdotes and Whimsical Yarns of the Old Time Bench and Bar.* Richmond: Dietz, 1934.

Hall, Virginius Cornick, Jr. *Portraits in the Collection of the Virginia Historical Society: A Catalogue.* Charlottesville: University Press of Virginia, 1981.

Hebert, Paul. *The Jefferson Hotel: The History of a Richmond Landmark.* Charleston: History Press, 2012.

Heinemann, Ronald L. "The 1923 Highway Bond Referendum." In *Encyclopedia Virginia,* edited by Brendan Wolfe. Virginia Foundation for the Humanities, 2010. www.EncyclopediaVirginia.org.

Heite, Edward F. "Judge Robert Ould." *Virginia Cavalcade* 14, no. 4 (Spring 1965): 10–19.

Herringshaw, Thomas William. *Herringshaw's Encyclopedia of American Biography of the Nineteenth Century.* Chicago: American Publishers' Association, 1898.

Hollan Catherine B. *Virginia Silversmiths, Jewelers, Watch- and Clockmakers, 1607–1860: Their Lives and Marks.* Mclean, Va.: Hollan, 2010.

Hutton, James V., Jr. "The One-Armed Hero of the Shenandoah." *Virginia Cavalcade* 19, no. 1 (Summer 1969): 4–11.

Janney, Caroline E. *Burying the Dead but Not the Past: Ladies Memorial Associations and the Lost Cause.* Chapel Hill: University of North Carolina Press, 2008.

Jurgens, Karri. "One of the Finest and Most Commodious, Major Dooley's Carriage House at Maymont." *Maymont Notes,* no. 3 (2003–4): 22–26.

Kimball, Gregg D. *American City, Southern Place: A Cultural History of Antebellum Richmond.* Athens: University of Georgia Press, 2000.

———. "Militias, Politics, and Patriotism: Virginia and the Union in Antebellum Richmond." *Virginia Cavalcade* 49, no. 4 (Autumn 2000): 158–77.

Klein, Maury. *The Great Richmond Terminal: A Study in Businessmen and Business Strategy.* Charlottesville: University Press of Virginia, 1970.

Lankford, Nelson. *Cry Havoc! The Crooked Road to Civil War, 1861.* New York: Viking, 2007.

———. *Richmond Burning: The Last Days of the Confederate Capital.* New York: Viking, 2002.

———. "Virginia Convention of 1861." In *Encyclopedia Virginia,* edited by Brendan Wolfe. Virginia Foundation for the Humanities, April 5, 2011. www.EncyclopediaVirginia.org.

Larsen, William. *Montague of Virginia: The Making of a Southern Progressive.* Baton Rouge: Louisiana State University Press, 1965.

Lewis, W. David. "Joseph Bryan and the Virginia Connection in the Industrial Development of Northern Alabama." *Virginia Magazine of History and Biography* 98, no. 4 (October 1990): 613–40.

———. *Sloss Furnaces and the Rise of the Birmingham District: An Industrial Epic.* Tuscaloosa: University of Alabama Press, 1994.

Lindgrun, James M. "First and Foremost a Virginian: Joseph Bryan and the New South Economy." *Virginia Magazine of History and Biography* 96, no. 2 (April 1988): 157–80.

Link, William A. *A Hard Country and a Lonely Place: Schooling, Society, and Reform in Rural Virginia, 1870–1920.* Chapel Hill: University of North Carolina Press, 1986.

Loth, Calder. "The Dooley Mausoleum at Maymont." *Maymont Notes,* no. 2 (Fall 2002): 4–7.

———, ed. *The Virginia Landmarks Register.* Charlottesville: University Press of Virginia, 1999.

Maddex, Jack P. *The Virginia Conservatives, 1869–1879: A Study in Reconstruction Politics.* Chapel Hill: University of North Carolina Press, 1970.

Manarin, Louis H., and Lee A. Wallace, Jr. *Richmond Volunteers: The Volunteer Companies of Richmond and Henrico County, Virginia 1861–1865.* Official Publication No. 26, Richmond Civil War Centennial Committee. Richmond: Westover, 1969.

Mays, David J. *The Pursuit of Excellence: A History of the University of Richmond Law School.* Richmond, Virginia: University of Richmond, 1970.

McCabe, W. Gordon. *Joseph Bryan: A Brief Memoir.* Richmond: W. E. Jones, 1909.

McCullough, David. *The Path between the Seas: The Creation of the Panama Canal, 1870–1914.* New York: Simon and Schuster, 1977.

McLeod, Norman C., Jr. "Not Forgetting the Land We Left: The Irish in Antebellum Richmond." *Virginia Cavalcade* 47, no. 1 (Winter 1998): 36–47.

McPherson, James M. *Battle Cry of Freedom: The Civil War Era.* New York: Oxford University Press, 1988.

Meagher, Margaret. *History of Education in Richmond.* Richmond: privately published, 1939.

Miller, Kerby A. *Emigrants and Exiles: Ireland and the Irish Exodus to North America.* New York: Oxford University Press, 1985.

Mitchell, Mary H. *Hollywood Cemetery: The History of a Southern Shrine.* Richmond: Library of Virginia, 1999.

Moger, Allen. "Railroad Practices and Policies in Virginia after the Civil War." *Virginia Magazine of History and Biography* 59 (1951): 432.

———. *Virginia: Bourbonism to Byrd, 1870–1925.* Charlottesville: University Press of Virginia, 1968.

Moore, James Tice. "Battle for the Medical College: Physicians, Politicians, and the Courts, 1882–1883." *Virginia Cavalcade* 31, no. 3 (Autumn 1981): 158–67.

———. *Two Paths to the New South: The Virginia Debt Controversy 1870–1883.* Lexington: University of Kentucky Press, 1974.

Morrill, Lily Logan. *A Builder of the New South: Notes on the Career of Thomas M. Logan by His Daughter.* Boston: Christopher, 1940.

Munford, Beverley Bland. *Virginia's Attitude toward Slavery and Secession.* New York: Longmans Green, 1909.

Munford, Robert Beverley, Jr. *Richmond Homes and Memories.* Richmond: Garrett and Massie, 1936.

Nicols, James L. *General Fitzhugh Lee: A Biography.* Lynchburg, Va.: H. E. Howard, 1989.

O'Leary, Elizabeth L. *From Morning to Night: Domestic Service in Maymont House and the Gilded Age South.* Charlottesville: University of Virginia Press, 2003.

Peters, John. *Richmond's Hollywood Cemetery.* Richmond: Valentine Richmond History Center, 2010.

————. *Tale of the Century: A History of the Bar Association of the City of Richmond 1885–1985.* Richmond: Bar Association of the City of Richmond, 1985.

Pilgrim, Dianne H., Richard N. Murray, and Richard Guy Wilson. *The American Renaissance: 1876–1917.* Exhibition catalogue. Brooklyn Museum, 1979.

Potterfield, T. Tyler. *Nonesuch Place: A History of the Richmond Landscape.* Charleston, S.C.: History Press, 2009.

Prince, Richard E. *Seaboard Air Line Railway: Steamboats, Locomotives, and History.* Bloomington: Indiana University Press, 2000.

Readnour, Harry Warren. "General Fitzhugh Lee, 1835–1905: A Biographical Study." Ph.D. diss., University of Virginia, 1971.

Richmond Chamber of Commerce. *The Advantages of Richmond, Virginia as a Manufacturing and Trading Center.* Richmond: published under the auspices of the Trade Committees of the Chamber of Commerce and Commercial Club, 1882.

————. *Richmond, the Pride of Virginia: An Historical City.* Philadelphia: Progress, 1900.

Ripley, William Z. *Railroads: Finance & Organization.* 1915. New York: Kraus, 1969.

Rusk, Emily. "Mothers and Grandmothers." *GRIVA [Genealogical Research Institute of Virginia] News & Notes* 23, no. 3 (March 2003): 41, 44–46, 52.

Ryan, Edward L. "Poplar Vale." *Virginia Magazine of History and Biography* 48, no. 3 (July 1940): 202–6.

Salmon, Emily J. "The Belle of the Nineties: Richmond's Jefferson Hotel, 1895–1995." *Virginia Cavalcade* 41 (Summer 1995): 4–13.

Salmon, Emily, and Edward D. C. Campbell, eds. *The Hornbook of Virginia History: A Ready-Reference Guide to the Old Dominion's People, Places and Past.* Richmond: Library of Virginia, 1994.

Scott, Anne Firor. *Natural Allies: Women's Associations in American History.* Urbana: University of Illinois Press, 1991.

————. *The Southern Lady: From Pedestal to Politics 1830–1930.* Chicago: University of Chicago Press, 1970.

Scott, Mary Wingfield. *Houses of Old Richmond.* New York: Bonanza, 1941.

————. *Old Richmond Neighborhoods.* 1950. Reprint, Richmond: The Valentine Museum, 1984.

Sentinel on the Hill: Monte Maria and One Hundred Years. Richmond: Monastery of the Visitation, 1966.

Shepard, Lee. "Sketches of the Old Richmond Bar: A. Judson Crane." *Richmond Quarterly* 6, no. 2 (Fall 1983): 12–15.

"The Sisters of Charity in Virginia, 1833–1870." In *The Nineteenth Century Educa-*

tion. Johns Hopkins University Studies in Education No. 27, p. 41. Daughters of Charity Archives, St. Joseph's Provincial House, Emmetsburg, Md.

Stanard, Mary Newton. *Richmond: Its People and Its Story.* Philadelphia: Lippincott, 1923.

Stover, John F. *The Railroads of the South: 1865–1900: A Study in Finance and Control.* Chapel Hill: University of North Carolina Press, 1955.

Strouse, Jean. *Morgan: American Financier.* New York: Random House, 1999.

Temple, K. Richmond. "John Skelton Williams: Richmonder of Vision." *Richmond Quarterly* 7, no. 2 (Fall 1984): 38–42.

Thomas, Emory M. *The Confederate State of Richmond: A Biography of the Capital.* Baton Rouge: Louisiana State University Press, 1998.

Thorpe, James. *Henry Edwards Huntington: A Biography.* Berkeley: University of California Press, 1994.

Treadway, Sandra Gioia. *Women of Mark: A History of the Woman's Club of Richmond, Virginia, 1894–1994.* Richmond: Library of Virginia, 1995.

Tyler, Lyon Gardiner. *Encyclopedia of Virginia Biography.* New York: Lewis Historical Publishing, 1915.

———. *Men of Mark in Virginia: Ideals of American Life. A Collection of Biographies of the Leading Men in the State.* Washington, D.C.: Men of Mark Publishing, 1906.

Tyler-McGraw, Marie. *At the Falls: Richmond, Virginia and Its People.* Chapel Hill: University of North Carolina Press, 1994.

Underhill, Marjorie Fay. "The Virginia Phase of the Ogden Movement: A Campaign for Universal Education." Master's thesis, University of Virginia, 1952.

Valentine, Elizabeth Gray. *Dawn to Twilight: Work of Edward V. Valentine.* Richmond: William Byrd, 1929.

Varon, Elizabeth R. *We Mean to Be Counted: White Women and Politics in Antebellum Virginia.* Chapel Hill: University of North Carolina Press, 1998.

Wallace, Lee, ed. *First Virginia Infantry.* Richmond, n.d.

Weaver, Jeffrey, and Lee Wallace, eds. *The Richmond Ambulance Committee, Herbig's Infirmary Company, and the Virginia Public Guard and Armory Band.* Lynchburg: H. E. Howard, 1985.

Weddell, Elizabeth Wright. *St. Paul's Church, Richmond, Virginia: Its Historic Years and Memorials.* 2 vols. Richmond: William Byrd, 1931.

Wheary, Dale. "A Baroque Sculpture in the Maymont House Collection." *Maymont Notes,* no. 2 (Fall 2002): 23–26.

———. *The Italian Garden at Maymont.* Booklet. Maymont Foundation, 2009.

———. "Maymont: Gilded Age Estate." *Maymont Notes,* no. 1 (Fall 2001): 9–14.

———. "Swannanoa: Summer Home of James and Sallie Dooley, 1913–1925." *Augusta [County] Historical Bulletin* 50 (2014): 19–34.

————. "A Tiffany & Company Tour de Force at Maymont," *Maymont Notes,* no. 3 (2003–4): 18–21.

Williams, Frances Leigh. *They Faced the Future: A Saga of Growth.* Richmond: State Planters Bank and Trust Company, 1951.

Winthrop, Robert P. *Architecture in Downtown Richmond.* Richmond: Junior Board of Historic Richmond Foundation, 1982.

Woodward, C. Vann. *Origins of the New South, 1877–1913: A History of the South.* Vol. 9. Edited by Wendell Holmes Stephenson and E. Merton Coulter. Baton Rouge: Louisiana State University Press, 1951.

Woolridge, William Charles. "The Sound and Fury of 1896: Virginia Democrats Face Free Silver." *Virginia Magazine of History and Biography* 75, no. 2 (1967): 97–108.

Younger, Edward, and James Tice Moore, eds. *The Governors of Virginia: 1860– 1978.* Charlottesville: University of Virginia Press, 1982.

Bentley, William, 218
Binford's hat store, Richmond, 43
black Conservatives, 97
Black Heritage Library Collection, 198
Black Warrior Coal Fields, Alabama, 135
Blair, A. Beirne, 196
Blair, Francis Preston, 94
Blair, Frank (Virginia attorney general),
    134–35
Blair, James P., 75
Blair & Company, 190–91
Board of Public Works (Virginia), 108
Bohannon, Sarah, and Richard L., 12
Books for Libraries Press, 198
Bosher, Kate Langley, 255n34
Bowie, Walter Russell, 220, 222
Boy Scouts, 215
Branch, Blythe, 141
Branch, James R., 97, 101
Branch, John Kerr, 182, 214
Branch, John Patteson, 127, 135, 141, 181,
    182, 183, 196, 243n3
Branch, Mary Cook (later, Munford),
    172–73, 192, 216
Branch, Melville, 211
Bratt, James, 95
Braxton, A. Caperton, 182
Breckinridge, John C., 43, 44
Brock, R. A., 233n24
Brock, Sallie, 60, 78, 80–81
Brown, J. Thompson, 106
Brown, John, 37
Brown, William Garl, Jr., 147
Bruton Parish Church, Williamsburg, 56
Bryan, Isobel (née Stewart), 121, 136
Bryan, John Stewart, 200
Bryan, Joseph: at constitutional conven-
    tion banquet, 183; and Grover Cleve-
    land banquet, 161; death of, 200;
    education, interest in, 192; founder,

board member, president, Common-
    wealth Club, 151; Jefferson Hotel
    and, 193; legal career, 121; on list of
    American millionaires, 183; Manhat-
    tan Club, 152; marriage, 121; planta-
    tion roots of, 219; as president of Vir-
    ginia Historical Society, 162; railroad
    and other investments with James
    Henry Dooley and Thomas Logan,
    2, 121–29, 135, 136, 141, 143–45, 147,
    148, 151, 152, 158, 162–63, 168, 187; in
    Roosevelt welcoming party, 194
Bryson, W. Hamilton, 105
Buchanan and Clifton Forge Railroad,
    115, 135
Buford, A. S. B., 129, 160, 243n3
Bull Run (Manassas), first battle of,
    50–53, 58
business and finance: Civil War, effects
    of, on, 49–50, 51, 53–54, 60, 69;
    James Henry Dooley as financial
    prognosticator, 155–57, 163–64,
    165, 186, 187, 204–5; economic re-
    covery in 1880s, 130; "great depres-
    sion" of 1903–4, 186–91; inflation
    of Confederate currency, 60, 68,
    74, 76; panic of 1833–34, 6; panic
    of 1837–38, 8; panic of 1857, 17, 28,
    33–34; panic of 1873 and depression
    of 1870s, 111–12, 114, 116–17, 119, 130;
    panic of November 1890, 159–60;
    panic of 1893, 148, 156, 157, 161–67,
    172; panic of 1907, 199; post–Civil
    War financial depression and recov-
    ery, 86–87; pre–Civil War anxiety
    in Richmond, effects of, on, 40–48;
    recession of mid-1880s, 136, 139; St.
    Paul, Minn., Virginians' business
    trip to, 140, 141–44; Vanderlip on
    US economy, 185–86, 187, 251n45;

Virginia House of Delegates, James Henry Dooley in, 107, 108–9, 112–13. *See also* hat manufacturing business; investments of James Henry Dooley; investments of John Dooley; *and specific business and financial institutions*

Butler, Benjamin, 126

Byrne, Mary (née Dooley; sister of John), 22

Byrne, Michael (brother-in-law of John), 22, 23, 26, 27–28, 32, 34, 35, 36, 78–79, 81–82

Cabell, Henry Landon, 174, 181

Callahan (police officer), 96

Cameron, William E. (governor of Virginia), 133–35

Cammack, Addison, 139

Campbell, James Alston, 182

Capitol Building, Richmond, 9, 16, 43, 73, 78, 109, 123, 178, 181

Capitol Square, Richmond, 6, 8, 9, 10, 16, 41, 42, 47, 67, 68, 71, 78, 80, 82, 100, 134, 179, 180, 194, 209, 215

Caravati, Charles M., 230n42, 233n23, 240n28

"Carrie's Rest," 203

Carrington, I., 10–11

Carrington, Isaac H., 132

Carter, Thomas H., 115–16

Catholics and Catholicism, 2, 5, 14, 21, 24–25, 34, 101, 116, 205, 220. *See also specific churches and organizations*

Central Lunatic Asylum for the Colored Insane, 111

Central Railway, 176

Central Southern Rights Associations, 38

Chamber of Commerce, Richmond, 100, 112, 114–15, 152, 176, 177, 179, 180, 191, 196

Chernow, Ron, 228n27

Chesapeake and Ohio (C&O) Railroad, 107, 109–10, 112–13, 125, 157, 178, 188, 201, 207, 254n34

Chicago, 22, 26, 32–33, 34, 36, 78–79, 81–82, 98, 142, 160, 162, 165

cholera epidemic of 1854, 24

Christian, E. D., 136–38, 153; bankruptcy, 172

Christian, Frank, 196

Christie, John, 103

Christmas celebrations, 66, 86

Citizen (New York City newspaper), 23

City Hall, Richmond, 80, 100, 106, 110

Civil War: Amnesty Proclamation and Oath, 81, 82–83, 236n9; Appomattox, surrender at, 79; business and financial effects of, 49–50, 51, 53–54, 60, 69; conscription, Confederate, 1, 54, 62, 72–73, 74; desertion, Confederate, 57, 62; Jack Dooley's military service in, 62, 65–67, 69–70, 75–76; James Henry Dooley's military service in, 54–57, 61–63, 233n24; John Dooley's military service in, 1–2, 48–54, 68; events leading up to, 18–19, 34, 37–48; Fort Sumter, 38, 46–47; general amnesty for Confederates, 92, 94; hat manufacturing for Confederate Army, 49; inflation of Confederate currency in, 60, 68, 74, 76; papal recognition of Confederacy, attempts to gain, 101; peace negotiations, 75; prisoners of war and prisoner exchanges, 61–62, 69–71, 75–76; railroads in, 49, 52, 59, 60–61, 67, 73, 76; Richmond Ambulance Committee, activities of, 2, 58–76; Richmond Evacuation Fire, 2, 77–78, 79, 119; secession of states from Union,

Daniel, John W. (politician), 111, 117, 156, 166, 194

Daughters of the American Revolution (DAR), 150, 151, 162

Davenport, Isaac, 112

Davis, Jefferson, 54, 63, 75, 76, 78, 79, 101, 119, 184

Dem Good Ole Times (Sallie Dooley), 3, 197–99

Democratic Hibernian Club, 94

Democratic Party, 11, 24–25, 26, 43, 44, 94, 203–4

Dennis, John B., 191

desertion, Confederate, 57, 62

devaluation/deflation of American currency, 155–56

diabetes, 205

Digges, Sir Dudley, 2

Digges, Edward, 2

Dillon, John, 122–23

direct trade, 18–19

Dispatch: before Civil War, 19, 25, 32, 40–42, 44, 45–47; during Civil War, 50–51, 53–57, 59, 66, 67, 73–75; Reconstruction era, 80, 86, 89, 91–93, 95–97, 100, 105, 106, 110, 113, 115, 117, 118, 237n42; post-Reconstruction era and "New South," 119, 126–28, 131, 133, 138–39, 147, 149, 153–54, 156, 161, 162, 163, 166–67, 170, 175; twentieth century, 176, 177, 180, 182, 186. See also *Times-Dispatch*

Dooley, Alice Elizabeth (sister of James Henry), 12, 119, 199, 209, 211, 221

Dooley, Alice Irina (sister of James Henry; died in infancy), 10, 199

Dooley, Ann (sister of John), 5, 6, 20, 36, 91

Dooley, Eliza (sister of John), 5, 36, 91

Dooley, Florence Catherine (later, Lewis; sister of James Henry), 14, 67, 73–74, 81, 91, 109, 211–13

Dooley, George J. (brother of James Henry), 8, 27–28, 30, 34, 43, 199

Dooley, James (grandfather of James Henry), 5

Dooley, James Henry (Jim), 1–3; on annexation of Maymont by City of Richmond, 152, 196–97; articles and pamphlets written by, 156, 161, 165–67, 185–87, 195–96, 203–4, 206–7; birth of, 9; business trip with father, 32–33; Civil War military service of, 54–57, 61–63, 233n24; courtship and marriage, 3, 94, 97–98, 102; death of, 218–20; debts from father's estate paid by, 218; deeds 212 to Sallie, 163; deeds Maymont to Sallie, 190; disability discharge certificate, 62–63; "Dooley bill," 152; Dooley Hospital, 214, 216–17; education, interest in, 183, 185, 192–93, 203–4, 206; Episcopal church and, 205, 220; European trips, 204, 205, 209; in Evacuation Fire, 77; Far West, 1888 trip to, 144–45; as financial prognosticator, 155–57, 163–64, 165, 186, 187, 204–5; as founder and board member of Commonwealth Club, 151; as founder of Westmoreland Club, 115, 151; hat business run by, during early Civil War, 50–51, 54; as head and primary financial support for Dooley family, 91, 95, 117–18, 166, 212–13; Ireland and Irish immigrants, interest in, 2, 89–90, 92–94, 100, 106, 122–23; in list of American millionaires, 183; love of books and read-

Dooley, Mary (later, Byrne; sister of John), 22

Dooley, Mary Helen (later, Jones; sister of James Henry), 8, 42, 49, 73, 117

Dooley, Mary Margaret (née McNamara; grandmother of James Henry), 5, 6, 8, 22

Dooley, Sallie (née Saidie May; wife of James Henry), 1; ancestry, 3; APVA, 150; "Autumn" (poem), 215–16; change of name from Saidie to Sallie, 102; charitable work of, 113–14, 172; courtship and marriage, 3, 94, 97–98, 102; in DAR and Colonial Dames, 150–51, 162, 172, 178, 182; death of, 222, 254n10; *Dem Good Ole Times,* 3, 197–99, 210; diabetes of, 205; European trips, 204, 205, 209; family papers burned after death of, 1; Far West, 1888 trip to, 144–45; Floral Carriage parade, 178–79; historic preservation movement, involvement in, 150–51, 162, 178; member of executive committee of Virginia Association Opposed to Woman's suffrage, 178, 208; owner of Maymont, 157; owner of 212 W. Franklin St., 131–32, 157; philanthropy of, 222; portrait, 147; purchase and sale of 212 West Franklin Street home, 129–30, 157; Richmond Art Club and, 192; Mrs. Roosevelt and, 195; Swannanoa (mountain vacation home), 1, 204, 205–6, 207–8, 215, 218; will of, 222; in Woman's Club, 172–73; women's suffrage, opposition to, 178, 208–9. *See also* Maymont

Dooley, Sally (later, Heaton; sister of John), 5, 26, 28, 35, 223n7

Dooley, Sarah (née McNamara; mother of James Henry), 1–2; blood relationship to husband, 6, 223n7; charitable works of, 114; in Civil War, 67; in Clay Club, 11, 41; courtship and marriage, 5–6, 223n7; death of, 199; as executrix of husband's will, 50, 91, 95; financial assistance for daughter Florence, 109; on Hollywood Memorial Association board, 88; house numbering in Richmond and, 35; illnesses of, 27–28, 34; immigration to US from Ireland, 2, 5–6, 223n7; letter from Georgetown treasurer handled by, 40; letters of James Henry Dooley to, 95, 98–99; portrait of, 36; women's rights and politics, interest in, 2, 9, 11

Dooley, Sarah Evelyn (Saidie; later, Sister Mary Magdalen; sister of James Henry), 24, 47, 67, 104–5, 116, 205, 220, 221

Dooley and Richardson's Hospital, Richmond, 61

"Dooley Bill," 152

Dooley hat manufacturing business. *See* hat manufacturing business

Dooley Hospital, 214, 216–18

Dooley Public Library bequest, 222

Dooley Scholarships at Richmond Art Club, 206

Dornin, Philip, 49

Dorr & Rade (piano builders, Richmond), 229n31

Doubleday, Page & Company, 3, 198

Douglas, Stephen A., 18, 25–26, 43

Douglas Association, 43

Dr. Socrates Maupin's Classical and Mathematical Academy for Boys, Richmond, 15–16, 20

Dramatic Association, Georgetown College, 32, 41

Drexel, Morgan & Company, 154, 157, 163
Duddy, Father, 40
Dun & Co., 12, 14, 17, 36, 187
dysentery, 53

Eagle Square, Richmond, 87
Earley, Father, 41
economic issues. *See* business and finance
education: of daughters of John and Sarah Dooley, 14, 67, 73–74, 81, 104–5; of Jackie Dooley, 30–32, 34, 36–38, 40–42, 48; James Henry Dooley's interest in, 183, 185, 192–93, 203–4, 206; John Dooley's interest in, 3, 9–10, 14, 24, 27; Josephine Houston, school run by, 166; of Nora Houston, 132, 166, 192; Progressive movement and, 182–83; the Woman's Club and, 172, 173. *See also specific schools, institutes, and associations*
education of James Henry Dooley: bills for, 40, 48, 78–79; graduation from Georgetown, 42, 50; honorary doctor of laws degree from Georgetown, 217; master's degree from Georgetown, 84; schooling, 2, 15–16, 20–21, 27; as undergraduate at Georgetown, 30–32, 34, 36–39, 40–42, 228n1
Elder, Anna (née May; sister of Sallie Dooley), 97
Elder, Fitzhugh (nephew of Sallie Dooley), 205–6
Elder, T. C. (brother-in-law of Sallie Dooley), 97, 98, 184–85
Eleventh Virginia Regiment, Confederate Army, 55
Ellis, Thomas H., 88
Ellyson's *Richmond Directory and Business Advertiser,* 18

Emancipation celebration, First African Baptist Church, Richmond, 78
Enders, John, 58, 63, 72
English, J. J., 218
English, William, 54, 111
Enoch W. Clark firm, 243n30
Enquirer, 13, 18, 56, 62, 63–64, 71, 102, 106–7, 115
Equal Suffrage League, 209
Europe, James Henry, and Sallie Dooley in, 204, 209
Evacuation Fire, Richmond, 2, 77–78, 79, 119, 151
Evans, Henry, 204
Examiner, 59, 60, 63–64, 72–73, 79
Exchange Hotel, Richmond, 13, 23, 47, 84, 87, 111, 123, 129
Executive Mansion, Richmond, 179

Fairfax, Henry Tennant, 182
Farmers' Bank of Virginia, 45, 84
Farmers' National Bank of Richmond, 84–85, 87
Fayette Artillery, 42, 47
Federal Reserve Act, 210; Richmond as site of Federal Reserve bank, 210–11
Fenians, 85
Fifth Corps, Army of the Potomac, 80
Financial Chronicle, 189–90
financial issues. *See* business and finance
First African Baptist Church, Richmond, 10, 15, 16, 20, 43, 45, 75, 78
First Annual Road Congress, American Association for Highway Improvement, 208
First Baptist Church, Richmond, 6, 10
First National Bank, Richmond, 80, 87, 215, 217
First Virginia Regiment: Confederate army, 1, 48, 49, 50, 53–57, 59, 65–66,

Johnson, Andrew, 81, 92, 236n19

Johnson, Bradley T., 114

Johnson, Joseph (governor of Virginia), 19

Johnson, Martha, 89

Johnston, George Ben, 173

Johnston, Helen, 173

Johnston, John W., 135, 137

Johnston, Mary, 255n34

Jones, J. B., 48

Jones, Mary Helen (née Dooley; sister of James Henry), 8, 42, 49, 73, 117

Jones, Robert "Tantie" McCandlish, 49, 66, 73, 98, 110, 117

Joseph Bryan Memorial Association, 200

Joynes, William A., 85

Kanawha & Michigan Railway Company, 201

Keiley, Anthony, 93, 100, 101–2, 123, 133

Keiley, John, 49

Kelly, Joseph, 95–97

Kemper, James L. (governor of Virginia), 110, 111

Kemper Kampaign Klub (KKK), 110

Kilpatrick, Judson, 71–72

Know-Nothing Party, 22, 23–26, 43, 94–95

Knoxville Gas Light Company, 129

Konservative Kampaign Klub, 114

Ku Klux Klan, 111

Laburnum, 200

Lamb, John, 196

Lambert, William (mayor of Richmond), 13, 19

Lancaster, Robert A., Sr., 148

Langhorne, Irene, 162

Law Greys (Baltimore regiment), 19

lawyer, James Henry Dooley as, 43–44, 74, 85–86, 89, 91–93, 95–97, 102–4, 109, 116, 119, 184–85, 237n42

Leading Pursuits and Leading Men (mercantile guide), 28

Lee, Fitzhugh (governor of Virginia), 140, 141, 142

Lee, Robert E., 37, 55, 68–69, 79, 140, 215

Lehman, Emanuel, 128

Letcher, John (governor of Virginia), 46, 66

Lewis, David, 138

Lewis, Florence (née Dooley; sister of James Henry), 14, 67, 73–74, 81, 91, 109, 211–13

Lewis, John (lieutenant governor of Virginia), 134

Lewis, L. L., 182

Lewis, William (Willie) Lynn (brother-in-law of James Henry Dooley), 91, 109, 117, 212–13

Liberty Loan campaigns, World War I, 214–15

Light Infantry Blues, 23, 37

Limerick, Ireland, 5, 15

Lincoln, Abraham, 43, 44, 45, 46, 47, 75, 78, 79–80

Lincoln, Tad, 78

Logan, Kate Virginia (née Cox), 121

Logan, Lily, 192

Logan, Thomas Muldrup, 2, 120–31, 133, 135–37, 145, 148, 153, 168, 183, 187, 211, 219

Long Island Railroad, 185

Longstreet, General, 52, 55, 65

Louisa Railroad, 17

Louisville and Nashville Railroad, 188

Lovenstein, Mr., 105

Lover, Samuel, 13, 66; *Handy Andy,* 13

McNamara, Sarah. *See* Dooley, Sarah

Meade, George, 80

Meagher, Thomas Francis, 15, 20, 22, 35

Mechanics Institute (earlier Mechanics Association), 3, 9–10, 24, 34, 46

Medical College of Virginia (MCV), 10, 12, 16, 125, 132–35, 214, 216–17

mental illness: Central Lunatic Asylum for the Colored Insane, James Henry Dooley as director of, 111; of John Dooley's sisters, 20, 36

Merchants and Mechanics Insurance Company, 124

Merchants' Insurance Company, 35–36, 60

Merchants National Bank, 111, 124, 215

Meredith, John A., 92–93

Metropolitan Hall, Richmond, 46, 47

Mexican War, 12, 15

Michard, Mr., 21

Middendorf, Oliver and Company (financial firm), 168, 187, 189, 191

Military District No. 1, Virginia as, 90

Miller, John M., 217

Millhiser, Moses, 122, 183

Milner Coal and Railroad Company, 136

Missouri Compromise, 18

Mitchel, James, 49, 55, 62, 67, 69

Mitchel, John, 15, 19–20, 22–23, 34, 61, 63–69, 72, 75, 76, 79, 84, 85, 106, 113; *History of Ireland since the Treaty of Limerick*, 85

Mitchel, John, Jr., 69

Mitchel, Willy, 63–64, 65, 66, 69

"Mitchel Memorial Meeting," 113

Mitchell, S.C., 193

Moncure, Richard C., 85

Monroe, James, reburial of, 34–35

Monroe Park, Richmond, 200

Montague, Andrew Jackson (governor of Virginia), 181–83, 192–93, 194

Montague, Betsie, 182, 194

Montague, Latane (lieutenant governor of Virginia), 48

Monte Maria, Monastery of the Visitation of Holy Mary, 116

Montgomery, Richard, 15

Montgomery Guard, 15, 19, 23, 28, 34–35, 37, 40, 42, 45–46, 48, 50–52, 53, 64

Moore, P. T., 41, 49–50

Moore & Caulfield, 98

Morgan, J. P., 146, 186

Mount de Chantal Visitation Academy, Wheeling, West Virginia, 104–5

Mount Hope (mental asylum), Baltimore, 20, 36, 91, 95

Mozart Hall, Richmond, 122, 123

Mulford, John, 83

Munford, Beverley, 172–73, 192

Munford, Hunton, Williams & Anderson (law firm), 196

Munford, Mary Cook Branch, 172–73, 192, 216

Murfee, Mr., 21

Murphy, D. Y., 49

Muto, Y., 207, 255n21

Myers, Gustavus, 238n2

Napoleonic Wars, 5

National Bank of Virginia, 87

National City Bank, New York City, 185, 201

nativism and Know-Nothing Party, 22, 23–26

New England Society of New York, 139

New Orleans, commemoration of Battle of, 45

"New South," 139–40, 142, 146, 184

Peyton, T. G., 157

Philonomosian Society, Georgetown College, 32

Pierpont, Francis H. (governor of Virginia), 81, 83–84

Pillsbury, Charles, John, and George, 142

Pius IX (pope), 101

Pizzini, Anthony, 122

Planters National Bank, 171

police brutality case, 95–97

polio, 217

political career of James Henry Dooley: Commonwealth attorney campaign, 100–101; Conservative Party, continuing role in, 124–25, 133; in Democratic party, 203–4; Dooley, "A National Constitutional Convention and Its Possible Consequences," 206–7; on free-trade features of McKinley law, 165–66; historic preservation lobbying of Sallie Dooley and, 178; Irish ancestry and, 106; Irish Conservatives and, 93–94; legal career and, 92–93, 104; nominating conventions, Conservative party, 110–11, 117; on railroad rate regulation, 181–82, 184, 194–96; on Richmond as Federal Reserve Bank site, 210–11; Richmond improvements, "Dooley Bill" on, 152; road improvement in Virginia, 169–71; Sherman Silver Purchase Act, comments on, 155–56, 161–62, 164, 165, 166; speeches on public issues, 101–2, 113; on tariff proposal of 1893, 166–67; Virginia constitutional convention of 1900–1902, 181–84; in Virginia House of Delegates, 2, 107–18

Polk, James K., 11

Possum Club, St. Paul, 142

Potts, Frank, 51–52

Powhatan Hotel, Richmond, 63

Preston, William Ballard, 46

prisoner-of-war exchange cartel, 61

Progressive movement, 170, 182–83

Prohibition, 203

Purcell, John B., 35, 75, 176

Purcell and Ladd Pharmaceutical Company, 35

Quakers, in Ireland, 14

R. E. Lee Camp No. 1, 184, 220

R. G. Dun & Co., 12, 14, 17, 36, 187

R. H. Maury & Co., 120

Radical Republicans, 90, 92, 93

Ragland, Edith Anne Pemberton, 210

railroads: bankruptcies, 112–13, 124, 126, 188, 190; in Civil War, 49, 52, 59, 60–61, 67, 73, 76; development and growth of, 6–7, 12, 17–18; direct trade and, 18–19; James Henry Dooley's investments in, 120–31, 135–39, 141–45, 147–48, 153–54, 156–57, 159, 162–63, 168, 173–80, 194–96, 201, 207, 218–19; John Dooley's investments in, 6–7, 12, 14, 17–18, 42, 124, 223n12; first Virginia railroad commissioner, choosing, 115–16; golden spike connecting Seaboard rails, ceremonial driving of, 179–80; rate regulation, 181–82, 184, 194–96; Richmond's industrial growth and expansion of, 107, 109–10, 112–13; teamster business, 119. See also specific railway lines and companies

Raleigh and Gaston Railroad, 175

Randolph, George Wythe, 25, 46, 68

Randolph and English, 218

Reading-Room Association, George-town College, 32, 38

Readjuster and Funder contingents, Conservative Party, 108, 114, 117, 133–35

Reconstruction Acts and Reconstruction in Virginia, 90

Relief Committee, Richmond, 79, 80

Republican Party, 43, 90, 92, 93

Richardson, William, 61

Richardson Romanesque, 151

Richmond, Va.: annexation of territory by, 152, 196–97; bar association (Marshall Association) for, 89; Confederate government evacuation of, 76; Dooley family moving to, 6; James Henry Dooley promoting, 152, 183–84; epidemics in, 24, 26; Evacuation Fire of 1865, 2, 77–78, 79, 119, 151; as Federal Reserve Bank site, 210–11; growth in 1850s, 16–17, 35; Home Guard, 62, 68, 71–72, 77; inauguration celebrations of 1893 in, 161; Irish affairs, interest in, 13–14, 15; Liberty Loan campaign in, 215; Lincoln visiting, 78; liquor and tobacco in city, orders to destroy, 77, 235n1; Maymont bequeathed to, 220–21, 222; militia companies, 12; National Governor's Conference of 1912 in, 209–10; numbering of houses in, 35; presidential elections of 1840 in, 9; presidential elections of 1844 in, 11; presidential elections of 1860 in, 42–43; prewar anxiety, pro-Southern sentiment, and their financial effects in, 40–48; railroad, beginnings of, 6–7; railroads, industrial growth and expansion of, 107, 109–10, 112–13; rebuilding, postwar, 80–88, 119,

183–84; Relief Committee, 79, 80; Roosevelt's visit to, 194–95; Southern Rights Association of, 18; surrender to Union Forces and military presence in, 78–88; telautograph exchange in, 159–60, 164–65; twentieth century celebrations, 178–79; "A Year in Richmond" 1913 calendar, 210. *See also specific locations and organizations*

Richmond Ambulance Committee, 2, 58–76, 82, 83, 91

Richmond and Allegheny Railroad, 125, 207

Richmond and Danville Extension Company, 128, 135, 136

Richmond and Danville Railroad, 2, 12, 14, 76, 114, 120–26, 128–31, 136–39, 162–63, 168, 171, 172, 182, 219, 223n12

Richmond and Louisa Railroad, 7, 17

Richmond and Petersburg Railroad, 7, 18, 73, 173

Richmond and St. Paul Land and Improvement Company, 141–44, 185, 200–201

Richmond and Washington Air Line, 177

Richmond and West Point Land, Navigation and Improvement Company, 153, 158, 171

Richmond and West Point Terminal Railway and Warehouse Company, 125–26, 128, 130–31, 136–39, 143, 152–53, 154, 156–57, 162–63, 166, 168, 171

Richmond and York River Railroad, 17, 59, 124, 158, 223n12

Richmond Architectural Iron-Works, 116

Richmond Art Club/Art Club of Richmond, 173, 192, 206, 209

Richmond Blues, 179

St. Peter's Ladies' Benevolent Society, 114

St. Vincent de Paul Society, 86, 91, 114

Stanard, Mary Newton, 255n34; *Richmond: Its People and Stories,* 150

Standard Oil Company, 130

Starke, Barry, 255n21

State (newspaper), 113, 129, 143–44, 146, 153, 154, 156, 162, 163

State Corporation Commission, 181–82, 184

Stevens, George W., 201, 207

Stevens M. Taylor & Co., 120

Stevenson, Adlai, 161

Stewart, Daniel, 243n3

Stewart, Isobel (later, Bryan), 121, 136

Stewart, John, 121, 243n3

Stuart, A. H. H., 46

Stuart, J. E. B., 215

Swamp Angels, 111

Swannanoa (Dooley mountain vacation home), 1, 204, 205–6, 207–8, 212, 215, 218

Sweet Springs, 91, 95

Swepson (banker), 129, 130

Taft, William Howard, 205, 208

Talbot & Bros. foundry, 17

Taylor, Mrs. Henry, 208

Taylor, Stevens M., 119–20

teamster business, 119

Teeling, John, 49

telautograph (fax machine prototype), 145–46, 148–49, 159–60, 164–65, 216

Temple, K. Richmond, 249n17

Terhune, Mary Virginia Hawes (Marion Harland), 150, 223n9, 230n36

Terminal Hotel, West Point, Va., 158

Texas (battleship), 171

Thorpe, James, 254n34

Tiffany, George S., 159

Tighe, Richard H. L., 20–21, 27, 31, 38

Times. See *New York Times; Richmond Times*

Times-Dispatch, 187, 188, 189, 190–91, 195, 196, 198, 200, 204–5, 210, 211, 219. See also *Dispatch; Richmond Times*

Tippecanoe Club, 9

Tobacco Association, Richmond, 110

transatlantic cable, 34

Tredegar Iron Works, 17, 35, 41, 47, 53–54, 112–13

Triennial Convention of the Episcopal Church, 193

Trigg, William R., 181

tuberculosis, 70, 94, 110, 132

Tucker, Beverley St. George, 56

Tucker, David H., 56, 62–63

Tuller, Walker K., 206, 254

Tuskegee Institute, Alabama, 185

Tweed, William M. "Boss," 104

Tyler, J. Hoge (governor of Virginia), 182

Tyler, John, 9, 48

Tyler, Lyon Gardiner, 233n24

Underwood Constitution, Virginia's adoption of, 101

Union Hotel, Richmond, 10

Union Pacific Railroad, 154

United States Colored Troops, 78

University Club, New York City, 152

University of Virginia, 20, 121

Ursuline Academy, Columbia, South Carolina, 67, 73–74

U.S. Supreme Court, 89

Valentine, Edward, 16, 173, 184

Valentine, Lila Meade, 209

Valley Railroad, 182

Williams, Robert Lancaster, 173
Williamsburg, Battle of, 55–57
Wilson, Woodrow, 209–10, 212, 214–15
Windsor Hotel, New York City, 155
Winston, P. B., 142
Wise, George D., 105
Wise, Henry A. (governor of Virginia), 24–25, 35, 37, 48, 72, 94–95, 113
Wise, Peyton, 105
Woman's Club, the, Richmond, 172–73
women: Dooley hat manufacturing business employing, 25, 49, 61; Virginia Association of Ladies for Erecting a Statue of Henry Clay (Clay Club), 11, 41; working in Richmond during Civil War, 232n15
women's rights and women's suffrage: Alice Dooley's interest in, 199; Jackie Dooley in school debate on, 36; James Henry Dooley refusing to sign petition in support of, 209; Sallie

Dooley's opposition to, 178, 208–9; Sarah Dooley's interest in, 2, 199; Josie and Nora Houston's interest in, 199; Nineteenth Amendment (granting suffrage to women), 208–9; presidential campaign of 1840 and, 9
World's Columbian Exposition (1893, Chicago), 160, 162, 165
World War I, 211–12, 214–16
Wright, Philip, 68
Wyatt, West, 89
Wynne, Colonel, 105

"Year in Richmond," 1913 calendar, 210
yellow fever epidemic of 1855, 26, 27
Yellowstone National Park, 144
Yosemite National Park, 144
Young Catholic Friend Society, 27
Young Guard, 37
Young Ireland movement, 15, 20
Yount (farmer), 203